ora pro nobis

O Maria sine labe concepta

qui ad te confugimus

THE RACCOLTA

OR

COLLECTION OF INDULGENCED

PRAYERS

& GOOD WORKS

THE RACCOLTA

OR

COLLECTION OF INDULGENCED

PRAYERS

& GOOD WORKS

By

Fr Ambrose St John

The 1910 Edition

Caritas Publishing

NIHIL OBSTAT: Henricus S. Bowden,
Censor Deputatus.

IMPRIMATUR: Edmundus Surmont,
Vicarius Generalis.

Westmonasterii, die 10 Maii, 1909.

"And therefore, O Lord, we must tremble before
Thy judgments, since Thy truth is neither mine,
nor his, nor another's, but belongs to all of us,
whom Thou call to have it in common, warning
us terribly not to hold it as specially for ourselves,
lest we be deprived of it. For whosoever claims to
himself as his own that which Thou appointed to
all to enjoy, and desires that to be his own which
belongs to all, is cast away from what is common
to all to that which is his own -- that is, from truth
to a lie." ~ St. Augustine, Confessions, Book XII,
Chapter 25:34.

Vademecum ISBN: 978-1-945275-11-1
Large Print ISBN: 978-1-945275-12-8

In the present volume all instances of *Holy Ghost* have
been changed to *Holy Spirit*. –The Publisher, 2025.

To the Modern Reader (2025)

This is a treasured *collection* – *raccolta* – of two thousand years of the Church's most powerful and sublime devotions. Pray using the very words of Saints, immersed in the deepest dynamics of the Holy Trinity, the Redemptive Sacrifice, the Communion of Saints. These prayers not only teach us how to pray, but they help to remake our modern, malformed interior dispositions in accordance with that which is most pleasing to His Divine Majesty.

In 1968, by a Decree of the Sacred Apostolic Penitentiary, most of these Indulgences were revoked. Nevertheless, they may still be prayed to immense benefit. We beseech our Holy Father, Pope Leo IV, who holds the Keys to this treasury, to restore these Indulgences to us, that we may most effectively *labora sicut bonus miles Christi Jesu.*

—*The Publisher, 2023*

Please note in the texts:

Pater - pray the *Our Father*.
Ave - pray the *Hail Mary*.
Gloria - pray the *Glory be*.
Credo - pray the *Apostle's Creed*.

To the holy souls in purgatory, all
especially who have been benefactors
of the congregation of the Oratory,
and are now in need of the prayers of
those whom on earth they aided to
love and serve God, this translation is
affectionately dedicated.

The Oratory, Edgbaston
November 2, 1857

CONTENTS

THE RACCOLTA

APPROBATION

MOST BLESSED FATHER, in order to promote thereby the piety of the faithful in England, Ambrose St John, Priest of the Oratory of St Philip Neri, in the Diocese of Birmingham, humbly prays for permission to print in English a translation of the book entitled *Raccolta di Orazioni, &c., alle quali sono annesse le SS. Indulgenze*, having first obtained the approbation of His Eminence the Cardinal Archbishop of Westminster; and also that the faithful who make use of this translation may gain all the Indulgences annexed to the original.

After an audience of the Holy Father, granted February 3, 1856, our most Holy LORD Pius IX, by Divine Providence Pope, on an application made by me, the undersigned Secretary of the Sacred Congregation for the Propagation of the Faith, has of his goodness answered by Rescript in favour of the grace, according to the terms of the petition, provided the translation be made from the last Roman edition, and it being understood that the Decree printed at the end of this edition remains in full force.

Given at Rome from the House of the same Sacred Congregation, on the day and year aforesaid.

Gratis, without any payment on any plea whatever.

AL. BARNABO, Secretary.

In the place of ✠ the seal.

WE approve of the Translation by virtue of the above Rescript of His Holiness.

N. CARDINAL ARCHBISHOP.

Westminster, October 23, 1857.

Preface to the Sixth Edition

In Memoriam
Ambrose St John

AMBROSE St John was the younger of the two sons of Henry St John, and grandson of St Andrew St John, D. D., Dean of Worcester, of the ancient family of St John of Staunton St John, Oxfordshire. He was born June 29, 1815, went to Westminster School, and afterwards graduated with Honours at Oxford. From Christ Church he entered the Anglican Ministry, and, after accepting a curacy under the Rev. Henry William Wilberforce, then incumbent of Bransgore, Hants, joined Dr Newman at Littlemore, where he remained till 1844.

He was received into the Church September 29, 1845, at Prior Park, near Bath, and accompanied Dr Newman to Rome, where the two converts were ordained Subdeacon together in the private chapel of Cardinal Franzoni May 26, 1847. Three days later they received the Diaconate at St John Lateran's, and the Priesthood the following day, Trinity Sunday. After a short novitiate they returned to England as Oratorians, and in the foundation of the Oratory in England by Father Newman Ambrose St John figures as his right hand at Maryvale, at Alcester Street, and finally at Edgbaston.

Bright and cheerful in aspect and manner, and many sided in his accomplishments, Father St John devoted himself most assiduously to the service of GOD and his neighbour in the Oratory. He was a typical son of St Philip, indefatigable alike in the confessional and in the pulpit, and a true father, whether to the Italian organ-grinders or to the poor factory girls of Birmingham. Later on, at Dr Newman's request, he sacrificed himself to the exacting work of the Oratory School, founded in 1859, of which as Headmaster from 1862, under the guidance of his Superior, he may be said to have laid the permanent foundations. His memory is held in grateful recollection by many old Oratory boys.

The translation of the *Raccolta* by Father St John was one of the first books of popular devotion issued by the Fathers of the Birmingham Oratory, and it supplied them with the congregational prayers, still in use in their church, for the Stations of the Cross, for the month of May, the Triduo and Novenas in preparation for the Feasts of our Lady, and similar devotions. The fifth edition of the book, brought out after Father St John's death, was printed in Birmingham by the direction and under the supervision of Cardinal Newman himself. Concurrently with the issue of the English *Raccolta* Father St John translated and published a work on Indulgences by the Abbate Dominico Sarra, Recorder of the Sacred Congregation of Indulgences and Holy Relics, a

handy popular treatise on the doctrine and use
of Indulgences published by authority at Rome.

This Edition has been conformed to the latest
Roman *Raccolta*, approved July 23, 1898, and the
Supplement, approved July 31, 1902; and contains
also the Indulgences and decisions since recorded
in the *Acta Sanctæ Sedis* up to the present time.

The immediate occasion of Father St John's
death was an act of neighbourly kindness, which
led him to assist one very hot day as Deacon at
the Festa of St Paul of the Cross, to which he
had been invited by the Passionist Fathers at
Harborne, his health being at the time very un-
certain. He had recently translated from the
German Dr. Fessler's *True and False Infallibility*,
a work approved by the Holy See, which Dr
Newman thought of great importance in the con-
troversy which had arisen out of Mr Gladstone's
Vaticanism; the work had been done against time,
and the effort, made in the midst of multifarious
duties, had proved a great strain. The High Mass
at Harborne was celebrated in a large conserva-
tory, then in use as a temporary church, and the
sun, beating down through the glass, brought on
a kind of sunstroke and brain fever, to which he
succumbed. Dr Newman in replying to a letter of
condolence says: "I do not like not to acknowledge your kind sympathy in my sorrow, but I am
so pulled down that I cannot write without bringing on a flood of tears not I trust from want of
resignation, but from love of him I have lost, so I
say only a few words. You who have undergone
bitter losses will make allowance for me."

Their friendship is recorded in the concluding sentences of the *Apologia*, in which that work is offered as a memorial of affection and gratitude to the Fathers of the Oratory: "And to you especially, dear Ambrose St John, whom GOD gave me when He took everyone else away; who are the link between my old life and my new; who have now for twenty one years been so devoted to me, so patient, so zealous, so tender; who have watched me so narrowly, who have never thought of yourself if I was in question."

Father St John was buried in the private cemetery of the Oratorian Fathers at Rednal, and Cardinal Newman left strict injunctions that he himself should be laid in his friend's grave. A single head-stone bears their brief epitaphs. In the present issue of the *Raccolta*, brought up to date, the editor would claim for them and for himself, from all who use this book, a remembrance in their prayers.

R.G.B.

The Oratory, Birmingham,
November 2, 1908.

ON INDULGENCES

PUNISHMENT, like a shadow, follows all sin, whether mortal or venial, and it is not usually remitted to the full when forgiveness is obtained.

Eternal punishment, incurred by mortal sin, is always remitted with the guilt, but *some* temporal punishment generally remains due to the justice of GOD. This temporal punishment is inflicted by GOD either in this life or in Purgatory; but a man may anticipate the divine justice by works of penance, or by means of Indulgences.

The *guilt*, then, of sin is one thing, the punishment another. The guilt is remitted when a man truly repents, either with or without the Sacrament of Penance; but though the punishment, or a portion of it, may be remitted with the guilt, some usually remains, as a debt of satisfaction, to be paid in this world or the next. This truth is clearly indicated in the sacramental penances which always accompany Absolution. These penances have, in course of time, under pressure of external circumstances, lost much of the severity which characterized them in earlier ages, but they still testify to the principle that after forgiveness satisfaction remains due. The comparative lightness of modern sacramental penances ought to suggest that they alone are not sufficient to satisfy the justice of GOD, and that they should be supplemented either by other penanc-

es, self-inflicted or patiently accepted at the hand
of GOD, or by some equivalent. And in the case of
sins forgiven either *indirectly* in the Sacrament,
or by means of contrition alone, the satisfaction
remaining due is left altogether to the individual's patience under chastisement from GOD, or
to his personal activity in applying himself either
to works of penance, or to some equivalent. That
equivalent is to be found in Indulgences.

What, then, is an Indulgence? An Indulgence is
the remission by the Church, on specified conditions, of the whole or a part of the debt of satisfaction remaining due for sin. The Church has
power to absolve from guilt; she has also power
to remit the punishment. The one she exercises
in the Sacrament of Penance; the other she exercises when she grants an Indulgence. And it is
clear from what has been said that an Indulgence
is supplemental to Absolution, and presupposes
the forgiveness of the guilt of sin.

Theologically considered, an Indulgence is not
a mere exercise of spiritual power and authority
on the part of the Church; it is truly a payment of
the debt, made out of her Treasury of satisfactory
merit; for in this are stored up the superabun-
dant merits of JESUS CHRIST, and the accumulated
merits of our Lady and all the Saints. With this
inexhaustible fund at her command, she has the
means of satisfying the debts due from her children to the justice of GOD.

In form, an Indulgence emanates from the
Pope; leaving out of account the limited power
exercised by Bishops in favour of their flocks and

by Cardinals, Nuncios and others; and it is registered in a Decree or Rescript of the Congregation of Indulgences, or some similar document. It attaches to a specified prayer or good work an additional satisfactory value, such value being expressed in the terms of an ancient canonical penance, viz., so many days, Quarantines (which lasted forty days), or years, to which the Indulgence is thereby declared to be equivalent. The earliest Indulgences were, in fact, remissions of these very penances.

Indulgences are either Plenary or Partial, according as a remission of all, or of part, of the debt of punishment due is granted. In either case the actual benefit obtained depends upon the dispositions of the penitent, and the *care and accuracy* he employs in fulfilling the conditions laid down. For the sake of clearness and facility of reference, the general and special conditions required for obtaining Indulgences are set out in tabular form below.

It only remains to add that, though the Church has no direct jurisdiction over the souls in Purgatory, she authorizes and encourages, as a work of supreme charity, the application of Indulgences, by way of suffrage, to the needs of those afflicted souls; and we may confidently assure ourselves that these suffrages are most acceptable to the Divine Majesty, and that what the Church would thus, as it were, indirectly loose in Purgatory is speedily loosed also in Heaven, amid the rejoicing of all the heavenly court, to the great glory of God, and to the incalculable benefit, as well of the suffering souls as of their earthly benefactors.

General Conditions required for all Indulgences.

1. STATE OF GRACE. (See Decisions 1, 2,)
2. INTENTION. (See Decisions 3, 4,)
3. Accuracy and DEVOTION in fulfilling the specified conditions. (See N.B.—ibid.)

Special Conditions usually required for Plenary, and sometimes for Partial, Indulgences.

I. CONFESSION.
II. COMMUNION.
III. VISIT to a church or public chapel.
IV. PRAYER according to the intention of the Pope.

N.B.—Too much stress cannot be laid on the importance of *carefully noting and exactly fulfilling* all that may be required for gaining a particular Indulgence. If there is any deviation, even though unintentional, from the strict letter of the specified conditions, no Indulgence can be gained.

To gain the *full benefit* of a Plenary Indulgence, it is necessary to have a true hatred of every, even venial, sin committed, and to be wholly free from all voluntary attachment to what is sinful.

NOTE.—In the case of gaining Indulgences *for the dead*, the necessity of a state of grace is questioned by some theologians, unless it is specified or implied in the Grant; and therefore, *in this particular case*, the necessity cannot be insisted upon as *absolutely certain*; nevertheless, in practice, a state of grace should *always* be considered of the first importance, *the opinion above quoted being only probable.*

The following decisions of the Congregations of Indulgences should be carefully noted:

DECISIONS OF THE SACRED CONGREGATION OF INDULGENCES

STATE OF GRACE

1. A state of grace ought to precede everything, but in case it should not, it must at least be attained before the last of the acts prescribed for the Indulgence is completed.

2. Although for Partial Indulgences Confession is not usually required as a condition, the usual formula being, "with at least a contrite heart," in case of conscious mortal sin it should precede the other acts; but in case of difficulty in getting to confession an act of true contrition with a firm purpose of confessing suffices. (December 17, 1870.) Under ordinary circumstances, the formula above quoted implies nothing more than a state of grace.

INTENTION

3. A general intention of gaining all Indulgences is sufficient. It should be renewed from time to time, say every morning.

4. By a further general intention all, or by a particular intention any, Indulgences may be applied to the Holy Souls in Purgatory, either to the

Holy Souls in general, or to individual souls (Ib.)
N.B.—Indulgences to be applicable to the holy
souls require a positive declaration to that effect
in the grant.

Confession

5.   Confession, when required as a condition, is
binding even on those who are not conscious of
mortal sin. (May 19, 1759)

6. The Confession, or Confession and
Communion, required as conditions may be
made on the day previous to that appointed
for an Indulgence, provided other acts remain
to be done on the day itself. (January 12, 1878.
6a. In cases of special feasts enriched with
Indulgences, and of those days when as in the
case of the Portiuncula many Indulgences can be
gained in succession; on account of the concourse
of penitents, the Confession can now be made, in
the first case, i.e. when a single Indulgence is in
question, two days, and in the second case three
days before the feast. (March 11, 1908.)

7.   Habitual weekly Confession, for those in a
state of grace, suffices for all Indulgences during
the week, except Jubilees. (March 12, 1855.)

8.   By weekly Confession is meant Confession
every seven days. (November 23, 1878, February
25, 1886.) N.B.—Daily Communicants are no longer required to make this weekly Confession. See
"Frequent Communion," No. 85, p. 84.

9.   In cases of devotion extending over a period
of days, the Confession and Communion may be

made any time within eight days after the end of such a period. (December 8, 1897.)

10. If the Bishop of the Diocese applies for it, a concession is made in favour of places where, through want of Confessors, people have a difficulty in getting to Confession before an indulgenced feast. In such cases, Confession made eight days before suffices, and covers all Indulgences during the period. (June 12, 1822;September 28, 1838; December 15, 1841.)

11. Under similar circumstances, and if the Bishop applies for the concession, the habitual Confession made once a fortnight, i.e. every thirteen days, suffices for all the Indulgences during the period. (November 23, 1878; February 25, 1886.)

12. Confession and Communion made on Easter Day satisfy for the Paschal precept and for the Indulgence attached to the Papal blessing given by the Bishop. (March 19, 1841.)

13. For a Jubilee, ordinary or extraordinary, a special Confession and Communion must be made. (May 10, 1844.)

COMMUNION

14. One Communion satisfies for all the Indulgences of the day. (May 29, 1841.)

15. The Paschal Communion satisfies for the Paschal precept and the Indulgence of the day. (May 10, 1844.)

16. Unless specially required, the Communion for an Indulgence attached to a particular church need not be made in that church. (May 19, 1759.)

17. In cases of chronic infirmity, or physical impediment, the Confessor can commute the Communion for some other good work. And this has been made applicable to Communities. (September 18, 1862; January 16, 1886.)

Visit to a Church or Public Chapel

18. Separate visits must be made for two or more Indulgences. (February 29, 1864.)

19. If the Communion be made in a church or chapel prescribed, or available for the visit, special prayer said at the time of Communion satisfies for one visit.

20. The chapels of monasteries, seminaries, and convents, to which the faithful have not public access, are not available for the visit. (August 22, 1842.)

21. Confessors can commute the visit in the case of chronic invalids, or those who cannot go out. And this has been made applicable to Communities. (September 18, 1862; June 16, 1886.)

22. The visit may be made before or after the other acts, i.e., any time from midnight to midnight, unless otherwise specified, e.g., from first Vespers on the vigil to sunset on the feast. (May 19, 1759; January 12, 1878.)

PRAYER ACCORDING TO THE POPE'S INTENTION

23. The Pope's intention always includes the following objects:
    i. The progress of the Faith and triumph of the Church.
    ii. Peace and union among Christian Princes and Rulers.
    iii. The conversion of sinners.
    iv. The uprooting of heresy.

These intentions may be fittingly recalled and prayed for after Communion, or at the visit; but a general intention of praying according to the mind of the Pope is sufficient; and any prayers may be used which are not already of obligation, e.g., the Little Hours of a priest's Office. (July 12, 1847; May 29, 1841.)

THE DEAF AND DUMB

24. Vocal prayer is commuted for devout elevation of mind and heart. (February 16, 1852.)

25. At public Devotions, presence and a devout attitude of mind and heart suffice. (Ibid.)

26. Confessors can commute private prayers for other external works. (Ibid.)

27. Vocal prayers may be said by signs or mentally, or they may be read over without articulation. (July 16, 1902).

GENERAL

28. Indulgenced prayers may be said in any language, provided that the version in the vernacular is a faithful rendering of the original; and this may be guaranteed, either by the Cardinal Prefect of the Congregation of Indulgences, or by one of

the Ordinaries of the country where the language in question is spoken. (December 20, 1884.)

29. Unless specially required, indulgenced prayers need not be said kneeling. (September 18, 1862.)

30. Unless otherwise declared, e.g., "from first Vespers on the vigil to sunset on the feast," the day is calculated from midnight to midnight. (January 12, 1878.)

31. Devotions which admit of being said alternately, such as the Angelus or Rosary, may be said by several persons together. (February 29, 1820.)

32. A prayer or good work, enriched with diverse Indulgences, must be repeated, if several Indulgences are to be gained, unless such repetition is impracticable, e.g. Communion, or unusual, e.g. Confession. (February 29, 1820; January 12, 1878.)

33. A Plenary Indulgence, granted for visiting a church on certain days, or doing some other pious work, can be gained only once a day, save that of the Portiuncula (March 7, 1678), and similar concessions granted T.Q.

34. An Indulgence attached to a visit to a church or chapel, even though described as *quotidiana plenaria*, can be gained once only in the year, unless it is clearly stated in the indult that it can be gained every day. (February 16, 1852.)

35. By feasts of our LORD, when spoken of in connexion with *Plenary* Indulgences, must be understood the Nativity, Circumcision, Epiphany, Easter, Ascension, and Corpus CHRISTI. And by feasts of our Lady must be understood the

Immaculate Conception, Nativity, Annunciation, Purification, and Assumption. (September 18, 1862.)

36. If *Partial* Indulgences are granted to "other" feasts of our Lord and our Lady, this must be understood of feasts which are common to the Universal Church.

37. In all cases by feasts of the Apostles are meant those feasts which commemorate their entrance into eternal life. (September 18, 1862.)

Rosaries, Medals, Etc.

38. Blessed objects can only be used by the person for whom they were originally blessed, or if blessed for distribution, can be passed on by that person to others; but they can go no further. They cannot be given away, or lent with the intention of transferring the Indulgences attached to them. If they be so dealt with, the Indulgences are lost, and the objects return to their original unblessed condition. They cannot be sold or exchanged. And if a person undertakes to get such objects blessed for others, he must be careful, if he wishes to receive payment for them, either to obtain the money before getting them blessed, or at least a precise commission to buy them, sufficient to determine the ownership of the goods. (February 6, 1657; January 10, 1839; July 16, 1887; July 10, 1896.)

Leaflets, Etc.

39. Anyone obtaining a grant of an Indulgence, of universal extension, must, under pain of nullity, present the original to the Secretary of the Sacred Congregation of Indulgences.

40. Thus all leaflets, circulars, little books or papers, purporting to contain prayers indulgenced for all the faithful, not to be found in the *Raccolta* (as distinguished from similar documents belonging to Confraternities, Pious Societies, etc., which are purposely omitted), are certainly spurious and worthless, unless they have annexed to them the approbation of the said Congregation. (January 22, 1858; January 8, 1861; January 19, 1756; April 14, 1856.)

N.B.—It follows from what has been said above, that only Indulgences granted to all the Faithful in general are to be found in the *Raccolta*, and that the Indulgences belonging to Confraternities, Pious Societies and the like, which are not therefore of universal extension, must be sought for elsewhere, in the Rules and Regulations of such Societies.

List of Abbreviations

Bl., Bull.
Bps., Congregation of Bishops and Regulars.
Br., Brief.
Res., Rescript.
Mem., Secretariate of Memorials.
Enc., Encyclical.
Con., Constitution.

Aff., — of Special Ecclesiastical Affairs.
Mot. pr., Motu proprio.
Pr. ma., Propria manu.
Bfs., — of Briefs.
Indul., Congregation of Indulgences
Sta., — of State.
Pen., Penitentiary.
Ind., — of the Index.
Off., Holy Office.
Rit., — of Rites.
A.S.S., Acta Sanctæ Sedis.
Prop., — of Propaganda.
T.Q., Toties quoties, i.e., any number of times.

THE RACCOLTA

INSTRUCTIONS

THE conditions, general and special, for gaining Indulgences, with the decisions of the Congregation of Indulgences which follow, should be carefully studied and often referred to.

2. Unless otherwise stated, e.g., "once a day," a partial Indulgence may be gained any number of times in succession. This is indicated by the letters T.Q.

3. To gain a "Plenary, once (or twice, etc.) a month," the prayer or act must be repeated daily for a month; and the Communion may be made, unless otherwise declared, on any day of the month, or within eight days after.

4. The Roman numerals, I, II, III, IV, placed after an Indulgence, indicate the special conditions, viz., I, CONFESSION; II, COMMUNION; III, VISIT to a church or public chapel; IV, PRAYER according to the Pope's intention (see pp. xi-xv).

5. The Reference Notes at the end of the book correspond with the Indulgences; and the dates are those of rescripts of the Congregation of Indulgences, unless otherwise noted (see p. xviii).

6. The Our FATHERS, Hail Mary's, and Glories prescribed for an Indulgence are indicated

throughout by the Latin *Pater noster*, *Ave Maria*, and *Gloria Patri*, or in short, *Pater*, *Ave*, and *Gloria*. They can of course be said in English, and this applies to similar references in Latin to familiar prayers, antiphons, etc.

N.B.—*All the Indulgences which follow, except those granted "in articulo mortis," i.e., for the point of death, and except those marked with an asterisk, are applicable to the holy souls in Purgatory* (S.C. Indul., Dec. 8. 1897).

I. THE HOLY TRINITY.

1. The Angelic Trisagion.

    i. 100 Days, once a day.
    ii. 100 Days, three times a day, on Sundays and during the Octave of Trinity Sunday.
    iii. Plenary, once a month. I, II, IV.

(See Instructions, p. 1.)

SANCTUS, Sanctus, Sanctus, DOMINUS DEUS exercituum: Plena est terra gloria tua: Gloria PATRI, Gloria FILIO, Gloria SPIRITUI SANCTO.

HOLY, Holy, Holy, LORD GOD of Hosts, earth is full of thy Glory, Glory be to the FATHER, Glory be to the SON, Glory be to the HOLY SPIRIT.

2. Gloria Patri seven times, said by three Persons.

    i. 100 Days, once a day.
    ii. Seven Years and Seven Quarantines, on Sundays.

iii. Plenary, twice a month, on any two Sundays. I, II, IV.

(See Instructions.)

In order to gain these Indulgences there must be a pious union of three persons, who shall agree to recite, either together or separately, thrice a day, morning, afternoon and evening, *Gloria Patri* seven times, and *Ave Maria* once, in honour of the Holy Trinity. Should any one of the three die, or cease to belong to the union, a substitute must be found.

3. Mass and Prayers in Thanksgiving for Our Lady's Privileges.

i. 300 Days, once a day.
ii. Plenary, twice a month. I, II, IV.

(See Instructions, p. 1.)

In this Devotion, originally restricted to the Church of Our Lady of Loreto in the Forum of Trajan, Rome, one Votive Mass of the Most Holy Trinity can be celebrated each day, and this in one church alone in any city or village; this church must be designated by the Ordinary. The Mass may be said on days when the Office is of an ordinary double festival. On days when the rite is a major double, or double of the second class, the Mass of the day must be said with a Commemoration of the Most Holy Trinity; this permission, however, does not extend to Sundays of the first class or doubles of the first class. This Mass may be applied according to the intention of benefactors, or for any other pious object, or in suffrage for the dead, even on days when the Rubric requires *Missa pro defunctio.*

Prayers to be said by priest and people after the Mass.

MOST Holy Trinity, FATHER, SON, and HOLY SPIRIT, Three Persons and one GOD, we adore Thee, and with all the love of our whole hearts we give Thee thanks for the high gifts and privileges granted to Mary most holy in her glorious and Immaculate Conception. Gloria PATRI *thrice*, and Ave Maria *once*.

MOST Holy Trinity, FATHER, SON, and HOLY SPIRIT, we adore Thee, and with all the love of our whole hearts we give Thee thanks for the high gifts and privileges granted to Mary most holy in her glorious Nativity. Gloria PATRI *thrice*, and Ave Maria *once*.

MOST Holy Trinity, FATHER, SON, and HOLY SPIRIT, we adore Thee, and with all the love of our whole hearts we give Thee thanks for the high gifts and privileges granted to Mary most holy in her glorious Presentation in the Temple. Gloria PATRI *thrice*, and Ave Maria *once*.

MOST Holy Trinity, FATHER, SON, and HOLY SPIRIT, we adore Thee, and with all the love of our whole hearts we give Thee thanks for the high gifts and privileges granted to Mary most holy in her glorious Annunciation. Gloria PATRI *thrice*, and Ave Maria *once*.

MOST Holy Trinity, FATHER, SON, and HOLY SPIRIT, we adore Thee, and with all the love of our whole hearts we give Thee thanks for the high gifts and privileges granted to Mary most holy in her glorious Visitation. Gloria PATRI *thrice*, and Ave Maria *once*.

MOST Holy Trinity, FATHER, SON, and HOLY SPIRIT, we adore Thee, and with all the love of our whole hearts we give Thee thanks for the high gifts and privileges granted to Mary most holy in her glorious Purification. Gloria Patri *thrice*, and Ave Maria *once*.

MOST Holy Trinity, FATHER, SON, and HOLY SPIRIT, we adore Thee, and with all the love of our whole hearts we give Thee thanks for the high gifts and privileges granted to Mary most holy in her most glorious Assumption. Gloria Patri *thrice*, and Ave Maria *once*.

LASTLY, we give Thee most hearty thanks, for that Thou hast exalted and glorified the most holy and most sweet name of Mary throughout the whole world.

Prayer to the most Holy Virgin.

MARY, dear Mother! Mother most amiable! tender Mother! Mother full of love and sweetness for thy clients and children! we pray thee, by this our loving act of thanksgiving to the Most Holy Trinity, obtain for all of us grace ever to employ the powers of our souls, and our bodily senses, to the honour and glory of GOD, one in Three Persons, directing all our actions to Him, and loving Him with pure hearts, even as thou didst love Him here on earth; that thus we may be able to attain to the enjoyment of Him in the bliss of heaven with thee for ever and ever.

Bless us in the name of the FATHER, and of the SON, and of the HOLY SPIRIT.

All say the Salve Regina *(See No. 184).*

℣. Let us bless the FATHER, SON, and HOLY SPIRIT.

℞. Let us praise and exalt Him above all for ever.

Let us pray.

ALMIGHTY and eternal GOD, who hast given to us thy servants grace by the confession

of the true faith to acknowledge the glory of the
eternal Trinity, and in the power of thy Majesty
to worship the Unity; grant, we beseech Thee,
that by the firmness of this our faith we may ever
be defended from all adversities. Through CHRIST
our LORD. ℟. Amen.

4. Gloria Patri thrice.

i. 100 Days, thrice a day, for saying morning, noon,
and evening, *Gloria Patri* thrice, in thanksgiving to
the Most Holy Trinity for the graces and privileges
granted to most holy Mary, especially in her glorious Assumption into heaven.

ii. Plenary, once a month. I, II, IV.

(See Instructions, p. 1.)

5. Prayers of Thanksgiving for Our Lady's As-sumption.

i. 300 Days, once a day.

ii. Plenary, once a month. I, II, IV.

(See Instructions, p. 1.)

Adore the eternal FATHER *with a* PATER, Ave, *and*
Gloria; *then say,*

I ADORE Thee, Eternal FATHER, my LORD and
my GOD, in union with all the heavenly host,
rendering Thee infinite thanks for every grace
and favour Thou hast granted to Mary, most holy
Virgin, thy well-beloved daughter, and, above all,
for that height of power to which Thou didst exalt her by her Assumption into heaven.

Adore the Eternal SON *with a* PATER, Ave, *and*
Gloria; *then say,*

I ADORE Thee too, Eternal SON, my GOD, my
LORD, and my REDEEMER, in union with all the

heavenly host, rendering Thee infinite thanks for every grace and favour Thou hast granted to Mary, Virgin most blessed, thy well-beloved Mother, and, above all, for the gift of highest wisdom with which Thou didst glorify her on her Assumption into heaven.

Adore the HOLY SPIRIT *with a* PATER, Ave, *and* Gloria; *then say,*

I ADORE Thee also, O HOLY SPIRIT, the PARACLETE, my GOD and my LORD, and in union with all the heavenly host I render Thee infinite thanks for every grace and favour Thou hast granted to the most blessed Virgin, thy most loving Spouse, and, above all, for that most perfect and divine charity with which Thou didst inflame her most holy and most pure heart in the act of her most glorious Assumption into heaven. In the name of thy most chaste Spouse, I humbly beg of Thee to grant me the grace of remission of all my most grievous sins which I have committed from the first moment when I was able to sin until this day, for all of which I grieve exceedingly, firmly purposing rather to die than ever again offend thy Divine Majesty; and relying on the high merits and most powerful protection of this thy most loving Spouse, I beg of Thee to grant me the most precious gift of thy grace and Divine love, by vouchsafing me those lights and special helps whereby thy eternal providence has determined to will my salvation, and to bring me to Thyself.

Then say three times,

HOLY Mary, all ye holy men and women, saints of GOD, intercede for us to our LORD, that we may merit his help and be saved. Amen.

To the Most Blessed Virgin.

I ACKNOWLEDGE thee and I venerate thee, most holy Virgin, Queen of Heaven, Lady and Mistress of the Universe, as Daughter of the Eternal FATHER, Mother of his well-beloved SON, and most loving Spouse of the HOLY SPIRIT. Kneeling at the feet of thy great Majesty, with all humility I pray thee, through that divine charity with which thou wast so bounteously enriched on thy Assumption into heaven, to vouchsafe me favour and pity, placing me under thy most safe and faithful protection, and receiving me into the number of thy happy and highly-favoured servants. Deign, Mother and Lady most tender, to accept my miserable heart, memory, will, powers, and senses, internal and external; govern them all in conformity to the good pleasure of thy Divine SON, as I intend by my every thought and deed to give thee glory and honour. And, by that wisdom with which thy well-beloved SON glorified thee, I pray and beseech thee to obtain for me light that I may clearly know myself and my own nothingness, and in particular my sins, that so I may hate and loathe them; and that I may discern the snares of the infernal enemy, and all his modes of attack, whether open or hidden. Above all, most tender Mother, I beg of thee the grace of N.

Say three times,

> Virgin of all virgins,
> To thy shelter take us,
> Gentlest of the gentle,
> Chaste and gentle make us.

Let us pray.

PARDON, O LORD, we beseech Thee, the sins of thy servants; that we, who of our own actions know not how to please Thee, may be saved by the intercession of the Mother of thy SON, our LORD. Through the same CHRIST our LORD. Amen.

May the almighty and merciful LORD, FATHER, SON, and HOLY SPIRIT, bless and preserve us. Amen.

6. Three Offerings of Thanksgiving—To obtain a Good Death.

i. 100 Days. T.Q.
ii. Plenary, once a month, at the end of the month. I, II, IV.

(See Instructions, p. 1.)

WE offer to the Most Holy Trinity the merits of JESUS CHRIST, in thanksgiving for the Most Precious Blood which He shed in the garden for us; and through those merits we beseech his Divine Majesty for pardon of our sins. PATER, Ave, Gloria.

WE offer to the Most Holy Trinity the merits of JESUS CHRIST, in thanksgiving for his most precious death endured on the Cross for us; and through those merits we beseech his Divine Majesty for the remission of the pains due to our sins. PATER, Ave, Gloria.

WE offer to the Most Holy Trinity the merits of JESUS CHRIST, in thanksgiving for his unspeakable charity, in descending from heaven to earth to take human flesh, and to suffer and die for us upon the Cross; and by those merits we beseech his Divine Majesty to bring our souls to the glory of heaven after our death. Pater, Ave, Gloria.

7. Triduo, or Novena (made at any time in public or private in honour of the Holy Trinity).

  i. Seven Years and Seven Quarantines every day of the Triduo or Novena.
  ii. Plenary, to those who shall keep such Novena or Triduo completely. I, II, III & IV.

  (See Instructions, p. 1.)

8. The Sign of the Cross.

  i. 50 Days. T.Q.
  ii. 100 Days, if made with Holy Water. T.Q.

  (See Instructions, p. 1.)

N.B.—The words must in either case be said.

In the name of the Father, and of the Son, and of the Holy Spirit.

9. Thanksgiving on New-Year's Eve.

Seven Years, IV.

  (See Instructions, p. 1.)

This Devotion consists of two half-hours, viz., the last of the old year and the first of the new, spent in thanksgiving to the Holy Trinity for benefits received, and in praying according to the intention of the Pope.

10. Prayer.

200 Days, once a day.

  (See Instructions, p. 1.)

OMNIPOTENTIA Patris, adjuva fragilitatem meam, et

OMNIPOTENCE of the Father, help my frailty, and rescue

e profundo miseriæ eripe me.

Sapientia FILII, dirige cogitationes, verba et actiones meas omnes.

Amor SPIRITUS SANCTI, esto cunctarum animæ meæ operationum principium, quo jugiter sint divino beneplacito conformes.

me from the depths of misery.

Wisdom of the SON, direct all my thoughts, words, and actions.

Love of the HOLY SPIRIT, be the source of all the operations of my soul, so that they may be entirely conformed to the divine will.

11. Acts of Adoration and Thanksgiving to the Blessed Trinity.

300 Days, once a day.

(See Instructions, p. 1.)

MOST Holy Trinity, FATHER, SON, and HOLY SPIRIT, behold us prostrate in thy divine presence. We humble ourselves profoundly, and beg of Thee pardon for our sins.

We adore Thee, Omnipotent FATHER, and with the outpouring of our hearts we thank Thee for having given us thy divine SON JESUS to be our REDEEMER, and for having left Him with us to the consummation of the world in the most august sacrament of the Holy Eucharist, in which mystery of faith and love He reveals to us the wonders of his Sacred Heart. Gloria PATRI.

O DIVINE Word, most adorable JESUS, we adore Thee in thy Sacrament, and with the outpouring of our hearts we thank Thee for having taken human flesh and for having made Thyself, for our redemption, Priest and Victim in the sacrifice of the Cross, a sacrifice which, by an excess of the love of thy adorable Heart, Thou dost renew every moment on our altars throughout the world. O supreme Priest, O divine Victim, grant that we may honour the sacrifice of the most holy Eucharist with the united homage of most holy Mary and of all thy Church, in triumph, in suffering, and in warfare. We offer ourselves wholly to Thee, and since thou dost deign to have victims associated with Thee, accept our offering, and, uniting it with thine, bless us. Gloria PATRI.

O DIVINE SPIRIT and PARACLETE, we adore Thee, and with the outpouring of our hearts, we thank Thee for having, with so much love for us, wrought the ineffable blessing of the Incarnation of the divine Word, a benefit which is continually being extended and increased in the most holy Eucharist. By this adorable mystery of the love of the Sacred Heart of JESUS, grant to us and to all sinners thy grace; pour out upon us and upon all redeemed souls thy holy gifts, but in a special manner bestow them upon the holy Church, the Spouse of JESUS CHRIST and our Mother, upon its visible head the supreme Pontiff, upon all the Cardinals, the Bishops and pastors of souls, on all priests, and on all the other ministers of the Sanctuary. Amen. Gloria PATRI.

12. Prayer to the Holy Trinity.

300 Days.* T.Q.

(See Instructions, p 1.)

I ADORE Thee, O my GOD, one GOD in three Persons; I annihilate myself before thy Majesty. Thou alone art being, life, truth, beauty, and goodness. I glorify Thee, I praise Thee, I thank Thee, and I love Thee, all incapable and unworthy as I am, in union with thy dear SON JESUS CHRIST, our SAVIOUR and our FATHER, in the mercifulness of his heart and through his infinite merits. I wish to serve Thee, to please Thee, to obey Thee, and to love Thee always, in union with Mary immaculate, Mother of GOD and our Mother, loving also and serving my neighbour for thy sake. Therefore, give me thy HOLY SPIRIT to enlighten, correct, and guide me in the way of thy commandments, and in all perfection, until we come to the happiness of heaven, where we shall glorify Thee for ever. Amen.

13. Renewal of Baptismal Vows.

Plenary. I, II, & IV.

(See Instructions, p. 1.)

This must be done solemnly and publicly, with ceremonial sanctioned by the Bishop, on Trinity Sunday.

II. ALMIGHTY GOD

14. Acts of Faith, Hope and Charity.

i. Seven Years and Seven Quarantines. T.Q.
ii. Plenary, once a month. I, II, IV.
iii. Plenary, *in articulo mortis,* (at the point of death), if frequently used during life.

(See Instructions, p. 1.)

N.B.—Any form of words may be used, provided that in each case it expresses the special motive peculiar to the virtue.

Act of Faith.

I MOST firmly believe, because GOD, who is the infallible Truth, hath so revealed to the Holy Catholic Church, and through the Church reveals to us, that there is one only GOD in three divine Persons, equal and distinct, FATHER, SON, and HOLY SPIRIT; that the SON became Man by taking to himself flesh and a human soul through the operation of the HOLY SPIRIT in the womb of the most pure Virgin Mary; that He died for us upon the Cross, rose again, ascended into heaven, and from thence shall come again at the end of the world to judge the living and the dead, to give Paradise for ever to the good and hell to the wicked; moreover, from the same motive I believe all that the same holy Church believes and teaches.

Act of Hope.

O MY GOD, because Thou art almighty, infinitely good and merciful, I hope that, by the merits of the Passion and Death of JESUS CHRIST our SAVIOUR, Thou wilt grant me eternal life, which Thou, most faithful, hast promised to all those who shall do the works of a good Christian, as I purpose to do by thy holy help.

Act of Charity.

O MY GOD, because Thou art the highest and most perfect good, I love Thee with my whole heart, and above all things; and rather than offend Thee, I am ready to lose all things; and moreover for thy love I love, and will love my neighbour as myself.

15. Chaplet of Acts of the Love of GOD.

i. 300 Days, once a day.
ii. Plenary, once a year, to those who say them at least ten times a month. I, II, IV.

(See Instructions, p. 1.)

O My GOD, and Sovereign Good, would that I had always loved Thee!

2. My GOD, I detest that time when I loved Thee not.

3. How could I ever live so long without thy holy love?

4. And Thou, too, my GOD, how couldst Thou bear with me?

5. My GOD, I give Thee thanks for thy great patience.

6. But now I desire to love Thee for ever.

7. I am content rather to die than love Thee not.

8. Take from me my life, O my GOD, if I am not to love Thee.

9. The grace I beg of Thee is to love Thee ever.

10. With thy love I shall be blessed. Gloria PATRI.

M Y GOD, I would see Thee loved by all.

2. Happy should I be, could I but shed my blood that all might love Thee.

3. He who loves Thee not is blind indeed.

4. My GOD, give him thy light.

5. Miserable indeed are they who love not Thee, the Sovereign Good.

6. My GOD, let me never be one of those wretched ones who love Thee not.

7. My GOD, be Thou my joy, and all my good.

8. I would be wholly thine for ever.

9. Who shall separate me from thy holy love?

10. Come, all ye creatures, love ye my GOD. Gloria PATRI.

MY GOD, I would I had a thousand hearts wherewith to love Thee.

2. I would that I had all hearts of all men wherewith to love Thee.

3. I would there were more worlds, that all might love Thee.

4. How blessed would he be who could love Thee with the hearts of all possible creatures!

5. Thou meritest, my GOD, to be so loved.

6. My heart is too poor, too cold, to love Thee.

7. Alas for the dead coldness of men in not loving their Sovereign Good!

8. Alas for the miserable blindness of the world which knows not Thee, who art true love.

9. O blessed inhabitants of heaven, who know and love him!

10. O blessed necessity of loving GOD! Gloria PATRI.

MY GOD, when will the time come that I shall burn with love for Thee?

2. Oh, then what happiness were mine!

3. But, since I know not how to love Thee, I will at least rejoice that there are so many others who love Thee with their whole hearts.

4. In particular I rejoice that Thou art loved by all angels and all saints in heaven.

5. With the hearts of all these I unite the love of my poor heart.

6. In a special manner I intend to love Thee with the love with which those Saints who loved Thee best have loved Thee.

7. Wherefore I intend to love Thee with the love wherewith St Mary Magdalene, St Catherine and St Teresa loved Thee.

8. With the love wherewith St Augustine, St Dominic, St Francis Xavier, St Philip Neri and St Louis Gonzaga loved Thee.

9. With the love wherewith thy Holy Apostles, especially St Peter, St Paul, and the beloved Disciple, loved Thee.

10. With that same love wherewith St Joseph the great Patriarch loved Thee. Gloria PATRI.

MOREOVER, I intend to love Thee with that love wherewith Mary most holy, loved Thee when on earth.

2. In particular with that love wherewith she loved Thee when she conceived thy Divine SON in her virgin womb, when she brought Him forth, when she suckled Him, and when she saw Him die.

3. Yet more, I intend to love Thee with that love wherewith she loves Thee, and will love Thee forever in heaven.

4. But to love Thee worthily, O my GOD of infinite goodness, not even this love suffices.

5. Wherefore I would love Thee as thy SON, the Divine Word made Man, did love Thee.

6. As He loved Thee when He was born.

7. As He loved Thee when He died upon the Cross.

8. As He loves Thee ever in those sacred tabernacles where He lies hid.

9. And with that love with which He loves Thee and will love Thee in heaven for all eternity.

10. Lastly, I would fain love Thee with that love with which Thou lovest thyself; but since that is impossible, grant me, O my GOD, of thy tender pity, that I may love Thee as far as I know how and am able, and as Thou art pleased that I should love Thee. Amen and Amen. Gloria PATRI.

Let us pray.

O GOD, who hast prepared invisible good things for them that love Thee, pour into our hearts such a desire of thy love, that we, loving Thee in all things and above all things, may attain thy heavenly promises, which exceed all that we can desire. Through CHRIST our LORD. Amen.

16. Prayer.

i. 40 Days. T.Q.
ii. 100 Years and 100 Quarantines, or saying it every Saturday for a month.

(See Instructions, p. 1.)

LOOSEN, O LORD, we pray Thee, in thy pity, the bonds of our sins, and by the intercession of the blessed Mary ever Virgin, Mother of GOD, St Joseph, the blessed Apostles Peter and Paul, and all saints, keep us thy servants and our abodes in all holiness; cleanse us, our relations, kinsfolk, and acquaintances from all vices; adorn us with all virtues; grant us peace and health; repel our enemies visible and invisible; curb our carnal desires; give us healthful seasons; bestow thy charity upon our friends and our enemies; guard thy holy City; preserve our Sovereign Pontiff N.; defend all prelates, princes, and Christian people from all adversity. Let thy blessing be ever upon us, and grant to all the faithful departed eternal rest. Through CHRIST our LORD. Amen.

17. Prayer of St Francis Xavier for the Conversion of Infidels.

300 Days, once a day.
(See Instructions, p. 1.)

AETERNE rerum omnium effector DEUS, memento abs te animas infidelium procreatas, easque ad imaginem et similitudinem tuam conditas. Ecce, DOMINE, in opprobrium tuum his ipsis infernus impletur. Memento JESUM FILIUM tuum pro illorum salute atrocissimam subiisse necem. Noli, quæso, DOMINE, ultra permittere, ut FILIUS tuus ab infidelibus contemnatur; precibus sanctorum virorum

ETERNAL GOD, the Maker of all things, remember that the souls of unbelievers have been created by Thee, and that they have been made after thy own image and likeness. Behold, O LORD, to thy dishonour, with these very souls hell is filled. Remember, O GOD, that for their salvation thy SON JESUS CHRIST underwent a most cruel death. O LORD, suffer not that thy SON be despised by unbelievers; appeased by the et Ecclesiæ sanctissimi FILII tui Sponsæ placatus, recordare misericordiæ tuæ, et oblitus idololatriæ et infidelitatis eorum, effice ut ipsi quoque agnoscant aliquando quem misisti DOMINUM JESUM CHRISTUM, qui est salus, vita, et resurrectio nostra; per quem salvati et liberati sumus: cui sit gloria per infinita sæcula sæculorum. Amen.

prayers of holy men and of the Church, the Spouse of thy most holy SON, remember thy own pity, and, forgetting their idolatry and their unbelief, bring to pass that they may at length acknowledge thy SON JESUS CHRIST, who is our salvation, life, and resurrection, through whom we are saved and set free; to whom be glory from age to age without end. Amen.

18. Prayer for Peace

i. i. 100 Days, T.Q.
ii. Plenary once a month. I, II, III, IV.
(See Instructions, p. 1.)

DA pacem, DOMINE, in diebus nostris: quia non est alius qui pugnet pro nobis nisi tu, DEUS noster.

℣. Fiat pax in virtute tua.

℞. Et abundantia in turribus tuis.

GIVE peace, O LORD, in our days; for there is none other that fighteth for us, but only Thou, our GOD.

℣. Let there be peace in thy strength, O LORD.

℞. And plenty in thy strong places.

Oremus.

DEUS, a quo sancta desideria, recta consilia, et justa sunt opera: da servis tuis illam, quam mundus dare non potest, pacem: ut et corda nostra mandatis tuis dedita, et hostium sublata formidine, tempora sint tua protectione tranquilla. Per CHRISTUM DOMINUM nostrum. Amen.

Let us pray.

O GOD, from whom proceed all holy desires, all right counsels and just works; grant unto us thy servants that peace which the world cannot give, that our hearts may be devoted to thy service, and that, being delivered from the fear of our enemies, we may pass our time in peace under thy protection. Through CHRIST our LORD. Amen.

19. Offerings for the Beginning of the Day and for Mass.

iii. Three Years, once a day for each prayer.
iv. Plenary, to those who say both the prayers every day or a month. I, II, III, IV.

(See Instructions, p. 1.)

At the Beginning of the Day.

O LORD GOD Almighty, behold me prostrate before Thee in order to appease Thee, and to honour thy Divine Majesty, in the name of all creatures. But how can I do this who am myself but a poor sinner? Nay, but I both can and will, knowing that Thou dost make it thy boast to be called FATHER of mercies, and for love of us hast given thy only-begotten SON, who sacrificed Himself upon the Cross, and for our sake doth continually renew that sacrifice of Himself upon our altars. And therefore do I—sinner, but penitent; poor, but rich in JESUS CHRIST—present myself before Thee, and, with the love of angels and of all thy saints, and with the tender affection of the Immaculate Heart of Mary, I offer to Thee in the name of all creatures the Masses which are now being celebrated, together with all those which have been celebrated, and which shall be celebrated to the end of the world. Moreover, I intend to renew the offering of them every moment of this day and of all my life, that I may thereby render to thy infinite Majesty an honour and a glory worthy of Thee, thus to appease thy indignation, to satisfy thy justice for our many sins, to render Thee thanks in proportion to thy benefits, and to implore thy mercies for myself and for all sinners, for all the faithful, living and dead, for thy whole Church, and principally for its visible Head, the Sovereign Pontiff, and lastly for all poor schismatics, heretics, and infidels, that they also may be converted and save their souls.

During, or (in the case of priests) before Mass.

ETERNAL FATHER, I offer to Thee the sacrifice which thy beloved SON JESUS made of Himself upon the Cross, and which He now renews upon this altar; I offer it to Thee in the name of all creatures, together with the Masses which have been celebrated, and which shall be celebrated in the whole world, in order to adore Thee, and to give Thee the honour which Thou dost deserve, to render to Thee due thanks for thy innumerable benefits, to appease thy anger, which our many sins have provoked, and to give Thee due satisfaction for them; to entreat Thee also for myself, for the Church, for the whole world, and for the blessed souls in purgatory. Amen.

20. An Offering.

100 Days, once a day.

(See Instructions, p. 1.)

ETERNAL FATHER, we offer Thee the Blood, Passion, and Death of JESUS CHRIST, and the sorrows of the most holy Mary and St Joseph, in payment for our sins, in suffrage for the holy souls in purgatory, for the wants of our holy Mother the Church, and for the conversion of sinners. Amen.

21. A Morning Offering.

i. 100 Days, once a day.
ii. Plenary, once a month, during the month. I, II, III, IV.

(See Instructions, p. 1.)

ETERNAL GOD, behold me prostrate before the immensity of thy majesty. I humbly adore Thee, and offer Thee all my thoughts, words, and works of this day. I intend to do everything for love of Thee, for thy glory, and for the fulfilment of thy divine will; in order to serve, praise, and bless Thee, to be enlightened in the mysteries of our holy faith, to secure my salvation, and to hope in thy mercy; to satisfy the divine justice for my many grievous sins, to assist the holy souls in purgatory, and to obtain the grace of a true conversion for all sinners. I desire, in fine, to do everything in union with that most pure intention which JESUS and Mary had during life, and which the saints now have in heaven, and the just on earth. Would that I could write down this intention with my own blood, and repeat it as often as there be moments in eternity! O my GOD, accept my goodwill; grant me thy holy blessing and efficacious grace never to commit a mortal sin throughout the course of my life, but particularly on this day, on which I desire and purpose to gain all the Indulgences which it is possible for me to gain, and to be present in spirit at all the Masses which will be celebrated today in the whole world, that I may apply them to the holy souls in purgatory, and free them from all pain. Amen.

22. An Act of Faith.

100 Days, once a day.

(See Instructions, p. 1.)

O MY GOD! I believe in Thee; I believe all that Thou hast revealed, and that the holy Catholic Church proposes for my belief. I believe, first, that the most blessed Virgin is truly the Mother of GOD; I believe firmly, and with all certainty, that she is at the same time mother and virgin, and that she is free from even the least actual sin. I also believe most firmly, and with all certainty, that by a singular grace and privilege of Almighty GOD, in view of the merits of JESUS CHRIST, the Saviour of the human race, Mary was, in the first instant of her conception, preserved free from all stain of original sin. I believe most firmly and with all certainty that when the Roman Pontiff speaks *ex cathedra* that is, when, fulfilling the office of chief pastor and teacher of all Christians, he, in virtue of his supreme and apostolic authority, defines a doctrine concerning faith or morals to be held by the universal Church by the divine assistance, promised him in the person of St Peter, possesses that infallibility with which the divine REDEEMER wished his Church to be endowed when defining matters of faith or morals; and, therefore, that such definitions of the Roman Pontiff are, of themselves, and not from the consent of the Church, irreformable. I believe all this, because thy holy Church, which is the pillar and ground of truth, which has never erred and can never err, proposes it to be believed.

23. Prayer of St Bonaventure.

100 Days, once a day.

(See Instructions, p. 1.)

DOMINE sancte, PATER omnipotens, æterne DEUS, propter tuam largitatem et FILII tui, qui pro me sustinuit passionem et mortem, et matris ejus excellentissimam sanctitatem, atque beati Francisci, et

O HOLY LORD, almighty FATHER, eternal GOD! through thy liberality and that of thy SON, who for me endured suffering and death, through the surpassing holiness of His Mother, and through the merits of omnium sanctorum merita, concede mihi peccatori, et omni tuo benencio indigno, ut te solum diligam, tuo amore semper sitiam, beneficium passionis continuo in corde habeam, meam miseriam recognoscam, et ab omnibus conculcari et contemni cupiam: nihil me contristet nisi culpa. Amen.

blessed Francis, and of all the saints, grant me, a sinner, undeserving of all thy benefits, that I may love Thee alone, and always thirst for thy love; that I may constantly feel in my heart the benefit of thy Passion; that I may acknowledge my misery, and desire to be trampled upon and despised by all men; that nothing but sin may sadden my heart. Amen.

24. Prayer.

100 Days, once a day.

(See Instructions, p. 1.)

O LORD Almighty, who permittest evil to draw good therefrom, hear our humble prayers, and grant that we remain faithful to Thee unto death. Grant us also, through the intercession of most holy Mary, the strength ever to conform ourselves to thy most holy Will.

25. Prayer of St Ignatius.

300 Days, once a day.
(See Instructions, p. 1.)

SUSCIPE DOMINE universam meam libertatem. Accipe memoriam, intellectum atque voluntatem omnem. Quidquid habeo vel possideo mihi largitus es: id tibi totum restituo, ac tuæ prorsus voluntati trado gubernandum. Amorem tui solum cum gratia tua dones, et dives sum satis, nec aliud quidquam ultra posco.

TAKE, O LORD, all my liberty. Receive my memory, understanding, and entire will. Thou hast bestowed on me whatever I have or possess: I give all back to Thee, and deliver it to Thee to be entirely subject to thy will. Only grant me thy love and thy grace, and I am rich enough and ask for nothing more.

26. Prayer.

200 Days, once a day.
(See Instructions, p. 1.)

THOU seest, O LORD, how on all sides the winds are let loose upon us, and the sea is growing rough with the violent commotion of the waves. Do Thou, we beseech Thee, who alone art able, command the winds and the waves. Restore to mankind that true peace which the world cannot give, the peace which comes of good order. Let men impelled by thy grace return to a right

and orderly course of life, practising again, as
they ought, love towards GOD, justice and charity
in dealing with their neighbour, temperance and
self control in their own lives. May thy kingdom
come, and may those who now vainly and labo-
riously seek for truth and salvation, far removed
from Thee, understand that they must live as thy
servants in subjection to Thee. Thy laws show
forth thy justice and paternal gentleness, and to
enable us to keep them, Thou dost freely supply
by thy grace the ready means. The life of man on
earth is a warfare, but "Thou dost thyself behold
the strife, "Thou dost help man to conquer, raise
him when he falls, and crown him when he is
victorious." St. Aug. in Ps. 32.

27. Prayer.

100 Days, once a day.
(See Instructions, p. 1.)

O LORD, who in the mystery of the glorious
Transfiguration of thy Divine SON, didst
deign to make resplendent the truth of the holy
Catholic Faith, and to confirm miraculously, by
thy very word, spoken from a cloud, our perfect
adoption as thy sons; we humbly beg of Thee to
grant that we may in truth become coheirs of this
same King of Glory, and share in thy everlasting
happiness. Amen.

28. Prayer for the Supreme Pontiff.

200 Days, once a day.

(See Instructions, p. 1.)

O LORD, in union with millions of believers, and prostrate here at thy feet, we pray Thee to save, defend, and long preserve the Vicar of CHRIST, the Father of the glorious society of souls, our own Father. Today and every day he prays for us, fervently offering to Thee the sacred Victim of love and peace. Turn then, O LORD, thy loving eyes upon us, who forgetful as it were of ourselves pray now above all things for him. Unite our prayers with his, and receive them into the bosom of thy infinite mercy, as a most sweet perfume of that living and efficacious charity, in which the children of the Church are united to their Father. All that he asks of Thee today we too ask for with him. Whether he sorrows or rejoices, or when he hopes or offers the Victim of love for his people, we would be united with him. We desire that the utterance of our souls should be one with his. Mercifully grant, O LORD, that no one of us be far from his mind and heart during the hour of his prayer, and when he offers to Thee the sacrifice of thy blessed SON. And in the moment that he, our most revered Pontiff, holding in his hands the very body of JESUS CHRIST, shall say to the people over the Chalice of benediction the words: *The peace of the Lord be ever with you,* do Thou, O LORD, cause thy most sweet peace to descend with a new and manifest power into our hearts, and upon all the nations of mankind. Amen.

29. Ejaculation of Resignation to the Will of GOD.

   i. 100 Days, once a day.
  ii. Plenary, once a year, to all who say it daily. I, II, IV.
 iii. Plenary, *in articulo mortis* (at the point of death), to those who, during life, shall have frequently recited this Ejaculation, provided that, worthily disposed, they accept death with resignation from the hands of GOD.

(See Instructions, p. 1.)

FIAT, laudetur, atque in æternum superexaltetur justissima, altissima, et amabilissima voluntas DEI in omnibus.

MAY the most just, most high, and most adorable will of GOD be in all things done, praised, and magnified forever.

30. Ejaculation.

50 Days. T.Q.

(See Instructions, p. 1.)

DEUS meus et omnia!

My GOD, and my all!

31. Invocation.

100 Days, once a day.

(See Instructions, p. 1.)

MY GOD, grant that I may love Thee, and as the sole reward of my love, grant that I may ever love Thee more and more.

32. Ejaculation.

   i. 300 Days, once a day.
   ii. Plenary, once a month, during the month. I, II, III, IV.

             (See Instructions, p. 1.)

MY GOD, my only good, Thou art all mine; grant that I may be all thine.

33. Ejaculation.

50 Days. T.Q. (If said devoutly on hearing a blasphemy.)

             (See Instructions, p. 1.)

DEUS sit benedictus.   Blessed be GOD.

34. Ejaculation.

300 Days. T.Q.

             (See Instructions, p. 1.)

MY GOD, unite all minds in the truth and all hearts in charity.

III. THE HOLY SPIRIT

35. The Hymn and Sequence.

i. 100 Days for each. IV. T.Q.
ii. 300 Days, on Whit Sunday, and its Octave for either. IV.
iii. Plenary, once a month for one, or other. I, II, IV.

(See Instructions, p. 1.)

Hymn.

VENI, Creator
SPIRITUS,
Mentes tuorum visita,
Imple superna gratia
Quæ tu creasti pectora.

COME, O Creator
SPIRIT blest!
And in oursouls take up
thy rest;
Come, with thy grace
and heavenly aid,
To fill the hearts which
Thou hast made.

Qui diceris PARACLITUS,
Altissimi Donum DEI,
Fons vivus, Ignis,
Charitas
Et spiritalis Unctio.

Great PARACLETE! to
Thee we cry:
O highest gift of GOD
most high!
O fount of life! O fire of
love!
And sweet Anointing
from above!

Tu, septiformis munere,
Digitus Paternæ dexteræ,
Tu rite promissum
PATRIS,
Sermone ditans guttura.

Thou in thy sevenfold
gifts art known!
Thee, Finger of GOD's
hand, we own;
The promise of the
FATHER Thou!

Who dost the tongue
with pow'r endow.

Accende lumen sensibus,
Infunde amorem cor-
dibus,
Infirma nostri corporis
Virtute firmans perpeti.

Kindle our senses from
above,
And make our hearts
o'erflow with love;
With patience firm, and
virtue high,
The weakness of our
flesh supply.

Hostem repellas longius,
Pacemque dones proti-
nus;
Ductore sic te prævio
Vitemus omne noxium.

Far from us drive the foe
we dread,
And grant us thy true
peace instead;
So shall we not, with
Thee for guide,
Turn from the path of
life aside.

Per te sciamus da
PATREM,
Noscamus atque FILIUM,
Teque utriusque SPIRITUM
Credamus omni tempore.

O, may thy grace on us
bestow
The FATHER and the SON
to know,
And Thee, through end-
less times confess'd,
Of Both th'eternal SPIRIT
blest.

DEO PATRI sit gloria
Ejusque soli FILIO,
Cum SPIRITU PARACLITO
Nunc et per omne sæcu-
lum. Amen.

All glory, while the ages
run,
Be to the FATHER and the
SON,
The same, O HOLY
SPIRIT, to Thee,
Now and through all
eternity. Amen.

Temp. Pasch.
DEO PATRI sit gloria,
Et FILIO, qui a mortuis
Surrexit, ac PARACLITO,
In sæculorum sæcula.
     Amen.

Paschal Time.
All glory while the ages
run
Be to the FATHER and the
SON,
Who rose from death;
the same to Thee,
O HOLY SPIRIT, eternally.
     Amen.

Sequence.
VENI, SANCTE SPIRITUS,
Et emitte cœlitus
Lucis tuæ radium.
Veni, PATER pauperum
Veni, dator munerum;
Veni, lumen cordium.

HOLY SPIRIT! LORD of
light!
From thy clear celestial
height,
Thy pure beaming radi-
ance give:
Come, Thou FATHER of
the poor!
Come, with treasures
which endure!
Come, Thou Light of all
that live!

Consolator optime,
Dulcis hospes animæ,
Dulce refrigerium.

Thou, of all consolers
best,
Visiting the troubled
breast,
Dost refreshing peace
bestow;

In labore requies,
In æstu temperies,

Thou in toil art comfort
sweet;
Pleasant coolness in the
heat;

In fletu solatium.

Solace in the midst of
woe.

O lux beatissima,
Reple cordis intima
Tuorum fidelium.

Light immortal! Light
Divine!
Visit Thou these hearts
of thine,
And our inmost being
fill:

Sine tuo numine
Nihil est in homine,
Nihil est innoxium.

If Thou take thy grace
away,
Nothing pure in man
will stay;
All his good is turn'd
to ill.

Lava quod est sordidum,
Riga quod est aridum,
Sana quod est saucium.

Heal our wounds our
strength renew;
On our dryness pour
thy dew;
Wash the stains of guilt
away:

Flecte quod est rigidum,
Fove quod est frigidum,
Rege quod est devium.

Bend the stubborn heart
and will;
Melt the frozen, warm
the chill;
Guide the steps that go
astray.

Da tuis fidelibus

Thou, on those who
evermore

In te confidentibus	Thee confess and Thee
Sacrum septenarium.	adore,
	In thy sevenfold gifts,
	descend:

Da virtutis meritum,	Give them comfort
Da salutis exitum,	when they die;
Da perenne gaudium.	Give them life with Thee
Amen.	on high;
	Give them joys which
	never end.
	Amen.

36. Novena of the Holy Spirit.

    i. 300 Days, each day.
    ii. Plenary, once during the Novena or eight succeed-
       ing days. I, II, IV.

              (See Instructions, p. 1.)
  This Novena may be made at any time, with any form
of prayers approved by competent ecclesiastical authority.

37. Novena for Pentecost.

    i. Seven Years and Seven Quarantines, each day.
    ii. Plenary, once during the Novena, Feast or Octave.
       I, II, IV.

              (See Instructions, p. 1.)
  This Novena may be made publicly or privately, and
the same Indulgences are granted for special prayers
said every day during the Octave. Any prayers to the
Holy Spirit may be used.

38. Gloria Patri seven times.

To obtain the Seven Gifts, for the Propagation of the Faith, and for the intention of the Pope. Seven Days. IV. T.Q.

(See Instructions, p. 1.)

39. Prayer for the Church.

300 Days, once a day.

(See Instructions, p. 1.)

O CREATOR SANCTE SPIRITUS, adesto propitius Ecclesiæ Catholicæ, eamque contra inimicorum incursus tua superna virtute robora et confirma; tua caritate, et gratia spiritum famulorum tuorum, quos unxisti, renova, ut in te clarificent PATREM FILIUM que ejus unigenitum JESUM CHRISTUM DOMINUM nostrum. Amen.

O HOLY SPIRIT, CREATOR, be propitious to the Catholic Church; and by thy heavenly power make it strong and secure against the attacks of its enemies; and renew in charity and grace the spirit of thy servants, whom Thou hast anointed, that they may glorify Thee and the FATHER and his only begotten SON, JESUS CHRIST, our LORD. Amen.

40. Prayer for the Propagation of the Faith.

100 Days, once a day.

(See Instructions, p. 1.)

SPIRITUS SANCTE, Spiritus veritatis, veni in corda nostra; da populis claritatem lucis tuæ, ut in fidei unitate tibi complaceant.

O HOLY SPIRIT, Spirit of Truth, come into our hearts; shed the brightness of thy light on all nations, that they may be one in Faith and pleasing to Thee.

41. Veni Sancte Spiritus, reple, etc.

300 Days. T.Q.

(See Instructions, p. 1.)

VENI SANCTE SPIRITUS, reple tuorum corda fidelium, et tui amoris in eis ignem accende.

COME, O HOLY SPIRIT, fill the hearts of thy faithful, and kindle in them the fire of thy love.

42. Chaplet of the Holy Spirit.

i. Seven Years and Seven Quarantines, once a day.
ii. Plenary, on the Feast, or during the Octave, of Pentecost, for all who make a practice of this Devotion. I, II, III, IV.

(See Instructions, p. 1.)

Short Act of Contrition.

I GRIEVE, O my GOD, for having sinned against Thee, because Thou art so good; and with the assistance of thy grace I will never sin again.

Come, O Creator SPIRIT blest, etc., (No. 35).

℣. Send forth thy SPIRIT, and they shall be created.

℟. And Thou shalt renew the face of the earth.
Let us pray.

O GOD, who didst instruct the hearts of the faithful by the light of the HOLY SPIRIT, grant us in the same SPIRIT to be truly wise and ever to rejoice in His consolation, through JESUS CHRIST our LORD. Amen.

FIRST MYSTERY. JESUS was conceived of the Virgin Mary by the power of the HOLY SPIRIT.

Meditation. "The HOLY SPIRIT shall descend upon thee, and the power of the most high shall overshadow thee, and therefore the Holy one that shall be born of thee shall be called the SON of GOD" (*St Luke i, 35*).

Application. Pray earnestly for the help of the divine SPIRIT and, through the intercession of Mary, for grace to imitate the virtues of JESUS CHRIST, who is the example of all virtue, and so to be conformed to the image of the SON of GOD. PATER *and* Ave *once*, Gloria *seven times*.

SECOND MYSTERY. The SPIRIT of GOD rests upon JESUS.

Meditation. "JESUS being baptized came forth immediately from the water, and behold the heavens were opened, and he saw the SPIRIT of GOD descend like a dove, and coming, stand over Him" (*St Matt, iii, 16*).

Application. Hold in the highest esteem the priceless gift of sanctifying grace, which the HOLY SPIRIT infused into your heart in Baptism. Keep the promises to the observance of which you have bound yourself. By continual exercise, increase Faith, Hope and Charity. Live always as becomes

children of GOD, and members of his true Church,
in order that after this life has run its course, you
may be worthy to receive your heavenly inheritance. PATER *and* Ave *once*, Gloria *seven times*.

THIRD MYSTERY. JESUS was conducted by the SPIR-
IT into the desert.

Meditation. "But JESUS, full of the HOLY SPIRIT,
retired from the Jordan, and was conducted by
the SPIRIT into the desert for forty days; and was
tempted by the Devil" (*St Luke iv, 1, 2*).

Application. Be always grateful for the seven gifts
given to you by the HOLY SPIRIT in Confirmation;
for the spirit of wisdom and understanding, of
counsel and fortitude, of knowledge and piety,
and of the fear of the LORD. Faithfully adhere to
your divine Guide, acting manfully in all the dangers of this life and in temptation, as becomes
a perfect Christian and a brave athlete of JESUS
CHRIST. PATER *and* Ave *once*, Gloria *seven times*.

FOURTH MYSTERY. The HOLY SPIRIT in the Church.

Meditation. "And suddenly there was a sound
from Heaven as of a mighty wind coming where
they were assembled; and they were all filled with
the HOLY SPIRIT, and began to discourse of the
wonderful works of GOD" (*Acts ii, 2, 4, 11*).

Application. Thank GOD for making you a child of
his Church which the divine SPIRIT, sent into the
world on the day of Pentecost, ever vivifies and
rules. Hear and obey the Supreme Pontiff, who
by the assistance of the HOLY SPIRIT is the infallible teacher, and the Church, which is the pillar
and foundation of truth. Hold fast her doctrines,
maintain her cause, defend her rights. PATER *and*

Ave *once*, Gloria *seven times*.

FIFTH MYSTERY. The HOLY SPIRIT in the soul of the just man.

Meditation. "Do you not know that your members are the temple of the HOLY SPIRIT, who is in you" (I *Cor. vi*, 19).

"Do not extinguish the SPIRIT" (I *Thess. v*, 19).

"And grieve not the HOLY SPIRIT of GOD, whereby you are sealed unto the day of redemption "(*Ephes. iv*, 30).

Application. Be ever mindful of the HOLY SPIRIT who is in you, and watch with all possible care over purity of soul and body. Faithfully obey his divine inspirations, so as to gather therefrom the fruits of the SPIRIT: Charity, joy, peace, benignity, goodness, longanimity, mildness, faith, modesty, continency, chastity. PATER *and* Ave *once*, Gloria *seven times*.

End with the Creed, as a profession of faith, and PATER *and* Ave *once according to the intention of the Pope.*

43. Prayer to the Holy Spirit.

300 Days, once a day.

(See Instructions, p. 1.)

O HOLY SPIRIT, divine spirit of light and love, I consecrate to Thee my understanding, heart and will, my whole being for time and for eternity. May my understanding be always submissive to thy heavenly inspirations, and to the teaching of the Catholic Church, of which Thou art the infallible Guide; may my heart be ever inflamed with love of GOD and of my neighbour; may my will be ever conformed to the divine will, and may my whole life be a faithful imitation of the life and virtues of our LORD and SAVIOUR JESUS CHRIST, to whom with the FATHER and Thee be honour and glory for ever. Amen.

IV. JESUS CHRIST

44. Rosary of Our Lord.

This Rosary is composed of the *Pater*, said thirty-three times in remembrance of the thirty-three years He lived on earth, and of the *Ave* five times in honour of his five most holy wounds; the first three of which are said, one at the beginning of each of the three divisions comprising the *Pater* said ten times; of the two remaining one *Ave* is said before saying *Pater noster* thrice in conclusion, and the other after saying them. This Rosary finishes with the *Credo* in honour of the holy Apostles.

In order to gain the following Indulgences it is necessary that—

The Rosary mbe blessed by the Reverend Fathers of the Camaldolese Order, either hermits or monks, or else by those who have apostolical authority to bless them.

Every one saying this Rosary should, according to his capacity, meditate on the mysteries of the life of our LORD JESUS CHRIST.

  i. 200 Years, every time, when said after Confession, or at least with firm resolution to confess.

 ii. 150 Years, to anyone who carries about him one of these Rosaries, and says it every Monday,

Wednesday, and Friday, and also on all Feasts of obligation. I, II.

iii. Plenary, once a year, to anyone who has made a practice of saying it at least four times a week. I, II.

iv. Plenary, once a month. I, II, IV.

v. Plenary, at the point of death, to anyone who shall then invoke in his heart, if he cannot do so with his lips, the most holy Name of JESUS; provided he has said this Rosary once during his illness with the intention of gaining this Indulgence; in the event of his recovery, he gains 200 Years.

vi. 20 Days, to anyone who shall carry about him one of these Rosaries, and invoke the adorable Name of JESUS after he has made an examination of conscience with contrition for his sins, and said thrice the *Pater* and thrice the *Ave* for the good estate of the Church.

vii. 20 Years. I, IV.

viii. 10 Years, to anyone who, having about him this Rosary, shall say thrice the *Pater* and thrice the *Ave*, as often as he does any spiritual or temporal good work in honour of our LORD JESUS CHRIST, the Blessed Virgin Mary, or some saint, or for the good of his neighbour.

ix. 200 Years, on the days of the Stations in Rome, to those who carry about them one of these Rosaries. If in Rome, they must visit the church of the Station, or if out of Rome, some other church. But in either case, if the visit cannot be made, the recitation of this Rosary, together with the Penitential Psalms, the Litanies and prayers, may be substituted.

* Plenary on Fridays in March. I, II.

(See Instructions, p. 1.)

Begin with an act of contrition.

First Decade.

THE Archangel Gabriel makes known to Mary the Incarnation of the Divine Word in her pure womb. Ave Maria.

1. The Son of God made man is born of Mary the Virgin in a stable. Pater noster.
2. The Angels rejoice and sing *Gloria in excelsis Deo.* Pater noster.
3. The shepherds hear the Angels' tidings, and come and adore Him. Pater noster.
4. He is circumcised the eighth day, and called by the most holy Name of Jesus. Pater noster.
5. Is adored by the Magi with offerings of gold, frankincense, and myrrh. Pater noster.
6. Is presented in the Temple, and foretold to be the Saviour of the world. Pater noster.
7. Flees from the persecution of Herod, and is carried into Egypt. Pater noster.
8. Herod finds him not, and murders the Innocents. Pater noster.
9. He is carried back by Joseph and his Mother into Nazareth, his home. Pater noster.
10. Disputes in the Temple with the doctors, being twelve years old. Pater noster.

(*Add* Eternal rest, *etc., if said for the departed. See No.* 414)

Second Decade.

Jesus is most obedient to the Blessed Virgin his Mother, and to St Joseph. Ave Maria.

1. When thirty years old, He is baptized by John in the Jordan. Pater noster.
2. Fasts forty days in the desert, and overcomes the tempter. Pater noster.

3. Practises and preaches his own holy law, whereby is life eternal. PATER noster.

4. Calls his disciples, who forthwith leave all and follow Him. PATER noster.

5. Works his first miracle of changing water into wine. PATER noster.

6. Heals the sick, makes the lame to walk, gives hearing to the deaf, sight to the blind, life to the dead. PATER noster.

7. Converts sinful men and women, and pardons their sins. PATER noster.

8. When the Jews persecute Him even unto death, He chastises them not, but sweetly chides them. PATER noster.

9. Is transfigured on Mount Thabor, in the presence of Peter, James and John. PATER noster.

10. Enters triumphant into Jerusalem sitting on an ass's colt, and drives the profaners from the Temple. PATER noster.

(Eternal rest, *etc.*, *as above.*)

THIRD DECADE.

JESUS takes leave of his most holy Mother before He goes to die for our salvation. Ave Maria.

1. Celebrates the last Paschal Supper, washes the Apostles feet. PATER noster.

2. Institutes the most holy Sacrament of the Eucharist. PATER noster.

3. Prays in the garden, sweats blood, and is comforted by an angel. PATER noster.

4. Is betrayed by Judas with a kiss, is taken and bound by the officers of justice as a great malefactor. PATER noster.

5. Is falsely accused, is buffeted and spit upon, and shamefully used before four tribunals. PATER noster.

6. Looks tenderly on Peter after he had thrice denied Him, and converts him; whilst Judas despairs, hangs himself, and is lost. PATER noster.

7. Is cruelly scourged at the pillar, and receives innumerable blows. PATER noster.

8. Is crowned with thorns, shown to the people, who cry, Crucify Him! Crucify Him! PATER noster.

9. Is condemned to die, carries the heavy cross with grievous pain upon his shoulders to Mount Calvary. PATER noster.

10. Is crucified between two thieves, dies after three hours' most painful agony, is wounded in the side with a lance, and is buried. PATER noster.

(Eternal rest, *etc.*, *as above.*)

JESUS rises the third day, and visits first of all Mary his most holy Mother. Ave Maria.

1. Appears to the three Marys, and bids them tell the disciples they have seen Him risen from the dead. PATER noster.

2. Appears to the disciples, shows them his most holy Wounds, makes Thomas touch them. PATER noster.

3. The fortieth day after his resurrection, blesses most holy Mary his Mother and all his disciples; then ascends into heaven. PATER noster.

Let us pray to the most holy Virgin to obtain for us also the blessing of her divine SON JESUS

CHRIST, now and at the hour of our death. Ave Maria.

(Eternal rest, *etc.*, *as above*.)

Then say the Credo in honour of the holy Apostles.

45. Invocation of the Holy Name.

i. 50 Days, every time anyone says to another:

Laudetur JESUS CHRISTUS.   Praised be JESUS CHRIST.

or answers: Amen, or,

In sæcula.   For evermore.

ii. 25 Days, every time anyone invokes the most holy Name of JESUS.

iii. Plenary, at the point of death, to anyone who has had the devout practice of saluting and answering as above, or of invoking often the said most holy Name, provided that he then invokes this holy Name at least in his heart, if he is unable to do so with his lips.

The same Indulgences to preachers and others who exhort the faithful to salute each other in this way, and to invoke frequently the most holy Names of JESUS and Mary.

(See Instructions, p. 1.)

46. Hymns and Psalms in Honour of the Holy Name.

To those who recite certain psalms whose initial letters compose the most holy Name of JESUS, together with certain hymns and prayers:

i. Seven Years and Seven Quarantines. T.Q.

ii. Plenary, once a month. I, II, IV.

iii. Plenary, on the Feast of the most holy Name of JESUS (the Second Sunday after Epiphany) to all who say them frequently in the course of the year. I, II, IV.

iv. Plenary, on the Feast of the Circumcision of our
LORD JESUS CHRIST, January I, and the Feast of JESUS
the Nazarene, October 23, for those who say them
for a month together. I, II, IV.

(See Instructions, p. 1.)

HYMN.

JESU, dulcis memoria,
   Dans vera cordi gaudia:
Sed super mel, et omnia,
Ejus dulcis præsentia.

Nil canitur suavius,
Nil auditur jucundius,
Nil cogitatur dulcius,
Quam JESUS, DEI Filius.

JESU, spes pœnitentibus,
Quam pius es petentibus!
Quam bonus te quærentibus!
Sed quid invenientibus!

Nec lingua valet dicere,
Nec littera exprimere:
Expertus potest credere,
Quid sit JESUM diligere.

Sis, JESU, nostrum gaudium,
Qui es futurum præmium!
Sit nostra in te gloria,
Per cuncta semper sæcula. Amen.

J. *Ant.* In Nomine JESU.
Psalm. xcix.

JUBILATE DEO omnis terra: * servite DOMINO
   in lætitia.
Introite in conspectu ejus, * in exultatione.

Scitote, quoniam Dominus ipse est Deus: * ipse fecit nos, et non ipsi nos.

Populus ejus, et oves pascuæ ejus: * introite portas ejus in confessione, atria ejus in hymnis; confitemini illi.

Laudate nomen ejus, quoniam suavis est Dominus, in æternum misericordia ejus: * et usque in generationem et generationem veritas ejus.

Gloria Patri, et Filio, *etc.*

Ant. In Nomine Jesu omne genu flectatur cœlestium, terrestrium, et infernorum.

E. *Ant.* Ego autem.
Psalm. xix.

EXAUDIAT te Dominus in die tribulationis: * protegat te nomen Dei Jacob.

Mittat tibi auxilium de sancto: * et de Sion tueatur te.

Memor sit omnis sacrificii tui: * et holocaustum tuum pingue fiat.

Tribuat tibi secundum cor tuum: * et omne consilium tuum confirmet.

Lætabimur in salutari tuo: * et in nomine Dei nostri magnificabimur.

Impleat Dominus omnes petitiones tuas: * nunc cognovi, quoniam salvum fecit Dominus christum suum.

Exaudiet ilium de cœlo sancto suo: * in potentatibus salus dexteræ ejus.

Hi in curribus, et hi in equis: * nos autem in nomine Domini Dei nostri invocabimus.

Ipsi obligati sunt, et ceciderunt: * nos autem surreximus, et erecti sumus.

Domine, salvum fac regem: * et exaudi nos in die, qua invocaverimus te.

Gloria Patri, etc.

Ant. Ego autem in Domino gaudebo, et exultabo in Deo Jesu meo.

S. Ant. Sanctum et terribile.

Psalm. xi.

Salvum me fac, Domine, quoniam defecit sanctus, * quoniam diminutæ sunt veritates a filiis hominum.

Vana locuti sunt unusquisque ad proximum suum: * labia dolosa, in corde, et corde locuti sunt.

Disperdat Dominus universa labia dolosa, * et linguam magniloquam.

Qui dixerunt: linguam nostram magnificabimus, labia nostra a nobis sunt: * quis noster Dominus est?

Propter miseriam inopum, et gemitum pauperum, * nunc exurgam, dicit Dominus.

Ponam in salutari: * fiducialiter agam in eo.

Eloquia Domini eloquia casta, * argentum igne examinatum, probatum terræ, purgatum septuplum.

Tu, Domine, servabis nos, et custodies nos * a generatione hac in æternum.

In circuitu impii ambulant: * secundum altitudinem tuam multiplicasti filios hominum.

Gloria Patri, *etc.*

Ant. Sanctum, et terribile Nomen ejus: initium sapientiæ timor Domini.

U. Ant. Vocabis Nomen ejus Jesus.

Psalm. xii.

USQUEQUO, DOMINE, oblivisceris me in finem? * usquequo avertis faciem tuam a me? Quamdiu ponam consilia in anima mea, * dolorem in corde meo per diem?

Usquequo exaltabitur inimicus meus super me? * respice, et exaudi me, DOMINE DEUS meus.

Illumina oculos meos, ne unquam obdormiam in morte; * nequando dicat inimicus meus: prevalui adversus eum.

Qui tribulant me, exultabunt, si motus fuero: * ego autem in misericordia tua speravi.

Exultabit cor meum in salutari tuo: cantabo DOMINO, qui bona tribuit mihi, * et psallam nomini DOMINI altissimi.

Gloria PATRI, *etc.*

Ant. Vocabis Nomen ejus JESUM: ipse enim salvum faciet populum suum a peccatis eorum.
S. *Ant.* Sitivit anima mea.
Psalm. cxxviii.

SÆPE expugnaverunt me a juventute mea: * dicat nunc Israel.

Sæpe expugnaverunt me a juventute mea: * etenim non potuerunt mihi.

Supra dorsum meum fabricaverunt peccatores: * prolongaverunt iniquitatem suam.

DOMINUS Justus concidit cervices peccatorum: * confundantur, et convertantur retrorsum omnes, qui oderunt Sion.

Fiant sicut fœnum tectorum, * quod priusquam evellatur, exaruit.

De quo non implevit manum suam, qui metit, * et sinum suum, qui manipulos colligit.

Et non dixerunt, qui præteribant: Benedictio DOMINI super vos: * benediximus vobis in nomine DOMINI.

Gloria PATRI, *etc.*

Ant. Sitivit anima mea ad Nomen sanctum tuum, DOMINE.

HYMN

JESU, Rex admirabilis
Et triumphator nobilis,
Dulcedo ineffabilis,
Totus desiderabilis.

Quando cor nostrum visitas,
Tune lucet ei veritas;
Mundi vilescit vanitas,
Et intus fervet charitas.

JESU, dulcedo cordium,
Fons vivus, lumen mentium,
Excedens omne gaudium
Et omne desiderium.

JESUM omnes agnoscite,
Amorem ejus poscite;
JESUM ardenter quærite,
Quærendo inardescite.

Te nostra, JESU, vox sonet,
Nostri te mores exprimant:
Te corda nostra diligant
Et nunc, et in perpetuum. Amen.

℣. Sit nomen DOMINI benedictum.
℟. Ex hoc nunc, et usque in sæculum.
Oremus.

DEUS, qui Unigenitum FILIUM tuum constituisti humani generis Salvatorem, et JESUM vo-

cari jussisti: concede propitius; ut cujus sanctum
Nomen veneramur in terris, ejus quoque aspec-
tu perfruamur in cœlis. Per eumdem CHRISTUM
DOMINUM nostrum. Amen.

47. Prayer for a Holy Death.

300 Days. T.Q.

(See Instructions, p. 1.)

DIVINE JESU, FILI DEI
incarnate, qui pro
nostra salute in stabulo
nasci, vitam in pauper-
tate, ærumnis et mise-
ria degere, et in crucis
doloribus mori digna-
tus es, divino tuo PATRI
dic, quæso, in momen-
to mortis meæ: PATER
ignosce ei; die matri tuæ
dilectæ: *Ecce filius tuus*;
die animæ meæ: *Hodie
eris mecum in Paradiso.*
DEUS meus, DEUS
meus, ne derelinquas
me in ilia hora. Sitio:
utique, DEUS meus,
anima mea sitit ad te,
qui es fons aquarum
viventium. Vita mea
præterit velut umbra;

DIVINE JESUS, incar-
nate SON of GOD,
who for our salvation
didst vouchsafe to be
born in a stable, to
pass thy life in poverty,
trials, and misery, and
to die amid the suf-
ferings of the Cross,
I entreat Thee in the
hour of my death, say
to thy divine FATHER:
"Father, forgive him" say
to thy beloved Mother:
"behold thy son"; say
to my soul: *"this day
thou shalt be with me
in Paradise."* My GOD,
my GOD, forsake me
not in that hour. *"I
thirst"*: truly, my GOD,
my soul thirsts af-
ter Thee, who art the

adhuc modicum et consummata erunt omnia. Quapropter, O SALVATOR mi adorabilis, ex hoc momento in omnem æternitatem, *in manus tuas commendo spiritum meum.* DOMINE JESU, accipe animam meam. Amen.

fountain of living waters. My life passes like a shadow; yet a little while and all will be consummated. Wherefore, O my adorable SAVIOUR, from this moment, for all eternity, *"into thy hands I commend my spirit."* LORD JESUS, receive my soul. Amen.

48. Prayer.

300 Days, once a day.

(See Instructions, p. 1.)

O JESU, vivens in Maria, veni et vive in famulis tuis, in SPIRITU sanctitatis tuæ, in plenitudine virtutis tuæ, in veritate virtutum tuarum, in perfectione viarum tuarum, in communione Mysteriorum tuorum, dominare omni adversæ potestati in SPIRITU tuo ad gloriam PATRIS. Amen.

O JESUS, who dost live in Mary, come and live in thy servants, in the spirit of thine own holiness, in the fullness of thy power, in the reality of thy virtues, in the perfection of thy ways, in the communion of thy Mysteries; have Thou dominion over every adverse power, in thine own SPIRIT, to the glory of thy FATHER. Amen.

49. Prayer.

100 Days, once a day.
(See Instructions, p. 1.)

O CLEMENTISSIME Jesu, salus, vita, resurrectio nostra tu solus es. Te ergo quæsumus ne derelinquas nos in augustiis et perturbationibus nostris, sed per agoniam cordis tui sanctissimi et per dolores matris tuæ immaculatæ tuis famulis subveni, quos pretioso sanguine redemisti.

O MOST compassionate Jesus! Thou alone art our salvation, our life, and our resurrection. We implore Thee, therefore, do not forsake us in our needs and afflictions, but by the agony of thy most Sacred Heart, & by the sorrows of thy immaculate Mother, succour thy servants whom Thou hast redeemed by thy most Precious Blood.

50. Prayer.

100 Days, once a day.
(See Instructions, p. 1.)

O GOOD Jesus! O most tender Jesus! O most sweet Jesus! O Jesus, Son of Mary the Virgin, full of mercy and kindness! O sweet Jesus, according to thy great mercy, have pity on me! O most merciful Jesus, I entreat Thee by that Precious Blood of thine, which Thou didst will to pour forth for sinners, to wash away all my iniquities, and to look upon me, poor and unworthy as I am, asking humbly pardon of Thee, and invoking this holy Name of JESUS. O Name of JESUS, sweet Name! Name of JESUS, Name of joy! Name of JESUS, Name of strength! Nay, what meaneth the Name of JESUS but SAVIOUR? Wherefore, O JESUS, by thine own holy Name, be to me JESUS, and save me. Suffer me not to be lost—me, whom Thou didst create out of nothing. O good JESUS, let not my iniquity destroy what thy almighty goodness made. O sweet JESUS, recognize what is thine own, and wipe away from me what is not of Thee! O most kind JESUS, have pity on me while it is the time of pity, and condemn me not when it is the time of judgment. The dead shall not praise Thee, LORD JESUS, nor all those who go down into hell. O most loving JESUS! O JESUS, most longed for by thine own! O most gentle JESUS! JESUS, JESUS, JESUS, let me enter into the number of thine elect. O JESUS, salvation of those who believe in Thee; JESUS, consolation of those who fly to Thee. JESUS, SON of Mary the Virgin, pour into me grace, wisdom, charity, chastity, and humility, that I may be able perfectly to love Thee, to praise Thee, to enjoy Thee, to serve Thee, and make my boast in Thee, together with all those who invoke thy Name, which is JESUS. Amen.

51. Prayer of St Thomas Aquinas.

(To be said before study or class.)
300 Days. T.Q.
(See Instructions, p. 1.)

CONCEDE mihi, misericors DEUS, quæ tibi placita sunt ardenter concupiscere, prudenter investigare, veraciter agnoscere et perfecte adimplere ad laudem et gloriam nominis tui. Amen.

O MERCIFUL GOD, grant that I may eagerly desire, carefully search out, truthfully acknowledge, and ever perfectly fulfil all things which are pleasing to Thee, to the praise and glory of thy Name. Amen.

52. Prayer of St Thomas Aquinas.

(Before writing, preaching, etc.)
200 Days, once a day.
(See Instructions, p. 1.)

CREATOR ineffabilis, qui de thesauris sapientiæ tuæ tres angelorum hierarchias designasti et eas super cælum empyreum miro ordine collocasti, atque universi partes elegantissime disposuisti.

INEFFABLE CREATOR, who, of the treasures of thy wisdom hast formed the nine choirs of Angels, and set them on high above the heavens in a wonderful order, and hast exquisitely fashioned and knit together

Tu inquam, qui verus fons luminis et sapientiæ diceris ac supereminens principium, infundere digneris super intellectus mei tenebras tuæ radium claritatis, duplices, in quibus natus sum, a me removens tenebras, peccatum scilicet et ignorantiam. Tu, qui linguas infantium facis disertas, linguam meam erudias, atque in labiis meis gratiam tuæ benedictionis infunde. Da mihi intelligendi acumen, retinendi capacitatem, addiscendi modum et facultatem, interpretandi subtilitatem, loquendi gratiam copiosam; ingressum instruas,progressum dirigas, egressum compleas, tu, qui es verus DEUS et homo. Qui vivis et regnas in sæcula sæculorum. Amen.

all parts of the universe; do Thou, who art the true fountain and one principle of light and wisdom, deign to shed the brightness of thy light upon the darkness of my understanding, and thus to disperse the twofold darkness of sin and ignorance wherein I was born. O Thou, who makest eloquent the tongues of babes, instruct my tongue, and pour forth on my lips the grace of thy blessing. Grant me acuteness in understanding what I read, power to retain it, subtlety to discern its true meaning, and clearness and ease in expressing it. Do Thou order my beginnings, direct and further my progress, complete and bless my ending; Thou who art true GOD and true Man, who livest and reignest world without end. Amen.

53. Petitions of St Augustine.

50 Days, once a day.

(See Instructions, p. 1.)

Domine Jesu, noverim me, noverim te. Nec aliquid cupiam nisi te. Oderim me et amem te. Omnia agam propter te. Humiliem me, exaltemte. Nihil cogitem nisi te. Mortificem me et vivam in te. Quæcunque eveniant accipiam a te. Persequar me, sequar te. Semperque optem sequi te. Fugiam me, confugiam ad te. Ut merear defendi a te. Timeam mihi, timeam te, Et sim inter electos a te. Diffidam mihi, fidam in te. Obedire velim propter te. Ad nihil afficiar nisi ad te. Et pauper sim propter te. Aspice me, ut diligam te. Voca me ut videam te. Et in æternum fruar te. Amen.

Lord Jesus, may I know myself and know Thee. And desire nothing save only Thee. May I hate myself and love Thee. May I do everything for the sake of Thee. May I humble myself and exalt Thee. May I think of nothing except Thee. May I die to myself and live in Thee. May I receive whatever happens as from Thee. May I banish self and follow Thee. And ever desire to follow Thee. May I fly from myself and fly to Thee, that I may deserve to be defended by Thee. May I fear for myself and fear Thee, and be among those who are chosen by Thee. May I distrust myself and trust in Thee. May I be willing to obey on account of Thee. May I cling to nothing but to Thee. May I be poor for the sake of Thee. Look upon me that I may love Thee. Call me that I may see Thee, and ever and ever enjoy Thee. Amen.

54. Prayer for the Conversion of Scandinavia.

300 Days, once a day.
(See Instructions, p. 1.)

O GOOD JESUS, prostrate at thy feet, we humbly implore Thee, by thy most sacred wounds and by the Precious Blood which Thou didst shed for the salvation of the whole world, that Thou wouldst deign to cast a look of pity on the peoples of Scandinavia, seduced from the Faith for so many centuries, and plunged in the darkness of heresy, separated from thy Church, deprived of the participation of the adorable Sacrament of thy Body and Blood, and of the other sacraments instituted by Thee, as the refuge of souls in life and in death. Remember, O REDEEMER of the world, that for these souls too Thou didst suffer bitter death, with the loss of all thy blood. Bring back, O good Shepherd, these wandering sheep of thine to the one fold and to the healthy pastures of thy Church, so that they may form with us one flock, tended by Thee, and by thy Vicar on earth, the supreme Pontiff, whom, in the person of the Apostle St Peter, Thou didst commission to feed thy sheep and thy lambs. Graciously hear, O good JESUS, the prayers which we offer Thee with the most lively trust in the love of thy Sacred

Heart, and to thy most holy Name be praise, glory, and honour, world without end. Amen.

55. Devotion to the Holy Name.

i. 300 Days. T.Q.
ii. Plenary, on the Sunday after the Epiphany, if said
daily, to all who visit a church where the Feast of
the Holy Name is being celebrated. I, II, IV.
iii. Plenary, to all who assist at the annual requiem for
those who were devout to the holy Name. I, II, IV.

(See Instructions, p. 1.)

Gloria PATRI *and* May the holy Name of JESUS
be infinitely blessed, *five times.*

56. Litany of the Holy Name of Jesus.

300 Days, once a day.
(See Instructions, p. 1.)

KYRIE eleison.
CHRISTE eleison.
KYRIE eleison.
JESU, audi nos.
JESU, exaudi nos
PATER de cœlis DEUS,
  miserere nobis.
FILI REDEMPTOR mundi
  DEUS, *miserere nobis.*
SPIRITUS SANCTE DEUS,
  miserere nobis.
SANCTA TRINITAS, unus
  DEUS, *miserere nobis.*

LORD, have mercy
on us.
CHRIST, have mercy on us.
LORD, have mercy on us.
JESUS, hear us.
JESUS, graciously hear us
GOD the FATHER of heav-
en, *have mercy on us.*
GOD the SON, REDEEMER
of the world, *have
mercy on us.*
GOD the HOLY SPIRIT,
have mercy on us.
Holy Trinity, one GOD,
have mercy on us.

JESU, FILI DEI vivi,
miserere nobis.
JESU, splendor PATRIS,
JESU, candor lucis
æternæ,
JESU, Rex gloriæ,
JESU, sol justitiæ,
JESU, Fili Mariæ Virginis,
JESU amabilis,
JESU admirabilis,
JESU, DEUS fortis,
JESU, PATER futuri sæculi,
JESU, magni consilii
Angele,
JESU potentissime,
JESU patientissime,
JESU obedientissime,
JESU, mitis et humilis
corde,
JESU, amator castitatis,
JESU, amator noster,
JESU, DEUS pacis,
JESU, auctor vitæ,
JESU, exemplar virtutum,
JESU, zelator animarum,
JESU, DEUS noster,
JESU, refugium nostrum,

miserere nobis.

JESUS, SON of the living
GOD,
JESUS, splendour of the
FATHER,
JESUS, brightness of
eternal light,
JESUS, King of glory,
JESUS, sun of justice,
JESUS, SON of the
Virgin Mary,
JESUS, most amiable,
JESUS, most admirable,
JESUS, the mighty GOD,
JESUS, the Father of the
world to come,
JESUS, the Angel of great
counsel,
JESUS, most powerful,
JESUS, most patient,
JESUS, most obedient,
JESUS, meek and humble
of heart,
JESUS, lover of chastity,
JESUS, lover of us,
JESUS, the GOD of peace,
JESUS, the Author of life,
JESUS, the example of
virtues,
JESUS, the zealous lover
of souls,
JESUS, our GOD,
JESUS, our refuge,

have mercy on us.

JESU, pater pauperum,

JESU, thesaure fidelium,

JESU, bone pastor,

JESU, lux vera,

JESU, sapientia æterna,

JESU, bonitas infinita,

JESU, via et vita nostra,

JESU, gaudium Angelorum

JESU, Rex Patriarcharum,

JESU, Magister Apostolorum,

JESU, Doctor Evangelistarum,

JESU, fortitudo Martyrum,

JESU, Lumen Confessorum,

JESU, puritas Virginum,

JESU, corona Sanctorum omnium,

Propitius esto, parce nobis, JESU.

Propitius esto, exaudi nos, JESU.

Ab omni malo, *libera nos*, JESU.

Ab omni peccato, *libera nos*, JESU.

miserere nobis.

JESUS, the father of the poor,

JESUS, the treasure of the faithful,

JESUS, the good shepherd,

JESUS, the true light,

JESUS, the eternal wisdom,

JESUS, infinite goodness,

JESUS, our way and our life,

JESUS, the joy of Angels,

JESUS, the King of Patriarchs,

JESUS, the Master of the Apostles,

JESUS, the Teacher of the Evangelists,

JESUS, the strength of Martyrs,

JESUS, the light of Confessors,

JESUS, the purity of Virgins,

JESUS, the crown of all Saints,

Be merciful unto us, spare us, O LORD JESUS.

Be merciful unto us, hear us, O LORD JESUS.

From all evil, JESUS, *deliver us.*

From all sin, JESUS, *deliver us.*

have mercy on us.

Ab ira tua,
Ab insidiis diaboli,
A spiritu fornicationis,
A morte perpetua,
A neglectu inspiratio-
num tuarum,
Per mysterium sanctæ
Incarnationis tuæ,
Per Nativitatem tuam,
Per Infantiam tuam,
Per divinissimam vitam
tuam,
Per labores tuos,
Per agoniam et passio-
nem tuam,
Per crucem et derelictio-
nem tuam,
Per languores tuos,
Per mortem et sepultur-
am tuam,
Per Resurrectionem
tuam,
Per Ascensionem tuam,
Per sanctissimam insti-
tutionem Eucharistiæ
tuæ,
Per gaudia tua,
Per gloriam tuam,

AGNUS DEI, qui tollis
peccata mundi, parce
nobis, JESU.

Libera nos, Jesu

From thy wrath,
From the snares of the
devil,
From the spirit of forni-
cation,
From everlasting death,
From the neglect of
thy inspirations,
Through the mystery
of thy holy Incarnation,
Through thy Nativity,
Through thy infancy,
Through thy most
divine life,
Through thy labours,
Through thy Agony and
Passion,
Through thy Cross and
dereliction,
Through thy sufferings,
Through thy Death and
burial,
Through thy
Resurrection,
Through thy Ascension,
By the most holy institu-
tion of thy Eucharist.
Through thy joys,
Through thy glory,

LAMB of GOD, who takest
away the sins of the
world, JESUS, spare us.

Jesus, deliver us.

Agnus Dei, qui tollis
peccata mundi, exaudi
nos, Jesu.
Agnus Dei, qui tollis
peccata mundi, misere-
re nobis, Jesu.
Jesu, audi nos.
Jesu, exaudi nos.

Oremus.

Domine Jesu Christe,
qui dixisti: Petite,
et accipietis; quærite,
et invenietis; pulsate,
et aperietur vobis: quæ-
sumus, da nobis petent-
ibus divinissimi tui am-
oris affectum, ut te toto
corde, ore et opere diliga-
mus, et a tua nunquam
laude cessemus.

Sancti Noministui,
Domine, timorem parit-
er et amorem fac nos
habere perpetuum, qui-
anunquam tua guberna-
tione destituis quos in
soliditate tuæ dilectionis
instituis. Qui vivis et regnas.

Lamb of God, who takest
away the sins of the
world, Jesus, graciously
hear us.
Lamb of God, who tak-
est away the sins of the
world, have mercy on us.
Jesus, hear us.
Jesus, graciously hear us.

Let us pray.

Lord Jesus Christ,
who hast said:
Ask, and ye shall re-
ceive; seek, and ye
shall find; knock, and
it shall be opened
unto you; grant, we
beseech Thee, to our
most humble suppli-
cations, the gift of thy
most divine love, that
we may ever love Thee
with our whole hearts,
words, and works, and
never cease praising
Thee.

O Lord, give us a per-
petual fear as well as
love of thy holy Name,
for Thou never ceasest
to govern those whom
thou foundest upon the
the solidity of thy love,
Who livest, *etc.*

57. Prayer for Grace to do the Will of God.

200 Days, once a day.
(See Instructions, p. 1.)

GRANT me, most kind JESUS, thy grace, that it may abide with me, labour with me, and persevere with me to the end.

Grant me ever to desire and to will that which is the more acceptable to Thee, and pleases Thee more dearly.

May thy will be mine, and my will ever follow thine, and be in closest accord with it.

May it be my one care to will and to be unwilling with Thee, and may I be unable to will or not will anything but what Thou willest or willest not.

58. Prayer for the Preservation of Faith.

300 Days, once a day.
(See Instructions, p. 1.)

O My REDEEMER, will that terrible moment ever come, when but few Christians will be found animated with a spirit of faith? that moment when, provoked to indignation, Thou wilt remove from us thy protection? The vices, the evil habits of our children, have perhaps irrevocably moved thy justice this very day to vengeance! O Thou who art the author and finisher of our faith, we conjure Thee, in the bitterness of our hearts, humbled and contrite, not to permit the beautiful light of faith to be extinguished in us. Be mindful of thy mercies of old, cast a compassionate regard upon that vine which Thou hast planted with thy

right hand, which was bedewed with the sweat
of the Apostles, watered with the precious blood
of thousands upon thousands of martyrs and the
tears of so many generous penitents, and made
fruitful by the prayers of so many confessors and
innocent virgins. O divine Mediator, have regard
for those zealous souls who incessantly raise
their hearts to Thee and pray for the maintenance
of that most precious treasure, the true Faith.
Suspend, O must just GOD, the decree of our reprobation, turn away thine eyes from our sins, and
fix them on the adorable blood, shed upon the
Cross as the price of salvation, and daily pleading
for it, on our behalf, upon our altars. Oh, preserve
us in the true Catholic Roman Faith. Infirmities
afflict us, annoyances wear us away, misfortunes
oppress us: but preserve to us thy holy faith; for,
endowed with this precious gift, we shall willingly bear every sorrow, and nothing can affect
our happiness. On the other hand, without this
supreme treasure of the faith, our misfortunes
will be unspeakable and immense. O good JESUS,
author of our faith, keep it pure; keep us safe
within the bark of Peter, faithful and obedient to
his successor, thy Vicar here on earth, that so the
unity of holy Church may be preserved, holiness
fostered, the Holy See kept free and protected,
and the universal Church extended, to the advan-
tage of souls. O JESUS, author of our faith, humble
and convert the enemies of thy Church; bestow
on all Kings and Christian Princes, and on all
the faithful, peace and true unity; strengthen and
maintain all in thy holy service, to the end that we

may live by Thee and die in Thee. Ah! my JESUS, author of our faith, in Thee I would live, and in Thee would I die. Amen.

59. Prayer for the Love of GOD.

50 Days, twice a day.

(See Instructions, p. 1.)

O My JESUS, Thou well knowest that I love Thee; but I do not love Thee enough: Oh! make me to love Thee more. O Love which burnest always and is never extinguished, my GOD, Thou who art Charity itself, kindle in my heart that divine fire which consumes the Saints and transforms them into Thee. Amen.

60. Prayer in Honour of the Holy Family.

200 Days, once a day.

(See Instructions, p. 1.)

FAC nos, Domine JESU, Sanctæ Familiæ tuæ exempla jugiter imitari, ut in hora mortis nostræ, occurrente gloriosa Virgine Matre tua cum beato Joseph, per te in æterna tabernacula recipi mere amur.

GRANT us, O LORD JESUS, faithfully to imitate the examples of thy Holy Family, so that in the hour of our death, in the company of thy glorious Virgin Mother and St Joseph, we may deserve to be received by Thee into eternal tabernacles.

61. Ejaculation.

100 Days. T.Q.

(See Instructions, p. 1.)

My Jesus, mercy!

62. Ejaculation of St Jerome Emilian.

i. 50 Days. T.Q.
ii. Plenary, on the Feast of the Saint, July 20, from
first Vespers, or during the Octave, if said at least
once a day for a year. I, II, III, IV.

(See Instructions, p. 1.)

DULCISSIME Jesu,
non sis mihi Judex
sed Salvator.

SWEETEST Jesus,
be to me not a
judge but a Saviour.

63. Ejaculation.

50 Days. T.Q. For saying or inducing others to say the
following.

(See Instructions, p. 1.)

Jesu, Deus meus,
super omnia amo
te.

Jesus, my God, I
love Thee above all
things.

64. Ejaculation.

100 Days, once a day.

(See Instructions, p. 1.)

Jesu, fili David, miserere mei (*Luc. xviii,*
38).

Jesus, Son of David,
have mercy on me.

65. Ejaculation.

100 Days. T.Q.

(See Instructions, p. 1.)

O LORD, preserve to us the Faith.

66. Ejaculation.

50 Days, once a day.

(See Instructions, p. 1.)

SALVATOR mundi, miserere nobis.

SAVIOUR of the world, have mercy on us.

67. Ejaculation.

100 Days, once a day.

(See Instructions, p. 1.)

DULCISSIME JESU, da mihi fidei, spei et caritatis augmentum, cor contritum et humiliatum.

MOST sweet JESUS, increase my faith, hope, and charity, and give me a humble and contrite heart.

68. Prayer to Jesus our Redeemer.

i. 300 Days, once a day.
ii. Plenary, once a month. I, II, III, IV.

(See Instructions, p. 1.)

O JESUS, SON of the living GOD, my SAVIOUR and REDEEMER, behold us prostrate at thy feet. We beg pardon, and make this act of reparation for all the blasphemies uttered against thy holy Name, for all the outrages committed against Thee in the most holy Sacrament of the altar, for all irreverence shown to thy most blessed and immaculate Mother, and for all the calumnies spoken against thy spouse, our holy Mother, the Catholic Church. O JESUS, who didst say: *whatever you shall ask the* FATHER *in my Name, that I will do*, we pray and beseech Thee for our brethren who are living in danger of sin, that Thou wouldst preserve them from the seductions of apostasy. Save them who stand over the abyss; give them light and knowledge of the truth, power and strength in the conflict against evil, and perseverance in faith and active charity. And therefore, most merciful JESUS, do we pray to the FATHER in thy Name, with whom Thou livest and reignest, in the unity of the HOLY SPIRIT, world without end. Amen.

69. Invocation.

300 Days. T.Q.

(See Instructions, p. 1.)

JESUS and Mary, *invoked with the heart, if not with the lips.*

70. Prayer for the Conversion of Sinners.

300 Days. T.Q.

(See Instructions, p. 1.)

O LORD JESUS, most merciful SAVIOUR of the world, we beg and beseech Thee, through thy most Sacred Heart, that all wandering sheep may now return to Thee, the Shepherd and Bishop of their souls. Who livest and reignest with GOD the FATHER and the HOLY SPIRIT, GOD for ever and ever. Amen.

71. Prayer to our Lord.

300 Days, once a day.
(See Instructions, p. 1.)

O UNCREATED Word, exemplar and creator of all things, redeemer of men, who didst bestow on blessed Albert a powerful mind to contemplate all beings in their dependence one on another, from GOD and his infinite perfections to the constellations of heaven, and the most minute of terrestrial creatures with all their wonderful qualities; grant that I too may understand, according to the humble proportion of my intellectual gifts, the bond which binds together the human sciences in their diversity, and the mutual assistance they can render one another in their common service of the one truth. Then shall I value them all, as well as those who cultivate the various branches of them, and I shall summon up in desire the blessed hour when all the learned shall agree to place their persevering labours, their acquired knowledge, and their many discoveries at the service of the Faith. I beg this favour of Thee, O LORD, for thy glory, for the honour of thy holy Church, and for the salvation of souls purchased by thy Precious Blood. Amen.

72. Prayer to Jesus, Lover of Children.

300 Days, once a day.
(See Instructions, p. 1.)

O JESUS, friend of children, who from thy most tender years didst grow visibly in wisdom and in grace before GOD and men; who at the age of

twelve wast seated in the Temple, in the midst of
the doctors, listening to them attentively, humbly asking them questions, and exciting their
admiration by the prudence and wisdom of thy
discourse; who didst receive so willingly the children, blessing them and saying to thy disciples:
*Let them come to Me, for of such is the Kingdom of
Heaven,* inspire me as Thou didst inspire Blessed
Peter Canisius, model and guide of the perfect
Catechist, with a profound respect and a holy affection for childhood, a taste and a marked devotion for instructing them in Christian doctrine, a
special aptitude in making them understand its
mysteries and love its beauties. I ask this of Thee,
through the intercession of the blessed Virgin
Mary. Amen.

V. THE CHILD JESUS

73. Christmas Day. To all who say or assist in Church at the Divine Office.

i. 100 Years, for 1, Matins; 2, Mass; 3, 1st Vespers; 4,
   Second Vespers. I, II.
ii. 40 Years, for each of the Hours, Prime, Terce, Sext,
   None, and for Compline. I, II.

(See Instructions, p. 1.)

74. Novena for Christmas.

i. 300 Days, each day.
ii. Plenary, on Christmas Day, or during the Novena
   or Octave. I, II, IV.

(See Instructions, p. 1.)

This Novena may be made once more, at any time during the year. Any form of prayers may be used.

75. Mysteries of the Holy Childhood.

    i. Plenary, on the twenty-fifth of every month, for assisting at these devotions in public. I, II, IV.
    ii. 300 Days, once a day on any other day.

(See Instructions, p. 1.)

℣. Incline unto my aid, O GOD.
℟. O LORD, make haste to help me.
℣. Glory be to the FATHER, *etc.*
    PATER noster.

I

JESUS, sweetest Child, who didst come down from the bosom of the FATHER for our Salvation, who wast conceived by the HOLY SPIRIT, who didst not abhor the Virgin's womb, and, the Word made flesh, didst take upon Thee the form of a servant; have mercy upon us.
℟. Have mercy on us, Infant JESUS, have mercy on us. Ave Maria.

II

JESUS, sweetest Child, who, through thy Virgin Mother, didst visit Saint Elisabeth, and fill thy forerunner the holy Baptist with the HOLY SPIRIT, sanctifying him whilst yet in his mother's womb; have mercy upon us.
℟. Have mercy, *etc.* Ave Maria.

III

JESUS, sweetest Child, who, shut up for nine months in thy Mother's womb, wast looked for with eager expectation by Mary and by Joseph, and wast offered to GOD the FATHER for the salvation of the world; have mercy upon us.

℟. Have mercy, *etc.* Ave Maria.

IV

JESUS, sweetest Child, born in Bethlehem of Mary ever Virgin, swathed in rags, laid in the manger, announced by angels, visited by shepherds; have mercy upon us. ℟. Have mercy, *etc.* Ave Maria.

> O JESUS, born of Virgin bright,
> Immortal glory be to Thee;
> Praise to the FATHER Infinite,
> And HOLY SPIRIT eternally.

℣. CHRIST is at hand.

℟. Come let us worship.

PATER noster.

V

JESUS, sweetest Child, wounded in thy circumcision the eighth day, called by the glorious Name of JESUS, and at once by thy Name and thy Blood foreshown as the SAVIOUR of the world; have mercy upon us. ℟. Have mercy, *etc.* Ave Maria.

VI

JESUS, sweetest Child, made known to the three Magi by a star, adored in the arms of thy Mother, presented with the mystic gifts of gold, frankincense, and myrrh; have mercy upon us. ℟. Have mercy, *etc.* Ave Maria.

VII

JESUS, sweetest Child, who wast presented in the Temple by thy Virgin Mother, who wast embraced by Simeon, and revealed to Israel by Anna the prophetess; have mercy upon us. ℟. Have mercy, *etc.* Ave Maria.

VIII

JESUS, sweetest Child, whom wicked Herod sought to slay, whom Joseph carried with Mary into Egypt, who wast taken from a cruel death and wast glorified by the blood of innocents; have mercy upon us. ℟. Have mercy, *etc.* Ave Maria.

IX

O JESUS, *etc.*, as above, ℣. and ℟. as above. PATER noster.
JESUS, sweetest Child, who didst dwell in Egypt with most holy Mary and the Patriarch holy Joseph until the death of Herod; have mercy upon us. ℟. Have mercy, *etc.* Ave Maria.

X

JESUS, sweetest Child, who didst return with Mary and Joseph out of Egypt into the land of Israel, who didst suffer many toils by the way, and didst enter into the city of Nazareth; have mercy upon us. ℟. Have mercy, *etc.* Ave Maria.

XI

JESUS, sweetest Child, who in the holy house at Nazareth didst remain subject to Mary and Joseph, didst dwell there most holily, wast wearied by poverty and labours, and didst advance in wisdom, age, and grace; have mercy upon us. ℟. Have mercy, *etc.* Ave Maria.

XII

JESUS, sweetest Child, at twelve years old brought to Jerusalem, sought for by Mary and Joseph with sorrow, and found with joy after three days amongst the doctors; have mercy upon us. ℟. Have mercy, *etc.* Ave Maria.

O JESUS, *etc.*, as above.

For Christmas Day and its Octave.

℣. The Word was made flesh. Alleluia,

℟. And dwelt among us. Alleluia.

The Alleluia *is omitted during the rest of the year.*

For the Epiphany and its Octave.

℣. CHRIST hath manifested Himself to us. Alleluia.

℟. Come, let us adore. Alleluia.

Let us pray.

ALMIGHTY and everlasting GOD, LORD of heaven and earth, who dost reveal thyself to little ones; grant, we beseech Thee, that we,. duly honouring the holy mysteries of thy SON, the Infant JESUS, and daily imitating Him in our lives, may come to the kingdom of Heaven promised by Thee to little children. Through the same JESUS CHRIST, *etc.* ℟. Amen.

76. Novena for the Twenty-fifth Day of every Month.

One Year, for each day of this Novena, made either in public or private, on nine days previous to the 25th day of any and each month.

(See Instructions, p. 1.)

First Offering.

ETERNAL FATHER, I offer to thy honour and glory, and for my own salvation, and for the salvation of all the world, the mystery of the Birth of our Divine SAVIOUR. Gloria PATRI.

Second Offering.

ETERNAL FATHER, I offer to thy honour and glory, and for my eternal salvation, the sufferings of the most holy Virgin and of St Joseph in that long and weary journey from Nazareth to Bethlehem; I offer Thee their pain in finding no place wherein to shelter themselves, when the SAVIOUR of the world was to be born. Gloria PATRI.

Third Offering.

ETERNAL FATHER, I offer to thy honour and glory, and for my eternal salvation, the stable where JESUS was born, the hard straw which served Him for a bed, the cold He suffered, the swaddling-clothes which bound Him, the tears He shed, and his tender infant cries. Gloria PATRI.

Fourth Offering.

ETERNAL FATHER, I offer to thy honour and glory, and for my eternal salvation, the pain which the divine Child JESUS felt in his tender infant body when He submitted it to the keen knife of circumcision; I offer Thee that Precious Blood which then first He shed for the salvation of the whole race of man. Gloria PATRI.

Fifth Offering.

ETERNAL FATHER, I offer to thy honour and glory, and for my eternal salvation, the humility, mortification, patience, charity and all the virtues of the Child JESUS; I thank Thee, and I love

Thee, and I bless Thee without end, for this ineffable mystery of the Incarnation of the divine Word. Gloria Patri.

℣. The Word was made flesh.

℟. And dwelt amongst us.

Let us pray.

O GOD, whose only-begotten SON was made manifest to us in the substance of our flesh; grant, we beseech Thee, that our souls may be inwardly renewed through Him, whom our eyes have seen externally like unto ourselves. Who liveth and reigneth with Thee for ever and ever. Amen.

77. Prayer before the Crib.

 i. 200 Days, once a day, if said in the Basilica of St Mary Major.
 ii. 100 Days, once a day, if said anywhere else.
   (See Instructions, p. 1.)

I ADORE Thee, O Word Incarnate, true SON of GOD from all eternity, and true SON of Mary ever Virgin in the fullness of time. When I adore thy divine Person, and the Humanity united to thy Divinity, I venerate the poor manger which welcomed Thee when an Infant, and which was truly the throne of thy love. I prostrate myself before it with the simplicity of the shepherds, with the faith of Joseph, with the love of Mary. I bow down in veneration of this precious memorial of our salvation with the same spirit of mortification, poverty and humility with which Thou, though the LORD of heaven and earth, didst choose for thyself a manger wherein to

lay thy tender infant limbs. And Thou, O LORD,
who in thine Infancy didst deign to lay thyself
in this manger, vouchsafe also to pour into my
heart a drop of that joy to which the sight of thy
lovely Childhood, and the miracles which accompanied thy Birth, gave rise. By that holy Birth, I
now implore Thee to grant to all the world peace
and goodwill, and in the name of the whole human race I render thanks and honour to GOD the
FATHER, and to GOD the HOLY SPIRIT, who with
Thee live and reign one GOD world without end.
Amen.

78. Prayer.

100 Days, once a day.

(See Instructions, p. 1.)

MOST dear LORD JESUS CHRIST, who, being
made an infant for us, wast willing to be
born in a cave, to free us from the darkness of
sin, to draw us to thyself, and to inflame us with
thy holy love; we adore Thee as our CREATOR and
REDEEMER, we accept and choose Thee for our
King and LORD, and for tribute we offer Thee all
the affections of our poor hearts. Dear JESUS, our
LORD and GOD, deign to accept this offering, and
that it may be worthy of thine acceptance, pardon us our faults, enlighten us, and inflame us
with that holy fire which Thou camest to bring
into the world and enkindle in men's hearts. May
our souls thus become a perpetual sacrifice in thy
honour. Grant that we may ever seek thy greater
glory here on earth, so that we may one day come

to rejoice in thy infinite loveliness in Heaven.
Amen.

79. The Month of January.

    i. 300 Days, each day, if the Devotions are public, in
a church or public chapel,
    ii. 100 Days, each day, if private.
    iii. Plenary, on the last day of the month, for daily at-
tendance at public devotions. I, II, IV.
              (See Instructions, p. 1.)
  Some devotion must be practised daily in honour of
the holy Name of JESUS.

VI. THE BLESSED SACRAMENT.

80. Novena for Corpus Christi.

    i. Seven Years and Seven Quarantines, each day.
    ii. Plenary, on the Feast or during the Novena or
Octave. I, II, IV.
              (See Instructions, p. 1.)
  The Novena may be made privately, with any pious
practice or publicly with devotions prescribed by the
Bishop.

81. Feast and Octave of Corpus Christi.

    i. 200 Days, on the vigil of the Feast of Corpus
CHRISTI, to all who, having confessed, shall fast, or
do some other good work enjoined them by their
confessor. I.
    ii. 400 Days, on the Feast, to all who, having con-
fessed, shall devoutly assist at or be present at First
or Second Vespers, Matins, or Mass. 160 Days for
each of the Little Hours Prime, Terce, Sext, None,
and for Compline. I.

iii. 200 Days, during the Octave, for each Vespers, Matins, and Mass. 80 Days, for each of the Little Hours, and for Compline.

iv. 200 Days, for accompanying the procession of the Blessed Sacrament on the Feast or during the Octave, to every priest who has said Mass, and to every layman who has gone to Communion praying according to the intention of the Pope.

(See Instructions, p. 1.)

82. Triduo on Friday, Saturday and Sunday, during the Octave of Corpus Christi.

i. Seven Years and Seven Quarantines, each day.
ii. Plenary, during the Triduo. I, II, IV.
iii. Plenary, on the Sunday. I, II, III, IV.

(See Instructions, p. 1.)

There must be each day a sermon, on the Holy Eucharist and Benediction. And on the Sunday a sermon, at the parochial Mass, on the Gospel and the Holy Eucharist. The devotions in the afternoon as above, with special sermon on frequent Communion, and the *Te Deum* before the *Tantum ergo*. The Bishop may transfer the Triduo to another time.

N.B.—This devotion is primarily for Cathedral Churches, but Bishops may order them, and specially the Sunday devotions, in other churches.

The Prayer, Dulcissime Jesu, must be said after the sermon during exposition on each day.

ᴏDULCISSIME JESU, qui in hunc mundum venisti, ut omnes animas vita ditares gratiæ tuæ, ad quam in illis servandam simulque fovendam in

ᴏSWEETEST JESUS, who came into this world to enrich the souls of all with thy grace, and who, in order to preserve and increase it augustissimo Eucharistiæ Sacramento salutare pharmacum earum infirmitatibus sanandis, et cibum divinum debilitati sustinendæ temetipsum quotidie præbes, te supplices deprecamur, ut super eas sanctum tuum spiritum benignus effundas; quo repletæ, lethali labe si quæ sint inquinatæ ad te revertentes, vitam gratiæ deperditam recuperent; quæ vero, te misericorditer largiente, jam tibi adhærent, quotidie, prout cui dabitur, ad tuam cœlestem dapem devote accedant, qua roboratæ, venialium culparum a se quotidie admissarum antidotum sibi comparare, vitamque gratiæ tuæ alere valeant, sicque magis magisque emundatæ, sempiternam in cœlis beatitudinem consequantur. Amen.

in them, didst in the most august Sacrament of the Eucharist, give thyself to be a salutary remedy for our infirmities and divine food to sustain our weakness; we humbly beg of Thee mercifully to pour out upon all men thy HOLY SPIRIT, which may enable them, if stained with any mortal guilt, to recover the life of grace lost by sin, and return to Thee; while those who through thy great mercy are still united with Thee may daily, so far as each may be able, approach thy heavenly table, where they may find strength, and an antidote for their daily faults, may nourish the life of grace within them, and, being more and more purified, may attain to everlasting happiness in Heaven. Amen.

83. Corpus Christi.

Plenary, for every visit, after the fashion of the Indulgence of the Portiuncula, made on Corpus CHRISTI, from first Vespers to sunset next day, to a church of the Congregation of the Blessed Sacrament. I, II, III, IV.

(See Instructions, p. 1.)

84. Act of Adoration during the Elevation.

Two Years, if made in church. One Year, if made in any other place.

(See Instructions, p. 1.)

Kneeling in prayer, when the bell rings at a conventual or parochial Mass.

85. Frequent Communion.

   i. Five Years, every time on Feast days, I, II, IV.
  ii. Ten Years, every time they communicate, to those who have the good habit of communicating at least once a month, on all the Feasts of our LORD, of the Blessed Virgin, of the Holy Apostles, and on the birthday of St John Baptist,
 iii. Plenary, once a year, to all such persons, on the day when the principal Feast of the city or country where they may happen to be is celebrated. I, II, IV.

(See Instructions, p. 1.)

N.B.—Those who are daily communicants, even though they miss once or twice a week, are not bound to confess weekly in order to gain all Indulgences, except Jubilees (Pius X, February 14, 1906).

86. Visit during the Forty Hours Exposition.

   i. Plenary, once during the Exposition. I, II, IV.
  ii. Ten Years and Ten Quarantines, for each other visit,
 iii. Indulgence of the Privileged Altar, to all the altars of a church during the time of Exposition there.

(See Instructions, p. 1.)

87. Visit during Exposition between Septuagesima Sunday and Ash Wednesday.

Plenary, to all who visit the Blessed Sacrament when exposed for three days in any church in any one or all of the weeks from Septuagesima up to Ash Wednesday; the same to those who shall visit it when exposed on the Thursday after Sexagesima Sunday, the day commonly called in Rome "Giovedì grasso." I, II, IV.

(See Instructions, p. 1.)

88. Prayers before the Blessed Sacrament.

iv. Plenary, on the first Thursday of every month. I, II, IV.
v. Seven Years and Seven Quarantines, on any other Thursday. I, II, IV.
vi. 100 Days, on any other day.

(See Instructions, p. 1.)

℣. We adore Thee, CHRIST, and we bless Thee,
℟. Because by thy holy Cross Thou hast redeemed the world.

I ADORE Thee, Eternal FATHER, and I give Thee thanks for the infinite love with which Thou didst deign to send thy only-begotten SON to redeem me, and to become the food of my soul. I offer Thee all the acts of adoration and thanksgiving that are offered to Thee by the angels and saints in Heaven and by the just on earth. I praise, love, and thank Thee with all the praise, love, and thanksgiving that are offered to Thee by thine own SON in the Blessed Sacrament; and I beg Thee to grant that He may be known, loved, honoured, praised, and worthily received by all, in this most divine Sacrament. PATER, Ave, Gloria.

I ADORE Thee, Eternal SON, and I thank Thee for the infinite love which caused Thee to become man for me, to be born in a stable, to live in poverty, to suffer hunger, thirst, heat, cold, fatigue, hardships, contempt, persecutions, the scourging, the crowning with thorns, and a cruel death upon the hard wood of the Cross. I thank Thee, with the Church militant and triumphant, for the infinite love with which Thou didst institute the most blessed Sacrament to be the food of my soul.

I adore Thee in all the consecrated hosts throughout the whole world, and I return thanks for those who know Thee not, and who do not thank Thee. Would that I were able to give my life to make Thee known, loved, and honoured by all, in this sacrament of love, and to prevent the irreverences and sacrileges that are committed against Thee! I love Thee, divine JESUS, and I desire to receive Thee with all the purity, love, and affection of thy blessed Mother, and with the love and affection of thy own most pure Heart. Grant, O most amiable spouse of my soul, in coming to me in this most holy Sacrament, that I may receive all the graces and blessings which Thou dost come to bestow on us, and let me rather die than receive Thee unworthily. PATER, Ave, Gloria.

I ADORE Thee, Eternal SPIRIT, and I give Thee thanks for the infinite love with which Thou didst work the ineffable mystery of the Incarnation, and for the infinite love with which Thou didst form the sacred body of our LORD JESUS CHRIST out of the most pure blood of the

Blessed Virgin Mary, to become in this Sacrament the food of my soul. I beg Thee to enlighten my mind, and to purify my heart and the hearts of all men, that they all may know this great benefit of thy love, and receive worthily this most blessed Sacrament. PATER, Ave, Gloria.

Tantum ergo, *with Versicle and Prayer.* (See p. 94.)

89. Acts of Adoration and Reparation.

300 Days. T.Q.

(See Instructions, p. 1.)

I

I ADORE Thee, my JESUS, in the Blessed Sacrament; I acknowledge Thee, true GOD and true Man. By this my act of adoration I intend to make Thee reparation for the coldness of so many of thy people, who pass before thy church-es, nay, before thy very tabernacle, where hour after hour Thou dost deign to dwell in loving impatience to communicate thyself to thy faithful, yet do not even bow the knee before Thee, but like the Israelites in the wilderness, seem by their indifference to loathe this heavenly manna. I offer Thee thine own most precious Blood which Thou didst shed from the wound in thy Left Foot, in reparation for this hateful coldness, and entering therein, I cry, and will never cease to cry:

Blessed and praised every moment

Be the most holy and divine Sacrament!

PATER, Ave, Gloria.

II

I PROFOUNDLY adore Thee, my JESUS; I acknowledge Thee present in the most holy Sacrament. By this act of adoration I would fain make amends for the forgetfulness of so many Christian people, who, when they see Thee go to the poor sick, to be their strength in their great journey to eternity, leave Thee unescorted, and hardly give Thee even one outward sign of homage. I offer Thee, in reparation for this coldness, that most precious Blood which Thou didst shed from the wound in thy Right Foot, and entering therein, I cry, and will never cease to cry:

Blessed and praised every moment
Be the most holy and divine Sacrament!
PATER, Ave, Gloria.

III

I PROFOUNDLY adore Thee, my JESUS, true Bread of life eternal; and by this my act of adoration I would fain make Thee compensation for all the wounds with which thy Sacred Heart bleeds daily to see the profanation of those churches wherein Thou dost vouchsafe to abide, beneath the sacramental species, to receive the love and adoration of thy people. I offer Thee, in reparation for all these irreverences, that most precious Blood which Thou didst shed from the wound in thy Left Hand, and, entering therein, I will ever cry:

Blessed and praised every moment
Be the most holy and divine Sacrament!
PATER, Ave, Gloria.

IV

IPROFOUNDLY adore Thee, my JESUS, Living
Bread come down from heaven; and by this act
of adoration I would fain make amends for all the
acts of irreverence which thy people day by day
commit whilst they assist at holy Mass, in which
bloodless Sacrifice Thou dost renew the very
Sacrifice which once Thou didst consummate on
Calvary for our salvation. I offer Thee, in reparation for all this ingratitude, that most precious
Blood which Thou didst shed from the wound
in thy Right Hand; and, entering therein, I unite
my voice with the voices of the holy angels who
adore around thy throne:

Blessed and praised every moment
Be the most holy and divine Sacrament!

PATER, Ave, Gloria.

V

IPROFOUNDLY adore Thee, my JESUS, true
Victim of expiation for our sins; and I offer Thee this act of adoration in compensation
for the sacrilegious outrages Thou dost receive
from so many of thy ungrateful people, who
dare to draw nigh to Thee and receive Thee in
Communion with mortal sin upon their souls.
In reparation for these hateful sacrileges, I offer
Thee those last drops of thy most precious Blood
which Thou didst shed from the wound in thy
Side; and, entering therein, I approach Thee with
acts of adoration, love, and thanksgiving, and,
with all holy souls who are devout to Thee in this
most holy Sacrament, I cry:

Blessed and praised every moment
Be the most holy and divine Sacrament!
PATER, Ave, Gloria.
Tantum ergo *with Versicle and Prayer.* (See p. 94.)

90. Act of Reparation and Ejaculations.

200 Days. T.Q.

(See Instructions, p. 1.)

JESUS, my GOD, my SAVIOUR, true GOD and true
Man, in that lowly homage with which the faith
itself inspires me, with my whole heart I adore and
love Thee in the most august Sacrament of the
Altar, in reparation for all the acts of irreverence,
profanation and sacrilege, which I myself may
ever have been so unhappy as to have committed,
as well as for all such like acts that ever have been
done by others, or that may be done in ages yet to
come. I adore Thee, my GOD, not indeed as Thou
deservest, nor as much as I am bound to adore,
but as far as I am able; and I would that I could
adore Thee with all the perfection of which a rea-
sonable creature is capable. Meantime I purpose
now and ever to adore Thee, not only for those
Catholics who adore and love Thee not, but also
for the conversion of all bad Christians, and of all
Heretics, Schismatics, Mohammedans, Jews and
idolaters. JESUS, my GOD, mayest Thou be ever
known, adored, loved and praised every moment,
in the most holy and divine Sacrament. Amen.

I ADORE Thee every moment, O living Bread of
Heaven, great Sacrament!

JESUS, Heart of Mary, I pray Thee send thy
blessing on my soul.

Holiest JESUS! loving SAVIOUR! I give Thee my heart.

91. One Hour's Prayer on Holy Thursday, Corpus Christi, and other Thursdays.

i. Plenary, to all who on Holy Thursday, either in public or private, shall for one hour practise some devotion in remembrance of the institution of the most holy Eucharist; to be gained after Confession and Communion on that day, or some day in the following week. I, II.

ii. Plenary, on the same conditions, on the Feast of Corpus CHRISTI. I, II

iii. 300 Days, on any other Thursday.

(See Instructions, p. 1.)

92. Visit to the Holy Sepulchre on Holy Thursday and Good Friday.

i. Ten Years and Ten Quarantines for each visit, IV.

ii. Plenary, on Holy Thursday or Easter Sunday. I, II, IV.

(See Instructions, p. 1.)

93. Prayer.

100 Days, once a day.

(See Instructions, p. 1.)

BEHOLD, my most loving JESUS, to what an excess thy boundless love has carried Thee. Of thine own Flesh and Precious Blood Thou hast made ready for me a divine banquet in order to give me all thyself. What was it that impelled Thee to this transport of love? It was thy Heart, thy loving Heart. O adorable Heart of my JESUS! burning furnace of Divine Love! within thy most

sacred wound receive Thou my soul; that in that
school of charity I may learn to requite the love
of that GOD who has given me such wondrous
proofs of his love. Amen.

94. The Hymn Pange Lingua, with Versicle and Prayer.

i. 300 Days, once a day.
ii. 100 Days, to those who say the *Tantum ergo* only,
with the Versicle and Prayer.
iii. Plenary, every year, on Holy Thursday, Corpus
CHRISTI, or one day in its Octave, and any one other
day in the year, for saying either *Pange lingua*, or
Tantum ergo with ℣. and Prayer at least ten times a
month. I, II, III, IV.

(See Instructions, p. 1.)

PANGE lingua gloriosi
Corporis Mysterium,
Sanguinisque pretiosi,
Quem in mundi pre-
  tium,
Fructus ventris generosi,
Rex effudit gentium.

Nobis datus, nobis natus
Ex intacta Virgine,
Et in mundo conver-
  satus

SING, my tongue,
the SAVIOUR's glory,
Of his Flesh the mystery
  sing;
Of the Blood, all price
  exceeding,
Shed by our immortal
  King,
Destin'd, for the world's
  redemption,
From a noble womb to
  spring.
Of a pure and spotless
Virgin
Born for us on earth
below,

Sparso verbi semine,
Sui moras incolatus
  Miro clausit ordine.

He, as Man with man
  conversing,
Stay'd, the seeds of truth
  to sow;
Then He clos'd in sol-
  emn order
Wondrously his life of
  woe.

In supremæ nocte cœnæ
Recumbens cum frat-
  ribus,
Observata lege plene
Cibis in legalibus,
Cibum turbæ duodenæ
Se dat suis manibus.

On the night of that Last
  Supper,
Seated with his chosen
  band,
He, the paschal Victim
  eating,
First fulfils the Law's
  command;
Then as food to all his
  brethren
Gives himself with his
  own hand.

Verbum caro, panem
  verum,
Verbo carnem efficit:
Fitque Sanguis CHRISTI
  merum,
Et si sensus deficit:
Ad firmandum cor
  sincerum
Sola fides sufficit.

Word made Flesh, the
  bread of nature
By his word to Flesh He
  turns;
Wine into his Blood He
  changes
What though sense no
  change discerns?
Only be the heart in
  earnest,
Faith her lesson
  quickly learns.

TANTUM ergo
Sacramentum
Veneremur cernui:
Et antiquum documen-
tum
Novo cedat ritui:
Præstet fides supple-
mentum
Sensuum defectui.

Genitori, Genitoque
Laus et jubilatio,
Salus, honor, virtus
quoque
Sit et benedictio:
  Procedenti ab utroque
Compar sit laudatio.
Amen.

℣. Panem de cœlo
  præstitisti eis.
℟. Omne delectamen-
  tum in se habentem.
Oremus.
DEUS, qui nobis sub
Sacramento mirabili
Passionis tuæ memoriam

DOWN in adoration
falling,
Lo! the sacred Host we
hail;
Lo! o'er ancient forms
departing,
Newer rites of grace
prevail;
Faith for all defects
supplying,
Where the feeble senses
fail.

To the everlasting
FATHER,
And the SON who reigns
on high,
With the HOLY SPIRIT
proceeding
Forth from each eter-
nally,
Be salvation, honour,
blessing,
Might, and endless
majesty.

℣. Thou gavest them
Bread from heaven,
℟. And therein was
sweetness of every
kind.
Let us pray.
O GOD, who under this
wonderful Sacrament

reliquisti: tribue, quæsumus, ita nos Corporis et Sanguinis tui sacra mysteria venerari, ut redemptionis tuæ fructum in nobis jugiter sentiamus. Qui vivis et regnas in sæcula sæculorum. Amen.

hast left unto us the memorial of thy Passion; grant us, we beseech Thee, so to venerate the sacred mysteries of thy Body and thy Blood that we may constantly experience within ourselves the fruit of thy redemption. Who livest and reignest, forever and ever. Amen.

95. Invocations.

i. 300 Days. T.Q.
ii. Seven Years, if said after Communion,
iii. Plenary, once a month. I, II, III, IV.
(See Instructions, p. 1.)

ANIMA CHRISTI, sanctifica me.
Corpus CHRISTI, salva me.
Sanguis CHRISTI, inebria me.
Aqua lateris CHRISTI, lava me.
Passio CHRISTI, conforta me.
O bone JESU, exaudi me.

SOUL of CHRIST, be my sanctification.
Body of CHRIST, be my salvation.
Blood of CHRIST, fill all my veins.
Water of CHRIST's side, wash out my stains.
Passion of CHRIST, my comfort be.
O good JESUS, listen to me.

Intra tua vulnera absconde me.	In thy wounds I fain would hide,
Ne permittas me separari a te.	Ne'er to be parted from thy side.
Ab hoste maligno defende me.	Guard me should the foe assail me.
In hora mortis meæ voca me,	Call me when my life shall fail me.
Et jube me venire ad te,	Bid me come to Thee above.
Ut cum sanctis tuis laudem te,	With thy Saints to sing thy love
In sæcula sæculorum.	World without end.
Amen.	Amen.

96. Prayer of St Alphonsus Liguori, to be said at a Visit to the most Holy Sacrament.

i. 300 Days. T.Q.
ii. Plenary, once a month. I, II, IV.

(See Instructions, p. 1.)

O MY LORD JESUS CHRIST, who for the love which Thou dost bear men dost remain night and day in this Sacrament, all full of tenderness and love, expecting, inviting, and receiving all those who come to visit Thee; I believe Thee present in the Sacrament of the Altar; I adore Thee in the depths of my own nothingness; and I thank Thee for all the graces which Thou hast granted me, especially for having vouchsafed to bestow thyself upon me in this Sacrament, for having given me thy own most holy Mother Mary for my advocate, and for having invited me to visit

Thee in this church. I pay my homage this day to thy adorable Heart, and I do so for the following three intentions: first, in thanksgiving for this great gift itself; secondly, as a reparation for all the injuries which Thou hast received from all thy enemies in this Sacrament; thirdly, by this visit I intend to adore Thee in all those places where Thou, sacramentally present, art least reverenced and most abandoned. My JESUS, I love Thee with my whole heart. I repent of having so many times heretofore displeased thy infinite goodness. By thy grace I resolve never to offend Thee more for the time to come; and at this present moment, poor sinner as I am, I consecrate myself wholly to Thee. I renounce for myself, and I give to Thee, my will, my affections, my desires, everything that I call my own. From this day forth do Thou with me, and with everything that belongs to me, whatever pleases Thee. I ask Thee only, and I wish only, for thy holy love, for final perseverance, and the perfect fulfilment of thy will. I commend to Thee the souls in purgatory, especially those who were most devoted to the most holy Sacrament, and to Mary most holy. Moreover, I commend to Thee all poor sinners. For this intention, O my dear SAVIOUR JESUS, I unite all my affections with the affections of thy most loving Heart; and thus united, I offer them to thy Eternal FATHER, and I entreat Him, in thy Name and for thy love, to accept and answer them.

97. Prayer.

100 Days, once a day.

(See Instructions, p. 1.)

DEAR JESUS, present in the Sacrament of the Altar, be for ever thanked and praised. Love, worthy of all celestial and terrestrial love! who, out of infinite love for me, ungrateful sinner, didst assume our human nature, didst shed thy most precious Blood in the cruel scourging, and didst expire on a shameful cross for our eternal welfare! Now, illumined with lively faith, with the outpouring of my whole soul and the fervour of my heart, I humbly beseech Thee, through the infinite merits of thy painful sufferings, give me strength and courage to destroy every evil passion which sways my heart, to bless Thee in my greatest afflictions, to glorify Thee by the exact fulfilment of all my duties, supremely to hate all sin, and thus to become a saint.

98. Visit to the Blessed Sacrament, with Pater, Ave, and Gloria five times, and Pater, Ave, and Gloria once for the intention of the Pope.

300 Days. T. Q.

(See Instructions, p. 1.)

99. Prayer for a Visit.

100 Days, once a day.

(See Instructions, p. 1.)

LOOK down, Holy FATHER and LORD, from thy sanctuary, and from heaven, thy dwelling-place on high, and behold this sacred Victim

which our great High Priest, thy holy Child, our
LORD JESUS, offers up to Thee for the sins of his
brethren; and be appeased for the multitude of
our transgressions. Behold, the voice of the Blood
of JESUS, our Brother, cries to Thee from the
Cross. Give ear, O LORD! Be appeased, O LORD!
Hearken, and do not tarry, for thine own sake, O
my GOD, for thy Name is invoked upon this city
and upon thy people; and deal with us according
to thy mercy. Amen.

℣. That Thou vouchsafe to defend, pacify, keep,
preserve, and bless this city,

℟. We beseech Thee to hear us.

100. Following the Blessed Sacrament.

i. 200 Days, to all who accompany the Blessed
Sacrament carried to the sick.

ii. 100 Days, for accompanying the Blessed
Sacrament on any other occasion.

(See Instructions, p. 1.)

101. Following the Blessed Sacrament to the Sick.

i. Seven Years and Seven Quarantines, to all who accompany the Blessed Sacrament with a light, and
pray according to the intention of the Pope.

ii. Five Years and Five Quarantines, to those who accompany it without a light, praying as above.

iii. Three Years and Three Quarantines, to those who,
being legitimately hindered from going themselves, send some one in their stead to carry a light.

iv. 100 Days, to those who cannot go, provided they
say one *Pater noster* and one *Ave Maria* for the intention of the Pope, while it is being carried to
the sick.

(See Instructions, p. 1.)

102. Prayer to be said during the Elevation in the Mass.

60 Days, once a day.

(See Instructions, p. 1.)

SALVE, salutaris Victima, pro me et omni Humano genere in patibulo crucis oblata.
Salve, pretiose Sanguis, de vulneribus crucifixi DOMINI nostri JESU CHRISTI profluens, et peccata totius mundi abluens.
Recordare, DOMINE, creaturæ tuæ, quam tuo pretioso sanguine redemisti.

HAIL, saving Victim, offered upon the scaffold of the Cross, for me, and for the whole human race.
Hail, Precious Blood streaming from the wounds of my crucified LORD JESUS CHRIST, washing away the sins of the whole world.
Remember, O LORD, thy servant, the work of thy hands, whom Thou hast redeemed with thy Precious Blood.

103. Ejaculation.

i. 100 Days, before the tabernacle. T.Q.
ii. 300 Days, at exposition. T.Q.
iii. 100 Days, for making a reverence passing a church or chapel where the Blessed Sacrament is reserved. T.Q.

(See Instructions, p. 1.)

JESUS, my GOD, I adore Thee here present in the Sacrament of thy love.

104. Act of Spiritual Communion of Saint Alphonsus Liguori.

60 Days, once a day.

(See Instructions, p. 1.)

MY JESUS, I believe that Thou art in the Blessed Sacrament. I love Thee above everything, and I long for Thee in my soul. Since I cannot now receive Thee sacramentally, come at least spiritually into my heart. As though Thou wert already come, I embrace Thee and unite myself entirely to Thee; allow me not to be separated from Thee.

JESUS, my good, my sweet love,
Wound, inflame this heart of mine.
So that it may be always and all on fire for Thee.

105. Act of Homage to Christ, our GOD and our King.

  i. Plenary, on Corpus CHRISTI, one day in the Octave, once during the forty hours, and on any two Thursdays in the year fixed by the Bishop. I, II, IV.
  ii. Seven Years and Seven Quarantines, on all other Thursdays.
  iii. 300 Days, once a day, for private recitation before the Blessed Sacrament.
  iv. 100 Days, once a day, for private recitation anywhere.

(See Instructions, p. 1.)

To be said by priest and people together during Exposition of the Blessed Sacrament.

O SWEET SAVIOUR and REDEEMER of mankind, JESUS CHRIST, who in the impenetrable designs of thine infinite wisdom bearest with the audacity of the impious and sufferest the violence of the wicked, reserving to thyself the sovereign right of judging the impious man and his perverse works, turn thy merciful regard upon thy children, who in the blindness of their hearts have turned from Thee in rebellion. With the eyes of a FATHER, and with the power of the sovereign King of the Universe, stretch forth thy hand to bless and regenerate modern society, which is rebelliously turning its back upon Thee, the King of Kings, LORD of LORDS. Be moved to compassion for thy people, whom Thou hast purchased with thy Blood, regenerated with thy grace, and exalted with thy love. Thou hast given them true liberty, Thou hast called them to the inheritance of thy FATHER, Thou hast numbered them among thy brethren; but in the delirium of their rebellion they have preferred the slavery of Satan, and live in abject misery, without joy, without hope.

O my LORD JESUS CHRIST, King of eternal glory, restorer of all things in heaven and on earth, supreme and omnipotent, who with infinite wisdom reunitest at thy feet things scattered and dispersed; enlighten the Kings of the earth, the rulers of nations; instil thy spirit into all civil institutions, into every form of government, into laws and armies; grant that all the powers of earth may recognize in Thee the majesty of the eternal GOD, the source from which all authority is derived; illuminate the nations that they may understand that Thou art the origin of rights and duties, that it is through Thee that the Kings of the earth rule, and that it is to Thee that Kings and people alike owe obedience. O most sweet

JESUS, who hast deigned to descend into this valley of tears, and to dwell with us, suffering and dying for the salvation of us sinners, and who in an excess of charity hast set up thy abode in the midst of men, hidden under the sacramental species, and who in the fullness of the Godhead, corporally present in our tabernacles, makest thyself the food and life of our souls; oh, receive the humble but sincere and profound homage of our hearts, offered in reparation for the falling away of the rebellious. We firmly believe in Thee and all that the faith infused into our hearts by the HOLY SPIRIT has revealed to us about Thee. We see in Thee the beginning and the end of all existing things, we adore Thee as the one true GOD, we wish to live only for Thee and in thy service. Do Thou, O LORD, save our brethren, reunite the scattered members of modern society gone astray, that we as brethren may together be one with Thee, as Thou art one with thy FATHER in Heaven. May thy will be done by all and in everything. May thy Majesty shine forth on the throne of thy earthly dominion, and the world confess Thee to be the true SON of GOD, through whom all things were created.

O JESUS, GOD of love, set free from his chains thy Vicar, the successor of Peter; re-establish him in the exercise of that liberty which Thou thyself didst give him, together with the supreme keys, that he might effectually carry on thy work of regenerating mankind; and so hasten on that longed-for day, in which Thou wilt be glorified by the return of Society to its paternal home. Gather together, O King of the nations, the sheep and the lambs under the care of the one shepherd. O LORD, do not abandon us; we are thy children, we love Thee; recognize us still as thy children, unworthy, yet ever thine; save us, and together with us, save Kings, Rulers, and Nations. Amen.

106. Hymn of St Thomas Aquinas.

100 Days, if said after Communion.
(See Instructions, p. 1.)

ADORO te devote, latens DEITAS,
Quæ sub his figuris vere latitas;
Tibi se cor meum totum subjicit,
Quia te contemplans, totum deficit.

Visus, tactus, gustus, in te fallitur,
Sed auditu solo tuto ere ditur;
Credo quidquid dixit DEI FILIUS,
Nil hoc verbo veritatis verius.

In cruce latebat sola DEITAS,
At hic latet simul et humanitas:

O GODHEAD hid, devoutly I adore Thee,
Who truly art within the forms before me;
To Thee my heart I bow with bended knee,
As failing quite in contemplating Thee.

Sight, touch, and taste in Thee are each deceived;
The ear alone most safely is believed:
I believe all the SON of GOD has spoken,
Than truth's own word there is no truer token.

GOD only on the Cross lay hid from view;
But here lies hid at once the manhood too:

Ambo tamen credens
  atque confitens,
Peto quod petivit latro
  pœnitens.

Plagas sicut Thomas
  non intueor,
Deum tamen meum te
  confiteor:
Fac me tibi semper
  magis credere,
In spem habere, te
  diligere.

O memoriale mortis
  DOMINI,
Panis vivus vitam
  præstans homini:
Præsta meæ menti de te
  vivere,
Et te illi semper dulce
  sapere.

Pie pelicane JESU
  DOMINE,
Me immundum munda
  tuo sanguine,
Cujus una stilla salvum
  facere
Totum mundum quit ab
  omni scelere.

And I, in both profess-
  ing my belief,
Make the same prayer as
  the repentant thief.

Thy wounds, as Thomas
  saw, I do not see:
Yet Thee confess my
  LORD and GOD to be:
Make me believe Thee
  ever more and more;
In Thee my hope, in
  Thee my love to store.

O Thou memorial of our
  LORD's own dying!
O living bread, to mor-
  tals life supplying!
Make Thou my soul
  henceforth on Thee
  to live;
Ever a taste of heavenly
  sweetness give.

O loving Pelican! O
  JESUS LORD!
Unclean I am, but
  cleanse me in thy
  blood!
Of which a single drop,
  for sinners spilt,
Can purge the entire
  world from all its guilt.

JESUM quem velatum nunc aspicio,	JESUS! whom for the present veil'd I see,
Oro, fiat illud, quod tam sitio,	What I so thirst for, oh, vouchsafe to me:
Ut te revelata cernens facie,	That I may see thy countenance unfolding,
Visu sim beatus tuæ gloriæ.	And may be blest thy glory in beholding.
Amen.	Amen.

107. Prayer.

300 Days, if said after Communion.
(See Instructions, p. 1.)

NOW full of delight is the sweetness of thy heavenly bread! How admirable is the tranquillity and how complete the peace of those who receive Thee, after detesting and sincerely confessing their sins. Be Thou blessed a thousand times, my JESUS! When I was in sin, I was unhappy. Now not only do I find my soul tranquil, but I seem to enjoy a very foretaste of the peace of Paradise. How true it is that our hearts are made for Thee, my beloved LORD, and that they rejoice only when they repose in Thee. I, then, render Thee thanks, and firmly purpose ever to fly sin and its occasions, to fix my abode in thy divine Heart, and thence to look for help to love Thee until death. Amen.

108. Ejaculation.

i. 100 Days, once a day.

ii. 100 Days, three times a day on Thursdays, and during the Octave of Corpus CHRISTI.
iii. Plenary, once a month. I, II, IV.
iv. 100 Days, during Mass, if said at each elevation.
v. 100 Days, at the ringing of the bell at the hours during the forty hours Exposition, or at other times, and at Benediction.

(See Instructions, p. 1.)

BLESSED and praised every moment
Be the most holy and divine Sacrament.

109. Ejaculation after Mass.

Seven Years and Seven Quarantines. This Indulgence holds good if the Prayer is said alternately with the priest.

(See Instructions, p. 1.)

MOST Sacred Heart of JESUS, have mercy on us. (*Thrice.*)

110. First Communicants and their Friends.

i. Plenary, to the third degree of relationship. I, II, IV.
ii. Seven Years and Seven Quarantines to others present.

(See Instructions, p. 1.)

111. Prayer for the Increase of Daily Communion.

i. 300 Days, once a day.
ii. Plenary, once a month. I, II, III, IV.

(See Instructions, p. 1.)

OSWEETEST JESUS, who camest into this world to give to all the life of thy grace, and who, to preserve and sustain it, didst will to be the daily remedy of our daily infirmities, and our daily food; humbly we pray Thee, by thy heart, all on fire with love of us, to pour out thy HOLY SPIRIT upon all, so that those who are unhappily in mortal sin may be converted to Thee, and recover the life of grace which they have lost; and those who by thy gift still live this divine life, may every day, when they are able, approach devoutly to thy holy table, where, in daily communion, receiving every day the antidote to their daily venial sins, and nourishing the life of grace in their hearts, and purifying more and more their souls, they may come at last to the enjoyment with Thee of eternal beatitude. Amen.

112. Prayer to our Lady of the Blessed Sacrament.

300 Days. T.Q.
(See Instructions, p. 1.)

O VIRGIN Mary, our Lady of the Blessed Sacrament, glory of the Christian people, joy of the universal Church, salvation of the world; pray for us, and awaken in all the faithful devotion to the Holy Eucharist in order that they may render themselves worthy to receive it daily.

113. Prayer to our Lord in the Blessed Sacrament.

300 Days. T.Q.
(See Instructions, p. 1.)

O UR sins, O LORD, darken our minds, and we lose the benefit of loving Thee as Thou deservest. Enlighten us with a ray of thy bright light. Thou art Friend, REDEEMER, Father of all who turn repentant to thy Heart; and we return to Thee sorrowing. Save us, O JESUS; provide out of thy infinite bounty for our miseries. O JESUS, we hope in Thee because we know that our salvation cost Thee thy life sacrificed upon the Cross, and induced Thee to dwell continuously in the Blessed Sacrament, in order to be united with us as often as we desire. We, O LORD, to thank Thee for the great love Thou bearest us, promise with the help of thy grace to receive Thee in the Blessed Sacrament as often as possible; to declare thy praises in church and in every place, without human respect. O LORD, confiding in thy Sacred Heart, we beseech Thee, to preserve in thy love those who love Thee, and to invite all to receive Thee daily at the altar in accordance with thy burning desire.

114. Prayers during a Procession of the Blessed Sacrament.

300 Days.

(See Instructions, p. 1.)

PATER, Ave, Gloria. *Then say ten times:*
℣. Let us every moment praise the most holy Sacrament.
℟. May our GOD, present in the Sacrament, be now and ever praised.
Repeat PATER, Ave, *etc., as often as needed.*

115. Prayer to be said at the Beginning of Mass.

i. 300 Days. T.Q.

ii. Plenary once a month, if said on every Sunday and holiday of obligation. I, II.

(See Instructions, p. 1.)

ETERNAL FATHER, I unite myself with the intentions and affections of our Lady of Sorrows on Calvary, and I offer Thee the sacrifice which thy beloved SON JESUS made of himself on the Cross, and now renews on this holy altar: 1. To adore Thee and give Thee the honour which is due to Thee, confessing thy supreme dominion over all things, and the absolute dependence of everything upon Thee, Thou who art our one and last end. 2. To thank Thee for innumerable benefits received. 3. To appease thy justice, irritated against us by so many sins, and to make satisfaction for them. 4. To implore grace and mercy for myself, for . . ., for all afflicted and sorrowing, for poor sinners, for all the world, and for the holy souls in Purgatory.

116. Ejaculation.

i. Seven Years and Seven Quarantines.* T.Q.
ii. Plenary, once a week, if used daily, II.*

(See Instructions, p. 1.)

DOMINUS meus, et DEUS meus.

MY LORD and my GOD.

These words are to be said with faith, piety, and love, while looking upon the Blessed Sacrament, either during the Elevation in the Mass, or when exposed on the altar.

VII. JESUS CRUCIFIED

117. The Stations of the Cross.

Those who perform devoutly the Stations of the Cross
may gain all the Indulgences which have ever been
granted by Popes to the faithful who visit in person
the sacred places in Jerusalem. It is not permitted to
specify definitely what these Indulgences are. All, however, who wish to gain them must bear in mind that the
Stations must be erected by one who has Faculties, and
that it is indispensably required of them to meditate,
according to their abilities, on the Passion of our LORD
and SAVIOUR JESUS CHRIST, and to go from one Station to
the other, so far as the number of persons engaged in
the devotion, and the space where the fourteen Stations
are erected, will admit, and this is all that is required for
the Indulgences.

Those who are sick, in prison, or at sea, or *in parlibus
infidelium*, or who are prevented in any other way from
visiting the Stations erected in churches or public ora-
tories, may gain the said Indulgences by reciting fourteen times *Pater noster* and *Ave Maria*, and at the end
of these, *Pater noster* and *Ave Maria* and *Gloria Patri*
five times, and one *Pater, Ave,* and *Gloria* besides, for
the Pope, "holding in their hands the while a crucifix"
blessed by the Father-General of the Order of the Friars
Minor Observants at the Convent of Ara Cœli, or else
by the Father-Provincial or any Father-Guardian, subject of the said Father-General, or any priest with Faculties from the said Father-General. These crucifixes,
so indulgenced, after they have been blessed, cannot be
sold or given away or lent for the purpose of enabling
others to gain the Indulgences of the Stations.

Devotions which may be used for the Stations.
(The pious reader may use any other devotions which are more to his mind.)
Begin with an act of contrition.

STATION I. JESUS condemned to death.

℣. Adoramuste, CHRISTE, et benedicimus tibi.

℣. We adore Thee, O CHRIST, and we bless Thee.

℟. Quia per sanctam Crucem tuam redemisti mundum.

℟. Because by thy holy Cross Thou hast redeemed the world.

My JESUS, oft have I signed thy death-warrant by my sins; save me by thy death from that death eternal I deserve. PATER, Ave.

℣. Miserere nostri, DOMINE.

℣. Have mercy on us, O LORD.

℟. Miserere nostri.

℟. Have mercy on us.

Passing on from one station to another, say, or sing,

Holy Mother, pierce me through,
In my heart each wound renew
Of my SAVIOUR crucified.

or the Stabat Mater (No. 238).

STATION II. JESUS receives his cross.

℣. Adoramus, *etc.*

My JESUS, who by thine own will didst take on Thee the Cross which I made for Thee by my sins; oh, make me know the weight of them, and sorrow for them ever while I live. PATER, Ave. ℣. Miserere.

STATION III. JESUS falls the first time beneath the Cross.

℣. Adoramus, *etc.*

My JESUS, the heavy burden of my sins has made
Thee fall down beneath the Cross. My JESUS, I
loathe them, I detest them, I beseech Thee to pardon them; aided by thy grace, I will never commit
them more. PATER, Ave. ℣. Miserere.

STATION IV. JESUS meets his Mother.
℣. Adoramus, *etc.*
  JESUS, most suffering! Mary, Mother most sorrowful! if for the past by sin I have caused you
pain and sorrow, yet by divine grace it shall be so
no more, but I will love you faithfully until death.
PATER, Ave. ℣. Miserere.

STATION V. Simon of Cyrene helps JESUS to carry
the Cross.
℣. Adoramus, *etc.*
  My JESUS, happy was that man of Cyrene who
aided Thee to bear the Cross. Happy shall I be if I
too aid Thee to bear the Cross, by suffering with
patience and goodwill the crosses Thou shalt
send me during life. My JESUS, give me grace to
do so. PATER, Ave. ℣. Miserere.

STATION VI. JESUS and Veronica.
℣. Adoramus, *etc.*
  JESUS most compassionate, who didst deign
to print thy sacred countenance upon the cloth
with which Veronica wiped the sweat from off
thy brow; print in my soul deep, I pray Thee, the
lasting memory of thy most bitter pains. PATER,
Ave. ℣. Miserere.

STATION VII. JESUS falls a second time.
℣. Adoramus, *etc.*

My JESUS, oft have I sinned, and by sin often made Thee fall beneath the Cross. Help me to use such efficacious means of grace that I may never fall again into sin. PATER, Ave. ℣. Miserere.

STATION VIII. JESUS comforts the women of Jerusalem.
℣. Adoramus, *etc.*

My JESUS, who didst comfort the pious women of Jerusalem who wept to see Thee so tormented; comfort my soul with thy mercy, for in thy mercy alone is my trust; oh, may I never frustrate it! PATER, Ave. ℣. Miserere.

STATION IX. Again a third time JESUS falls.
℣. Adoramus, *etc.*

My JESUS, by all the bitter woe Thou didst endure when a third time Thou didst fall beneath the heavy Cross, oh, never, never let me fall away; but rather let me die than ever mortally sin again. PATER, Ave. ℣. Miserere.

STATION X. JESUS stripped and given gall to drink.
℣. Adoramus, *etc.*

My JESUS, who wast stripped of thy clothes and given gall to drink, strip me of love for things of earth, and make me loathe all that savours of the world and sin. PATER, Ave. ℣. Miserere.

STATION XI. JESUS nailed to the Cross.
℣. Adoramus, *etc.*

My JESUS, by those agonizing pains Thou didst endure when the hard nails pierced thy tender hands and feet and fixed them to the Cross, oh, make me ever crucify my flesh with the spirit of true Christian penance. PATER, AVE. ℣. Miserere.

STATION XII. JESUS dies upon the Cross.
℣. Adoramus, *etc.*
My JESUS, three hours didst Thou hang in agony upon the Cross, and then didst die for me; let me die before I sin again, and if I live, may I live to love Thee and to serve Thee faithfully. PATER, AVE. ℣. Miserere.

STATION XIII. JESUS taken from the Cross and laid in Mary's bosom.
℣. Adoramus, *etc.*
Mary, Mother most sorrowful, the sword of grief went through thy soul when thou didst see thy dear SON JESUS lying lifeless in thy bosom; ask for me hatred of sin, which was the cause of his death and made thee suffer so much; and then obtain for me grace to live a true Christian life, and save my soul. PATER, AVE. ℣. Miserere.

STATION XIV. JESUS laid in the tomb.
℣. Adoramus, *etc.*
My JESUS, beside Thee in the tomb I desire that I may ever remain as one dead; and if I live, I wish to live only to Thee, that so one day I may come with Thee to taste of the bliss of heaven, fruit of thy Passion and most painful death. Amen. PATER, AVE. ℣. Miserere.

Oremus.
DEUS, qui Unigeniti FILII tui pretioso sanguine vivificæ crucis vexillum

Let us pray.
GOD, who by the Precious Blood of thy only-begotten SON didst

sanctificare voluisti; concede, quæsumus, eos, qui ejusdem sanctæ crucis gaudent honore, tua quoque ubi que protectione gaudere. Per eundem CHRISTUM DOMINUM nostrum. ℞. Amen.

sanctify the standard of the Cross; grant, we beseech Thee, that all those who rejoice in the glory of the same Holy Cross may at all times and places feel the gladness of thy protection. Through the same CHRIST our LORD. ℞. Amen.

End with one PATER, Ave, *and* Gloria *for the intention of the Sovereign Pontiff.*

118. Chaplet of the Stations of the Cross.

Indulgences, the same as for the Stations, if hindered from making the Stations.

This Chaplet, invented by Louisa Borgiotti, co-founder of the Nazarene Sisters, consists of *Pater, Ave,* and *Gloria,* twenty times, one for each Station, five for the five wounds, and one for the intention of the Pope. The beads must be blessed by a Priest of the Missions.

If several persons say the Chaplet together, it is sufficient if one has beads. A similar privilege attaches to Crucifixes blessed by the Friars Minor.

119. The "Scala Santa" in Rome.

i. Nine Years, for each of the twenty-eight steps of the Scala Santa.

N.B.—The two stairs on either side are similarly indulgenced on All Saints, during the Octave of All Souls, from Christmas to the Epiphany, and during Lent. The ascent must be made on the knees, with a contrite heart and meditation on the Passion of our LORD.

ii. Plenary, as often as the ascent is made. I, II, IV. T.Q.

(See Instructions, p. 1.)

120. Pious Exercise on Fridays.

100 Days, to all who when the church bell rings on Friday at three in the afternoon, or at any other hour fixed by custom, kneel and say five times *Pater noster* and *Ave Maria*, in memory of the Passion of our LORD, praying according to the intention of the Pope.

(See Instructions, p. 1.)

121. Devotions in Honour of the Five Wounds.

i. 100 Days, once a day.
ii. Plenary, twice a year—that is, on the two Feasts, first, that of the Invention (May 3), and, secondly, that of the Exaltation of the Holy Cross (September 14)—to all who shall say these prayers at least ten times a month. I, II.
iii. Seven Years and Seven Quarantines, once a day, to those who say these prayers from Passion Sunday to Holy Saturday inclusive.
iv. Plenary on Easter Day to those who have said the prayers daily during the period mentioned. I, II.

(See Instructions, p. 1.)

Act of Contrition.

AS I kneel before Thee on the Cross, most loving SAVIOUR of my soul, my conscience tells me it was I who nailed Thee to that Cross with these hands of mine, as often as I have fallen into mortal sin, wearying Thee with my monstrous ingratitude. My GOD, my chief and most perfect Good, worthy of all my love, seeing Thou hast ever loaded me with blessings, I cannot now undo my misdeeds, as I would most willingly, but I can and will loathe them, grieving greatly for having offended Thee who art infinite Goodness.

And now, kneeling at thy feet, I will try at least to compassionate Thee, to give Thee thanks, to ask of Thee pardon and contrition; wherefore with heart and lips I say:

To the First Wound of the Left Foot.

HOLY wound of the Left Foot of my JESUS, I adore Thee! I compassionate Thee, O my JESUS, for that most bitter pain which Thou didst suffer. I thank Thee for the love whereby Thou wast wearied in overtaking me on the way to ruin, and didst bleed amid the thorns and brambles of my sins. I offer to the Eternal FATHER the pain and love of thy most sacred humanity, in atonement for my sins, all which I detest with sincere and bitter contrition. PATER, Ave, Gloria.

> Holy Mother, pierce me through;
> In my heart each wound renew
> Of my SAVIOUR crucified.

To the Second Wound, of the Right Foot.

HOLY wound of the Right Foot of my JESUS, I adore Thee! I compassionate Thee, O my JESUS, for that most bitter pain which Thou didst suffer. I thank Thee for the love which pierced Thee with such torture and shedding of blood in order to punish my wanderings and the guilty pleasures I have granted to my passions. I offer the Eternal FATHER all the pain and love of thy most sacred humanity, and I pray unto Him for grace to weep over my transgressions with burning tears, and to enable me to persevere in the good which I have begun, without ever swerving again from my obedience to the Commandments of my GOD. PATER, Ave, Gloria.

> Holy Mother, *etc.*

To the Third Wound, of the Left Hand.

HOLY wound of the Left Hand of my JESUS, I adore Thee! I compassionate Thee, O my JESUS, for that most bitter pain which Thou didst suffer. I thank Thee for having, in thy love, spared me the scourges and eternal damnation which my sins have merited. I offer to the Eternal FATHER the pain and love of thy most sacred humanity, and I pray Him to teach me how to turn to good account my span of life, and bring forth in it worthy fruits of penance, and so disarm the angry justice of my GOD. PATER, Ave, Gloria.

Holy Mother, *etc.*

To the Fourth Wound, of the Right Hand.

HOLY wound of the Right Hand of my JESUS, I adore Thee! I compassionate Thee, O my JESUS, for that most bitter pain which Thou didst suffer. I thank Thee for thy graces lavished on me with such love, in spite of all my miserable obstinacy. I offer to the Eternal FATHER all the pain and love of thy most sacred humanity, and I pray Him to change my heart and its affections, and make me do all my actions in accordance with the will of GOD. PATER, Ave, Gloria.

Holy Mother, *etc.*

To the Fifth Wound, of the sacred Side.

HOLY wound in the side of my JESUS, I adore Thee! I compassionate Thee, O my JESUS, for the cruel insult Thou didst suffer. I thank Thee, my JESUS, for the love which suffered thy side and heart to be pierced, that so the last drops of blood and water might issue forth, making my redemption to abound. I offer to the Eternal FATHER this outrage, and the love of thy most sacred humanity, that my soul may enter once for all into that most loving Heart, eager and ready to receive the greatest sinners, and from it may never more depart. PATER, Ave, Gloria.

Holy Mother, *etc.*

To the most Holy Virgin, Mother of Sorrows.

MARY, Virgin Mother of GOD, Martyr of love and sorrow, in that thou didst witness the pains and torments of JESUS; truly didst thou concur in the great work of my redemption, first by thy innumerable afflictions, and then by the offering thou didst make to the Eternal FATHER of his and thy only-begotten for a holocaust and victim of propitiation for my sins. I thank thee for that love, well-nigh infinite, through which thou didst bereave thyself of the fruit of thy womb, very GOD and very Man, to save me, sinner that I am; let thy intercession, which never returneth to thee void, interpose with the FATHER and the SON for me; that I may steadily amend my evil ways, and never by further faults crucify afresh my loving SAVIOUR; that so, persevering in his grace until death, I may obtain eternal life through the merits of his painful Passion and Death upon the Cross. Ave Maria, *thrice.*

Let us pray.

O LORD JESUS CHRIST, who at the sixth hour of the day didst, for the redemption of the world, mount the scaffold of the Cross, and shed thy Precious Blood for the remission of sins;

we humbly beseech Thee grant us that after our death we may joyfully enter the gates of Paradise.

We beseech Thee, O LORD JESUS CHRIST, that now, and at the hour of our death, blessed Mary ever Virgin, thy Mother, may intercede for us, through whose most holy soul the sword passed in the hour of thy Passion. Through Thee, JESUS CHRIST, SAVIOUR of the world, who with the FATHER and the HOLY SPIRIT livest and reignest for ever and ever. Amen.

122. Devotion of the Seven Words.

Seven Years and Seven Quarantines. T.Q.
(See Instructions, p. 1.)

℣. Deus, in adjutorium meum intende.

℟. DOMINE, ad adjuvandum me festina.

℣. Gloria PATRI, *etc.*

℣. O GOD, come to my assistance.

℟. O LORD make haste to help me.

℣. Glory be to the FATHER, *etc.*

FIRST WORD: *Father, forgive them; for they know not what they do.*

℣. Adoramuste, CHRISTE, et benedicimus tibi.

℟. Quia per sanctam crucem tuam redemisti mundum.

℣. We adore Thee, O CHRIST, and we bless Thee.

℟. Because by thy holy Cross Thou hast redeemed the world.

JESUS, my love! who for love of me didst hang in agony upon the Cross, there by thy pains to pay the penalty of my sins, and didst open thy divine mouth to obtain for me the pardon of

them from Eternal Justice; O JESUS, pity all the
faithful who are now in their last agony, and pity
me when I too shall be in mine. By the merits of
thy most Precious Blood shed for our salvation,
vouchsafe unto us all such lively sorrow for our
sins that at our death we may breathe forth our
souls into the bosom of thy infinite mercy. Gloria
PATRI, *thrice*.

℣. Miserere nostri,   ℣. Have mercy on us, O
DOMINE.   LORD.

℟. Miserere nostri.   ℟. Have mercy on us.

My GOD, I believe in Thee, I hope in Thee, I love
Thee. I repent of my sins, because by them I have
offended Thee.

SECOND WORD: *This day shalt thou be with Me in
Paradise.*

℣. We adore Thee, *etc.*

JESUS, my love! who for love of me didst hang
in agony upon the Cross, and with such readiness and bounty didst respond to the faith of
the good thief, who in thy humiliations acknowledged Thee to be the SON OF GOD, and didst assure unto him the Paradise prepared for him; oh,
pity all the faithful who are in their last agony,
and pity me when I too shall be in mine. By the
merit of thy most Precious Blood, wake up in our
souls such firm and steadfast faith as shall never
waver at any suggestion of the evil one; that so we
also may obtain the prize of holy Paradise. Gloria
PATRI, *thrice*.

℣. Have mercy, *etc.*   My GOD, *etc.*

THIRD WORD: *Behold thy Mother! Behold thy Son.*

℣. We adore Thee, *etc.*

Jesus, my love! who for love of me didst hang in agony upon the Cross, and, unmindful of thine own sorrows, didst leave us thy own most holy Mother as the pledge of thy love, that through her intercession we might seek Thee with confidence in our greatest straits; have pity on all the faithful who are in their last agony, and pity me when I too shall be in mine. By the inward martyrdom of thy dear Mother, quicken in our hearts a firm hope in the infinite merits of thine own most Precious Blood, that so we may escape the sentence of eternal death, which we have merited by our sins. Gloria PATRI, *thrice.*

℣. Have mercy, *etc.* My GOD, *etc.*

FOURTH WORD: *My GOD, my GOD, why hast Thou forsaken Me?*

℣. We adore Thee, *etc.*

Jesus, my love! who for love of me didst hang in agony upon the Cross, and, whilst suffering after suffering was heaped upon Thee, with all thy bodily pain didst bear with infinite patience the most afflicting desolation of spirit, being forsaken by thine Eternal FATHER; pity all the faithful who are in their last agony, and pity me when I too shall be in mine. By the merits of thy most Precious Blood, grant us all thy grace, that we may suffer with patience the pain and anguish of our last agony, and so, joining our pains with thine, be made partakers of thy glory in Paradise. Gloria PATRI, *thrice.*

℣. Have mercy, *etc.* My GOD, *etc.*

FIFTH WORD: *I thirst.*

℣. We adore Thee, *etc.*

JESUS, my love! who for love of me didst hang in agony upon the Cross, and who, insatiable in thy thirst for insults and sufferings, didst will yet more and more to suffer, that all men might be saved, showing thereby that all the torrent of thy Passion was not enough to quench the thirst of thy most loving Heart; pity all the faithful who are in their last agony, and pity me when I too shall be in mine. By the merits of thy most Precious Blood, kindle in our hearts such fire of charity, as may make them burn to be made one with Thee for all eternity. Gloria PATRI, *thrice*.

℣. Have mercy, *etc.* My GOD, *etc.*

SIXTH WORD: *It is consummated.*

℣. We adore Thee, *etc.*

JESUS, my love! who for love of me didst hang in agony upon the Cross, and from this pulpit of truth didst announce that the work of our redemption was finished—that work through which, from children of wrath and perdition, we become GOD's children and the heirs of heaven; pity all the faithful who are in their last agony, and pity me when I too shall be in mine. By the merits of thy most Precious Blood, detach us wholly from the world and from ourselves, and at the moment of our agony grant us grace to offer Thee with all our hearts the sacrifice of our life, in expiation for our sins. Gloria PATRI, *thrice*.

℣. Have mercy, *etc.* My GOD, *etc.*

SEVENTH WORD: *Father, into Thy hands I commend My spirit.*

℣. We adore Thee, *etc.*

JESUS, my love! who for love of me didst hang in agony upon the Cross, and who in accomplishment of the great sacrifice didst accept the will of thine Eternal FATHER, commending thy spirit into his hands, and so didst bow thy head and die; pity all the faithful who are in their last agony, and pity me when I too shall be in mine. By the merits of thy most Precious Blood, give us in our agony an entire conformity to thy divine will, that ready to live or die as it please Thee, we may desire nothing so much as that thine adorable will may ever find its full accomplishment in us. Gloria PATRI, *thrice.*

℣. Have mercy, *etc.* My GOD, *etc.*

Prayer to the Holy Virgin, Mother of Sorrows

MOST Holy Mother of sorrows, by that intense martyrdom which thou didst suffer at the foot of the Cross during the three hours of the agony of JESUS, deign to aid us all, children of thy sorrows, in our last agony, that by thy prayers we may pass from our bed of death to adorn thy crown in Paradise. Ave Maria, *thrice.*

Maria, mater gratiæ,	Mother of mercy,
Mater misericordiæ,	Mother of grace,
Tu nos ab hoste protege,	Mary, help a fallen race;
Et mortis hora suscipe.	Shield us when the foe is nigh,
	And receive us when we die.
℣. A subitanea et improvisa morte,	℣. From sudden and unprepared death,
℟. Libera nos, DOMINE.	℟. Deliver us, O LORD.

℣. Ab insidiis diaboli,
℟. Libera nos, DOMINE.
℣. A morte perpetua,
℟. Libera nos, DOMINE

Oremus.

DEUS, qui ad humani generis salutem in dolorosissima FILII tui morte exemplum et subsidium constituisti; concede, quæsumus, ut in extreme mortis nostræ periculo tantæ charitatis effectum consequi et ipsius Redemptoris gloriæ consociari mereamur. Per eundem CHRISTUM DOMINUM nostrum. ℟. Amen.

℣. From the snares of the devil,
℟. Deliver us, O LORD.
℣. From everlasting death,
℟. Deliver us, O LORD.

Let us pray.

GOD, who for the salvation of the human race hast, in the most bitter death of thy SON, made for us both an example and a refuge; grant, we beseech Thee, that in the last peril, at the hour of our death, we may merit to obtain the full effect of his great charity, and be made partakers of our REDEEMER's glory. Through the same JESUS CHRIST our LORD. ℟. Amen.

End with the three ejaculations,

JESUS, Mary, and Joseph, I give you my heart and my soul.

JESUS, Mary, and Joseph, assist me in my last agony.

JESUS, Mary, and Joseph, may I breathe forth my soul with you in peace.

123. The Three Hours on Good Friday and any other Friday.

i. Plenary, on Holy Thursday or during Easter Week, to all who shall, either in public or private, practise this devotional exercise on Good Friday from noon to three o'clock, either by meditating according to their abilities on the sufferings of JESUS CHRIST during the three hours He hung on the Cross, and on the seven words He then uttered, or else, instead of meditation, by reciting psalms, hymns, or other prayers. I, II, IV.

ii. 200 Days, any Friday in the year, to every one who, in remembrance of, and out of devotion to, the agony of our Blessed LORD, shall spend some time in prayer, as above. IV.

iii. Plenary, once every month, on the last Friday, to everyone who has meditated and prayed every previous Friday in the month, in the way just mentioned. I, II, IV.

(See Instructions, p. 1.)

124. Devotion for Lent.

i. 300 Days, for each of the seven Fridays in Lent. I, II, IV.

ii. Plenary, on any one of these Fridays. I, II, IV.

iii. 300 Days, to every one who shall make use of this devotion on any other Friday in the year. IV.

iv. Plenary, if any one shall practise it on seven consecutive Fridays at any time in the year; to be gained on any one of those Fridays. IV.

(See Instructions, p. 1.)

To all who visit a public church or chapel, and say before a representation of JESUS crucified, in memory of the Passion, *Pater, Ave* and *Gloria* seven times, praying according to the Pope's intention.

125. The Prayer, Deus, qui pro Redemptione, etc.

i. 300 Days, once a day.
ii. Plenary, once a month, on one of the last three days. I, II, IV.

(See Instructions, p. 1.)

O GOD, who to redeem the world didst vouchsafe to be born amongst men, to be circumcised, rejected by the Jews, betrayed by the traitor Judas with a kiss, to be bound with cords, and as an innocent lamb to be led to the slaughter; who didst suffer thyself to be shamelessly exposed to the gaze of Annas, Caiphas, Pilate and Herod; to be accused by false witnesses, tormented by scourges and insults, crowned with thorns, smitten with blows, defiled with spittings, to have thy divine countenance covered, to be struck with a reed, to be stripped of thy clothes, nailed to and raised high upon a Cross between two thieves, to be given gall and vinegar to drink, and then pierced with a lance; do Thou, O LORD, by these most sacred sufferings, which I, unworthy as I am, yet dare to contemplate, by thy holy Cross and by thy bitter Death, free me from the pains of hell, and vouchsafe to bring me to Paradise, whither Thou didst lead the thief who was crucified with Thee, my JESUS, who with the FATHER and the HOLY SPIRIT livest and reignest GOD for ever and ever. Amen. PATER, Ave *and* Gloria *five times.*

126. Chaplet of the Five Wounds.

i. One Year, once a day.
ii. Plenary, three times a year, that is, on any one Friday in March, on the Feasts of the Invention

and Exaltation of the Holy Cross, or on any one day in the Octaves of these Feasts, to all who shall have practised the devotion of saying this Chaplet at least ten times each month. I, II, IV.

The Sovereign Pontiff Pius IX extended this Plenary Indulgence to the Feasts of the Nativity, Circumcision and Epiphany of our LORD JESUS CHRIST, the Feasts of His Most Holy Name, Easter Sunday, the Ascension, Corpus CHRISTI and the Transfiguration, or any one day in the Octaves of these Feasts. I, II, III, IV.

iii. Seven Years and Seven Quarantines, daily, to all who shall say this Chaplet from Passion Sunday to Holy Saturday inclusive; Plenary, when they fulfil the Paschal precept.

This Chaplet consists of five sets of five beads each; and at each one of these beads, in memory of the Five Wounds of JESUS CHRIST, one *Gloria Patri* is to be said; and at the end of each set of five, one *Ave Maria* is added in honour of our Lady's sorrows.

The condition of gaining all these Indulgences is, that the Chaplets used should be blessed by the most reverend the Father-General of the Congregation of Discalced Clerics of the Passion (Passionists), or by some other priest of the Congregation to whom the General has communicated the faculty received by him; after they have been blessed, they cannot be sold or lent, or given away to others, etc., for the purpose of communicating to them the Indulgences.

(See Instructions, p. 1.)

127. Prayer, En Ego.

Plenary, when said before any representation of JESUS crucified. I, II, IV.

(See Instructions, p. 1.)

EN EGO, O bone et dulcissime Jesu, ante conspectum tuum genibus me provolvo, ac maximo animi ardore te oro atque obtestor ut meum in cor vividos fidei, spei, et charitatis sensus, atque veram peccatorum meorum pœnitentiam, eaque emendandi firmissimam voluntatem velis imprimere: dum magno animi affectu, et dolore tua quinque Vulnera mecum ipse considero, ac mente contemplor, illud præoculis habens, quod jam in ore ponebat tuo David propheta de te, O bone Jesu: *Foderunt manus meas et pedes meos; dinumeraverunt omnia ossa mea.* (Ps. xxi, 17, 18.)

O GOOD and sweetest Jesus, before thy face I humbly kneel, and with the greatest fervour of spirit I pray and beseech Thee to vouchsafe to fix deep in my heart lively sentiments of faith, hope and charity, true contrition for my sins, and a most firm purpose of amendment; whilst I contemplate with great sorrow and affection thy five wounds, and ponder them over in my mind, having before my eyes the words which, long ago, David the prophet spoke in his own person concerning Thee, my Jesus: *They have pierced my hands and my feet; they have numbered all my bones.* (Ps. xxi, 17,18.)

128. Prayers of St Pius V, with the Apostles'

Creed five times.

    i. 60 Days, T.Q., provided that the faithful, while say-
ing these prayers, known as the Five *Credos* of St
Pius, intend to apply them according to the intention of the Pope.

    ii. Plenary, once a month. I, II, III, IV.

           (See Instructions, p. 1.)

I

O MY Lord Jesus Christ crucified, Son of the
most Blessed Virgin Mary, open thine ears,
and listen to me as Thou didst listen to the
Eternal Father on Mount Tabor. Credo.

II

O MY Lord Jesus Christ crucified, Son of the
most Blessed Virgin Mary, open thine eyes,
and look upon me as Thou didst look from the
tree of the Cross upon thy dear Mother sorrowing and afflicted. Credo.

III

O MY Lord Jesus Christ crucified, Son of the
most Blessed Virgin Mary, open thy blessed
mouth, and speak to me as Thou didst speak to St
John when Thou gavest him for son to thine own
most beloved Mother. Credo.

IV

O MY Lord Jesus Christ crucified, Son of the
most Blessed Virgin Mary, open thine arms
and embrace me as Thou didst open them upon
the Cross to embrace the whole human race.
Credo.

V

O MY Lord Jesus Christ crucified, Son of the
most Blessed Virgin Mary, open thy Heart and

receive therein my heart, and hear me in all that
I ask of Thee, if so be it be agreeable to thy most
holy will. Credo.

129. Invocation of St Thomas Aquinas to the Cross.

300 Days, once a day.
(See Instructions, p. 1.)

CRUX mihi cer-
ta salus. Crux est
quam semper adoro.
Crux DOMINI mecum.
Crux mihi refugium.

THE Cross is my
sure salvation. The
Cross I ever adore. The
Cross of my LORD is
with me. The Cross is
my refuge.

130. Prayers of St Clare of Assisi.

300 Days, once a day.
(See Instructions, p. 1.)

I. To the Wound in the Right Hand.

PRAISE be to Thee, O JESUS CHRIST, for the
most sacred wound in thy Right Hand. By
this adorable wound, and by thy most sacred
Passion, pardon me all the sins I have committed
against Thee in thought, word and deed, and all
negligence in thy service, and all sensuality for
which I have been to blame whether asleep or
awake. Grant that I may be able to recall with devotion thy most pitiful death and sacred wounds;
grant me the grace to mortify my body, and so to
offer a pledge of my gratitude to Thee, who livest and reignest world without end. Amen. PATER
noster, Ave Maria.

II. To the Wound in the Left Hand.

PRAISE and glory be to Thee, O sweetest JESUS CHRIST, for the most sacred wound in thy Left Hand. By this adorable wound, have mercy on me, and deign to root out of my heart everything displeasing to Thee. Give me the victory over thy perverse enemies, so that with thy grace I may be able to overcome them; and by the merits of thy most pitiful death save me from all the dangers of my present and future life; and then, grant that I may share thy glory in heaven, who livest and reignest for ever and ever. Amen. PATER noster, and Ave Maria.

III. To the Wound in the Right Foot.

PRAISE and glory be to Thee, O sweet JESUS CHRIST, for the most sacred wound in thy Right Foot; and by that adorable wound, grant me grace to do penance for my sins. And by thy most pitiful death I devoutly beg of Thee to keep me, thy poor servant, united, night and day, to the holy will, and to remove afar off every misfortune of body and soul. And when the day of wrath shall come, receive me into thy mercy, and lead me to eternal happiness. Who livest and reignest world without end. Amen. PATER noster, Ave Maria.

IV. To the Wound in the Left Foot.

PRAISE and glory be to Thee, most merciful JESUS CHRIST, for the most sacred wound in thy Left Foot; and by this adorable wound, grant me the grace of a full pardon, that with thine aid I may deserve to escape the sentence of eternal reprobation. I pray Thee, moreover, by thy most holy death, O my loving REDEEMER, that I may be able before my death to receive the sacrament of thy Body and Blood, after confession of my sins, and with perfect repentance and purity of body and mind. Grant that I may merit also to receive the holy anointing, for my eternal salvation, O LORD, who liveth and reigneth world without end. Amen. PATER noster, Ave Maria.

V. To the Wound in the sacred Side.

PRAISE and glory be to Thee, most loving JESUS CHRIST, for the most sacred wound in thy Side, and by that adorable wound, and by thy infinite mercy, which Thou didst make known in the opening of thy Breast to the soldier Longinus, and so to us all, I pray Thee, O most gentle JESUS, that having redeemed me by baptism from original sin, so now by thy Precious Blood, which is offered and received throughout the world, deliver me from all evils, past, present and to come. And by thy most bitter death give me a lively faith, a firm hope, and a perfect charity, so that I may love Thee with all my heart, and all my soul, and all my strength; make me firm and steadfast in good works, and grant me perseverance in thy service, so that I may be able to please Thee always. Amen. PATER noster, Ave Maria.

℣. We adore Thee, O CHRIST, and we bless Thee.

℞. Because by thy death and Blood Thou hast redeemed the world.

Let us pray.

ALMIGHTY and everlasting GOD, who by the five wounds of thy SON, our LORD JESUS CHRIST, hast redeemed the human race, grant to thy suppliants that we who daily venerate those wounds may, by the shedding of his Precious

Blood, be freed from sudden and everlasting death. Through the same CHRIST our LORD. Amen.

131. Hymn, Vexilla Regis.

100 Days, once a day.

(See Instructions, p. 1.)

VEXILLA Regis
prodeunt:
Fulget crucis mysterium,
Qua vita mortem per-
tulit,
Et morte vitam protulit.

Quæ vulnerata lanceæ
Mucrone diro, criminum
Ut nos lavaret sordibus,
Manavit unda et san-
guine.

Impleta sunt, quæ
concinit
David fideli carmine,
Dicendo nationibus:
Regnavit a ligno DEUS.

FORTH comes the
Standard of the
King:
All hail, thou Mystery
ador'd!
Hail, Cross! on which
the Life himself
Died, and by death our
life restor'd.

On which our SAVIOUR'S
holy side,
Rent open with a cruel
spear,
Of blood and water
pour'd a stream,
To wash us from defile-
ment clear.

O sacred Wood! in thee
fulfill'd
Was holy David's truth-
ful lay!
Which told the world,
that from a Tree,
The LORD should all the
nations sway.

Arbor decora et fulgida, Most royally empurpled o'er,
Ornata regis purpura,
Electa digno stipite How beautiful thy stem doth shine,
Tam sancta membra tangere. How glorious was its lot to touch
Those limbs so holy and divine!

Thrice blest, upon whose arms outstretched

Beata, cujus brachiis The SAVIOUR of the world reclined;
Pretium pependit sæculi,
  Statera facia corporis, Balance sublime! upon whose beam
Tulitque prædam tartari. Was weigh'd the ransom of mankind.

O Crux, ave spes unica, Hail, Cross! thou only hope of man,
Gentis redemptæ gloria! Sign of redemption's glorious day,

In Passiontide:

Hoc Passionis tempore Hail, on this holy Passion day.

In Paschal Time:

Paschale quæ fers gaudium, That bearest Paschal joy this day.

On the Exaltation of Cross (September 14):

In hac triumphi gloria Amid the triumph of this day.
Piis adauge gratiam,
Reisque dele crimina. To saints increase the
Te, fons salutis Trinitas, grace they have!

Collaudet omnis spir-
itus:
Quibus crucis victoriam
Largiris, adde præmium.
                    Amen.

From sinners purge
their guilt away.
Salvation's spring, blest
Trinity,
Be praise to Thee
through earth and
skies:
Thou through the
Cross the victory
Dost give; oh, also give
the prize.
                    Amen.

132. Prayer to Our Lord scourged at the Pillar.

100 Days, once a day.
                    (See Instructions, p. 1.)

MY divine SAVIOUR, what didst Thou become, when for love of souls Thou didst
allow thyself to be bound to the column? Oh, how
literally was then fulfilled the word of the prophet, that from head to foot Thou shouldst be all
one wound, and such as not to be recognized for
what Thou wast. What shame when they stripped
Thee of thy clothes! What torment under the
tempest of blows, multiplied without measure!
What a profusion of blood from thy streaming
wounds!

But it was neither the injustice of the Roman
governor nor the cruelty of the soldiers that
scourged Thee, but my sins. O miserable pleasures which have cost Thee such pains! O hardness of heart, when, knowing Thee to be tormented for my sake, I have gone on offending
Thee!

From today, then, it shall be so no more. Bound to Thee with eternal bonds and fastened with Thee to the column, as long as my life endures, I will make satisfaction to thy offended justice. By the column to which Thou wast bound, by the scourges which furrowed thy innocent flesh, by the blood Thou didst shed in such abundance, have pity, O LORD, have pity, on me in my desolation. Release me this day from the snares of the tempter and preserve me from them for ever; and at the end of this exile, receive me in heaven. Amen.

133. Ejaculation.

100 Days, once a day.

(See Instructions, p. 1.)

ADORAMUS te, sanctissime DOMINE JESU CHRISTE, benedicimus tibi; quia per sanctam crucem tuam redemisti mundum.

WE adore Thee, most holy LORD JESUS CHRIST, we bless Thee; because by thy holy Cross Thou hast redeemed the world.

134. Invocation.

100 Days, once a day.

(See Instructions, p. 1.)

ECCE Crucem DOMINI ✠ fugite partes adversæ, vicit Leo de tribu Juda, radix David, Alleluia.

BEHOLD the Cross of the LORD, ✠ flee ye adversaries, the Lion of the tribe of Juda has conquered, the root of David. Alleluia.

135. Prayer to Our Lord on the Cross.

i. 300 Days, once a day.
ii. Plenary, twice a year. I, II.

(See Instructions, p. 1.)

JESU mi crucifixe, suscipe benignus precem quam nunc pro meæ mortis articulo tibi fundo, quando ilia jam appetente, omnes mei sensus deficient.

Cum igitur, dulcissime JESU, mei oculi languidi et demissi te non amplius respicere poterunt, memento illius succensi aspectus, quem nunc tibi converto, et miserere mei.

Cum labia mea arefacta non amplius tuas sacratissimas plagas osculari poterunt, memento illorum osculorum, quæ nunc tibi figo, et miserere mei.

Cum manus meæ frigidæ non amplius tuam crucem amplecti poterunt, memento sensus, quo nunc hoc

MY crucified JESUS, mercifully accept the prayer which I now make to Thee for help in the moment of my death, when at its approach all my senses shall fail me.

When therefore, O sweetest JESUS, my weary and downcast eyes can no longer look up to Thee, be mindful of the loving gaze which now I turn on Thee, and have mercy on me.

When my parched lips can no longer kiss thy most sacred wounds, remember then those kisses which now I imprint on thee, and have mercy on me.

When my cold hands can no longer embrace thy Cross forget,

ago, et miserere mei.

Et cum tandem mea lingua tumens et immobilis non amplius loqui poterit, memento meæ invocationis hujus momenti.

JESU, Joseph, Maria, vobis commendo animam meam.

not the affection with which I embrace it now, and have mercy on me.

And when, at length, my swollen and lifeless tongue can no longer speak, remember that I called upon Thee now.

JESUS, Joseph, Mary, to you I commend my soul.

136. Prayer to Jesus Dead.

300 Days, T.Q

(See Instructions, p. 1.)

O JESUS, who in thy bitter Passion didst become the reproach of men and the man of sorrows, I venerate thy sacred face on which shone the grace and sweetness of the Divinity, now for my sake changed into the likeness of a leper. But under this deformity I perceive thy infinite love, and I am overwhelmed with the desire of loving Thee and making Thee beloved by all men. The tears which stream from thy eyes seem as precious pearls, which I love to gather up, in order to purchase with their infinite value the souls of poor sinners.

O JESUS, thy face is the only beauty which ravishes my heart. I am content not to see here below the sweetness of thy look, not to feel the ineffable delight of a kiss of thy mouth; but oh! I beseech Thee print on me thy divine likeness, and inflame me with thy love, so that it may rapidly consume me, and I may soon come to see thy glorious face in Heaven. Amen.

137. Prayer for a Happy Death.

100 Days, once a day.

(See Instructions, p. 1.)

O JESUS, while adoring thy last breath, I pray Thee to receive mine. In the uncertainty whether I shall have the command of my senses, when I shall depart out of this world, I offer Thee from this moment my agony and all the pains of my passing away. Thou art my FATHER and my SAVIOUR, and I give back my soul into thy hands. I desire that my last moment may be united to the moment of thy death, and that the last beat of my heart may be an act of pure love of Thee. Amen.

VIII. THE PRECIOUS BLOOD

138. Chaplet of the Precious Blood.

i. Seven Years and Seven Quarantines, once a day.
ii. Plenary, once a month. I, II, IV.

(See Instructions, p. 1.)

This Chaplet consists of seven Mysteries, in which we meditate upon the seven times in which JESUS CHRIST shed his Blood for us; at each Mystery except the last we say *Pater noster* five times, and *Gloria Patri* once; and at the last, *Pater noster* thrice, and *Gloria Patri* once; thus making up the number of 33, by saying the

Pater noster thirty-three times in remembrance of the thirty-three years of our Lord's life. End with the prayer, "Most Precious Blood," etc.

N.B.—These Indulgences can be gained by merely saying thirty-three *Pater Nosters* and, if the person is capable of meditating, reflecting on the Mysteries.

THE CHAPLET

℣. Deus, in adjutorium meum intende.

℣. O God, come to my assistance.

℟. Domine, ad adjuvandum me festina.

℟. O Lord make haste to help me.

℣. Gloria Patri, *etc.*

℣. Glory be to the Father, *etc.*

℟. Sicut erat, *etc.*

℟. As it was in the beginning, *etc.*

First Mystery.

THE first time our loving Saviour shed his Precious Blood for us was on the eighth day after his birth, when he was circumcised in order to fulfil the law of Moses. While, then, we reflect that Jesus did this to satisfy the justice of God for our lax ways, let us rouse ourselves to sorrow for them, and promise, with the help of his all-powerful grace, to be henceforth truly chaste in body and in soul. Pater noster *five times, and* Gloria Patri *once.*

℣. Te ergo quæsumus tuis famulis subveni quos pretioso Sanguine redemisti.

℣. We beseech Thee, therefore, help thy servants, whom Thou hast redeemed with thy Precious Blood.

Second Mystery.

NEXT, in the Garden of Olives, Jesus shed his Blood for us in such quantity that it bathed the earth around. He did this at the sight of the ingratitude with which men would meet his love. Let us, then, repent sincerely that we have hitherto corresponded so ill with the countless blessings of God, and resolve to make good use of his graces and inspirations. Pater noster *five times, and* Gloria Patri *once.*

℣. Te ergo quæsumus, ℣. We beseech Thee, *etc.* *etc.*

Third Mystery.

NEXT, in his cruel scourging, Jesus shed his Blood when his flesh was so torn that streams of Blood flowed from every part of his body, all of which he offered all the time to his Eternal Father in payment of our impatience and our softness. How comes it, then, that we do not curb our anger and love of self? Henceforth we will try our best to bear our troubles well, and, despising self, take peacefully the injuries which men may do us. Pater noster *five times, and* Gloria Patri *once.*

℣. Te ergo quæsumus, ℣. We beseech Thee, *etc* *etc.*

Fourth Mystery.

AGAIN, from the sacred Head of Jesus, Blood poured down when it was crowned with thorns, in punishment of our pride and evil thoughts. Shall we, then, continue to nurture haughtiness, foster foul imaginations, and feed

the wayward will within us? Henceforth let there
be ever before our eyes our utter nothingness,
our misery, and our weakness; and with generous
hearts let us resist all the temptations of the devil.
PATER noster *five times, and* Gloria PATRI *once.*

℣. Te ergo quæsumus, ℣. We beseech Thee,
etc.   *etc.*

FIFTH MYSTERY.

WHAT streams of Precious Blood did not
our loving LORD pour forth from his veins
when laden with the heavy Cross on that most
grievous journey to Calvary! The very streets and
ways of Jerusalem, through which He passed,
were watered with it! This He did in satisfaction
for the scandals and bad example by which his
own creatures had led others astray. Who can
tell how many of us are of this unhappy number? Who knows how many he himself alone
has, by his own bad example, brought down to
hell? And what have we done to remedy this evil?
Henceforth let us at least do all we can to save
souls by word and by example, making ourselves
a pattern to all of goodness and a holy life. PATER
noster *five times, and* Gloria PATRI *once.*

℣. Te ergo quæsumus, ℣. We beseech Thee,
etc.   *etc.*

SIXTH MYSTERY.

MORE, and still more Precious Blood did
the REDEEMER of mankind shed in his bar-
barous Crucifixion; when, his veins being rent
and arteries burst, there rushed forth in a torrent,

from his hands and his feet, that saving balm of life eternal, to pay for all the crimes and enormities of a lost world. Who, after this, would continue in sin, and so renew the cruel crucifixion of the SON of GOD? Let us weep bitterly for our bad deeds done, and detest them before the feet of the sacred minister of GOD; let us amend our evil ways, and henceforth begin a truly Christian life, with the remembrance ever in our hearts of all the Blood which our salvation cost the SAVIOUR of men. PATER noster *five times, and* Gloria PATRI *once.*

℣. Te ergo quæsumus, ℣. We beseech Thee, *etc.* *etc.*

SEVENTH MYSTERY.

LAST of all, after his death, when his sacred Side was opened by the lance, and his loving Heart was wounded, JESUS shed Blood, and with it there came forth water, to show us how his Blood was all poured out to the last drop for our salvation. Oh, the great goodness of our redeeming LORD! Who will not love Thee, SAVIOUR of my soul? What heart will not consume itself away for love of Thee, who hast done all this for our redemption? The tongue wants words to praise Thee; so let us invite all creatures upon earth, all angels and all saints in Paradise, and most of all our dear Mother Mary, to bless, praise, and celebrate thy most Precious Blood. Glory to the Blood of JESUS! Now and ever throughout all ages. Amen. PATER noster *thrice, and* Gloria PATRI *once.*

℣. Te ergo quæsumus, *etc.*

℣. We beseech Thee, *etc.*

Prayer.

MOST Precious Blood of life eternal! price and ransom of the world! drink and bath of the soul! ever pleading the cause of man before the throne of Mercy; I adore Thee most profoundly; I would, if I were able, make Thee some compensation for the outrages and wrongs Thou dost ever suffer from men, and especially from those who dare in their rashness to blaspheme Thee. Who will not bless this Blood of value infinite? Who does not feel himself on fire with the love of JESUS, who shed it all for us? What should I be but for this Blood, which hath redeemed me? And what drew Thee, Thou Precious Blood, from the veins of my LORD, even to the last drop? It was love. O boundless love, which gave to us this saving balsam! O balsam beyond all price, streaming forth from the fount of immeasurable love! Give to all hearts, all tongues, power to praise, celebrate, and thank Thee, now and ever, and throughout all eternity. Amen.

℣. Redemisti nos, Domine, in Sanguine tuo:
℟. Et fecisti nos Deo nostro regnum.

℣. Thou hast redeemed us, O Lord, with thy Blood,
℟. And hast made us a kingdom to our God.

Oremus.

Let us pray.

OMNIPOTENS sempiterne Deus, qui unigenitum Filium tuum

ALMIGHTY and everlasting God, who hast appointed thine

mundi Redemptorem constituisti, ac ejus Sanguine placari voluisti; concede nobis, quæsumus, salutis nostræ pretium ita venerari, atque a præsentis vitæ malis ejus virtute defendi in terris, ut fructu perpetuo lætemur in cœlis. Qui tecum vivit et regnat, *etc*. Amen.

only-begotten Son the Saviour of the world, and hast willed to be appeased by his Blood; grant us, we beseech Thee, so to venerate this Blood, the price of our salvation, and so to be defended on earth by its power from the evils of this present life, that in heaven we may be made glad by its everlasting fruit. Who liveth and reigneth, *etc*. Amen.

139. Prayer.

300 Days, once a day.
(See Instructions, p. 1.)

Most Precious Blood, *etc*. (See previous.)

140. Devout Aspirations.

100 Days, once a day.
(See Instructions, p. 1.)

GLORY be to Jesus!
Who in bitter pains
Pour'd for me the life-blood
From his sacred veins.

Grace and life eternal

In that Blood I find;
Bless'd be his compassion,
Infinitely kind!

Bless'd through endless ages
Be the precious stream,
Which from endless torment
Doth the world redeem.

There the fainting spirit
Drinks of life her fill;
There, as in a fountain,
Laves herself at will.

Oh, the Blood of CHRIST!
It soothes the FATHER's ire,
Opes the gate of heaven,
Quells eternal fire.

Abel's blood for vengeance
Pleaded to the skies,
But the Blood of JESUS
For our pardon cries.

Oft as it is sprinkled
On our guilty hearts,
Satan in confusion
Terror-struck departs.

Oft as earth exulting
Wafts its praise on high,
Hell with terror trembles,
Heaven is filled with joy.

Lift ye, then, your voices;
Swell the mighty flood;
Louder still and louder,
Praise the Precious Blood!

141. Seven Offerings, in reparation for all the outrages received by Our Lord in the Precious Blood.

    i. 300 Days. T.Q.
    ii. Plenary, once a month. I, II, IV.
                (See Instructions, p. 1.)

I

ETERNAL FATHER! I offer Thee the merits of the Precious Blood of JESUS, thy well-beloved SON, my SAVIOUR and my GOD, for the propagation and exaltation of my dear Mother, thy Holy Church; for the safety and prosperity of her visible head, our chief pastor the Bishop of Rome; for the cardinals, bishops, and pastors of souls, and for all the ministers of the sanctuary. Gloria PATRI.

Blessed and praised for evermore be JESUS, who hath saved us with his Blood,

II

ETERNAL FATHER! I offer Thee the merits of the Precious Blood of JESUS, thy well-beloved SON, my SAVIOUR and my GOD, for the peace and concord of Catholic kings and princes, for the humiliation of the enemies of our holy Faith, and for the welfare of all Christian people. Gloria PATRI.

Blessed and praised, *etc.*

III

ETERNAL FATHER! I offer Thee the merits of the Precious Blood of JESUS, thy well-beloved SON, my SAVIOUR and my GOD, for the repentance of unbelievers, the uprooting of heresy, and the conversion of sinners. Gloria PATRI.

Blessed and praised, *etc.*

IV

ETERNAL FATHER! I offer Thee the merits of the Precious Blood of JESUS, thy well-beloved SON, my SAVIOUR and my GOD, for all my relations, friends, and enemies; for the poor, the sick, and the afflicted, and for all those for whom Thou, my GOD, knowest that I ought to pray, or wouldst have me pray. Gloria PATRI.
Blessed and praised, *etc.*

V

ETERNAL FATHER! I offer Thee the merits of the Precious Blood of JESUS, thy well-beloved SON, my SAVIOUR and my GOD, for all who this day are passing to the other life; that thou wouldst save them from the pains of hell, and admit them quickly to the possession of thy glory. Gloria PATRI.
Blessed and praised, *etc.*

VI

ETERNAL FATHER! I offer Thee the merits of the Precious Blood of JESUS, thy well-beloved SON, my SAVIOUR and my GOD, for all those who love this great treasure, for those who join with me in adoring it and honouring it, and for those who strive to spread devotion to it. Gloria PATRI.
Blessed and praised, *etc.*

VII

ETERNAL FATHER! I offer Thee the merits of the Precious Blood of JESUS, thy well-beloved SON, my SAVIOUR and my GOD, for all my wants, spiritual and temporal; in suffrage for the holy souls in purgatory, and chiefly for those who

were most devout lovers of this Blood, the price
of our redemption, and of the sorrows and pains
of our dear Mother, most holy Mary. Gloria PATRI.
Blessed and praised, *etc.*

Glory be to the Blood of JESUS, now and for ever,
and throughout all ages! Amen.

142. Act of Oblation in thanksgiving for blessings received.

    i. 100 Days. T.Q.
    ii. Plenary, once a month. I, II, IV.
               (See Instructions, p. 1.)

ETERNAL FATHER! we offer Thee the most
Precious Blood of JESUS, shed for us with
such great love and bitter pain from his Right
Hand; and through the merits and the efficacy
of that Blood, we entreat Thy Divine Majesty to
grant us thy holy benediction, in order that we
may be defended thereby from all our enemies,
and be set free from every ill; whilst we say, May
the blessing of Almighty GOD, FATHER, SON and
HOLY SPIRIT descend upon us and remain with us
for ever. Amen. PATER, Ave *and* Gloria.

143. Month consecrated to the Precious Blood
(which may begin on any day of the year).

    i. Seven Years and Seven Quarantines daily to all
    who assist at the public devotions.
    ii. Plenary, to all who shall assist at public devotions
    at least ten times in the month; this they may gain
    in the course of the said month, or on one of the
    eight days immediately following it. I, II, III, IV.
    iii. 300 Days, daily, to those who shall practise this
    devotion in private, with devout prayers and acts
    in honour of the Precious Blood.

iv. Plenary, to those who shall practise it in private
for a month together; to be gained on the last day
of the month, or one of the next eight days. I, II,
III, IV.

(See Instructions, p. 1.)

144. Prayer to Jesus of Nazareth.

200 Days, once a day.

(See Instructions, p. 1.)

BEHOLD me at thy feet, O JESUS of Nazareth;
behold the most miserable of creatures, who
presents himself before Thee, humbled and penitent. Have mercy on me, O LORD, according to
thy great mercy. I sinned, and my sins were committed against Thee, O GOD of infinite bounty. O
JESUS, hear my prayers, graciously hear, O loving
FATHER, the requests I lay at thy feet: cast a favourable look on my soul, Thou who art the loving FATHER of men, the Supreme Judge, the King
of Heaven and of earth, the true benefactor of the
wretched. Come then to my assistance, O JESUS
of Nazareth. Grant me the graces which I ask of
Thee, kneeling at thy feet. My soul belongs to
Thee, because Thou hast created and redeemed
it with thy Precious Blood. May thy work not be
in vain. Turn, O loving FATHER, thy regard upon
me and bless me. O GOD of mercy, have pity on
me; pardon me, who am thy son; deal not severely
with me; give me tears of repentance; pardon me
as Thou didst pardon the penitent thief; watch
over me from the height of Heaven and bless me.
Amen.
End with the Apostles Creed.

145. Ejaculation.

i. 300 Days. T.Q.
ii. Plenary, once a month. I, II, IV.
(See Instructions, p. 1.)

To be said in reparation for blasphemies.

ETERNAL FATHER, by the most Precious Blood of JESUS CHRIST, glorify his most holy Name, according to the intention and the desires of his adorable Heart.

146. Offering.

100 Days. T.Q.
(See Instructions, p. 1.)

ETERNAL FATHER! I offer Thee the Precious Blood of JESUS CHRIST in satisfaction for my sins, and for the wants of Holy Church.

IX. THE SACRED HEART

147. Visit to a Representation of the Sacred Heart, exposed for public veneration.

Seven Years and Seven Quarantines. IV.
(See Instructions, p. 1.)

148. Act of Oblation to be made before a Representation of the Sacred Heart.

i. 100 Days, once a day.
ii. Plenary, once a month. I, II, IV.
(See Instructions, p. 1.)

MY loving JESUS, out of the grateful love I bear Thee, and to make reparation for my unfaithfulness to grace, I (N.N.) give Thee my heart, and I consecrate myself wholly to Thee; and with thy help I purpose never to sin again.

149. Acts of Devotion.

i. 300 Days, once a day.
ii. Plenary, once a month. I, II, IV.

(See Instructions, p. 1.)

I. The Word was made Flesh, and dwelt amongst us.

ETERNAL Word, made Man for love of us, humbly kneeling at thy feet we adore Thee with the deepest veneration of our souls; and in order that we may repair our ingratitude for this great benefit of thy Incarnation, we unite ourselves to the hearts of all those who love Thee, and together with them we offer Thee our humble loving thanksgiving. Pierced by the excess of humility, goodness, and sweetness which we behold in thy Divine Heart, we beseech Thee to give us thy grace, that in our lives we too may imitate these virtues so dear to Thee. PATER, Ave, and Gloria.

II. He was crucified also for us; suffered under Pontius Pilate, and was buried.

JESUS our loving SAVIOUR, humbly kneeling at thy feet we adore Thee with the deepest veneration of our souls; and, in order that we may give Thee proof of the sorrow we feel at our insensibility to the outrages and sufferings which thy loving Heart made Thee undergo for our salvation in thy painful Passion and Death, we here unite ourselves with the hearts of all those who love Thee, and together with them we give thanks unto Thee with our whole soul. We wonder at the boundless patience and generosity of thy Divine Heart; and we entreat Thee to fill our hearts with such a spirit of Christian penance as may enable us courageously to embrace suffering, and to make thy Cross our great comfort and all our glory. PATER, Ave, *and* Gloria.

III. Thou didst give them bread from heaven to eat, containing in itself all sweetness.

JESUS, who dost burn with love for us, humbly kneeling at thy feet we adore Thee with the deepest veneration of our souls; and, in order to make Thee reparation for the outrages which thy divine Heart daily receives in the most holy Sacrament of the Altar, we unite ourselves with the hearts of all those who love Thee, and give Thee tenderest thanks. We love in thy divine Heart this thy incomprehensible fire of love towards thy Eternal FATHER, and we entreat Thee to inflame our hearts with ardent charity towards Thee and towards our neighbour. PATER, Ave, *and* Gloria.

LASTLY, O most loving JESUS, we pray Thee, by the sweetness of thy Divine Heart, convert the sinner, console the afflicted, help the dying, lighten the pains of the souls in purgatory. Make all our hearts one in the bonds of true peace and charity, deliver us from sudden and unforeseen death, and grant us a death holy and peaceful. Amen.

℣. Heart of JESUS, burning with love of us,
℟. Inflame our hearts with love of Thee.
Let us pray.

GRANT, we beseech Thee, Almighty GOD, that we who glory in the most Sacred Heart of thy well-beloved SON, and call to mind the chief benefits of his heavenly charity towards us, may be gladdened by the operation and the fruit of those graces in our souls. Through the same CHRIST, *etc.*

O Divine Heart of my JESUS! I adore Thee with all the powers of my soul; I consecrate them to Thee for ever, together with all my thoughts, my words, my works, and my whole self. I purpose to offer to Thee, as far as I am able, acts of adoration, love, and glory, like unto those which Thou dost offer to thine Eternal FATHER. I beseech Thee, be Thou the reparation for my transgressions, the protector of my life, my refuge and asylum in the hour of my death. By thy sighs, and by that sea of bitterness in which Thou wast immersed for me throughout the whole course of thy mortal life, grant me true contrition for my sins, contempt of earthly things, an ardent longing for the glory of heaven, trust in thy infinite merits, and final perseverance in thy grace.

Heart of JESUS, all love! I offer Thee these humble prayers for myself, and for all who unite with me in spirit to adore Thee; vouchsafe, of thy infinite goodness, to receive and to answer them, and especially for that one of us who shall first end this mortal life. Sweet Heart of my SAVIOUR, pour down upon him, in the agony of death, thine inward consolations; place him in thy sa-

cred wounds; cleanse him from every stain in that
furnace of love, that so Thou mayest open to him
speedily the entrance into thy glory, there to intercede with Thee for all those who yet tarry in
their land of exile.

Most Holy Heart of my most loving JESUS, I purpose to renew these acts of adoration and these
prayers for myself, miserable sinner that I am,
as well as for all who are associated with me to
adore Thee, every moment while I live, down to
the last instant of my life. I recommend to Thee,
my JESUS, the Holy Church, thy well-beloved
Spouse, our own true Mother, the souls that undergo thy justice, all poor sinners, those who are
in affliction, the dying, and all mankind, let not
thy Blood be shed in vain for them; and, last of
all, vouchsafe to receive my poor prayers for the
relief of the souls in purgatory, and, above all, for
those who in the course of their life were wont
devoutly to adore Thee.

Most loving heart of Mary, which, amongst the
hearts of all creatures of GOD, art at once the most
pure, most inflamed with love for JESUS, and most
compassionate towards us poor sinners, gain for
us from the Heart of JESUS our REDEEMER all the
graces which we ask of thee. Mother of mercies,
one single throb, one beat of thy heart, all on fire
with love towards the Heart of JESUS, has power
to console us to the full. Only grant us this favour
and the Heart of JESUS, out of that filial love It had
and will ever have for thee, will not fail to hear
and answer us. Amen.

150. Chaplet.

i. 300 Days. T.Q.
ii. Plenary, once a month. I, II, IV.

(See Instructions, p. 1.)

℣. O God, come to my assistance.
℟. O Lord, make haste to help me.
℣. Glory be, *etc.*
℟. As it was, *etc.*

I

MY most loving Jesus, when I ponder over thy most Sacred Heart, all tenderness and sweetness for sinners, then doth my heart rejoice, and I am filled with hope of thy kind welcome. But, ah me, my sins! how many and how great! With Peter and with Magdalen, I bewail and abhor them, because they are an offence to Thee, my Sovereign Good. Oh, grant me pardon for them all. I pray thy Sacred Heart that I may rather die than offend Thee again, and may live only to love Thee. Pater *once,* Gloria *five times, in honour of the Sacred Heart, then:*

Sweet Heart of my Jesus,
Make me love Thee ever more and more.

II

MY Jesus, I bless thy most humble Heart; and I give thanks unto Thee, who in making It my model dost urge me with strong pleadings to imitate It, and also, at the cost of so many humiliations, dost vouchsafe thyself to point out and smooth for me the way to follow Thee. Fool and ungrateful that I am, how have I wandered far away from Thee! Pardon me, my Jesus! Take away from me all hateful pride and ambition, that with lowly heart I may follow Thee, my JESUS, amidst humiliations, and so gain peace and salvation. Strengthen me, Thou who canst, and I will ever bless thy Sacred Heart. PATER *once*, Gloria *five times, in honour of the Sacred Heart*, then:

Sweet Heart, *etc.*

III

MY JESUS, I marvel at thy most patient Heart, and I give Thee thanks for all the wondrous examples of unwearied patience which Thou hast left us. It grieves me that these examples still have to reproach me for my excessive delicacy, shrinking from every little pain. Pour, then, into my heart, O dear JESUS, a fervent and constant love of suffering and the cross, of mortification and of penance, that, following Thee to Calvary, I may with Thee attain the joys of Paradise. PATER *once*, Gloria *five times, in honour of the Sacred Heart*, then:

Sweet Heart, *etc.*

IV

DEAR JESUS, beside thy most gentle Heart I set my own, and shudder to see how unlike mine is to thine. How am I wont to fret and grieve when a hint, a look, or a word thwarts me! Pardon all my violence, and give me for the future grace to imitate in every contradiction thy unalterable meekness, that so I may enjoy an everlasting holy peace. PATER *once*, Gloria *five times, in honour of the Sacred Heart*, then:

Sweet Heart, *etc.*

v

LET us sing praise to JESUS for his generous Heart, Conqueror of death and hell; for well It merits every praise. Still more than ever confounded am I, looking upon my coward heart, which dreads even a rough word or injurious taunt. But it shall be so with me no more. My JESUS, I pray Thee for such strength that, fighting and conquering self on earth, I may one day rejoice triumphantly with Thee in heaven. PATER once, Gloria *five times, in honour of the Sacred Heart*, then:

Sweet Heart, *etc.*

NOW let us turn to Mary, and dedicating ourselves yet more and more to her, and trusting in her Mother's heart, we say to her: By all the virtue of thy most sweet heart obtain for me, great Mother of GOD, our Mother Mary, a true and enduring devotion to the Sacred Heart of JESUS, thy SON, that, bound up in every thought and affection in union with his Heart, I may fulfil each duty of my state, serving JESUS ever more with readiness of heart, and specially this day.

℣. Heart of JESUS, burning with love or us,

℟. Inflame our hearts with love of Thee.

Let us pray.

LORD, we beseech Thee, let thy HOLY SPIRIT kindle in our hearts that fire of charity which our LORD JESUS CHRIST, thy SON, sent forth from his inmost Heart upon this earth, and willed that it should burn exceedingly. Who liveth and reigneth with Thee, in the unity of the same HOLY SPIRIT, GOD for ever and ever. Amen.

151. Visit to any Church or Public Oratory where the Feast of the Sacred Heart is being kept.

Plenary, I, II, IV.

(See Instructions, p. 1.)

The Indulgences granted for Corpus CHRISTI, in the case of the divine offices celebrated during solemn Exposition (section VI on the Blessed Sacrament), may be gained on the Feast of the Sacred Heart, even if transferred. The Feast may be transferred with leave of the Ordinary.

152. Novena of the Sacred Heart.

    i. 300 Days, each day.
    ii. Plenary, during the Novena or Octave. I, II, IV.

(See Instructions, p. 1.)

This Novena may be made for the Feast of the Sacred Heart, and once during the year as well, with any form of prayers approved by competent ecclesiastical authority.

153. Prayer for those in their agony.

    i. 100 Days. T.Q.
    ii. Plenary, once a month, if said thrice daily, at three
       distinct intervals. I, II, III, IV.

(See Instructions, p. 1.)

O CLEMENTISSIME JESU, amator animarum; obsecro te, per agoniam cordis tui sanctissimi, et per dolores Matris tuæ Immaculatæ, lava in sanguine tuo

O MOST merciful JESUS, Lover of souls: I pray Thee, by the agony of thy most Sacred Heart, and by the sorrows of thy Immaculate Mother, cleanse in thine own peccatores totius mundi, nunc positos in agonia et hodie morituros. Amen.

Blood the sinners of the whole world who are now in their agony and to die this day. Amen.

Cor JESU, in agonia factum, miserere morientium.

Heart of JESUS, once in agony, pity the dying.

154. Month of June.

    i. Seven Years and Seven Quarantines, each day.
    ii. Plenary, during the month or first eight days of July. I, II, III, IV.
For i and ii any form of devotion, public or private, may be used. If it be in public, ten attendances suffice for the plenary Indulgence. If in private, the devotion must be practised daily throughout the month.
    iii. Plenary, T.Q., on June 30, every time a visit is made to a church where the Month of the Sacred Heart has been solemnly observed. I, II, IV.
    iv. 500 Days, to promoters of this devotion whenever they do any good work calculated to propagate or make better observed this Month of the Sacred Heart.
    v. Plenary, to the same persons for every Communion made in June. The privilege of the Gregorian altar is conferred on the preacher of the month and the Rector of the church where the month has been duly observed, available for their Masses on June 30.

(See Instructions, p. 1.)

N.B.—The solemn observance of June contemplated in III, IV, and V implies discourses, either daily, or at least for eight days, after the manner of spiritual exercises.

The Month may be concluded on the last Sunday of the month.

It may be observed in the semi-public chapels of seminaries, communities, etc.

It may be transferred to another month by leave of the bishop.

155. Acts of Homage to the Eucharistic Heart of Jesus.

200 Days, for each of the four Acts. T.Q.

(See Instructions, p. 1.)

N.B.—This Devotion does not substantially differ from the ordinary Devotion to the Sacred Heart. It merely emphasizes the Act of Supreme love of that Heart in bestowing the gift of the Holy Eucharist upon us.

I. Prayer.

HEART of JESUS in the Eucharist, sweet companion in our exile, *I adore Thee.*

Eucharistic Heart of JESUS,

Heart solitary,

Heart humiliated,

Heart abandoned,

Heart forgotten,

Heart despised,

Heart outraged,

Heart ignored by men,

Heart, lover of our hearts,

Heart desirous of being loved,

Heart patient in waiting for us,

Heart eager to hear us,

Heart longing to be prayed to,

Heart source of new graces,

Heart wrapped in silence, desiring to speak to souls,

Heart, the sweet refuge of the hidden life,

Heart, teacher of the secrets of union with GOD,

Heart of him who sleeps, yet ever watches,

I adore Thee.

Eucharistic Heart of JESUS, have pity on us.

JESUS Victim, I desire to console Thee.

I unite myself to Thee, and sacrifice myself with Thee.

I annihilate myself in thy presence.

I would forget myself to be mindful of Thee.

I would be forgotten and despised for love of Thee.

And be neither understood nor loved, unless by Thee.

I will silence myself to listen to Thee,

I will abandon myself to lose myself in Thee.

Grant that I may thus appease thy thirst, the thirst for my sanctification and salvation, and that being purified I may bestow on Thee a pure and true love.

I would not longer weary thy patience; take possession of me, I give myself to Thee.

I offer Thee all my actions, my intellect to be illuminated by Thee, my heart to be guided by Thee, my will to be made strong, my soul and body to be nourished, my misery to be lightened.

Eucharistic Heart of my JESUS, whose blood is the life of my soul, may it be no longer I that live, but do thou alone live in me. Amen.

II. Act of Consecration.

JESUS, adorable LORD, hidden in thy Sacrament of love, Thou who abidest with us to sweeten our exile, should I not occupy myself in consoling Thee in thine? To Thee who givest me thy heart, how should I not offer Thee mine?

Truly, to give myself to Thee is to benefit myself; it is to find an ineffable treasure, a heart, loving, disinterested, and faithful, such as I would wish my own to be. I cannot be for ever receiving, and giving nothing in return. Dear LORD, I could never vie with Thee in generosity, but I love Thee; deign to accept my poor heart, and though it is worthless, yet because Thou lovest it, it may become something by thy grace; make it good and take it into thy custody.

Eucharistic Heart of JESUS, I consecrate to Thee all the powers of my soul, and all the powers of my body; I desire to apply myself to the work of knowing Thee and loving Thee ever more and more, in order to make Thee better known and loved by others. I would do nothing except what tends to thy glory, nor act in anything but as thy divine FATHER wills. I consecrate to Thee all the moments of my life in a spirit of adoration before thy real presence, in a spirit of thanksgiving for this incomparable gift, of reparation for our cruel indifference, and of incessant supplication, so that our prayers offered to Thee, with Thee, and in Thee may rise to the throne of divine mercy pure and efficacious, and for GOD's eternal glory. Amen.

III. Ejaculation.

EUCHARISTIC Heart of JESUS, on fire with love of us, inflame our hearts with love of Thee.

IV. Act of Reparation.

EUCHARISTIC Heart of my GOD, living and beating under the veil of the sacred species, I adore Thee.

Moved afresh with love for the immense benefit of the divine Eucharist, penetrated with sorrow for my ingratitude, I humble and annihilate myself in the still greater abyss of thy mercies.

Thou didst choose me from childhood; Thou didst not despise my infirmity; Thou didst descend into my poor heart, and giving it happiness and peace, didst invite it to mutual love; and I have lost all, by being unfaithful to Thee, O JESUS, my LORD. I have allowed my spirit to become dissipated and my heart to grow cold; I have listened to my own voice and have forgotten Thee.

Thou wouldst have been my guide, my counsellor, protector of my life, and I, allowing my passions to destroy the sweet attraction of thy presence, have lost sight of Thee and forgotten Thee.

In the salutary trials of our probation, in times of joy and consolation, in my difficulties and necessities, instead of having recourse to Thee, I have gone after creatures and have forgotten Thee.

I have forgotten Thee in deserted tabernacles, where thy love languishes, in the churches of towns where Thou art outraged in the hearts of the indifferent and sacrilegious, and in my own sinful heart, O JESUS, as well when I approached to receive Thee, as after receiving Thee.

Eucharistic Heart of my SAVIOUR, the delight of my first Communion and of the days of my fidelity, I surrender to Thee. Return! Return! draw me to Thyself afresh. Pardon me yet again this time; and I shall hope everything in the strength of thy love.

Glorious Archangel St Michael and thou, O beloved disciple St John, offer to JESUS this my act of reparation, and be propitious to me. Amen.

156. Daily Act of Oblation.

100 Days, once a day.
(See Instructions, p. 1.)

O LORD JESUS CHRIST, in union with that divine intention with which Thou didst on earth offer praises to GOD through thy Sacred Heart, and now dost continue to offer them in all places in the Sacrament of the Eucharist, and wilt do so to the end of the world, I most willingly offer Thee, throughout this entire day without the smallest exception, all my intentions and thoughts, all my affections and desires, all my words and actions, that they may be conformed to the most sacred heart of the blessed Virgin Mary ever Immaculate.

157. Act of Consecration of B. Margaret Mary.

i. 300 Days, once a day.
ii. Plenary, once a month. I, II, III, IV.
(See Instructions, p. 1.)

I N.N., give and consecrate to the Sacred Heart, of our LORD JESUS CHRIST my person and my life, my actions, penances, and sufferings, not wishing to make use of any part of my being for the future except in honouring, loving, and glorifying that Sacred Heart.

It is my irrevocable will to be entirely his, and
to do everything for his love, renouncing with
my whole heart whatever might displease Him. I
take Thee then, O most Sacred Heart, as the sole
object of my love, as the protector of my life, as
the pledge of my salvation, as the remedy of my
frailty and inconstancy, as the repairer of all the
defects of my life, and as my secure refuge in the
hour of death.

Be then, O Heart of goodness, my justification
before GOD the FATHER, and remove far from me
the thunderbolts of his just wrath. O Heart of
love, I place my whole confidence in Thee. While
I fear all things from my malice and frailty, I hope
all things from thy goodness.

Consume then in me whatever can displease or
be opposed to Thee, and may thy pure love be so
deeply impressed upon my heart that it may be
impossible that I should ever be separated from
Thee, or forget Thee.

I implore Thee, by all thy goodness, that my
name may be written in Thee, for in Thee I wish
to place all my happiness and all my glory, living
and dying in very bondage to Thee. Amen.

158. Devotions for Fridays.

i. Plenary on the first Friday of the month. I, II, IV.
ii. Seven Years and Seven Quarantines, on other
Fridays. I, II, IV.

(See Instructions, p. 1.)

All that is required is that some time should be spent
in meditating on the infinite goodness of the Sacred
Heart.

159. Ejaculation.

100 Days, once a day.
(See Instructions, p. 1.)

MAY the Heart of Jesus be loved everywhere.

160. Ejaculation.

300 Days. T.Q.
(See Instructions, p. 1.)

JESUS, meek and humble of heart, make my heart like unto thine.

161. Ejaculation.

100 Days, once a day.
(See Instructions, p. 1.)

MAY the Heart of Jesus in the most Blessed Sacrament be praised, adored, and loved with grateful affection, at every moment, in all the Tabernacles of the world, even to the end of time. Amen.

162. Ejaculation.

i. 300 Days. T.Q.
ii. Plenary, once a month. I, II, III, IV.
(See Instructions, p. 1.)

Sweet Heart of my Jesus,
Make me love Thee ever more and more!

163. Ejaculation.

300 Days, once a day.
(See Instructions, p. 1.)

DULCE cor Jesu, sis amor meus.

SWEET Heart of Jesus be my love.

164. Ejaculation.

100 Days, once a day.

(See Instructions, p. 1.)

COR JESU flagrans amore nostri, inflamma cor nostrum amore tui.

HEART of JESUS burning with love of us, inflame our hearts with love of Thee.

165. Litany of the Sacred Heart.

300 Days, once a day.

(See Instructions, p. 1.)

KYRIE eleison.
CHRISTE eleison.
KYRIE eleison.
CHRISTE, audi nos.
CHRISTE, exaudi nos.

PATER de cœlis DEUS,
miserere nobis.
FILI REDEMPTOR mundi
DEUS, *miserere nobis.*
SPIRITUS SANCTE DEUS,
miserere nobis.
Sancta Trinitas, unus
DEUS, *miserere nobis.*
Cor JESU, FILII PATRIS
æterni, *miserere nobis.*

LORD, have mercy on us.
CHRIST, have mercy on us.
LORD, have mercy on us.
CHRIST, hear us.
CHRIST, graciously hear us
GOD the FATHER of heaven, *have mercy on us.*
GOD the SON, REDEEMER of the world, *have mercy on us.*
GOD the HOLY SPIRIT, *have mercy on us.*
Holy Trinity, one GOD, *have mercy on us.*
Heart of JESUS, SON of the eternal FATHER, *have mercy on us.*

Cor JESU, in sinu Virginis Matris a SPIRITU SANCTO formatum,

Cor JESU, Verbo DEI substantialiter uniturn,

Cor JESU, majestatis infinitæ,

Cor JESU, templum DEI sanctum, Cor JESU, tabernaculum Altissimi,

Cor JESU, domus DEI et porta cœli,

Cor JESU, fornax ardens caritatis,

Cor JESU, justitiæ et amoris receptaculum,

Cor JESU, bonitate et amore plenum,

Cor JESU, virtutum omnium abyssus,

Cor JESU, omni laude dignissimum,

Cor JESU, rex et centrum omnium cordium,

Cor JESU, in quo sunt omnes thesauri sapientiæ et scientiæ,

Cor JESU, in quo habitat omnis plenitude Divinitatis,

miserere nobis.

Heart of JESUS, formed in the womb of the Virgin Mother by the HOLY SPIRIT,

Heart of JESUS, united substantially with the Word of GOD,

Heart of JESUS, of infinite majesty,

Heart of JESUS, holy temple of GOD,

Heart of JESUS, tabernacle of the Most High,

Heart of JESUS, house of GOD and gate of Heaven,

Heart of JESUS, glowing furnace of charity,

Heart of JESUS, vessel of justice and love,

Heart of JESUS, full of goodness and love,

Heart of JESUS, abyss of all virtues,

Heart of JESUS, most worthy of all praise,

Heart of JESUS, King and centre of all hearts,

Heart of JESUS, in which are all the treasures of wisdom and knowledge,

have mercy on us.

Cor Jesu, in quo Pater sibi bene complacuit,

Cor Jesu, de cujus plenitudine omnes nos accepimus,

Cor Jesu, desiderium collium æternorum,

Cor Jesu, patiens et multæ misericordiæ,

Cor Jesu, dives in omnes qui invocant te,

Cor Jesu, fons vitæ et sanctitatis,

Cor Jesu, propitiatio pro peccatis nostris,

Cor Jesu, saturatum opprobriis,

Cor Jesu, attritum propter scelera nostra,

Cor Jesu, usque ad mortem obediens factum,

Cor Jesu, lancea perforatum,

Cor Jesu, fons totius consolationis,

Cor Jesu, vita et resurrectio nostra,

miserere nobis.

Heart of Jesus, in which dwelleth all the fullness of the Divinity,

Heart of Jesus, in which the Father is well pleased,

Heart of Jesus, of whose fullness we have all received,

Heart of Jesus, desire of the eternal hills,

Heart of Jesus, patient and rich in mercy,

Heart of Jesus, rich to all who invoke Thee,

Heart of Jesus, fount of life and holiness,

Heart of Jesus, propitiation for our sins,

Heart of Jesus, saturated with revilings,

Heart of Jesus, crushed for our iniquities,

Heart of Jesus, made obedient unto death,

Heart of Jesus, pierced with a lance,

Heart of Jesus, source of all consolation,

Heart of Jesus, our life and resurrection,

have mercy on us.

Cor Jesu, pax et reconciliatio nostra,

Cor Jesu, Victima peccatorum,

Cor Jesu, salus in te sperantium,

Cor Jesu, spes in te morientium,

Cor Jesu, deliciæ Sanctorum omnium,

miserere nobis.

Agnus Dei, qui tollis peccata mundi, parce nobis Domine.

Agnus Dei, qui tollis peccata mundi, exaudi nos Domine.

Agnus Dei, qui tollis peccata mundi, miserere nobis.

℣. Jesu mitis et humilis corde.

℟. Fac cor nostrum secundum cor tuum.

Oremus.

OMNIPOTENS sempiterne Deus, respice in cor dilectissimi Filii tui et in laudes et satisfactiones, quas in nomine peccatorum tibi

Heart of Jesus, our peace and reconciliation,

Heart of Jesus, Victim for our sins,

Heart of Jesus, salvation of those who hope in Thee,

Heart of Jesus, hope of those who die in Thee,

Heart of Jesus, delight of all saints,

have mercy on us.

Lamb of God, who takest away the sins of the world, spare us, O Lord.

Lamb of God, who takest away the sins of the world, graciously hear us, O Lord.

Lamb of God, who takest away the sins of the world, have mercy on us,

℣. Jesus meek and humble of heart,

℟. Make our hearts like to thine.

Let us pray.

ALMIGHTY and everlasting God, graciously regard the heart of thy persolvit, iisque misericordiam tuam petentibus, tu veniam concede placatus in nomine ejusdem FILII tui JESU CHRISTI, qui tecum vivit et regnat in unitate SPIRITUS SANCTI DEUS, per omnia sæcula sæculorum. Amen.

well-beloved SON and the acts of praise and satisfaction which He renders Thee on behalf of us sinners, and through their merit grant pardon to us who implore thy mercy in the name of thy SON JESUS CHRIST, who liveth and reigneth with Thee in the unity of the HOLY SPIRIT, world without end. Amen.

166. Prayer to the Sacred Hearts of Jesus and Mary for the Conversion of Jews and Turks.

100 Days, once a day.
(See Instructions, p. 1.)

O MOST loving and beloved Heart of JESUS, prostrate before Thee we fervently beseech Thee to extend over the Church and throughout the world those streams of living water, which flow from Thee as from an inexhaustible fountain springing up into eternal life. O JESUS, SON of David and SON of the living GOD, have compassion upon us, the children of thy pierced Heart. O take not from us the gift of thy most holy faith, though we deserve as much for our sins and ingratitude; hide not thyself from our eyes, Thou who art the true light and our one hope; but re-

main with us, O LORD, while the darkness of error
grows thicker, and fill us with the fire of charity,
which Thou camest on earth to bring, and desirest to be enkindled in the hearts of all men.

O JESUS, sacrificed for us upon the altar of the
Cross, draw us to Thee, and with us draw the
Jews and Turks, for whom also Thou hast shed
thy Blood to the last drop.

May this Blood, once invoked by some in male-
diction, descend in benediction upon their heads
and save them. May this Blood, despised and
profaned by other nations, give forth for these a
cry for mercy and purify them. Succour, O LORD,
we implore Thee, the poor sons of Isaac and
Ishmael, for whom Thou wouldst again undergo
thy dolorous Passion and death. We appeal on
their behalf to those most holy wounds in thy
Hands and Feet and Side, which Thou dost keep
ever fresh and open, as the price of the world's
redemption. To their powerful pleadings are united those which issue from the heart of thy most
sweet Mother. That heart, transfixed with a sword
of grief, plunged in a sea of suffering, tormented
with thine at the foot of the Cross, we offer to
Thee, O JESUS, for the salvation of all those unhappy souls.

O sweet heart of Mary, do Thou speak to JESUS as
we ourselves know not how to speak, and He will
hear thee, so that even if a miracle be necessary
to overcome the resistance of those for whom we
pray, we ask it of thee, O Virgin Immaculate, by
that immense love which Thou bearest to JESUS.

Only deign to appear to the Jews and Turks as Thou didst once appear to Ratisbonne, and, at a signal from thy right hand, like him they will be suddenly converted.

Oh! may the day soon come when the Holy Trinity shall reign through thee in all hearts, and all shall know, love and adore in spirit and in truth the blessed fruit of thy womb, JESUS, who, with the FATHER and the HOLY SPIRIT, liveth and reigneth world without end. Amen.

167. Prayer.

100 Days, once a day.
(See Instructions, p. 1.)

O DIVINE Heart of JESUS, grant, we beseech Thee, eternal rest to the souls in purgatory, the final grace to those who shall die today, true repentance to sinners, the light of the faith to pagans, and thy blessing to me and mine. To Thee, O most compassionate Heart of JESUS, I commend all these souls, and I offer to Thee on their behalf all thy merits, together with the merits of thy most holy Mother and of all the saints and angels, and all the sacrifices of the holy Mass, Communions, prayers and good works, which shall be accomplished today throughout the Christian world.

168. Ejaculation.

50 Days, once a day.
(See Instructions, p. 1.)

All praise, honour and glory to the divine Heart of JESUS.

169. Little Office of the Sacred Heart.

    i. 200 Days, once a day. IV.
    ii. Plenary, once a month. I, II, III, IV.
            (See Instructions, p. 1.)

170. Prayer to the Eucharistic Heart.

    i. 300 Days, during Exposition.
    ii. Plenary, once a month. For daily recitation and half
    hour's adoration once a week. I, II.

O EUCHARISTIC Heart, O sovereign love of our LORD JESUS, who hast instituted the august Sacrament, in order to dwell here below with us and to give to our souls thy Flesh as food and thy Blood as drink, we confidently trust, O LORD JESUS, in the supreme love which instituted the most holy Eucharist; and here, in the presence of this Victim, it is just that we should adore, confess, and exalt this love, as the great store-house of the life of thy Church. This love is an urgent invitation for us, as though Thou didst say to us: "See how I love you! giving you my Flesh as food, and my Blood as drink; I desire by this union to excite your charity, I desire to unite you to myself, I desire to effect the transformation of your souls into my crucified Self, I who am the Bread of eternal life. Give me then your hearts, live in my life, and you shall live in GOD." We recognise, O LORD, that such is the appeal of thy Eucharistic Heart, and we thank Thee for it, and we desire earnestly to respond to it. Grant us the grace to be keenly

alive to this supreme love, with which, before thy
Passion, Thou didst invite us to receive and feed
upon thy sacred Body. Print deeply on our souls
the firm determination to respond faithfully to
this invitation. Give us devotion and reverence
whereby we may honour and receive worthily the
gift of thy supreme love, and of thy Eucharistic
Heart. Grant that we may thus be able, with thy
grace, to celebrate profitably the remembrance of
thy Passion, to make reparation for our offences and our coldness, to nourish and increase our
love for Thee, and to keep ever living within our
hearts this seed of a blessed immortality. Amen.

171. Prayer to the Sacred Heart.

i. 300 Days, once a day.
ii. Plenary, once a month. I, II, IV.

(See Instructions, p. 1.)

O MOST sacred Heart of JESUS, pour down thy
blessings abundantly upon thy Church, upon
the Supreme Pontiff, and upon all the clergy;
give perseverance to the just, convert sinners,
enlighten unbelievers, bless our parents, friends
and benefactors, help the dying, free the souls in
Purgatory, and extend over all hearts the sweet
empire of thy love. Amen.

172. Consecration of the Family to the Sacred Heart.

Plenary, on the day of consecration, and every year on
the day of renewal. II

(See Instructions, p. 1.)

SACRED Heart of JESUS, who didst manifest to Blessed Margaret Mary the desire of reigning in Christian families, we today wish to proclaim thy most complete regal dominion over our own. We would live in future with thy life, we would cause to flourish in our midst those virtues to which Thou hast promised peace here below, we would banish far from us the spirit of the world which Thou hast cursed; and Thou shalt reign, over our minds in the simplicity of our faith, and over our hearts by the whole-hearted love with which they shall burn for Thee, the flame of which we shall keep alive by the frequent reception of thy divine Eucharist.

Deign, O divine Heart, to preside over our assemblings, to bless our enterprises, both spiritual and temporal, to dispel our cares, to sanctify our joys, to alleviate our sufferings. If ever one or other of us should have the misfortune to afflict Thee, remind him, O Heart of JESUS, that Thou art good and merciful to the penitent sinner. And when the hour of separation strikes, when death shall come to cast mourning into our midst, we will all, both those who go and those who stay, be submissive to thy eternal decrees. We will console ourselves with the thought that a day will come when the entire family, reunited in Heaven, can sing for ever thy glories and thy mercies.

May the immaculate heart of Mary and the glorious Patriarch, St Joseph, present this consecration to Thee, and keep it in our minds all the days of our life. All glory to the Heart of JESUS, our King and our FATHER.

173. Prayer to the Sacred Heart.

    i. 200 Days. T.Q.
    ii. Plenary, on the Immaculate Conception, if said every day for a year. I, II, III, IV.

          (See Instructions, p. 1.)

LET us, with Mary Immaculate, adore, thank, pray to and console the most sacred and well-beloved Eucharistic Heart of JESUS.

174. Ejaculation.

100 Days. T.Q.

          (See Instructions, p. 1.)

OUR Lady of the Sacred Heart, pray for us.

175. Ejaculation.

    i. 300 Days. T.Q.
    ii. Plenary, once a month. I, II, IV.

          (See Instructions, p. 1.)

SACRED Heart of JESUS, I trust in Thee.

176. Ejaculation.

300 Days. T.Q.

          (See Instructions, p. 1.)

EUCHARISTIC Heart of JESUS, have mercy on us.

177. Ejaculation.

300 Days. T.Q.

          (See Instructions, p. 1.)

COR JESU Eucharisticum, cordis sacerdotalis exemplar, miserere nobis.

EUCHARISTIC Heart of JESUS, model of the priestly heart, have mercy on us.

178. Ejaculation.

300 Days. T.Q.

(See Instructions, p. 1.)

SACRED Heart of JESUS, thy Kingdom come!

179. Ejaculation.

300 Days. T.Q.

(See Instructions, p. 1.)

DIVINE Heart of JESUS, convert sinners, save the dying, set free the holy souls in Purgatory.

180. Ejaculation of B. Margaret Mary.

300 Days. T.Q.

(See Instructions, p. 1.)

O HEART of love, I place all my trust in Thee: for though I fear all things from my weakness, I hope all things from thy mercies.

X. MARY.

A. MARY — GENERAL.

181. The Rosary of St Bridget.

This Chaplet is said in honour of the sixty-three years
which, it is said, the most holy Mary lived on earth: it
is composed of six divisions, each division consisting
of the *Pater* once, *Ave* ten times, and *Credo* once; after these, one *Pater* more is said, and *Ave* thrice. Thus
in all the *Pater* will be said seven times, to mark the
number of Seven Dolours and Seven Joys; and the *Ave*
sixty-three times, to make up the full number of sixty-three years. The following Indulgences may all (except ii and vi) be gained by saying five out of the six
decades.

It is requisite, in order to gain these Indulgences, that
the Chaplet, being made either of six or of five decades,
should be blessed by the superiors of the monastic
houses or other priests of the Order of St Saviour, otherwise the Order of St Bridget, or by one with the necessary faculties.

    i. 100 Days for each *Pater*, 100 Days for each *Ave*,
      and 100 Days for each *Credo*, for those who say
      at least five decades simultaneously with other
      Indulgences.

    ii. Seven Years and Seven Quarantines, for saying six
      decades.

N.B.—Whenever this Rosary is said with others, each
person may gain the Indulgences i and ii precisely the
same as when the said Rosary is said by one person
alone.

    iii. Plenary, to all who shall say at least five decades
      daily for a year, on any one day in the year. I, II, IV.

iv. Plenary, on the usual conditions, on the Feast of St Bridget (October 8), to all who say the said Rosary of five decades at least once a week. I, II, III, IV.

v. Plenary, to all who, having confessed and communicated, or being at least contrite, shall have been accustomed to say this Rosary, as in No. iv, when, *in articulo mortis*, recommending their souls to GOD, they say the holy name JESUS with their hearts, if unable to do so with their lips. I, II (if possible).

vi. Plenary, once a month, for saying five decades. I, II, III, IV.

vii. 40 Days, to all who carry this Rosary with them, if, at the tolling of the bell for a passing soul, they kneel down and pray for that soul.

viii. 20 Days, to all who carry this Rosary, whenever, in a contrite spirit, they make examination of conscience, and say thrice *Pater* and *Ave*.

ix. 100 Days, to all who carry this Rosary whenever they hear Mass, or assist at a sermon, or accompany the Most Holy Viaticum, or bring back any sinner into the way of salvation, or do any other good work in honour of our LORD JESUS CHRIST, the Blessed Virgin, or St Bridget, provided they say also the *Pater* and *Ave* thrice.

(See Instructions, p. 1.)

182. The Angelus and Regina Cœli.

i. Plenary, once a month, to all who, every day, at the sound of the bell, morning, noon, or evening, shall say on their knees the Angelus. I, II, IV.

ii. 100 Days, every time that they say the Angelus.

(See Instructions, p. 1.)

N.B.—These Indulgences are not suspended in the Holy Year of the Jubilee. The *Angelus* is to be said standing, every Sunday in the year, beginning from first Vespers, that is, Saturday evening; in Paschaltide (i.e., from Holy Saturday at midday to midday on Saturday before Trinity Sunday inclusive), the *Regina Cœli*, etc., is said instead, standing, with its proper ℣., ℟., and prayer; those, however, who do not know the *Regina* cœli may obtain the same Indulgences by saying the *Angelus* as above. Religious of both sexes, or others who live in community, if they cannot say the *Angelus* nor *Regina Cœli* at the sound of the bell as aforesaid, by reason of their being engaged upon some work prescribed by their rule or constitution, may obtain the above-named Indulgences, provided that immediately on the conclusion of their respective duties they say the *Angelus* or *Regina cœli*. Moreover, the faithful who happen to be dwelling where there is no such bell, may obtain the above-named Indulgences if, at the hours specified or thereabouts, they say the *Angelus* or *Regina Cœli*, according to the season.

These Indulgences may be gained by saying five *Hail Marys*, three times, by those who do not know and cannot read the proper prayers.

On Saturdays in Lent, at noon, the *Angelus* is to be said standing.

℣. Angelus DOMINI nuntiavit Mariæ.

℞. Et concepit de SPIRITU SANCTO. Ave Maria.

℣. Ecce ancilla DOMINI,

℞. Fiat mihi secundum verbum tuum. Ave Maria.

℣. Et Verbum caro factum est.

℞. Et habitavit in nobis. Ave Maria.

℣. The angel of the LORD declared unto Mary.

℞. And she conceived of the HOLY SPIRIT. Ave Maria.

℣. Behold the handmaid of the LORD.

℞. Be it done unto me according to thy word. Ave Maria.

℣. And the Word was made Flesh.

℞. And dwelt among us. Ave Maria.

℣. Ora pro nobis, sancta DEI Genitrix.
℟. Ut digni efficiamur promissionibus CHRISTI.
Oremus.

GRATIAM tuam quæsumus, DOMINE, mentibus nostris infunde: ut qui, angelo nuntiante, CHRISTI FILII tui Incarnationem cognovimus, per Passionem ejuset Crucem ad resurrectionis gloriam perducamur. Per eundem CHRISTUM DOMINUM nostrum. ℟. Amen.

REGINA cœli, lætare. Alleluia.
Quia quem meruisti portare. Alleluia.
Resurrexit sicut dixit. Alleluia.
Ora pro nobis DEUM. Alleluia.
℣. Gaude et lætare, Virgo Maria. Alleluia.

℣. Pray for us, O Holy Mother of GOD.
℟. That we may be made worthy of the promises of CHRIST.
Let us pray.

POUR forth, we beseech Thee, O LORD, thy grace into our hearts; that we, to whom the Incarnation of CHRIST thy SON was made known by the message of an angel, may by his Passion and Cross be brought to the glory of his resurrection. Through the same CHRIST our LORD. ℟. Amen.

QUEEN of Heaven, rejoice. Alleluia.
For He whom thou wast made worthy to bear. Alleluia.
Hath risen, as He said. Alleluia.
Pray for us to GOD. Alleluia.
℣. Rejoice and be glad, O Virgin Mary. Alleluia.

℞. Quia surrexit Dominus vere. Alleluia. Oremus.

Deus, qui per resurrectionem Filii tui Domini nostri Jesu Christi mundum lætificare dignatuses; præsta, quæsumus, ut per ejus Genitricem Virginem Mariam perpetuæ capiamus gaudia vitæ. Per eundem Christum Dominum nostrum. ℞. Amen.

℞. For the Lord hath risen indeed. Alleluia. Let us pray.

O God, who through the resurrection of thy Son our Lord Jesus Christ hast vouchsafed to give joy to the whole world; grant us, we beseech Thee, that, through the intercession of the Virgin Mary his Mother, we may obtain the joys of eternal life. Through the same Christ our Lord. Amen.

183. Invocation of the Name of Mary.

25 Days. T.Q.

(See Instructions, p. 1.)

184. The Salve Regina and Sub Tuum Præsidium.

To all the faithful who, being moved by a spirit of true religion to make some reparation for the injuries done to the honour of Mary, Mother of God, and to the saints, and to defend and propagate the worship and veneration of their sacred images and pictures, shall to this end say at morn the *Salve Regina*, etc., with the ℣℣. *Dignare me*, etc., and *Benedictus Deus in sanctis suis*, and at even, *Sub tuum præsidium*, etc., with the same versicles.

i. 100 Days, once a day.

ii. Seven Years and Seven Quarantines, on Sundays.
iii. Plenary, twice a month, on any two Sundays in the month. I, II, IV.
iv. Plenary, on every Feast of our blessed Lady, and on the Feast of All Saints. I, II, IV.
v. Plenary, *in articulo mortis*, at the point of death, to all who have been accustomed during life to say the prayers, provided they have been to Confession and Communion, or are at least contrite in heart.

(See Instructions, p. 1.)

MORNING.

SALVE, Regina, Mater misericordiæ, vita, dulcedo, et spes nostra, salve. Ad te clamamus, exules filii Hevæ; ad te suspiramus, gementes et flentes in hac lacrymarum valle. Eia ergo, Advocata nostra, illos tuos misericordes oculos ad nos converte; et JESUM, benedictum fructum ventris tui, nobis post hoc exilium ostende, O clemens, O pia, O dulcis Virgo Maria.

℣. Dignare me laudare te, Virgo sacrata.

Hail Holy Queen, Mother of Mercy, Hail our Life, our Sweetness, and our Hope! To thee do we cry, poor banished children of Eve; to thee do we send up our sighs, mourning and weeping in this vale of tears. Turn, then, most gracious Advocate, thine eyes of mercy towards us; and after this our exile, show unto us the blessed Fruit of thy womb, JESUS, O clement, O loving, O sweet Virgin Mary.

℣. Make me worthy to praise thee, O Holy Virgin.

℟. Da mihi virtutem contra hostes tuos.
℣. Benedictus Deus in sanctis suis.
℟. Amen.

EVENING.

SUB tuum præsidium confugimus, Sancta Dei Genitrix; nostras deprecationes ne despicias in necessitatibus nostris, et a periculis cunctis libera nos semper, Virgo gloriosa et benedicta.
℣. Dignare me laudare te, Virgo sacrata.
℟. Damihi virtutem contra hostes tuos.
℣. Benedictus Deus in sanctis suis.
℟. Amen.

℟. Give me strength against thine enemies.
℣. Blessed be God in his saints.
℟. Amen.

WE fly to thy patronage, O Holy Mother of God despise not thou our petitions in our necessities, but deliver us always from all dangers, O glorious and blessed Virgin.
℣. Make me worthy to praise thee, O Holy Virgin.
℟. Give me strength against thine enemies.
℣. Blessed be God in his saints.
℟. Amen.

185. Prayers of St Alphonsus Liguori for everyday of the Week, with Ave Maria thrice.

i. 300 Days, once a day.
ii. Plenary, once a month. I, II, IV.
(See Instructions, p. 1.)

PRAYER FOR SUNDAY.

MOTHER of my God, look down upon a poor sinner, who has recourse to thee and puts his trust in thee. I am not worthy that thou shouldst even cast thine eyes upon me; but I know that thou, beholding JESUS thy SON dying for sinners, dost thyself yearn exceedingly to save them. O Mother of Mercy, look on my miseries and have pity upon me. Men say thou art the refuge of the sinner, the hope of the desperate, the aid of the lost; be thou, then, my refuge, hope, and aid. It is thy prayers which must save me. For the love of JESUS CHRIST be thou my help; reach forth thy hand to the poor fallen sinner who recommends himself to thee. I know that it is thy joy to aid the sinner when thou canst; help me now, thou who canst help. By my sins I have forfeited the grace of GOD and my own soul. I place myself in thy hands; oh, tell me what to do that I may regain the grace of GOD, and I will do it. My SAVIOUR bids me go to thee for help; He wills that I should look to thy pity; that so, not only the merits of thy SON, but thine own prayers too, may unite to save me. To thee, then, I have recourse: pray thou to JESUS for me; and make me experience how great good thou canst do for one who trusts in thee. Be it done unto me according to my hope. Amen.

Then say thrice Ave Maria *to the Blessed Virgin Mary, in reparation for the blasphemies uttered against her.*

PRAYER FOR MONDAY.

MOST holy Mary, Queen of Heaven, I who was once the slave of the Evil One now dedicate myself to thy service for ever; and I offer myself, to honour and to serve thee as long as I live. Accept me for thy servant, and cast me not away from thee as I deserve. In thee, O my Mother, I place all my hope. All blessing and thanksgiving be to GOD, who in his mercy giveth me this trust in thee. True it is, that in past time I have fallen miserably into sin; but by the merits of JESUS CHRIST, and by thy prayers, I hope that GOD has pardoned me. But this is not enough, my Mother. One thought appals me; it is, that I may yet lose the grace of GOD. Danger is ever nigh; the devil sleeps not; fresh temptations assail me. Protect me, then, my Queen; help me against the assaults of my spiritual enemy. Never suffer me to sin again, or to offend JESUS thy SON. Let me not by sin lose my soul, heaven, and my GOD. This one grace, Mary, I ask of thee; this is my desire; this may thy prayers obtain for me. Such is my hope. Amen. Ave Maria *thrice*.

PRAYER FOR TUESDAY.

MOST holy Mary, Mother of Goodness, Mother of Mercy, when I reflect upon my sins and upon the moment of my death, I tremble and am confounded. O my sweetest Mother, in the Blood of JESUS, in thy intercession, are my hopes. Comforter of the sad, abandon me not at that hour; fail not to console me in that affliction. If even now I am so tormented by remorse for the sins I have committed, the uncertainty of my pardon, the danger of a relapse, and the strictness of the Judgment, how will it be with me then? O my Mother, before death overtake me, obtain for me great sorrow for my sins, a true amendment, and constant fidelity to GOD for the remainder of my life. And when at length my hour is come, then do thou, Mary, my hope, be thyself my aid in those great troubles wherewith my soul will be encompassed. Strengthen me, that I may not despair when the enemy sets my sins before my face. Obtain for me at that moment grace to invoke thee often, so that with thine own sweet name and that of thy most holy SON upon my lips I may breathe forth my spirit. This grace thou hast granted to many of thy servants; this, too, is my hope and my desire. *Ave Maria thrice.*

PRAYER FOR WEDNESDAY.

MOTHER of GOD, most holy Mary, how often by my sins have I merited hell! Long ago, perhaps, judgment would have gone forth against my first mortal sin, hadst not thou in thy tender pity delayed the justice of GOD, and afterwards attracted me by thy sweetness to have confidence in thy prayers. And oh, how very often should I have fallen in the dangers which beset my steps hadst not thou, loving Mother that thou art, preserved me by the graces thou, by thy prayers, didst obtain for me. But oh, my Queen, what will thy pity and thy favours avail me, if after all I perish in the flames of hell? If there was once a time when I loved thee not, yet now, next to GOD, I love thee before all. Wherefore, henceforth and for ever, suffer me not to turn my back upon thee and upon my GOD, who through thee has granted me so many mercies. O Lady, most worthy of all love, let it not be that I, thy child, should be doomed to hate and to curse thee for ever in hell. Thou wilt surely never endure to see thy servant lost who loves thee. O Mary, say not that I ever can be lost! Yet lost I shall assuredly be if I abandon thee. But who could ever have the heart to leave thee? Who can ever forget thy love? No, it is impossible for that man to perish who faithfully recommends himself to thee, and has recourse to thee. Only leave me not, my Mother, in my own hands, or I am lost! Let me but cling to thee! Save me, my hope! save me from hell; or, rather, save me from sin, which alone can condemn me to hell. Ave Maria *thrice*.

PRAYER FOR THURSDAY.

QUEEN of heaven, who sittest enthroned above all the choirs of the angels nighest to GOD, from this vale of miseries I, a poor sinner, say to thee, "Hail, Mary," praying thee in thy love to turn upon me those gracious eyes of thine. See, Mary, the dangers among which I dwell, and shall ever have to dwell whilst I live upon this earth. I may yet lose my soul, Paradise, and GOD. In thee, Lady, is my hope. I love thee; and I sigh after the time when I shall see thee and praise thee in Paradise. O Mary, how soon will the happy day come when I shall see myself safe at thy feet? When shall I kiss that hand, which has dispensed to me so many graces? Alas, it is too true, my Mother, that I have ever been very ungrateful during my whole life; but if I get to Heaven, then I will love thee there every moment of a whole eternity, and make thee reparation in some sort for my ingratitude by ever blessing and praising thee. Thanks be to GOD, for that He hath vouch-safed me this hope through the Precious Blood of JESUS, and through thy powerful intercession. This has been the hope of all thy true lovers; and no one of them has been defrauded of his hope. No, neither shall I be defrauded of mine. O Mary, pray to thine own SON JESUS, as I too pray to Him, by the merits of his Passion, to strengthen and increase this hope. Amen. Ave Maria *thrice*.

PRAYER FOR FRIDAY.

O MARY, thou art the noblest, highest, purest, fairest creature of GOD, the holiest of all crea-tures! Oh, that all men knew thee, loved thee, my Queen, as thou deservest to be loved! Yet great is my consolation, Mary, in that there are bless-ed souls in the courts of heaven, and just souls still on earth, whose hearts thou leadest captive with thy beauty and thy goodness. But above all I rejoice in this, that our GOD Himself loves thee alone more than all men and angels together. I too, O loveliest Queen, I, miserable sinner, dare to love thee, though my love is too little; I would I had a greater love, a more tender love; this thou must gain for me, since to love thee is a great mark of predestination, and a grace which GOD grants to those who shall be saved. Moreover, O my Mother, when I reflect upon the debt I owe thy SON, I see He deserves of me an immeasur-able love. Do thou, then, who desirest nothing so much as to see Him loved, pray that I may have this grace—a great love for JESUS CHRIST. Obtain it, thou who obtainest what thou wilt. I covet not goods of earth, nor honours, nor riches, but I desire that which thine own heart desires most—to love my GOD alone. Oh, can it be that thou wilt not aid me in a desire so acceptable to thee? No, it is impossible! Even now I feel thy help; even now thou prayest for me. Pray for me, Mary, pray; nor ever cease to pray, till thou dost see me safe in Paradise, where I shall be certain of possessing and of loving my GOD and thee, my dearest Mother, for ever and for ever. Amen. *Ave Maria thrice.*

PRAYER FOR SATURDAY.

MOST holy Mary, I know the graces which thou hast obtained for me, and I know the ingratitude which I have shown thee. The ungrateful man is unworthy of favours, and yet for all this I will not distrust thy mercy. O my great Advocate, have pity on me. Thou, Mary, art the stewardess of every grace which GOD vouchsafes to give us sinners, and therefore did He make thee so mighty, rich, and kind, that thou mightest succour us. I *will* that I may be saved: in thy hands I place my eternal salvation, to thee I consign my soul. I *will* to be associated with those who are thy special servants: reject me not. Thou goest up and down seeking the wretched, to console them. Cast not away, then, a wretched sinner who has recourse to thee. Speak for me, Mary; thy SON grants what thou askest. Take me beneath thy shelter, and it is enough for me; for with thee to guard me I fear no ill—no, not even my sins, because thou wilt obtain GOD's pardon for them; no, nor yet evil spirits, because thou art far mightier than hell; no, nor my Judge JESUS CHRIST, for at thy prayer He will lay aside his wrath. Protect me, then, my Mother; obtain for me pardon of my sins, love of JESUS, holy perseverance, a good death, and heaven. It is too true, I merit not these graces; yet do thou only ask them of our GOD and I shall obtain them. Pray, then, to JESUS for me. Mary, my Queen, in thee I trust; in this trust I rest, I live; and with this trust I *will* that I may die. Amen. Ave Maria *thrice*.

186. Month of May.

   i. 300 Days, for each day, to all who shall honour the Blessed Virgin, during the month of May (in public or in private), with prayer or other devotion.
   ii. Plenary, once in the month (or on one of the first eight days of June), to all who keep up this devotion every day during the month. I, II, IV.

             (See Instructions, p. 1.)

187. Psalms in Honour of the Name of Mary.

   i. Seven Years and Seven Quarantines. T.Q.
   ii. Plenary, once a month. I, II, IV.
   iii. Plenary, on the Sunday in the Octave of our Lady's Nativity (the Feast of her Name), if said often during a year. I, II, IV.

             (See Instructions, p. 1.)

M. *Ant.* Mariæ nomen cunctas illustrat ecclesias, cui fecit magna, qui potens est, et sanctum nomen ejus.
Cantic. B.M.V. *Luc.* i.
MAGNIFICAT * anima mea DOMINUM.

   Et exultavit spiritus meus * in DEO salutari meo.

   Quia respexit humilitatem ancillæ suæ: * ecce enim ex hoc beatam me dicent omnes generationes.

Quia fecit mihi magna, qui potens est, * et sanctum nomen ejus.

Et misericordia ejus a progenie in progenies * timentibus eum.

Fecit potentiam in brachio suo: * dispersit superbos mente cordis sui.

Deposuit potentes de sede, * et exaltavit humiles.

Esurientes implevit bonis, * et divites dimisit inanes.

Suscepit Israel puerum suum, * recordatus misericordiæ suæ.

Sicut locutus est ad patres nostros, * Abraham et semini ejus in sæcula.

Gloria Patri, *etc.*

Ant. Mariæ nomen.

℞. *Ant.* A solis ortu ortu usque ad occasum laudabile nomen Domini, et Mariæ matris ejus.
Psalm. cxix.

AD DOMINUM, cum tribularer, clamavi: * et exaudivit me.

Domine, libera animam meam a labiis iniquis,* et a lingua dolosa.

Quid detur tibi, aut quid apponatur tibi, * ad linguam dolosam?

Sagittæ potentis acutæ, * cum carbonibus desolatoriis.

Heu mihi, quia incolatus meus prolongatus est! habitavi cum habitantibus Cedar: * multum incola fuit anima mea.

Cum his, qui oderunt pacem, eram pacificus: * cum loquebar illis, impugnabant me gratis.

Gloria Patri, *etc.*
Ant. A solis.

℞. *Ant.* Refugium est in tribulationibus Mariæ nomen omnibus illud invocantibus.
Psalm. cxviii.

RETRIBUE servo tuo, vivifica me: * et custodiam sermones tuos.

Revela oculos meos, * et considerabo mirabilia de lege tua.

Incola ego sum in terra, * non abscondas a me mandata tua.

Concupivit anima mea desiderare justificationes tuas * in omni tempore.

Increpasti superbos: * maledicti qui declinant a mandatis tuis.

Aufer a me opprobrium, et contemptum, * quia testimonia tua exquisivi.

Etenim sederunt principes, et adversus me loquebantur: * servus autem tuus exercebatur in justificationibus tuis.

Nam et testimonia tua meditatio mea est: * et consilium meum justificationes tuæ.

Adhæsit pavimento anima mea: * vivifica me secundum verbum tuum.

Vias meas enuntiavi, et exaudisti me: * doce me justificationes tuas.

Viam justificationum tuarum instrue me, * et exercebor in mirabilibus tuis.

Dormitavit anima mea præ tædio: * confirma me in verbis tuis.

Viam iniquitatis amove a me, * et de lege tua miserere mei.

Viam veritatis elegi: * judicia tua non sum oblitus.

Adhæsi testimoniis tuis, DOMINE: * noli me con-
fundere.

Viam mandatorum tuorum cucurri, * cum
dilatasti cor meum.

GLORIA PATRI, *etc.*

Ant. Refugium est.

I. *Ant.* In universa terra admirabile est nomen
tuum, O Maria.
Psalm. cxxv.

IN convertendo DOMINUS captivitatem Sion, *
facti sumus sicut consolati.

Tunc repletum est gaudio os nostrum, * et lingua nostra exultatione.

Tunc dicent inter gentes: * magnificavit
DOMINUS facere cum eis.

Magnificavit DOMINUS facere nobiscum: * facti
sumus lætantes.

Converte, DOMINE, captivitatem nostram, * sicut
torrens in austro.

Qui seminantin lacrymis,*in exultatione me-
tent.

Euntes ibant, et flebant, * mittentes seminasua.

Venientes autem venient cum exultatione * por-
tantes manipulos suos.

GLORIA PATRI, *etc.*

Ant. In universa terra.

II. *Ant.* Annuntiaverunt cœli nomen Mariæ, et
viderunt omnes populi gloriam ejus.
Psalm. cxxii.

AD te levavi oculos meos, * qui habitas in cœlis.

Ecce sicut oculi servorum * in manibus dominorum suorum.

Sicut oculi ancillæ in manibus dominæ suæ: * ita oculi nostri ad DOMINUM DEUM nostrum, donec misereatur nostri.

Miserere nostri, DOMINE, miserere nostri, *quia multum repleti sumus despectione.

Quia multum repleta est anima nostra, * opprobrium abundantibus, et despectio superbis.

GLORIA PATRI, *etc.*

Ant. Annuntiaverunt.

℣. Sit nomen Virginis Mariæ benedictum.

℟. Ex hoc nunc et usque in sæculum.

Oremus.

CONCEDE, quæsumus, omnipotens DEUS, ut fideles tui, qui sub sanctissimæ Virginis Mariæ Nomine et protectione lætantur; ejus pia intercessione a cunctis malis liberentur in terris, et ad gaudia æterna pervenire mereantur in cælis. PER CHRISTUM DOMINUM, *etc.*

188. Twenty-five Days Preparation for the Nativity, after the example of St Catharine of Bologna.

i. 100 Days, each day.
ii. Plenary, to those who shall have practised it for at least twenty days. I, II, III, IV.

(See Instructions, p. 1.)

Prayer to be said every day.

IN lowly reverence at thy feet we kneel, great Mother of our GOD, most holy Mary, advocate of sinners; humbly praying thee, by the merits of the Precious Blood of thy Divine SON, shed for us sinners, and by the intercession of thy well-beloved servant, Catharine, to gain for us by thy prayers true fervour of spirit in this holy exercise, and the grace to walk in the way of all thy virtues, after the example of St Catharine, to the honour and glory of JESUS CHRIST, thine only SON our SAVIOUR. Forget our monstrous ingratitude, look not upon our sins, but rather find for us a refuge in the depths of thy loving kindness; and having regard to that love wherewith thou didst ever love thy faithful servant Catharine, obtain for us the remission of our sins, so that we may confidently hope to attain all that we desire for our spiritual wants. Amen.

FOR THE FIRST DAY.

IN imitation of St Catharine, we purpose now to praise the great Mother of our GOD, honouring her Sacred Delivery, and saying to her forty Angelic Salutations and forty Benedictions, thereby to obtain her powerful aid at the hour of our death, and a true contrition for our sins, that so we may pass from this land of our pilgrimage to eternal joys.

FOR THE OTHER DAYS.

IN imitation of St Catharine, let us continue to praise the great Mother of our GOD, honouring her Sacred Delivery with forty Angelic Salutations and forty Benedictions, to obtain thereby her powerful aid at the hour of our death, and true contrition for our sins, that so we may pass from this land of our pilgrimage to eternal joys.

FOR THE LAST DAY.

IN imitation of St Catharine, today we end this exercise praising the great Mother of our GOD, and honouring her Sacred Delivery, with forty Angelic Salutations and forty Benedictions, to obtain thereby her powerful aid at the hour of our death, and true contrition for our sins, that so we may pass from this land of our pilgrimage to eternal joys.

FIRST DECADE.

WHILST saying for the first time Ave Maria ten times and the ten Benedictions, we meditate on the ineffable mystery of the Incarnation of the Eternal Word, and the great dignity of the Virgin who was elected to be the Mother of the Most High.

Ave Maria *ten times, and after each* Ave,

Blessed be the hour, Mary, when thou didst become Mother of JESUS, SON of GOD.

SECOND DECADE.

WHILST saying for the second time Ave Maria ten times and the ten Benedictions, we meditate on the humility of the King of heaven, who chose for his birthplace a poor stable, and on the joy of Mary when she first saw the Only-begotten of the FATHER, the Fruit of her womb.

Ave Maria *ten times, and after each* Ave,

Blessed be the hour, Mary, when thou didst bring forth JESUS the SON of GOD.

THIRD DECADE.

WHILST saying for the third time Ave Maria ten times and the ten Benedictions, we contemplate the exact carefulness of Mary, as she fulfilled perfectly the parts both of Martha and of Magdalen, contemplating her SON as her REDEEMER, and at the same time ministering to Him as her Child.

Ave Maria *ten times, and after each Ave,*

Blessed be the hour, Mary, when thou didst nourish at thy breast JESUS, SON of GOD.

FOURTH DECADE.

WHILST saying for the fourth time Ave Maria ten times and the ten Benedictions, we meditate upon the great reverence with which Mary embraced and pressed to her very heart rather than to her bosom, kissed, and adored her GOD and ours, incarnate for love of us; and moved thereby with profound reverence and devout affection we say,

Ave Maria *ten times, and after each Ave,*

Blessed be that hour, Mary, when thou didst embrace JESUS, SON of GOD.

Then say,

PRAISE be to our GOD, because in imitation of

St Catherine, we { have begun (*first day*) / are continuing (*other days*) / have ended (*last day*) } this holy exercise.

We beseech the Queen of Angels that for these our thousand Angelic Salutations and thousand Benedictions which { we are saying / have said (*last day*) } the Mother may obtain of the Infant which is born of her these two special blessings, viz., the first, in life, grace truly to repent of our sins; the second, in death, certainty of salvation. Wherefore

let everyone here present say heartily with St
Catharine:

Turn, then, most gracious Advocate, thine eyes
of mercy towards us; and after this our exile show
unto us the blessed Fruit of thy womb, JESUS, O
clement, O loving, O sweet Virgin Mary. Then the
Litany B.V.M. (see next page), *and then,*

℣. Make me worthy to praise thee, Virgin ever
blessed.

℟. Give me strength against thine enemies.

Let us pray.

GOD, who by the message of an angel didst will
that thy Divine Word should take to Himself
human flesh in the womb of the Blessed Virgin
Mary; grant unto us thy suppliants that we, who
believe her to be verily and indeed Mother of
GOD, may be aided by her intercession with Thee.
Visit us, O LORD, we beseech Thee, and purify our
hearts; that our LORD JESUS CHRIST thy SON may,
when He comes with all his saints, find a dwelling-place prepared for Himself within us. Who
with Thee liveth and reigneth for ever and ever.

℟. Amen.

189. The Litany of Loreto.

i. 300 Days. T.Q.
ii. Plenary, to all who say it daily, on the Immaculate
Conception, the Nativity, the Annunciation, the
Purification, and the Assumption. I, II, III, IV.

(See Instructions, p. 1.)

Kyrie eleison.
Christe eleison.
Kyrie eleison.
Christe, audi nos.
Christe, exaudi nos.
Pater de cœlis Deus,
Fili Redemptor mundi Deus,
Spiritus Sancte Deus,
Sancta Trinitas, unus Deus,

miserere nobis.

Lord, have mercy on us.
Christ, have mercy on us.
Lord, have mercy on us.
Christ, hear us.
Christ, graciously hear us
God the Father of heaven,
God the Son, Redeemer of the world,
God the Holy Spirit,
Holy Trinity, one God,

have mercy on us.

Sancta Maria,
Sancta Dei Genitrix,
Sancta Virgo virginum,
Mater Christi,
Mater divinæ gratiæ,
Mater purissima,
Mater castissima,
Mater inviolata,
Mater intemerata,
Mater amabilis,
Mater admirabilis,
Mater boni consilii,
Mater Creatoris,
Mater Salvatoris,
Virgo prudentissima,

ora pro nobis.

Holy Mary,
Holy Mother of God,
Holy Virgin of virgins,
Mother of Christ,
Mother of divine grace,
Mother most pure,
Mother most chaste,
Mother inviolate,
Mother undefiled,
Mother most amiable,
Mother most admirable,
Mother of Good Counsel,
Mother of our Creator,
Mother of our Saviour,
Virgin most prudent,

pray for us.

Virgo veneranda,
Virgo prædicanda, Virgo potens,
Virgo clemens, Virgo fidelis,
Speculum justitiæ,
Sedes sapientiæ,
Causa nostræ lætitiæ,
Vas spirituale,
Vas honorabile,
Vas insigne devotionis,
Rosa mystica,
Turris Davidica,
Turris eburnea,
Domus aurea,
Fœderis arca,
Janua cæli,
Stella matutina,
Salus infirmorum,
Refugium peccatorum,
Consolatrix afflictorum,
Auxilium Christianorum,
Regina Angelorum,
Regina Patriarcharum,
Regina Prophetarum,
Regina Apostolorum,
Regina Martyrum,
Regina Confessorum,
Regina Virginum,
Regina Sanctorum omnium,

ora pro nobis.

Virgin most venerable,
Virgin most renowned,
Virgin, most powerful,
Virgin most merciful,
Virgin most faithful,
Mirror of justice,
Seat of wisdom,
Cause of our joy,
Spiritual Vessel,
Vessel of honour,
Vessel of singular devotion,
Mystical Rose,
Tower of David,
Tower of ivory,
House of gold,
Ark of the covenant,
Gate of heaven,
Morning-star,
Health of the sick,
Refuge of sinners,
Comforter of the afflicted,
Help of Christians,
Queen of Angels,
Queen of Patriarchs,
Queen of Prophets,
Queen of Apostles,
Queen of Martyrs,
Queen of Confessors,
Queen of Virgins,
Queen of all saints,

pray for us.

Regina sine labe origina-
li concepta,
Regina Sacratissimi
Rosarii,
AGNUS DEI, qui tollis
peccata mundi, parce
nobis DOMINE.
AGNUS DEI, qui tollis
peccata mundi, exaudi
nos DOMINE.
AGNUS DEI, qui
tollis peccata mundi,
miserere nobis.

Queen conceived with-
out original sin,
Queen of the most holy
Rosary,
LAMB of GOD, who takest
away the sins of the
world, spare us, O LORD.
LAMB of GOD, who takest
away the sins of the
world, graciously hear
us, O LORD.
LAMB of GOD, who takest
away the sins of the
world, have mercy on us.

190. Prayer of St Alphonsus.

  i. 300 Days, once a day.
  ii. Plenary, once a month. I, II, IV.
      (See Instructions, p. 1.)
Say the prayer for Wednesday (No. 185). Then the
Salve Regina thrice.

191. Three Offerings.

  i. 300 Days. T.Q.
  ii. Plenary, once a month. I, II, IV.
      (See Instructions, p. 1.)

MOST Holy Virgin, I venerate thee with my
whole heart above all angels and saints in
Paradise, as the Daughter of the Eternal FATHER,
and I consecrate to thee my soul with all its powers. Ave Maria.

MOST Holy Virgin, I venerate thee with my whole heart above all angels and saints in Paradise, as the Mother of the Only-begotten SON, and I consecrate to thee my body with all its senses. Ave Maria.

MOST Holy Virgin, I venerate thee with my whole heart above all angels and saints in Paradise, as the Spouse of the HOLY SPIRIT, and I consecrate to thee my heart and all its affections, praying thee to obtain for me from the ever-blessed Trinity all that is necessary for my salvation. Ave Maria.

192. Prayer, with Ave Maria, thrice, etc.

100 Days, once a day.

(See Instructions, p. 1.)

VIRGIN most holy, Mother of the Word Incarnate, Treasurer of graces, Refuge of us poor sinners; we fly to thy maternal love with lively faith, and we ask thee to obtain for us grace ever to do the will of GOD and thine own. Into thy most holy hands we commit the keeping of our hearts; beseeching thee for health of soul and body, in the certain hope that thou, our most loving Mother, wilt hear our prayer. Wherefore with lively faith we say, Ave Maria *thrice*.

Let us pray.

DEFEND, O LORD, we beseech Thee, us thy servants, through the intercession of the Blessed Mary ever-Virgin, from all infirmity both of body and soul; and mercifully protect from the snares of enemies those who, with their whole

heart, prostrate themselves before Thee. Through
CHRIST our LORD. Amen.

193. Prayer, O Excellentissima.

i. 100 Days, once a day.
ii. Plenary, once a month, on the last day, or one of
eight succeeding days. I, II, III, IV.
(See Instructions, p. 1.)

O MOST excellent, glorious, most holy and
ever inviolate blessed Virgin Mary, Mother
of our LORD JESUS CHRIST, Queen of the world,
and Mistress of all creatures! Thou who forsakest
no one, despisest no one, who leavest in sadness
none who seek help at thy hands with pure and
lowly hearts; do not despise me because of the
number and hatefulness of my sins, do not abandon me on account of my grievous iniquities nor
on account of the hardness and uncleanness of
my heart. Do not refuse me, thy servant, a share
in thy favour and thy love. Hear me, a wretched
sinner, who trusts in thy mercy and pity. Help
me, O most loving Virgin Mary, in all my perils
and needs, and obtain for me from thy beloved
SON, Almighty GOD and our LORD JESUS CHRIST,
the forgiveness of all my sins, the grace of the
fear and love of thee, health and chastity of body,
and deliverance from all the dangers which beset
both soul and body.

In the last moments of my life be thou my kind
helper, and save from eternal darkness, and from
evil of every kind, my poor soul, and the souls
of my parents, brothers, sisters, friends, relatives,
and benefactors, together with the souls of all the

faithful, both living and dead; through the grace
of Him whom for nine months thou didst bear in
thy most holy womb, and whom thou didst place
with thy holy hands in the manger, JESUS CHRIST
our LORD, to whom be all honour given for endless ages. Amen.

194. Prayer.

i. 100 Days, once a day.
ii. Plenary, once a month, on last day of the month, or
within eight days. I, II, III, IV.

(See Instructions, p. 1.)

VIRGIN Mother of GOD, most holy Mary,
safe refuge of sinners! to thee, who art, after
GOD, our hope and consolation in this place of
exile, to thee I have recourse with sincere confidence, though most undeserving of thy patronage. I know, on the one hand, how much I
stand in need of being converted from my very
heart; yet, on the other, the heinousness of my
crimes strikes me with terror. To thee, then, I betake myself to thee who art our sovereign mediator with thy dear SON JESUS, as He is with his
Eternal FATHER. To thee, after JESUS, must I look
for my amendment. Vouchsafe then, O Mother
of Mercy, to obtain for me the grace of a true
and lasting conversion. I wish to change my life
entirely. In this I am sincere; but my evil habits
and the ill use I have made of so many saving
inspirations, the multitude and heinousness of
my sins, and the bonds by which the world holds
me, while they render amendment difficult, call
for thy special assistance. Grant it to me in spite

of my unworthiness. In thee I trust; do thou not reject me. Although deserving of eternal punishment, I throw myself at thy feet, sorrowful and repentant. My sins, I own, have taken from me the strength which grace imparts, have cast me out from among the adopted sons of GOD, have deprived me of the right to everlasting happiness, and drawn on me instead the wrath of heaven. Tell me what I must do to regain the friendship of thy SON JESUS. Beg of Him, by his Precious Blood, his bitter Passion, and cruel death on the Cross, to pardon my offences, and He will pardon them. Tell Him thy desire for my salvation, and He will save me. But as I can still fall into sin and lose the life of grace amid the dangers which encompass me, ever watch thou over me, and I shall surely triumph over the enemies who incessantly work for my ruin. Instil into my heart a lively faith, a firm hope, an ardent charity, and all the virtues suitable to my state of life; and obtain for me constancy in good, and final perseverance. In fine, be thou my loving Mother here below, and my advocate at the hour of death, that I may be of the number of those to whom thy divine SON shall say: "Come, ye blessed of my FATHER, possess the kingdom prepared for you." Amen.

195. The Crown of Twelve Stars.

i. 100 Days. T.Q.
ii. Plenary, once a month. I, II, IV.
(See Instructions, p. 1.)

ALL praise and thanksgiving be to the ever-blessed Trinity, who hath shown unto us

Mary, ever-Virgin, clothed with the sun, with the moon beneath her feet, and on her head a mystic crown of twelve stars. ℟. For ever and ever. Amen.

Let us praise and give thanks to GOD the FATHER, who elected her for his daughter. ℟. Amen. PATER noster.

Praise be to GOD the FATHER, who predestined her to be the Mother of his SON. ℟. Amen. Ave Maria.

Praise be to GOD the FATHER, who preserved her from all stain in her conception. ℟. Amen. Ave Maria.

Praise be to GOD the FATHER, who on her birthday adorned her with his choicest gifts. ℟. Amen. Ave Maria.

Praise be to GOD the FATHER, who gave her Joseph for her pure spouse and companion. ℟. Amen. Ave Maria *and* Gloria PATRI.

Let us praise and give thanks to GOD the SON, who chose her for his Mother. ℟. Amen. PATER noster.

Praise be to GOD the SON, who became Incarnate in her womb, and abode there nine months. ℟. Amen. Ave Maria.

Praise be to GOD the SON, who was born of her and was nourished at her breast. ℟. Amen. Ave Maria.

Praise be to GOD the SON, who in his childhood willed that Mary should teach Him. ℟. Amen. Ave Maria.

Praise be to GOD the SON, who revealed to her the mysteries of the redemption of the world. ℟. Amen. Ave Maria *and* Gloria PATRI.

Let us praise and give thanks to GOD the HOLY SPIRIT who made her his spouse. ℟. Amen. PATER noster.

Praise be to GOD the HOLY SPIRIT, who revealed to her first his name of HOLY SPIRIT. ℟. Amen. Ave Maria.

Praise be to GOD the HOLY SPIRIT, through whose operation she became at once Virgin and Mother. ℟. Amen. Ave Maria.

Praise be to GOD the HOLY SPIRIT, through whom she became the living temple of the Most Holy Trinity. ℟. Amen. Ave Maria.

Praise be to GOD the HOLY SPIRIT, by whom she was exalted in Heaven high above all creatures. ℟. Amen. Ave Maria *and* Gloria PATRI.

For the Holy Catholic Church, for the propagation of the faith, for peace among Christian princes, and for the uprooting of heresies, let us say Salve Regina, *etc.* (No. 184.)

196. The Memorare.

i. 300 Days. T.Q.
ii. Plenary, once a month. I, II, III, IV.
(See Instructions, p. 1.)

MEMORARE, O piissima Virgo Maria, non esse auditum a sæculo quemquam ad tua currentem præsidia, tua implorantem auxilia,

REMEMBER, O most gracious Virgin Mary, that never was it known that anyone who fled to thy protection, implored thy help, or sought tua petentem suffragia, esse derelictum. Ego tali animatus confidentia, ad te, Virgo virginum, Mater, curro, ad te venio, coram te gemens peccator assisto; noli, Mater Verbi, verba mea despicere, sed audi propitia, et exaudi. Amen.

thy intercession, was left unaided. Inspired with this confidence, I fly unto thee, O Virgin of virgins, my mother; to thee I come, before thee I stand, sinful and sorrowful; O Mother of the Word Incarnate, despise not my petitions; but in thy clemency hear and answer me. Amen.

197. Prayer, Ave Augustissima.

i. 300 Days. T.Q.
ii. Plenary, once a month. I, II, III, IV.
    (See Instructions, p. 1.)

HAIL, thou that art most venerable, Queen of Peace, most holy Mother of GOD; through the Sacred Heart of JESUS, thy SON, the Prince of Peace, procure for us the cessation of his anger, that so He may reign over us in peace. Remember, O most gracious Virgin Mary, that never was it known that any one who sought thy prayers was forsaken by GOD. Inspired with this confidence, I come unto Thee. Despise not my petitions, O Mother of the Incarnate Word; but in thy loving-kindness hear and answer me, O merciful, O sweet Virgin Mary.

198. The Tota Pulchra, etc.

i. 300 Days, once a day.

ii. Plenary, on the Immaculate Conception, Nativity, Purification, Annunciation, and Assumption. I, II, III, IV.

(See Instructions, p. 1.)

Tota pulchra es Maria, *etc.; with ℣. ℟. and Prayer,* Deus qui per immaculatam, p. 216.

199. Five Novenas for the Principal Feasts of Our Lady.

These Novenas maybe said in public or private.
  i. 300 Days, each day.
  ii. Plenary on the Feast or during the Octave. I, II, IV.
(See Instructions, p. 1.)
N.B.—The prayers for the intention of the Pope are to be addressed to "GOD and to our Lady."

I. NOVENA FOR THE IMMACULATE CONCEPTION. *Begins November 29.*

VENI SANCTE SPIRITUS, reple tuorum corda fidelium, et tui amoris in eis ignem accende.
℣. Emitte SPIRITUM tuum, et creabuntur.
℟. Et renovabis faciem terræ.
Oremus.

DEUS qui corda fidelium SANCTI SPIRITUS illustratione docuisti, da nobis in eodem SPIRITU recta

COME, O HOLY SPIRIT, fill the hearts of thy faithful and kindle in them the fire of thy love.
℣. Send forth thy SPIRIT and they shall be created;
℟. And Thou shalt renew the face of the earth.
Let us pray.

O GOD, who hast taught the hearts of the faithful by the

sapere et de ejus semper consolatione gaudere. Per CHRISTUM DOMINUM nostrum. ℟. Amen.

light of the HOLY SPIRIT, grant us by the same SPIRIT to relish what is right, and evermore to rejoice in his consolation. Through CHRIST our LORD. ℟. Amen.

Preparatory Prayer to be said each day.

VIRGIN most pure, conceived without sin, all fair and stainless in thy Conception; glorious Mary, full of grace, Mother of my GOD, Queen of Angels and of men, I humbly venerate thee as Mother of my SAVIOUR, who, though He was GOD, taught me by his own veneration, reverence, and obedience to thee, the honour and homage that are due to thee. Vouchsafe, I pray thee, to accept this Novena which I dedicate to thee. Thou art the safe refuge of the penitent sinner; it is very fitting, then, that I should have recourse to thee. Thou art the Mother of Compassion; then wilt thou surely be moved with pity for my many miseries. Thou art my best hope after JESUS; thou canst not but accept the loving confidence that I have in thee. Make me worthy to be called thy son, that so I may dare to cry unto thee: *Show thyself a mother.*

Ave Maria *nine times, and* Gloria PATRI *once.*

Prayer for the First Day.

BEHOLD me at thy sacred feet, O Immaculate Virgin. I rejoice with thee, because from all eternity thou wast elected to be the Mother of the Eternal Word, and wast preserved stainless from the taint of original sin. I praise and bless the Most Holy Trinity, who poured out upon thy soul in thy Conception the treasure of that privilege. I humbly pray thee to obtain for me grace effectually to overcome the sad effects produced in my soul by original sin; make me wholly victorious over them, that I may never cease to love my GOD.

Then say or sing the Litany of the Blessed Virgin, (No. 189), *or else,*

℣. Tota pulchra es Maria,

℟. Tota pulchra es Maria.

℣. Et macula originalis non est in te

℟. Et macula originalis non est in te

℣. Tu gloria Jerusalem.

℟. Tu lætitia Israel.

℣. Tu honorificentia populi nostri.

℟. Tu advocata peccatorum.

℣. O Maria.

℟. O Maria.

℣. Virgo prudentissima.

℟. Mater clementissima.

℣. Ora pro nobis.

℣. All fair art thou, O Mary.

℟. All fair art thou, O Mary.

℣. The original stain is not in thee.

℟. The original stain is not in thee.

℣. Thou art the glory of Jerusalem.

℟. Thou art the joy of Israel.

℣. Thou art the honour of our people.

℟. Thou art the advocate of sinners.

℣. O Mary.

℟. O Mary.

℣. Virgin most prudent.

℟. Mother most clement.

℣. Pray for us.

℟. Intercede pro nobis
ad Dominum Jesum
Christum.

℟. Intercede for us
with our Lord Jesus
Christ.

After the Litany or Hymn as above, say,

℣. In Conceptione tua,
Virgo, immaculata
fuisti.

℣. In thy conception,
O Virgin, thou wast
immaculate.

℟. Ora pro nobis
Patrem, cujus Filium
peperisti.
Oremus.

℟. Pray for us to the
Father, whose Son
was born of thee.
Let us pray.

Deus qui per
Immaculatam
Virginis Conceptionem
dignum Filio tuo habi-
taculum praeparasti:
quaesumus ut qui ex
morte ejusdem Filii
tui praevisa eam ab
omni labe praeservas-
ti, nosquo que mun-
dos ejus intercessione
ad te pervenire con
cedas. Per Christum
Dominum nostrum.
Amen.

O God, who through
the Immaculate
Conception of a Virgin
didst prepare a worthy
dwelling place for Thy
Son, we beseech Thee,
who by the death of
that Son, foreseen by
Thee, didst preserve
her from all stain of
sin, to grant that by
her intercession we
also maybe purified,
and so may come to
Thee. Through Christ
our Lord. Amen.

Deus omnium fi-
delium pastor et
rector, famulum tuum
N., quem pastorem
ecclesiae tuae praeesse

O God, the Shepherd
and Ruler of all the
faithful, graciously
look down upon thy

voluisti, propitius respice; da ei quæsumus, verbo et exemplo, quibus præest, proficere, ut ad vitam una cum grege sibi credito perveniat sempiternam.

DEUS refugium nostrum et virtus, adesto piis ecclesiæ tuæ precibus, auctor ipse pietatis; et præsta, ut quod fideliter petimus efficaciter consequamur. Per CHRISTUM DOMINUM nostrum, ℟. Amen.

servant N., whom Thou hast chosen to be the Pastor of thy Church; and grant him, we beseech Thee, both by word and example, so to direct those over whom Thou hast placed him, that together with the flock entrusted to his care, he may attain eternal life.

O GOD, our refuge and strength, who art the author of all holiness, listen to the pious prayers of thy Church, and grant that what we ask in faith we may effectually obtain, through CHRIST our LORD. ℟. Amen.

The same order is to be observed on the other days of the Novena, the prayer for the day alone being changed.

Prayer for the Second Day, November 30.

MARY, unsullied lily of purity, I rejoice with thee, because from the first moment of thy Conception thou wast filled with grace, and hadst given unto thee the perfect use of reason. I thank and adore the ever blessed Trinity, who gave thee those high gifts. Behold me at thy feet overwhelmed with shame to see myself so poor in grace. O Thou who wast filled full of heavenly grace, grant me a portion of that same grace, and make me a partaker in the treasures of thy Immaculate Conception.

Prayer for the Third Day, December 1.

MARY, mystic rose of purity, I rejoice with thee at the glorious triumph thou didst gain over the serpent by thy Immaculate Conception, in that thou wast conceived without original sin. I thank and praise with my whole heart the ever blessed Trinity, who granted thee that glorious privilege; and I pray thee to obtain for me courage to overcome every snare of the great enemy, and never to stain my soul with mortal sin. Be thou always mine aid, and enable me with thy protection to obtain the victory over all the enemies of man's eternal welfare.

Prayer for the Fourth Day, December 2.

MARY Immaculate Virgin, mirror of holy purity, I rejoice exceedingly to see how from thy Immaculate Conception there were infused into thy soul the most sublime and perfect virtues with all the gifts of the most HOLY SPIRIT. I thank and praise the ever blessed Trinity who bestowed upon thee these high privileges, and I beseech thee, gracious Mother, obtain for me grace to practise every Christian virtue, and so to become worthy to receive the gifts and graces of the HOLY SPIRIT.

Prayer for the Fifth Day, December 3.

MARY, bright moon of purity, I congratulate thee in that the mystery of thy Immaculate Conception was the beginning of salvation to the human race, and was the joy of the whole world. I thank and bless the ever blessed Trinity who did so magnify and glorify thy person. I entreat thee to obtain for me grace so to profit by the death and passion of thy dear SON, that his Precious Blood may not have been shed upon the Cross for me in vain, but that after a holy life I may be saved.

Prayer for the Sixth Day, December 4.

MARY Immaculate, brilliant star of purity, I rejoice with thee, because thy Immaculate Conception brought exceeding joy to all the angels of Paradise. I thank and bless the ever blessed Trinity, who enriched thee with this privilege. Enable me also one day to take part in this heavenly joy, praising and blessing thee in the company of angels, world without end. Amen.

Prayer for the Seventh Day, December 5.

MARY Immaculate, rising morn of purity, I rejoice with thee, and I am filled with admiration at beholding thee confirmed in grace and rendered sinless from the first moment of thy Conception. I thank and praise the ever blessed Trinity, who elected thee alone from all mankind for this special privilege. Holiest Virgin, obtain for me so entire and lasting a hatred of sin, the worst of all evils, that I may rather die than ever again commit a mortal sin.

Prayer for the Eighth Day, December 6.

MARY, Virgin, sun without stain, I congratulate thee and I rejoice with thee, because GOD gave thee in thy Conception a greater and more abundant grace than He gave to all his angels and his saints together, even when their merits were most exalted. I thank and admire the immense beneficence of the ever blessed Trinity, who hath dispensed to thee alone this privilege. Oh, enable me too to correspond with the grace of GOD, and never more to receive it in vain; change my heart, and help me to begin in earnest a new life.

Prayer for the Ninth Day, December 7.

IMMACULATE Mary, living light of holiness, model of purity, Virgin and Mother, as soon as thou wast conceived, thou didst profoundly adore thy GOD, giving him thanks, because by means of thee the ancient curse was blotted out, and blessing was again come upon the sinful sons of Adam. Let this blessing kindle in my heart love towards GOD; and do thou inflame my heart still more and more, that I may ever love Him constantly on earth, and afterwards eternally enjoy Him in heaven, there to thank and praise Him more and more fervently for all the wondrous privileges conferred on thee, and to rejoice with thee for thy high crown of glory.

II. NOVENA FOR OUR LADY'S NATIVITY (*Beginning August 30*).

Come, O HOLY SPIRIT, *etc.*, (No. 199, I., up to and including the Preparatory Prayer).

MOST holy Mary, elect and predestined from all eternity by the most Holy Trinity to be Mother of the only-begotten SON of the Eternal FATHER, foretold by the Prophets, expected by the Patriarchs, desired by all nations, Sanctuary and living temple of the HOLY SPIRIT, sun without stain, conceived free from original sin, Mistress of Heaven and of Earth, Queen of Angels: humbly prostrate at thy feet we give thee our homage, rejoicing that the year has brought round again the memory of thy most happy Nativity; and we pray thee with all our hearts to vouchsafe in thy goodness now to come down again and be reborn spiritually in our souls, that, led captive by thy loveliness and sweetness, they may ever live united to thy most sweet and loving heart.

So now whilst we salute thee nine times, we will direct our thoughts to the nine months which thou didst pass enclosed in thy mother's womb; and we will devoutly say:

We hail thee, O Mary, who tracing thy descent from the royal house of David, didst come forth to the light of Heaven with high honour from the womb of holy Anna, thy most happy mother. Ave Maria.

We hail thee, heavenly babe, white dove of purity; who in spite of the serpent wast conceived free from original sin. Ave Maria.

We hail thee, bright morn; who, forerunner of the heavenly Sun of Justice, didst bring the first light to earth. Ave Maria.

We hail thee, Elect; who, like the untarnished Sun, didst burst forth in the dark night of sin. Ave Maria.

We hail thee, beauteous Moon; who didst shed light upon a world wrapped in the thickest darkness of paganism. Ave Maria.

We hail thee, dread warrior-child; who, in thyself a host, didst put to flight all hell. Ave Maria.

We hail thee, fair soul of Mary; who from eternity wast possessed by GOD. Ave Maria.

We hail thee, dear child, and we humbly venerate thy most holy infant body, the sacred swaddling-clothes wherewith they bound thee, the sacred crib wherein they laid thee, and we bless the hour and the day when thou wast born. Ave Maria.

We hail thee, much beloved infant, adorned with every virtue immeasurably above all saints, and therefore worthy Mother of the SAVIOUR of the world; who, having been made fruitful by the HOLY SPIRIT, didst bring forth the WORD Incarnate. Ave Maria.

Let us pray.

O MOST lovely infant, who by thy holy birth hast comforted the world, made glad the Heavens, struck terror into hell, brought help to the fallen, consolation to the sad, salvation to the weak, joy to all men living; we entreat thee, with the most fervent love and gratitude, to be spiritually reborn in our souls by means of thy most holy love; renew our spirit in thy service, rekindle in our hearts the fire of charity, bid all virtues blossom there, that so we may find more and more favour in thy gracious eyes. Mary! be thou our Mary, and may we feel the saving power of thy sweetest name; may it ever be our comfort to call on that name in all our troubles; may it be our hope in dangers, our shield in temptation, and our last utterance in death. men Mariæ mel in ore, melos in aure, et jubilus in corde. Amen. Let the name of Mary be honey in the mouth, melody in the ear, joy in the heart. Amen.

Here follows the Litany, (No. 189.) Then say:

℣. Nativitas tua, Dei Genitrix Virgo
℞. Gaudium annuntiavit universo mundo.
Oremus.

Famulis tuis, quæsumus Domine, cælestis gratiai munus impertire; ut quibus Beatæ Virginis partus extitit salutis exordium, nativitatis ejus votiva solemnitas pacis tribuat incrementum.
Deus, omnium fidelium, *and* Deus refugium *etc.* (*p. 217-218*).

℣. Your Nativity, O Virgin Mother of God
℞. Hath brought joy to the whole world.
Let us pray.

Grant to us thy servants, we beseech Thee, O Lord, the gift of heavenly grace; that to all those for whom the delivery of the Blessed Virgin was the beginning of salvation, this her votive festival may give increase of peace.
O God, the Shepherd and Ruler, *and* O God our refuge, *etc.*, (*p. 217-218*).

III. Novena for the Annunciation *(Beginning March 16)*.

Come, O Holy Spirit, *etc*., (No. 199, I., up to and including the Preparatory Prayer).

I VENERATE and I admire thee, most holy Virgin Mary, as the humblest of all the creatures of God on the very day of thy Annunciation, when God Himself exalted thee to the most sublime dignity of his own Mother. O mighty Virgin, enable me, wretched sinner that I am, to know the depths of my own nothingness, and at once with all my heart to humble myself before all men. Ave Maria.

Mary, most holy Virgin, when thou wast saluted by Gabriel the Archangel, and the message from God was conveyed to thee, and thou wast exalted by God above all the Choirs of the Angels, then thou didst humbly say, "Behold the handmaid of the Lord." Oh, obtain for me true humility and angelic purity, enabling me so to live on earth that I may ever be worthy of the blessing of God. Ave Maria.

O Virgin ever blessed, I rejoice with thee because solely by thy humble *Fiat* thou didst draw from the bosom of the Eternal Father the divine Word into thy own pure bosom. Draw then ever my heart to God; and with God draw grace into my heart, that I may ever bless thy *Fiat*, and cry with devotion, "O mighty *Fiat*! O efficacious *Fiat*! O *Fiat* to be venerated above all *Fiats*" (*St Thomas of Villanova*). Ave Maria.

O Virgin Mary, on the day of thy Annunciation thou wast found by Gabriel the Archangel quick and ready to do GOD's will, when it pleased the most Holy Trinity to await thy consent in order to redeem the world. Enable me in every good and bad fortune to turn to GOD with resignation and say: Be it done unto me according to thy word. Ave Maria.

Most holy Mary, I well understand that thy obedience made the union between thy GOD and thee more intimate than shall ever again be possible for any other creature: ("No creature could be in closer union with GOD." *B. Albertus Magnus*). I am confounded to see how sin has separated me from GOD. Help me then, kind Mother, truly to do penance for my sins, that thy own loving JESUS may yet once more live in me and I in Him. Ave Maria.

Most holy Mary, thou wast troubled by reason of thy modesty, when Gabriel the Archangel stood before thee in thy house; but I, when I come before thee, am troubled because of my great pride; wherefore do thou in thy incomparable humility, "which brought forth GOD for men, reopened Paradise, and set the captive souls free from hell beneath" (*S. Aug. Sermo de Sanct.*), draw me, I pray thee, out of the deep pit of my sins, and enable me to save my soul. Ave Maria.

Most holy Virgin, though I have an unhallowed tongue, I have the boldness to salute thee all hours of the day: "Hail, hail Mary, full of grace." I pray thee from my heart to replenish my soul with a little of that grace wherewith the HOLY SPIRIT, when He overshadowed thee, filled thee to the full. Ave Maria.

Most holy Mary, "The LORD is with thee"; I know by faith that the great GOD who has been ever with thee from thy Conception, is, by his Incarnation in thy purest womb, made still more closely one with thee; make it thy care, I pray thee, that I may ever be one in heart and soul with that same dear LORD JESUS, by means of his sanctifying grace. Ave Maria.

Most holy Mary, "Blessed art thou amongst women"; pour out upon my heart and soul thy heavenly blessing, as thou thyself wast ever blessed of GOD among all women; for I have this sure hope, that if, my dear Mother, thou wilt bless me while I live, then when I die I shall be blessed of GOD in the everlasting glory of Heaven. Ave Maria.

Then say the Litany, (No. 189), *and then:*

℣. Angelus DOMINI nuntiavit Mariæ.
℟. Et concepit de SPIRITU SANCTO.

Oremus.

DEUS qui de beatæ Mariæ Virginis utero Verbum tuum, angelo nuntiante carnem suscipere voluisti: præsta supplicibus tuis, ut qui vere eam Genitricem DEI credimus, ejus apud te intercessionibus adjuvemur.

℣. The angel of the LORD declared unto Mary,
℟. And she conceived of the HOLY SPIRIT.

Let us pray.

O GOD, who by the message of an angel didst will that the divine Word should take flesh of the Blessed Virgin Mary; grant unto us thy suppliants that we, who believe her to be truly the Mother of GOD, may be helped by her intercession with Thee.

DEUS, omnium fideli-   O GOD, the Shepherd
um, *and* Deus refugium, and Ruler, *and* O God our
etc. (*p. 217-218*).   refuge, *etc.*, (*p. 217-218*).

IV. NOVENA FOR THE PURIFICATION (*Beginning
January 24*).

Come, O HOLY SPIRIT, *etc.*, (No. 199, I., up to and
including the Preparatory Prayer).

MOST holy Virgin, bright mirror of all virtues, the forty days after thy delivery were
no sooner passed than thou, though the purest
of all virgins, didst will to be presented in the
Temple to be purified; oh, help us then to keep
our hearts unstained by sin, that so we too may
be made worthy one day to be presented to our
GOD in Heaven. Ave Maria.

Virgin most obedient, at thy presentation in the
Temple, thou didst willingly offer the sacrifice
customary among women; enable us so to follow
thy example, that we may make ourselves a living
sacrifice to GOD by practising every virtue. Ave
Maria.

Virgin most pure, thou didst despise the reproach of men, observing the precepts of the Law;
ask for us grace always to keep our hearts pure,
whatever the world may think of us. Ave Maria.

Virgin most holy, by offering thy SON, the
Divine Word, to his Eternal FATHER, thou didst
make Heaven glad; present our poor hearts to
GOD, that by his grace they may be kept free from
mortal sin. Ave Maria.

Virgin most humble, in consigning JESUS into
the arms of the holy old man Simeon, thou didst

fill his spirit full of heavenly joy; consign our hearts to GOD, that He may fill them full of his HOLY SPIRIT. Ave Maria.

Virgin most diligent, in ransoming thy SON JESUS according to the Law, thou didst co-operate in the salvation of the world; ransom our poor hearts from the slavery of sin, that they may be ever pure in the sight of GOD. Ave Maria.

Virgin most clement, on hearing the prophecy of Simeon foretelling thy woes, thou didst at once resign thyself to the good pleasure of thy GOD; make us always resigned to the dispositions of his Providence, and enable us to bear all troubles with patience. Ave Maria.

Virgin most compassionate, when thou didst fill the soul of Anna the prophetess with light, by means of thy Divine SON, thou didst make her magnify the mercies of GOD by recognizing JESUS as the REDEEMER of the world; enrich our spirits too with heavenly grace, that we may joyfully reap in full measure the fruits of our LORD's Redemption. Ave Maria.

Virgin most resigned, although thou didst feel thine own soul transfixed with sorrow, foreseeing all the bitter Passion of thy SON, yet knowing the grief of Joseph thy spouse for all thy sufferings, thou didst console him with holy words; pierce through and through our souls with true sorrow for our sins, that we may one day come to rejoice with thee in everlasting bliss, partakers of thy glory. Ave Maria.

Then say the Litany, (No. 189), *and then:*

℣. Responsum accepit Simeon a Spiritu Sancto.

℟. Non visurum se mortem nisi videret Christum Domini.

Oremus.

OMNIPOTENS sempiterne Deus, majestatem tuam supplices exoramus, ut sicut unigenitus tuus cum nostræ carnis substantia in Templo est præsentatus, ita nos facias purificatistibi mentibus præsentari.

Deus, omnium fidelium, *and* Deus refugium *etc.*, (p. 217-218).

℣. Simeon received answer from the Holy Spirit.

℟. That he should not see death till he had seen the Christ of the Lord.

Let us pray.

ALMIGHTY, everlasting God, we humbly pray thy Majesty that, as thine only-begotten Son was presented in the Temple in the substance of our flesh, so Thou wouldst enable us to present ourselves before thee with clean hearts.

O God, the Shepherd and Ruler, *and* O God our refuge, *etc.*, (p. 217-218).

V. Novena for the Assumption (*Beginning August 6*).

First Day, August 6.

Come, O Holy Spirit, *etc.*, (No. 199, I., up to and including the Preparatory Prayer).

Hymn.,

O GLORIOSA virginum Sublimis inter sidera,

O QUEEN of all the virgin choir, Enthroned above the starry sky;

Qui te creavit parvulum
Lactente nutris ubere.

Who with pure milk
from thy own breast
Thy own CREATOR didst
supply.

Quod Heva tristis
  abstulit
Tu reddis almo germine:
Intrent ut astra flebiles,
Cæli recludis cardines.

What man hath lost in
hapless Eve,
Thy sacred womb to
man restores;
Thou to the sorrowing
here beneath
Hast opened heaven's
eternal doors.

Tu regis alti janua,
Et aula lucis fulgida:
Vitam datam per
  Virginem
Gentes redemptæ
  plaudite.

Hail, O refulgent Hall of
Light!
Hail, Gate sublime of
Heaven's high King!
Through Thee re-
deemed to endless life,
Thy praise let all the
nations sing.

JESU, tibi sit gloria,
Qui natus es de Virgine,
Cum PATRE et almo
  SPIRITU
In sempiterna sæcula.
Amen.

O JESUS, born of Virgin
bright
Immortal glory be to
Thee;
Praise to the FATHER
infinite,
And HOLY SPIRIT eternal-
ly. Amen.

*The glory of Mary in death, in that she was well
prepared to die.*

LET us meditate how glorious Mary was at the moment of her death, because in life she was so well prepared to die; first by reason of her ardent longing to see her GOD and to be again united to her SON; and next, by the unapproachable merit of her consummate perfection. Then, reflecting how different we are from Mary in our practice of preparation for our death, let us say:

MOST holy Virgin, who in order to prepare thyself for a holy death, didst live in continual desire of the beatific vision; oh, take from us all vain desires for the frail things of earth. Ave Maria *thrice*.

Most holy Virgin, who in order to prepare thyself for a holy death didst in life ever sigh to be united to thy Son JESUS; obtain for us fidelity to JESUS even unto death. Ave Maria *thrice*.

Most holy Virgin, who, in preparation for a holy death, didst attain an unapproachable height of merit and of virtue; intercede for us that we may know that virtue and the grace of GOD alone will lead us to salvation. Ave Maria *thrice*.

Let us now give praise to Mary, so prudent in preparing for death; and whilst we exalt her glory, we will unite with the nine Choirs of Angels, who, on her Assumption into Heaven, escorted her, praising her with the first Choir:

Then say the Litany, (No. 189), *and then:*

℣. Exaltata est Sancta DEI Genitrix.

℟. Super Chores Angelorum ad cælestia regna.

℣. The Holy Mother of GOD is exalted.

℟. Into the heavenly kingdom above the Angel Choirs.

Oremus.

FAMULORUM tuorum, quæsumus DOMINE, delictis ignosce: ut qui tibi placere de actibus nostris non valemus, Genitricis FILII tui DOMINI nostri intercessione salvemur.

DEUS, omnium fidelium, and Deus refugium etc. (p. 217-218).

Let us pray.

WE beseech Thee, O LORD, to pardon the shortcomings of thy servants; that we who by our own works are not able to please Thee, may be saved by the intercession of the Mother of thy SON, our LORD JESUS CHRIST.

O GOD, the Shepherd and Ruler, and O God our refuge, etc., (p. 217-218).

Second Day, August 7.

Come, O HOLY SPIRIT, etc., (No. 199, I., up to and including the Preparatory Prayer). O Queen of all, etc., p. 230.

The glory of Mary in death, in that she was assisted by her Son Jesus and the Apostles.

Let us meditate how glorious Mary was at her death, in that, according to the teaching of holy writers, she was comforted not only by the apostles and saints, but also by her dear SON JESUS; and whilst we contemplate the unspeakable joy which filled her soul at this grace granted to her alone, let us entreat her for ourselves:

GLORIOUS Virgin, who for thy consolation didst merit to die in the blessed company of apostles and saints: obtain for us, that when we breathe forth our souls we may feel thy presence and that of our holy patrons, assisting us. Ave Maria *thrice.*

Glorious Virgin, who at the moment of thy death wast comforted by the sight of thy dear SON JESUS: oh, pray for us, that at that awful moment we too may be comforted by receiving JESUS in the most holy Viaticum. Ave Maria *thrice*.

Glorious Virgin, who didst surrender thy spirit into the arms of JESUS: assist us, that we also, in life and in death, may surrender our souls into the arms of JESUS, and that we may always desire that his most holy will be done. Ave Maria *thrice*.

Come then, let us magnify the glory of Mary, assisted at her death by her SON JESUS and his apostles, and join in jubilee at her triumph, with the second Choir of the heavenly host:

Then say the Litany, *(No. 189), and then:*

℣. Exaltata est Sancta DEI Genitrix.
℟. Super Chores Angelorum ad cælestia regna.
Oremus.

FAMULORUM tuorum, quæsumus DOMINE, delictis ignosce: ut qui tibi placere de actibus nostris non valemus, Genitricis FILII tui DOMINI nostri intercessione salvemur.

℣. The Holy Mother of GOD is exalted.
℟. Into the heavenly kingdom above the Angel Choirs.
Let us pray.

WE beseech Thee, O LORD, to pardon the shortcomings of thy servants; that we who by our own works are not able to please Thee, may be saved by the intercession of the Mother of thy SON, our LORD JESUS CHRIST.

Third Day, August 8.

Come, O HOLY SPIRIT, *etc.,* (No. 199, I., up to and including the Preparatory Prayer). O Queen of all, *etc.,* p. 230.

The glory of Mary in death, in that she died in an ecstasy of love.

Let us meditate how glorious the holy Mary was in her death, because she died in a very ecstasy of the love of GOD; and desiring that we too may be strengthened by that holy fire of love, let us ask for her help.

MARY, most happy Virgin, who didst die of the vehemence of the love of GOD; make it thy care that in our hearts, as GOD wills, there be lit up this living fire of his love. Ave Maria thrice.

Mary, most happy Virgin, who dying of divine love didst teach us what our love of GOD ought to do; pray for us, that we may never abandon our GOD in life or death. Ave Maria *thrice.*

Mary, most happy Virgin, who in leaving this mortal life, by virtue of an ecstasy of love didst make known the fire which ever burnt in thy heart, obtain for us at least a spark of that same fire, to give us true sorrow for our sins. Ave Maria *thrice.*

Let us with the third Choir of Angels now exalt the ineffable glory of Mary inflamed with the love of her GOD:

The Litany, (No. 189), ℣., ℟. *and prayers as above* p. 234:

Fourth Day, August 9.

Come, O HOLY SPIRIT, *etc.,* (No. 199, I., up to and including the Preparatory Prayer). O Queen of all, *etc.,* p. 230.

The glory of Mary after death in her dead body.

Let us meditate how glorious Mary was in her dead body, because it was adorned with marvelous splendour and majesty, and spread around an odour of sanctity, which was the very fragrance of Paradise, and because innumerable miracles were wrought at the sight of it. Then, thinking on our own misery, let us pray:

O LADY, most pure, who by reason of thy virginal purity didst merit the glory of being so bright and so majestic in thy body after death; obtain for us the strength to detach ourselves from every foul spirit of impurity. Ave Maria *thrice.*

O Lady most pure, who by reason of thy rare virtue didst from thy dead body spread around the sweetness of Paradise; make it thy care that we may edify our neighbour by our life, and never more by our bad example become a stumbling block to others. Ave Maria *thrice.*

O Lady most pure, at the sight of whose holy body numberless bodily infirmities were cured; intercede for us, that by thy prayers all our spiritual ills may be healed. Ave Maria *thrice.*

Come, let us rejoice in the glory given to the dead body of Mary, magnifying her with the fourth Choir of Angels:

The Litany, (No. 189), ℣., ℟. *and prayers as above* p. 234:

Fifth Day, August 10.

Come, O HOLY SPIRIT, *etc.*, (No. 199, I., up to and including the Preparatory Prayer). O Queen of all, *etc.*, p. 230.

The glory of Mary after death in the resurrection of her body.

Let us meditate how glorious Mary was after death, since by the power of the Highest her body, raised again to life, forthwith acquired the four gifts of brightness, agility, subtlety and impassibility; and filled with consolation at the excellence of her glory, let us invoke her:

O LADY exalted, who wast so gloriously raised to life again by thy GOD; help us so to live on earth, that we also may rise again like unto thee in the last judgment day. Ave Maria *thrice.*

O Lady exalted, to whose risen body were given the gifts of brightness and subtlety, by reason of the bright example and humility of thy life on earth; pray for us, that all contemptuous affectation may be taken from us; that so our souls, being freed from all self-love, may be adorned with humility. Ave Maria *thrice.*

O Lady exalted, whose risen body was glorified by the gifts of agility and impassibility, by reason of thy spiritual zeal and patience while on earth; obtain for us courage valiantly to mortify our bodies, and patiently to curb all our disordinate inclinations. Ave Maria *thrice.*

Then let us render due praise to Mary, and magnify the glory which adorned her risen body; while, with the fifth Choir, we exalt her:

The Litany, (No. 189), ℣., ℟. *and prayers as above* p. 234:

Sixth Day, August 11.
Come, O HOLY SPIRIT, *etc.,* (No. 199, I., up to and
including the Preparatory Prayer). O Queen of all,
etc., p. 230.
*The glory of Mary after death in her Assumption into
Heaven.*

Let us meditate how gloriously Mary was tak-
en up to Heaven, being escorted thither by many
legions of the heavenly host and of blessed souls
drawn by her merits out of Purgatory; and rejoicing in that majestic triumph, let us with all humility offer to her our supplications:

GREAT Queen, who wast assumed so royally
into the Kingdom of eternal peace; obtain
for us that all sordid, earthly thoughts be taken
away from us, and our hearts be fixed upon the
contemplation of the unchangeable happiness of
Heaven. Ave Maria *thrice.*

Great Queen, who wast assumed to Heaven
amidst a company of the Angelic Hierarchy; obtain for us strength to overcome the wiles of all
our enemies, and that we may lend a docile ear to
the counsels of that good angel who continually
assists and governs us. Ave Maria *thrice.*

Great Queen, who wast assumed to Heaven
most gloriously, in the company of souls drawn
by thy merits out of Purgatory; free us from the
slavery of sin, and make us worthy to praise thee
for all eternity. Ave Maria *thrice.*

Let us not cease to applaud the royal triumph
of Mary; and uniting our homage with the sixth
Choir of angels, let us honour the singular glory
of her Assumption into Heaven:
The Litany, (No. 189), ℣., ℟. *and prayers as above*
p. 234:

Seventh Day, August 12.

Come, O HOLY SPIRIT, *etc.,* (No. 199, I., up to and including the Preparatory Prayer). O Queen of all, *etc.,* p. 230.

The glory of Mary after death in her exaltation as Queen of Heaven.

Let us meditate how glorious Mary is in Heaven, because she is enthroned there as Queen of the universe, "and is ever receiving homage and veneration from countless hosts of angels and of saints; and assisting at her royal throne, let us implore her aid:

*S*OVEREIGN Queen of the universe, who for thy incomparable merit art raised to such high glory in the heavens; in thy pity look upon our miseries, and rule us with the gentle sway of thy protection, Ave Maria *thrice.*

Sovereign Queen of the universe, who art ever receiving worship and homage from all the heavenly host; accept, we pray thee, these our invocations, offered with such reverence as befits thy dignity and greatness. Ave Maria *thrice.*

Sovereign Queen of the universe, by that glory which thou hast by reason of thy high place in Heaven; vouchsafe to take us into the number of thy servants, and obtain for us grace that with quick and ready will we may faithfully keep the precepts of GOD our LORD. Ave Maria *thrice.*

Let us take part in the joy of the angels praising Mary, and rejoice with the seventh Choir, because we know that she is raised to the dignity of Queen of the universe.

The Litany, (No. 189), ℣., ℟. *and prayers as above* p. 234:

Eighth Day, August 13.

Come, O HOLY SPIRIT, *etc.*, (No. 199, I., up to and including the Preparatory Prayer). O Queen of all, *etc.*, p. 230.

The glory of Mary after death in the crown which decks her brow.

Let us meditate how glorious Mary is in Heaven by reason of the royal crown wherewith her divine SON has crowned her, and for the full knowledge which she now has of the deep mysteries of GOD, past, present and to come; and full of veneration for the incomparable honour bestowed upon our Queen, let us have recourse to her and say:

QUEEN unrivalled, who in Heaven above dost enjoy the high glory of being crowned by thy divine SON with a royal diadem; help us to share thy matchless virtues, and ask for us that, purified in heart, we may be made worthy to be crowned with thee in Paradise. Ave Maria *thrice.*

Queen unrivalled, in the full knowledge granted thee of all things on earth; for thy own glory's sake obtain pardon for our past evil deeds, that we may never offend again by froward tongue or wanton thought. Ave Maria *thrice.*

Queen unrivalled, whose desire it is to see men pure and clean of heart, that so they may be made worthy of thy GOD; obtain for us forgiveness of our sins, and help us, that all our looks, words and deeds may please his heavenly Majesty. Ave Maria *thrice.*

Let us then purify our hearts, in order that we may be worthy to give praise to Mary; and to the glory she possesses in that bright crown which decks her royal brow, let us add humble tokens of our love, rejoicing in union with the eighth Choir:

The Litany, (No. 189), ℣., ℟. *and prayers as above* p. 234:

Ninth Day, August 13.

Come, O HOLY SPIRIT, *etc.*, (No. 199, I., up to and including the Preparatory Prayer). O Queen of all, *etc.*, p. 230.

The glory of Mary after death in her patronage of man.

Let us meditate how glorious Mary is in Heaven by reason of her patronage of man, and for the power she has to aid him with great watchfulness in all his necessities; wherefore with lively confidence in the patronage of the very Mother of our GOD, let us implore her aid.

MARY, our most powerful patroness, whose glory it is in Heaven to be the advocate of man; oh! take us from the hands of the enemy and place us in the arms of our GOD and CREATOR. Ave Maria *thrice.*

Mary, our most powerful patroness, who being in Heaven the advocate of men wouldst that all men should be saved; make it thy care that none of us succumb at the thought of our past relapses into sin. Ave Maria *thrice.*

Mary, our most powerful patroness, who to fulfil thy office dost love to be continually invoked by men; obtain for us such true devotion that we may ever call upon thee in life, and above all at the awful moment of our death. Ave Maria *thrice.*

Now with all our hearts let us celebrate the glories of Mary; and consoled at having Mary for our advocate in Heaven, let us join in praising her with the ninth Choir of angels:

The Litany, (No. 189), ℣., ℟. *and prayers as above*
p. 234:

200. Eleven Novenas in Honour of Our Lady.

At any time of the year, with any form of prayer approved by competent ecclesiastical authority.
   i. 300 Days each day.
  ii. Plenary, once during the Novena or Octave. I, II, IV.
           (See Instructions, p. 1.)

In honour of (1) the Immaculate Conception; (2)
the Nativity B.V.M.; (3) the Presentation B.V.M.;
(4) the Annunciation B.V.M.; (5) the Visitation
B.V.M.; (6) the Sacred Delivery of Mary and Birth
of Jesus; (7) the Purification B.V.M.; (8) the Seven
Dolours B.V.M.; (9) the Assumption B.V.M.; (10)
the Sacred Heart of Mary and her Patronage; and
(11) for the Feast of the Most Holy Rosary.

201. One Ave and Prayer, O Domina Mea! for Victory in Temptations, especially those against Chastity.

   i. 100 Days, once a day, if said morning and evening.
  ii. Plenary, once a month. I, II, III, IV.
          (See Instructions, p. 1.)

Ave Maria.

O DOMINA mea! O Mater mea! Tibi me totum offero, atque ut me tibi probem devotum,

O My Queen! my Mother! I give thee all myself, and,
to show my devotion to thee, I consecrate to
thee this day my eyes,

consecro tibi hodie oculos meos, aures meas, os meum, cor meum, plane me totum. Quoniam itaque tuus sum, O bona Mater, serva me, defende me, ut rem ac possessionem tuam.

ears, mouth, heart, my entire self. Wherefore, O loving Mother, as I am thy own, keep me, defend me, as thy property and possession.

202. Prayer, O Beata Virgo.

50 Days. T.Q.

(See Instructions, p. 1.)

MARY, Virgin ever blessed! who can worthily praise thee or give thanks to thee, who, by that wondrous assent of thy will, didst rescue a fallen world? What honours can the weakness of our human nature pay to thee, which by thy intervention alone has found the way to restoration? Accept, then, such poor thanks as we have here to offer, though they are unequal to thy merits; and, receiving our vows, obtain by thy prayers the remission of our offences. Carry thou our prayers within the sanctuary of the heavenly audience, and bring forth from it the medicine of our reconciliation. Through thee may those sins become pardonable, the release from which through thee we ask of GOD, and that be granted which we demand with confidence. Accept what we offer, grant us what we seek, spare us what we fear, for thou art the sole hope of sinners. Through thee we hope for the forgiveness of our faults, and in thee, most blessed Virgin, is the hope of our reward. Holy Mary, succour the wretched, help the faint-hearted, comfort the sorrowful, pray for the people, shield the clergy, intercede for all women consecrated to GOD, let all feel thy aid who keep thy holy commemoration. Be thou at hand, ready to aid our prayers, when we pray; and bring back to us the answers we desire. Make it thy care to intercede ever for the people of GOD—thou who, blessed of GOD, didst merit to bear the REDEEMER of the world, who liveth and reigneth for ever and ever. Amen.

203. Prayer of St Alphonsus to be said before a representation of Our Lady.

i. 300 Days. T.Q.
ii. Plenary, once a month. I, II, IV.
(See Instructions, p. 1.)

MOST holy Mary, Immaculate Virgin and Mother, to thee who art the Mother of my LORD, the refuge of sinners, I, who am the most miserable of all, have recourse today. I adore thee, O great Queen, and I thank thee for the many favours thou hast done me up to now, especially for having preserved me from hell, which I have so often deserved. I love thee, most dear Lady; and by the love I bear thee I promise to desire ever to serve thee and to do all I can to make thee loved by others. I place all my hopes in thee, all my salvation. Accept me for thy servant and shelter me under thy mantle, O thou Mother of mercy. And since thou art so powerful with GOD, free me from all temptations, or obtain for me strength to overcome them as long as I live. Of thee I ask true love of JESUS CHRIST. Through thee I hope to die a good death. O Mother, by the love thou bearest to GOD, I pray thee to help me always, but specially in the last moment of my life. Do not leave me until thou seest me safe in Heaven, there to bless thee and sing thy mercies for all eternity. This is my hope. Amen.

204. Prayer for a Good Death.

100 days, once a day.

(See Instructions, p. 1.)

O MARY, conceived without stain, pray for us who fly to thee. Refuge of sinners, Mother of those who are in their agony, leave us not in the hour of our death, but obtain for us perfect sorrow, sincere contrition, remission of our sins, a worthy reception of the most holy Viaticum, the strengthening of the Sacrament of Extreme Unction, so that we may be able to stand with safety before the throne of the just but merciful Judge, our GOD and our REDEEMER. Amen.

205. Psalms and Prayers of St Bonaventure for every day in the week.

i. Seven Years and Seven Quarantines, once a day, for reciting, in any language, the psalms and prayers for each day, according to the order of the days of the week, from the Book entitled, *The Daily Tribute of Loving Prayers and Praises for each day in the week to the Immaculate Mother of God*, etc.

ii. Plenary, on the accustomed conditions, on the Feast of the Immaculate Conception and once during its

Octave, on the Feast of St Joseph, St Bonaventure
(July 14), and on any one day at pleasure during the
month of May, to those of the faithful who for one
month previous to these days shall have said daily
the above Psalms and Prayers. I, II, III, IV.

(See Instructions, p. 1.)

206. Chaplet of the Twelve Privileges of Our Lady.

i. 300 Days, once a day.
ii. Plenary, once a month. I, II, III, IV.

(See Instructions, p. 1.)

In the Name of the FATHER and of the SON and of
the HOLY SPIRIT. Amen.

℣. O GOD, come to my assistance.
℟. O LORD, make haste to help me.
Glory be to the FATHER, *etc.*

HAIL to thee, purest, holiest Mother of JESUS.
We humbly pray thee, by thy predestination,
whereby thou wast even from all eternity elected
Mother of GOD; by thy Immaculate Conception,
whereby thou wast conceived without stain of
original sin; by thy most perfect resignation,
whereby thou wast ever conformed to the will
of GOD; and, lastly, by thy consummate holiness,
whereby throughout thy whole life thou didst
never commit one single fault: we pray thee to
become our advocate with our LORD, that He may
pardon our many sins, which are the cause of
his wrath. And thou, O FATHER Almighty, by the
merits of these privileges vouchsafed to this thy
well-beloved Daughter, hear her supplications for
us, and pardon us, her clients.

Spare, O LORD, spare thy people. PATER *once*, Ave
four times, Gloria *once*.

By thy holy and Immaculate Conception deliver
us, glorious Virgin Mary.

HAIL to thee, purest, holiest Mother of JESUS.
We humbly pray thee, by the most holy
Annunciation, when thou didst conceive the
Divine Word in thy womb; by thy most happy
delivery, in which thou didst experience no pain;
by thy perpetual virginity, which thou didst unite
with the fruitfulness of a mother; and, lastly, by
the bitter martyrdom which thou didst undergo
in our SAVIOUR'S death: we pray thee to become
our mediatrix, that we may reap the fruit of the
Precious Blood of thy SON. And Thou, O Divine
SON, by the merit of these privileges granted to
thy well-beloved Mother, hear her supplications,
and pardon us, her clients.

Spare, O LORD, spare thy people. PATER *once*, Ave
four times, Gloria *once*.

By thy holy and Immaculate Conception deliver
us, glorious Virgin Mary.

HAIL to thee, purest, holiest Mother of JESUS.
We humbly pray thee, by the joys which thou
didst feel in thy heart at the Resurrection and
Ascension of JESUS CHRIST; by thy Assumption
into Heaven, whereby thou wast exalted above all
the Choirs of the Angels; by the glory which GOD
has given thee to be Queen of all saints; and, lastly, by that most powerful intercession, whereby
thou art able to obtain all that thou dost desire:
we pray thee, obtain for us true love of GOD. And
Thou, O HOLY SPIRIT, by the merits of these privi-

leges of thy well-beloved Spouse, hear her supplications, and pardon us her clients. Amen.

Spare, O LORD, spare thy people. PATER *once*, Ave *four times*, Gloria *once*.

By thy holy and Immaculate Conception deliver us, glorious Virgin Mary.

Antiphon. Thy Conception, Virgin Mother of GOD, brought joy to the whole world, for of thee was born the Sun of Justice, CHRIST our GOD, who, loosing the curse, bestowed the blessing, and, confounding death, gave unto us eternal life.

℣. In thy Conception, Virgin Mary, thou wast Immaculate.

℟. Pray to the FATHER for us, whose SON JESUS, conceived by the HOLY SPIRIT, thou didst bring forth.

Let us pray.

GOD of mercy, GOD of pity, GOD of tenderness, who, pitying the affliction of thy people, didst say to the angel smiting them, "Withhold thy hand"; for the love of thy glorious Mother, at whose precious breast thou didst sweetly find an antidote to the venom of our sins, bestow on us the help of thy grace, that we may be freed from all evil, and mercifully protected from every onset of destruction. Who livest and reignest for ever and ever. Amen.

207. Prayer for the Conversion of Heretics and Schismatics.

300 Days, once a day.

(See Instructions, p. 1.)

*O*MARY, Mother of mercy and Refuge of sinners, we beseech thee to look with pitying eyes on heretical and schismatical nations. Do thou, who art the Seat of wisdom, illuminate their minds, wretchedly involved in the darkness of ignorance and sin, that they may know the Holy, Catholic, Apostolic, Roman Church to be the only true Church of JESUS CHRIST, out of which no sanctity or salvation can be found. Finally, complete their conversion by obtaining for them the grace to believe every truth of our holy Faith, and to submit to the Sovereign Roman Pontiff, the Vicar of JESUS CHRIST on earth, that thus, being soon united to us by the bonds of divine charity, they may make with us but one fold under one and the same pastor, and that we may thus, O glorious Virgin, all sing exultingly for ever, "Rejoice, O Virgin Mary! alone thou hast destroyed all heresies in the whole world." Amen. Ave Maria *thrice*.

208. Prayer for the Conversion of Greek Schismatics.

i. 300 Days, once a day.
ii. Plenary, once a month. I, II, III, IV.
(See Instructions, p. 1.)

*O*IMMACULATE Virgin Mary, we thy servants, and sons of the holy Catholic and Roman Church, full of confidence in thy powerful protection, humbly beseech thee that thou wouldst deign to implore of the HOLY SPIRIT, by the honour and glory of his eternal Procession from the FATHER and the SON, the abundance of his gifts for our separated brethren, the Greek schismatics, that, enlightened by his vivifying grace, they may re-enter into the bosom of the Catholic Church, under the infallible guidance of her supreme pastor and teacher, the Sovereign Roman Pontiff; and that thus, sincerely re-united to us by the indissoluble bonds of the same faith and the same charity, they may, with us, glorify, by the practice of good works, the most august Trinity, and at the same time honour thee, O Virgin Mother of GOD, full of grace, now and through all ages. Amen. Ave Maria *thrice*.

209. Act of Reparation.

i. 300 Days, once a day.
ii. Plenary, once a month. I, II, III, IV.
     (See Instructions, p. 1.)

MOST glorious Virgin Mary, Mother of GOD, and our mother, look with pity upon us poor sinners, who, afflicted with so many miseries surrounding us in this life, feel ourselves cut to the heart by the many horrible insults and blasphemies which we are often constrained to hear uttered against thee, O Immaculate Virgin. Oh, how these impious sayings offend the infinite Majesty of GOD, and JESUS CHRIST his only begotten SON! How they provoke his anger, and give us cause to fear the terrible effects of his vengeance! If the sacrifice of our lives could avail against such outrages and blasphemies, very willingly would we make it, for we desire, most holy Mother, to love and honour thee with all our hearts, such being the will of GOD. And just be-

cause we love thee, we will do whatever lies in
our power to make thee loved and honoured by
all. And do thou, Mother of pity, supreme consoler of the afflicted, accept this act of reparation
offered to thee, in our name and in the name of
all our families, and on behalf of those who, not
knowing what they say, impiously blaspheme
thee; that so, by obtaining from GOD their conversion, thy glorious compassion, thy power, and
thy great mercy may become more manifest, and
they too may join with us in proclaiming thee
blessed amongst women, the Immaculate Virgin,
the most compassionate Mother of GOD. Ave
Maria *thrice*.

210. Prayer.

100 Days, once a day.

(See Instructions, p. 1.)

O POWERFUL Virgin, who alone hast destroyed all heresies throughout the world, deliver the Christian world from the snares of the
devil, and have compassion on the souls deceived
by diabolical cunning, that laying aside all heretical guilt, the hearts of the erring may be converted and return to the unity of the Catholic Faith,
through thy intercession with our LORD JESUS
CHRIST thy SON, who liveth and reigneth with
GOD the FATHER in the unity of the HOLY SPIRIT,
GOD for ever and ever. Amen.

211. Prayer.

300 Days, once a day.

(See Instructions, p. 1.)

O MARY, who, crowned with stars, hast for a footstool under thy feet the moon, and for thy throne the wings of angels; turn thy eyes upon this valley of sorrows, and listen to the voice of one who puts his hope and refuge in thee. Thou dost now enjoy the infinite sweetness of Paradise, but in the midst of joy and splendour thou bearest always in thy inmost heart the recollection of what thou didst suffer in this life. Thou hast tried the needs of this exile, and therefore knowest how bitterly flow the days of those who live in sorrow.

Ever in thy remembrance rises up a mount covered with armed men and the dregs of the people; thou hearest ever a voice, so well known by thee, which says to thee: "O Lady, behold, in my place, thy son." And these thoughts move thee to profound tenderness, and thou dost realize, O blessed one, that on that mountain and with those words thou wast destined to be the Mother of the living.

Without thee what would life be to the unhappy children of Adam. Each one of them has a sorrow which tries him, a grief which overwhelms, a wound which torments. And all have recourse to thee, as to a port of safety, to a fount of complete refreshment. When the waves lash themselves into fury, the wayfarer turns to thee and prays for calm. To thee has recourse the orphan who, like a flower in the wilderness, lies exposed to the whirlwind of life. To thee pray the poor who want their daily bread; and not one of them remains without help and consolation. But if all find in thee aid and refreshment, what shall we say, to whom thou art wont to appear, glorious as thou art in heaven.

O Mary, mother of all, enlighten our minds, soften our hearts, so that this most pure love which streams from thy eyes may be poured forth on every side, and produce those marvellous fruits which thy SON prepared for by shedding his Blood, whilst thou didst suffer the most cruel pangs at the foot of the Cross.

212. Office of the Blessed Virgin.

    i. Seven Years and Seven Quarantines, once a day.
    ii. Plenary, once a month. I, II.
    iii. 300 Days, once a day, for Matins and Lauds only,
    iv. 50 Days, for each Little Hour, for Vespers, and for Compline.

The Indulgences attached to this Office are extended to the recitation of it in the vernacular only in case of private recitation.

Private recitation includes recitation by communities in their private chapels or even in their churches, if the doors are closed to the public.

213. Hymn, Ave Maris Stella.

300 Days, once a day.

        (See Instructions, p. 1.)

AVE maris stella,
Dei Mater alma
Atque semper virgo,
Felix cæli porta.

HAIL thou star of the ocean!
Portal of the sky!
Ever Virgin Mother
Of the LORD most high!

Sumens illud Ave
Gabrielis ore,
Funda nos in pace,
Mutans Evæ nomen.

Oh! by Gabriel's *Ave*,
Utter'd long ago,
Eva's name reversing,
Stablish peace below.

Solve vincla reis,
Prefer lumen cæcis,
Mala nostra pelle,
Bona cuncta posce.

Break the captive's fetters;
Light on blindness pour;
All our ills expelling,
Every bliss implore.

Monstra te esse matrem,
Sumat per te preces,
Qui pro nobis natus,
Tulit esse tuus.

Show thyself a Mother
Offer Him our sighs,
Who for us incarnate
Did not thee despise.

Virgo singularis,
Inter omnes mitis,
Nos culpis solutos,
Mites fac et castos.

Virgin of all virgins!
To thy shelter take us:
Gentlest of the gentle!
Chaste and gentle make us.

Vitam præsta puram,
Iter para tutum,
Ut videntes Jesus,
Semper collætemur.

Still as on we journey,
Help our weak endeavour;
Till with thee and Jesus
We rejoice for ever.

Sit laus Deo Patri,
Summo Christo decus,
Spiritui Sancto,
Tribus honor unus.
Amen.

Through the highest
heaven,
To the Almighty Three,
Father, Son, and Spirit,
One same glory be.
Amen.

214. Reparation for Blasphemy against Our Lady.

300 Days. T.Q.

(See Instructions, p. 1.)

O MARY, bless this house, where thy name is ever held in benediction. All glory to Mary ever Immaculate, ever Virgin, blessed among women, the Mother of our LORD JESUS CHRIST, Queen of Paradise.

215. The Magnificat.

   i. 100 Days, once a day.
   ii. Seven Years and Seven Quarantines, once on Saturdays.

(See Instructions, p. 1.)

MAGNIFICAT:*anima mea DOMINUM. Et exultavit spiritus meus:* in DEO salutari meo

Quia respexit humilitatem ancillæ suæ: * ecce enim ex hoc beatam me dicent omnes generationes.

Quia fecit mihi magna qui potens est: * et sanctum nomen ejus.

Et misericordia ejusa progenie in progenies: * timentibus eum.

Fecit potentiam in brachio suo: * dispersit superbos mente cordis sui.

My soul doth magnify: the LORD. And my spirit hath rejoiced: in GOD my Saviour.

For He hath regarded the humility of his handmaid: for behold from henceforth all generations shall call me blessed.

For He that is mighty hath done great things unto me: and holy is his name.

And his mercy is from generation to generation: unto them that fear Him.

Deposuit potentes de sede: * et exaltavit humiles.
Esurientes implevit bonis: * et divites dimisit inanes.
Suscepit Israel puerum suum: * recordatus misericordiæ suæ.
Sicut locutus est ad patres nostres: * Abraham, et semini ejus in sæcula. Gloria PATRI, etc.

He hath shewed strength with his arm: He hath scattered the proud in the imagination of their heart.
He hath put down the mighty from their seat: and hath exalted the humble.
He hath filled the hungry with good things: and the rich He hath sent empty away.
He hath upholden his servant Israel: being mindful of his mercy.
As He spake unto our fathers: to Abraham and his seed for ever.
Glory be to the FATHER, etc.

216. Prayer of St Aloysius Gonzaga.

200 Days, once a day.
(See Instructions, p. 1.)

O HOLY Mary, my mistress, into thy blessed trust and special custody, and into the bosom of thy mercy I this day, every day, and in the hour of my death, commend my soul and my body: to thee I commit all my anxieties and miseries, my life and the end of my life, that by thy most holy intercession and by thy merits all my actions may be directed and disposed according to thy will and that of thy Son. Amen.

217. Prayer for England.

    i. 300 Days. T.Q.
    ii. Plenary, once a month. I, II, III, IV.
                    (See Instructions, p. 1.)

O BLESSED Virgin Mary, Mother of God, and our most gentle Queen and Mother, look down in mercy upon England thy Dowry, and upon us all who greatly hope and trust in thee. By thee it was that Jesus our Saviour and our hope was given unto the world; and He has given thee to us that we might hope still more. Plead for us thy children, whom thou didst receive and accept at the foot of the Cross, O sorrowful Mother. Intercede for our separated brethren, that with us in the one true fold they may be united to the supreme Shepherd, the Vicar of thy Son. Pray for us all, dear Mother, that by faith fruitful in good works we may all deserve to see and praise God together with thee in our heavenly home. Amen.

218. Prayer for Reunion.

   300 Days, once a day.
                    (See Instructions, p. 1.)

O IMMACULATE Virgin, who wast preserved by a singular privilege of grace from original sin, look with pity on our separated brethren, who are still thy children, and recall them to the centre of unity. They have, even from afar, preserved a most tender devotion towards thee, O Mother;

do thou, who art so generous, reward them for it by obtaining for them the grace of conversion. Victorious over the infernal serpent from the first moment of thy being, renew, now that the necessity is more urgent, thy triumphant progress, as of old. If our unhappy brethren continue in separation from our common FATHER, it is the work of the enemy; do thou, then, unmask his wiles, put his forces to rout, and let his victims see that it is impossible to obtain salvation except in union with the successor of St Peter. Do thou, who from the first in the plenitude of thy gifts didst glorify Him who worked such great wonders in thee, glorify thy SON, bringing back into his one fold his strayed sheep, making them subject to the guidance of the universal Shepherd, his Vicar on earth; and may it be thy glory, O Virgin, as well to have rooted out of the world all errors, as to have put an end to schisms, and so to have restored peace to the world.

219. Aspiration.

40 Days. T,Q.

(See Instructions, p. 1.)

O DOMINA mea! O Mater mea! memento me esse tuum. Serva me, defende me, ut rem et possessionem tuam.

MY Lady and my Mother, remember I am thine; protect and defend me as thy property and possession.

220. Ejaculation.

100 Days, once a day.

(See Instructions, p. 1.)

MARY, Mother of GOD and Mother of mercy, pray for us, and for the departed.

221. Three Invocations with Ave thrice.

100 Days, once a day.
(See Instructions, p. 1.)

VIRGO ante partum, ora pro nobis. Ave Maria.
Virgo in partu, ora pro nobis. Ave Maria.
Virgo post partum, ora pro nobis. Ave Maria.

THOU who wast a Virgin before thy delivery, pray for us. Ave Maria.
THOU who wast a Virgin in thy delivery, pray for us. Ave Maria.
THOU who wast a Virgin after thy delivery, pray for us. Ave Maria.

222. Ejaculation of St Philip Neri.

50 Days, once a day.
(See Instructions, p. 1.)

MARY, Virgin Mother of GOD, pray to JESUS for me.

223. Chaplet of the Seven Joys of Our Lady.

  i. All who, in churches of the Franciscans, join in the public recitation of this chaplet, gain all the Indulgences granted to members of the Order.
  ii. Plenary, on each of the Feasts of the Seven Joys, the greater Feasts of our Lady, or on any day within the Octaves, to all who recite the chaplet. I, II.
  iii. Plenary, once a month, if said every Saturday. I, II.
  iv. Plenary, *in articulo mortis*, at the point of death, to all who carry the beads about and say them frequently. I, II (if possible) or with at least contrition

and resignation, and the invocation of the Holy Name, in the heart, if not with the lips.

v. 300 Years, on other Feasts of our Lady.
vi. 200 Years, on holidays of obligation.
vii. 70 Years and 70 Quarantines, on any day.
viii. 10 Years to all who do any good work for the glory of GOD and the benefit, spiritual or temporal, of their neighbour, or who say *Ave* seven times in honour of the Joys, if they carry the beads about and say them frequently.

N.B.—The beads must be blessed by the Franciscan Minister-General, or a priest duly authorized by him (single decades may be said separately during the course of the day.)

(See Instructions, p. 1.)

(1) The Annunciation. (2) The Visitation. (3) The Nativity. (4) The Adoration of the Magi. (5) The Finding in the Temple. (6) The Resurrection. (7) The Assumption.

224. Ejaculation.

Before the Blessed Sacrament exposed.
300 Days. T.Q.

(See Instructions, p. 1.)

OUR Lady of the most holy Sacrament, pray for us.

225. Ejaculation.

300 Days. T.Q.

(See Instructions, p. 1.)

MARY, our hope, have pity on us.

226. Ejaculation.

300 Days. T.Q.

(See Instructions, p. 1.)

MARY sorrowing, Mother of all Christians, pray for us.

227. Ejaculation.

300 Days. TQ.

(See Instructions, p. 1.)

MOTHER of love, of sorrow, and of mercy, pray for us.

228. Prayer to Our Lady.

300 Days, once a day.

(See Instructions, p. 1.)

O MOTHER of mercy, help of Christians, faithful handmaid of divine providence, treasurer of all graces, remember that never was it known that those who devoutly had recourse to thee were left without consolation. Wherefore, I prostrate myself humbly before thee, trusting in thy heart of pity and in thy most generous watchfulness, and beg of thee to hear my prayers.

Obtain for me holy prudence, and graces in all my spiritual needs, and also that temporal prudence necessary for spending my days in this vale of tears.

I commend most fervently to thy loving and maternal heart Holy Church, the Supreme Pontiff, the conversion of souls, the propagation of the Catholic Faith, as well as the chosen spouses of our LORD who are suffering in the cruel flames of Purgatory, that they may quickly be consoled with eternal refreshment. Amen.

229. Prayer to Our Lady.

300 Days. T.Q.

(See Instructions, p. 1.)

MARIA Mater misericordiæ, Mater et Filia illius qui PATER est misericordiarum et DEUS totius consolationis,[1] Dispensatrix thesaurorum Filii tui,[2] Ministra DEI,[3] Mater summi Sacerdotis CHRISTI, Sacerdos pariter et Altare,[4] Sacrarium immaculatum Verbi DEI,[5] Magistra Apostolorum omnium et Discipulorum CHRISTI;[6] protege Pontificem Maximum, intercede pro nobis et pro sacerdotibus nostris, ut Summus Sacerdos CHRISTUS JESUS conscientias nostras purificet, et digne ac pie ad sacrum

MARY, Mother of mercy. Mother and daughter of Him who is the FATHER of mercies and the GOD of all consolation,[1] Dispenser of the treasures of thy SON,[2] Handmaiden of GOD,[3] Mother of the supreme High-Priest, CHRIST, at once Priest and Altar,[4] immaculate Treasure house of the Word of GOD,[5] Mistress of all the Apostles and Disciples of CHRIST;[6] protect the Supreme Pontiff, intercede for us and for our priests, that the High Priest JESUS CHRIST may purify our consciences, so that we may worthily and convivium suum accedamus.

O Virgo Immaculata, quæ non modo dedisti nobis panem cælestem CHRISTUM in remissionem peccatorum,[7] sed es tu ipsa hostia acceptissima DEO litata,[8] et gloria sacerdotum,[9] quæque teste beatissimo famulo tuo S. Antonino, quamvis sacramentum ordinis non acceperis, quidquid tamen dignitatis et gratiæ in ipso confertur, de hoc plena fuisti; unde merito Virgo Sacerdos[10] prædicaris; respice super nos et super sacerdotes Filii tui, purifica nos, salva nos, sanctifica nos, ut ineffabiles sacramentorum thesauros sancte suscipiamus, et æternam animarum nostrarum salutem consequi mereamur. Amen.

piously approach his holy banquet.

O Immaculate Virgin, who not only gavest us CHRIST, to be our bread from Heaven, for the remission of sins,[7] but art thyself a most acceptable victim offered to GOD,[8] and the glory of the priesthood,[9] who according to the testimony of thy most blessed servant St Antoninus, although thou didst not receive the Sacrament of Order, art filled with whatever of dignity and grace is conferred by it; wherefore deservedly art thou proclaimed Virgin Priest;[10] look down upon us and on the priests of thy SON; purify, sanctify, save us, that receiving the ineffable gifts of the sacraments, we may deserve to obtain the eternal salvation of our souls. Amen.

Mater misericordiæ, ora pro nobis.	Mother of mercy, pray for us.
Mater æterni Sacerdotis CHRISTI JESU, ora pro nobis.	Mother of the eternal Priest, CHRIST JESUS, pray for us.
Regina cleri, ora pro nobis.	Queen of the clergy, pray for us.
Maria Virgo Sacerdos, ora pro nobis.	Mary, Virgin Priest, pray for us.

1. Richard of St Laurence. 2. St Bernard. 3. Bernard de Busto. 4. St Epiphanius. 5. Blosius. 6. St Thomas of Villanova. 7. St Epiphanius. 8. St Andrew of Crete. 9. St Ephrem. 10. Br. of Pius IX, August 25, 1873.

B. MARY SORROWING

230. The Rosary of the Seven Dolours.

This Chaplet consists of seven divisions, in memory of our Lady's seven sorrows, on which we are to meditate, if we can, saying the *Pater noster* once and the *Ave Maria* seven times at each division, then ending with *Ave* thrice in honour of our Lady's tears.

To gain *any* of the following Indulgences beads must be used, though in the case of several persons saying the rosary together it is sufficient if the person leading the devotion uses them. They must have been blessed by a Servite Father or another with special faculties. To gain viii and ix the beads must have been blessed by a Servite Father.

For the benefit of those who for any reason are prevented from meditating on the mysteries of the Seven Dolours while they recite the Chaplet, i, ii, iii, vi, vii and viii can be gained by merely reciting the *Paters* and *Aves*. To gain iv, v and ix each mystery must be named and meditated on.

i. Seven Years and Seven Quarantines for the entire Chaplet. T.Q.

ii. 100 Days for each *Pater* and *Ave*, if the entire Chaplet is said.

iii. 200 Days for each *Pater* and *Ave* to every one who, having confessed, or at least made a firm resolution to confess, says this Chaplet in a Servite church, or says it anywhere on Fridays, or during Lent, or on the Feast and during the Octave of the Seven Dolours.

iv. 200 Years to those who shall say it after examination of conscience and Confession, and pray according to the intention of the Pope.

v. Plenary to all who say it four times a week, on any one day in the year when they say this Chaplet after Confession and Communion.

vi. Plenary once a month. I, II, IV.

vii. Ten Years to those who keep one of these Chaplets about them and are in the habit of saying it frequently, every time that after Confession and Communion they shall hear Mass, be present at a sermon, accompany the Blessed Sacrament to the sick, make peace between enemies, bring a sinner to repentance, recite devoutly *Pater* and *Ave* seven times or do any spiritual or temporal work of mercy in honour of our LORD, the Blessed Virgin, or their patron saint.

viii. 100 Years to all who say this Chaplet, having confessed or at least made a firm resolution to confess.

ix. 150 Years every Monday, Wednesday, Friday and Feast of obligation for reciting this Chaplet after Confession to those who habitually carry it about with them.

(See Instructions, p. 1.)

WAY OF SAYING THE CHAPLET.

Act of Contrition.

O My LORD, Thou who alone art most worthy of my love, behold me standing before thy Divine Presence utterly overwhelmed by the thought of the many grievous injuries I have done Thee. I ask thy pardon for them with my whole heart, repenting of them purely for love of Thee, and at the thought of thy great goodness hating and loathing them above every evil of this life. As I would rather have died a thousand times than have offended Thee, so now I am most firmly resolved to die a thousand deaths rather than offend Thee again. My crucified Jesus, I firmly purpose to cleanse my soul as soon as possible by thy most Precious Blood in the Sacrament of Penance. And thou, most tender Virgin, Mother of mercy and Refuge of sinners, do thou obtain for me by virtue of thy bitter pains, the pardon of sin which I desire; whilst, praying according to the mind of so many holy Pontiffs in order to obtain the Indulgences granted to this thy holy Rosary, I hope thereby to obtain remission of all pains due to my sins.

With this confidence in my heart, I meditate on the *First* Sorrow, when Mary, Virgin Mother of my God, presented Jesus her only Son in the Temple, laid Him in the arms of holy and aged Simeon, and heard his prophetic word, *"The sword of grief shall pierce thy soul,"* foretelling thereby the Passion and Death of her Son Jesus. Pater *once,* Ave *seven times.*

The *Second* Sorrow of the Blessed Virgin was when she was obliged to fly into Egypt by reason of the persecution of cruel Herod, who impiously sought to slay her well beloved Son. Pater *once,* Ave *seven times.*

The *Third* Sorrow of the Blessed Virgin was when, after having gone up to Jerusalem at the Paschal Feast with Joseph her spouse and JESUS her beloved SON, she lost Him on the way back to her poor house, and for three days bewailed the loss of her only Love. PATER *once*, Ave *seven times*.

The *Fourth* Sorrow of the Blessed Virgin was when she met her dear SON JESUS carrying to Mount Calvary on his tender shoulders the heavy Cross whereon He was to be crucified for our salvation. PATER *once*, Ave *seven times*.

The *Fifth* Sorrow of the Blessed Virgin was when she saw her SON JESUS raised upon the hard tree of the Cross, and blood flowing from every part of his sacred Body, and then beheld Him die after three hours agony. PATER *once*, Ave *seven times*.

The *Sixth* Sorrow of the Blessed Virgin was when she saw the lance pierce the sacred Side of JESUS, her beloved SON, the nails withdrawn, and his holy Body laid in her purest bosom. PATER *once*, Ave *seven times*.

The *Seventh* and last Sorrow of the Blessed Virgin, Queen and Advocate of us, her servants, miserable sinners, was when she saw the Holy Body of her SON buried in the grave. PATER *once*, Ave *seven times*.

Then say Ave *thrice in veneration of the tears which Mary shed in her sorrows, to obtain thereby true sorrow for sins and the holy Indulgences attached to this pious exercise.*

℣. Pray for us, Virgin most sorrowful.

℟. That we may be made worthy of the promises of Christ.

Let us pray.

GRANT, we beseech Thee, O Lord Jesus Christ, that the most blessed Virgin Mary, thy Mother, may intercede for us before the throne of thy mercy, now and at the hour of our death, whose most holy soul was transfixed with the sword of sorrow in the hour of thine own Passion. Through Thee, Jesus Christ, Saviour of the world, who livest and reignest, *etc.* Amen.

231. One Hour's Prayer.

Plenary, once in the year, to all the faithful, who, after Confession and Communion, on any one day should make one hour's prayer in honour of the sorrows of most holy Mary, meditating on them, or reciting prayers adapted to this devotion.

(See Instructions, p. 1.)

232. Devotions in honour of the Sorrowful Heart of Mary.

300 Days. T.Q.

(See Instructions, p. 1.)

℣. O God, come to my assistance.

℟. O Lord, make haste to help me.

Glory be to the Father, *etc.*

I COMPASSIONATE thee, sorrowing Mary, in the affliction of thy tender heart at the prophecy of the holy old man Simeon. Dear Mother, by thy heart then so afflicted, obtain for me the virtue of humility and the gift of holy fear of God. Ave Maria.

ICOMPASSIONATE thee, sorrowing Mary, in the anxiety which thy sensitive heart underwent in the flight and sojourn in Egypt. Dear Mother, by thy heart then made so anxious, obtain for me the virtue of liberality, especially towards the poor, and the gift of pity. Ave Maria.

ICOMPASSIONATE thee, sorrowing Mary, in the trouble of thy anxious heart, when thou didst lose thy dear SON JESUS. Dear Mother, by thy heart then so troubled, obtain for me the virtue of holy chastity and the gift of knowledge. Ave Maria.

ICOMPASSIONATE thee, sorrowing Mary, in the shock thy maternal heart underwent when JESUS met thee carrying his Cross. Dear Mother, by thy loving heart then so overwhelmed, obtain for me the virtue of patience and the gift of fortitude. Ave Maria.

ICOMPASSIONATE thee, sorrowing Mary, in the martyrdom thy generous heart bore so nobly whilst thou didst stand by JESUS in his agony. Dear Mother, by thy heart then so martyred, obtain for me the virtue of temperance and the gift of counsel. Ave Maria.

ICOMPASSIONATE thee, sorrowing Mary, in the wound of thy tender heart when the sacred Side of JESUS was pierced with the lance. Dear Mother, by thy heart then so transfixed, obtain for me the virtue of fraternal charity and the gift of understanding. Ave Maria.

ICOMPASSIONATE thee, sorrowing Mary, in the pang felt by thy loving heart when the Body of JESUS was buried in the grave. Dear Mother, by all the bitterness of desolation thou didst then experience, obtain for me the virtue of diligence and the gift of wisdom. Ave Maria.

℣. Pray for us, Virgin most sorrowful.

℟. That we may be made worthy of the promises of Christ.

Let us pray.

Grant, we beseech Thee, (p. 268) *etc.*

233. Devotions for Holy Week and Fridays.

i. Plenary, to all who from three o'clock on Good Friday until mid-day on Holy Saturday, either in public or private, spend one hour, or at least half an hour, in honour of our Lady sorrowing, in meditation or vocal prayer having reference to her sorrows, the Indulgence to be gained when the Paschal precept is fulfilled. I, II.

ii. 300 Days, in any other week, between three o'clock on Friday and Sunday morning.

iii. Plenary, once a month, to all who practise this devotion weekly. I, II.

(See Instructions, p. 1.)

234. Ave Maria, etc., seven times.

i. 300 Days, once a day.

ii. Plenary, once a month. I, II, IV.

(See Instructions, p. 1.)

After each Ave, *say:*

SANCTA Mater, istud agas,
Crucifixi fige plagas
Cordi meo valide

HOLY Mother, pierce me through;
In my heart each wound renew
Of my Saviour crucified.

235. Devotions during the Carnival.

i. 300 Days, each time, to those who shall assist at any devout exercise in honour of the Sorrows of most holy Mary, in order to make reparation for the sins committed during the Carnival, on the last ten days of the Carnival, in any church, or private or public chapel.

ii. Plenary, to those who shall assist at this pious exercise for at least five out of the ten days. I, II, IV.

(See Instructions, p. 1.)

236. Stations of Our Lady's Dolours.

The Stations must be erected and blessed by the Prior-General of the Servites, his Vicars or other ecclesiastics duly authorized by him, in a church or public chapel.

To all who in public or in private, passing from one to the other, meditate on the Dolours, or recite prayers in honour of them:

i. Seven Years and Seven Quarantines, once a day.

ii. Plenary, after making the Stations on seven days. I, II, IV.

(See Instructions, p. 1.)

237. The Month of September.

To those who daily practise some special devotion to our Lady Sorrowing

i. 300 Days, each day.

ii. Plenary, during the month or succeeding eight days. I, II, IV.

(See Instructions, p. 1.)

238. Hymn, Stabat Mater.

100 Days, T.Q.

(See Instructions, p. 1.)

STABAT Mater
Dolorosa
Juxta crucem lacrymosa
Dum pendebat Filius
Cujus animam ge-
   mentem,
Contristatam et dolen-
   tem,
Pertransivit gladius.

O quam tristis et afflicta
Fuit illa benedicta
Mater Unigeniti!
Quæ mœrebat, et
   dolebat,
Pia Mater dum videbat
Nati pœnas incliti.

Quis est homo qui non
   fleret
Matrem CHRISTI si
   videret
In tanto supplicio?
Quis non posset con-
   tristari

AT the cross her
station keeping,
Stood the mournful
   Mother weeping,
Close to JESUS to the last:
Through her heart, his
   sorrow sharing,
All his bitter anguish
   bearing,
Now at length the sword
   had passed.

Oh, how sad and sore
   distressed
Was that Mother, highly
   blest,
Of the sole begotten
   One!
CHRIST above in torment
   hangs;
She beneath beholds the
   pangs
Of her dying glorious
   SON.

Is there one who would
   not weep,
'Whelmed in miseries
   so deep,
CHRIST's dear Mother to
   behold?
Can the human heart
   refrain

CHRISTI Matrem contem-
plari
Dolentem cum Filio.

From partaking in her
pain
In that Mother's pain
untold?

Pro peccatis suæ gentis
Vidit JESUM in tormentis,
Et flagellis subditum.
Vidit suum dulcem
Natum Moriendo
desolatum,
Dum emisit spiritum.

Bruised, derided, cursed,
defiled,
She beheld her tender
Child,
All with bloody scourges
rent;
For the sins of his own
nation,
Saw Him hang in des-
olation
Till his spirit forth He
sent.

Eja Mater, fons amoris,
Me sentire vim doloris
Fac, ut tecum lugeam.
Fac, ut ardeat cor meum
In amando CHRISTUM
DEUM
Ut sibi complaceam.

O thou Mother! fount
of love!
Touch my spirit from
above,
Make my heart with
thine accord;
Make me feel as thou
hast felt;
Make my soul to glow
and melt
With the love of CHRIST
my LORD.

Sancta Mater, istud agas,

Holy Mother, pierce me
through;

Crucifixi fige plagas
Cordi meo valide.
Tui Nati vulnerati,
Tam dignati pro me pati,
Pœnas mecum divide.

In my heart each wound
 renew
Of my Saviour crucified;
Let me share with thee
 his pain,
Who for all my sins was
 slain,
Who for me in torment
 died.

Fac me tecum pie flere,
Crucifixo condolere,
Donec ego vixero,
Juxta crucem tecum stare
Et me tibi sociare
In planctu desidero.

Let me mingle tears
 with thee,
Mourning Him who
 mourned for me,
All the days that I may
 live:
By the cross with thee
 to stay;
There with thee to weep
 and pray
Is all I ask of thee to give.

Virgo Virginum
 præclara,
Mihi jam non sis amara,
Fac me tecum plangere.
Fac, ut portem Christi
 mortem,
Passionis fac consortem,
Et plagas recolere.

Virgin of all virgins best,
Listen to my fond
 request:
Let me share thy grief
 divine;
Let me to my latest
 breath
In my body bear the
 death
Of that dying Son of
 thine.

Fac me plagis vulnerari,
Fac me cruce inebriari,
Et cruore Filii.
Flammis ne urar suc-
        census,
Per te, Virgo, sim de-
        fensus
In die judicii.

Wounded with his every
        wound,
Steep my soul till it hath
        swooned
In his very Blood away;
Be to me, O Virgin,
        nigh,
Lest in flames I burn
        and die
In his awful judgment
        day.

CHRISTE, cum sit hinc
        exire,
Da per Matrem me
        venire
Ad palmam victoriæ.
Quando corpus mori-
        etur,
Fac ut animæ donetur
Paradisi gloria.
                    Amen.

CHRIST, when Thou shalt
        call me hence,
Be thy Mother my
        defence,
Be thy Cross my victory:
While my body here
        decays,
May my soul thy good-
        ness praise
Safe in Paradise with
        Thee.
                    Amen.

239. Prayer.

200 Days, once a day.
            (See Instructions, p. 1.)

MARY, most holy Virgin and Queen of
Martyrs, would that I could be transported
to Heaven, there to contemplate the honours bestowed on thee by the Blessed Trinity and by all

the heavenly court. But since I am still a pilgrim in this valley of tears, accept from me, thy unworthy and sinful servant, the most sincere homage and the most complete act of submission which a human being is capable of making to thee. In thy adorable heart, transfixed with so many swords of grief, I lay, once for all, my poor soul; receive me as the companion of thy sorrows, and do not allow me ever to be separated from that Cross on which thy only SON breathed forth his blessed Soul for me. With thee, O Mary, will I suffer all the trials, contradictions and infirmities with which it may please thy Divine SON to visit me in this life. I offer all to thee in memory of those sorrows which thou didst endure in thy life on earth; so that every thought of my mind, every beating of my heart, may henceforth be an act of compassion for thy sorrows and an act of rejoicing in the glories which thou dost now enjoy in Heaven. Therefore, dear Mother, while I now compassionate thee and rejoice to see thee thus glorified, do thou have compassion on me, and reconcile me with thy SON JESUS, so that I may be able to return and be thy true and faithful son. Come on my last day to assist me in my agony, as thou didst once assist at that of thy Divine SON, so that from this cruel exile I may come to share in thy glory in Heaven. Amen.

240. Prayer.

200 Days, once a day.

(See Instructions, p. 1.)

O MOST holy Virgin and Mother, whose soul a sword of grief went through in the Passion

of thy Divine SON, and who in his glorious
Resurrection wast filled with unending joy at his
triumph; intercede for us thy suppliants, that we
may become so truly partakers in the adversities of the Church and the trials of the Supreme
Pontiff, that we may deserve to share in the consolations they desire, in the charity and peace of
the same CHRIST our LORD. Amen.

C. MARY IMMACULATE

241. Chaplet of the Immaculate Conception.

   i. 300 Days. T.Q.
   ii. Plenary, once a month. I, II.
                  (See Instructions, p. 1.)

IN the name of the FATHER and of the SON and of
the HOLY SPIRIT. Amen.

First Set of Beads.
   Blessed be the Holy and Immaculate Conception
of the most Blessed Virgin Mary. PATER *once,* Ave
four times and Gloria *once.*

Second Set. Blessed, *etc., as before.* PATER, *etc.,
as before.*

Third Set. Blessed, *etc., as before.* PATER, *etc., as
before.*

242. Seven Sundays in Honour of the Immacu-
late Conception.

   i. Seven Years, on each of any seven consecutive
      Sundays. (Once a year.)
   ii. Plenary, on the seventh Sunday. I, II, III, IV.

(See Instructions, p. 1.)
Some special Prayer must be said.

243. The Little Office of the Immaculate Conception.

300 Days. T.Q.

(See Instructions, p. 1.)
The Latin and English Text may be obtained in separate form from Messrs Burns and Oates.

244. Antiphon, Versicle and Prayer.

100 Days. T.Q.

(See Instructions, p. 1.)

Ant. Hæc est virga in qua nec nodus originalis, nec cortex actualis culpæ fuit.

℣. In Conceptione tua, Virgo, immaculata fuisti.

℟. Ora pro nobis PATREM, cujus FILIUM peperisti.

Oremus.

DEUS qui per Immaculatam Virginis Conceptionem dignum Filio tuo habitaculum præparasti; quæsumus, ut qui ex morte ejusdem FILII tui

Ant. This is the rod in which was neither knot of original sin nor rind of actual guilt.

℣. In thy Conception, O Virgin, thou wast immaculate.

℟. Pray for us to the FATHER, whose SON thou didst bring forth.

Let us pray.

O GOD, who, by the Immaculate conception of the Virgin, didst prepare a worthy habitation for thy SON; we beseech Thee that, prævisa eam ab omni labe præservasti, nos quoque mundos ejus intercessione ad te pervenire concedas. Per eumdem CHRISTUM DOMINUM nostrum. ℞. Amen.

as in view of the death of that SON Thou didst preserve her from all stain of sin, so Thou wouldst enable us, being made pure by her intercession, to come unto Thee. Through the same CHRIST our LORD. ℞. Amen.

245. Ejaculation.

100 Days. T.Q.
(See Instructions, p. 1.)

In Conceptione tua, Virgo Maria, immaculata fuisti. Ora pro nobis PATREM, cujus FILIUM JESUM de SPIRITU SANCTO conceptum peperisti.

In thy Conception, O Virgin Mary, thou wast immaculate. Pray for us to the FATHER, whose SON JESUS CHRIST conceived of the HOLY SPIRIT thou didst bring forth.

246. Ejaculation.

100 Days, once a day.
(See Instructions, p. 1.)

TO thee, O Virgin Mother, who wast never defiled with the slightest stain of original or actual sin, I commend and entrust the purity of my heart.

247. Ejaculation.

100 Days, once a day.
(See Instructions, p. 1.)

O MARY, who didst enter the world free from stain, do thou obtain for me from GOD, that I may pass out of it free from sin.

248. Ejaculation.

300 Days. T.Q.
(See Instructions, p. 1.)

BLESSED be the holy and Immaculate Conception of the most blessed Virgin Mary, Mother of GOD.

249. Invocation.

100 Days, once a day.
(See Instructions, p. 1.)

O MARY, conceived without sin, pray for us who have recourse to thee.

250. Invocation.

100 Days, once a day.
(See Instructions, p. 1.)

SANCTA Virgo Maria Immaculata, Mater Dei, Mater nostra, tu pro nobis loquere ad Cor Jesu, qui tuus Filius est et frater noster.

MOST holy and Immaculate Virgin Mary, Mother of GOD and our Mother, speak on our behalf to the Heart of JESUS, who is thy SON and our Brother.

251. Devotion to the Crown of Living Stars.

100 Days. T.Q.

(See Instructions, p. 1.)

A contribution must be made during the year to the Institute of St Zita in Lucca for the rescue of Chinese and African children.

O MARY Immaculate! come to our aid, and help the little infidel children. Ave Maria.

252. Prayer to Our Lady Immaculate.

300 Days, once a day.

(See Instructions, p. 1.)

MOST holy Virgin, who wast pleasing to the LORD and became his Mother, immaculate in body and spirit, in faith and in love, look kindly on the wretched who implore thy powerful patronage. The wicked serpent, against whom was hurled the first curse, continues fiercely to attack and ensnare the unhappy children of Eve. Do thou, then, O Blessed Mother, our Queen and advocate, who from the first instant of thy Conception didst crush the head of the enemy, receive the prayers which, united with thee in one single heart, we implore thee to present at the throne of GOD, that we may never fall into the snares which are laid out for us, and may all arrive at the port of salvation; and, in so many dangers, may the Church and Christian society sing once again the hymn of deliverance, of victory, and of peace. Amen.

253. First Saturdays in Honour of the Immaculate Conception.

Plenary on each Saturday (or Sunday). I, II, IV.

(See Instructions, p. 1.)

Some time of the day must be devoted to prayer, vocal or mental, in honour of Mary Immaculate, and the practice must be kept up for twelve consecutive first Saturdays (or Sundays); otherwise the Indulgences will not be gained.

254. Consecration to Our Lady by Blessed Louis Mary Grignon de Montfort.

Plenary if said on the Immaculate Conception and April 28. I, II, III, IV.

(See Instructions, p. 1.)

O ETERNAL and incarnate Wisdom, O most sweet and adorable JESUS, true GOD and true Man, only SON of the Eternal FATHER and of Mary ever Virgin, I adore Thee profoundly, in the bosom and in the splendour of thy FATHER through eternity, and in the virginal womb of Mary thy most perfect Mother during the time of thy Incarnation.

I return Thee thanks for that Thou didst annihilate thyself, taking upon Thee the form of a servant, to rescue me from the cruel slavery of the devil. I praise and glorify Thee, for that Thou didst willingly become subject to Mary thy holy Mother in all things, in order to make me through her thy faithful slave. But, alas! ungrateful and faithless that I am in not keeping the promises I solemnly made to Thee in my Baptism, I have not fulfilled any of my obligations. I do not deserve to be called thy child or thy slave, and since there is nothing in me which does not merit thy reprobation and thy wrath, I dare no longer approach alone thy holy and august Majesty. Therefore it is that I have recourse to the intercession of thy most holy Mother, whom Thou hast given me to be my intercessor with Thee, and it is by this means that I hope to obtain from Thee the grace of contrition, the pardon of my sins, and the gift of abiding wisdom.

I salute thee, then, O Mary Immaculate, living tabernacle of the Divinity, where the eternal Wisdom lies hidden to be adored by angels and men. I salute thee, O Queen of heaven and of earth, beneath whose sway are subject all things that are lower than GOD. I salute thee, O secure refuge of sinners, whose mercy fails no one; graciously respond to the desires which I have for divine wisdom, and receive the vows and offerings which my nothingness makes to thee to obtain it.

I, N____, a faithless sinner, renew and ratify this day at thy hands my baptismal vows. I renounce for ever Satan, his works and pomps, and I give myself wholly to JESUS CHRIST, the incarnate Wisdom, to carry my cross after Him all the days of my life, and, in order that I may be more faithful to Him than I have hitherto been, I choose thee this day, O Mary, in the presence of the heavenly court, for my Mother and Mistress.

I deliver and consecrate to thee, as a bond slave, my body and my soul, my possessions interior and exterior, and even the value of all my good actions, past, present and to come, leaving thee the entire and full right to dispose of me and of all that belongs to me without exception, according to thy good pleasure, to the greater glory of GOD, for time and eternity.

Receive, O loving Virgin, this offering of bondage which I make to thee, in honour of and in union with the subjection which the eternal Wisdom gave to thy Maternity, as an act of homage before the power which thou and thy SON have over me, a worm and miserable sinner, in thanksgiving for the privileges which the Holy Trinity has bestowed on thee. I protest that I desire henceforth, as thy veritable slave, to seek thy honour and obey thee in all things. O Mother most admirable, present me to thy dear SON as his eternal slave, so that, having redeemed me through thee, He may receive me from thee. O Mother of mercy, obtain for me from GOD the gift of true wisdom, and also, to that end, the grace to place myself among the number of those who love thee, and whom thou dost cherish and protect as thy children and slaves. O faithful Virgin, make me a perfect disciple in all things, imitator and slave of the eternal Wisdom JESUS CHRIST, thy SON, so that by thy intercession I may come to the plenitude of his years on earth and of his glory in heaven. Amen.

255. The Miraculous Medal and Ejaculation.

100 Days. T.Q. (See Instructions.)
This Indulgence may be gained by those only who wear the miraculous medal blessed by a duly authorized priest.

O MARY, conceived without sin, pray for us who have recourse to thee.

256. Prayer of St Alphonsus for Purity.

300 Days, twice a day, morning and evening.
(See Instructions, p. 1.)

Ave Maria *thrice, and after each:*

PER tuam Immaculatam Conceptionem, O Maria, redde purum corpus meum et sanctam animam meam.

BY thy Immaculate Conception, O Mary, make my body pure, and my soul holy.

D. THE SACRED HEART OF MARY

257. Prayer and Act of Praise.

i. 60 Days, once a day.
ii. Plenary, to those who say it every day for a year, on each of the following three Feasts of our Lady, viz., the Nativity, Assumption, and her Sacred Heart, provided they visit a church or altar dedicated to the Blessed Virgin, and pray for the intention of the Sovereign Pontiff. I, II, III, IV.
iii. Plenary, *in articulo mortis*, at the point of death, to all who in life have said this prayer every day. I, II (or at least with contrition).

(See Instructions, p. 1.)

The Prayer.

HEART of Mary, Mother of GOD and our Mother, Heart most amiable, on which the adorable Trinity ever gazes with complacency, worthy of all the veneration and tenderness of angels and of men; Heart most like the Heart of

JESUS, whose most perfect image thou art; Heart full of goodness, ever compassionate towards our miseries; vouchsafe to thaw our icy hearts, that they may be wholly changed to the likeness of the Heart of JESUS. Infuse into them the love of thy virtues, inflame them with that blessed fire with which thou dost ever burn. In thee let the Holy Church find safe shelter; protect it and be its sweet asylum, its tower of strength, impregnable against every inroad of its enemies. Be thou the road leading to JESUS; be thou the channel whereby we receive all graces needful for our salvation. Be thou our help in need, our comfort in trouble, our strength in temptation, our refuge in persecution, our aid in all dangers; but especially in the last struggle of our life, at the moment of our death, when all hell shall be unchained against us to snatch away our souls: in that dread moment, that hour so terrible, whereon our eternity depends, ah, then, most tender Virgin, make us feel how great is the tenderness of thy maternal Heart, and how mighty thy power with the Heart of JESUS, opening to us a safe refuge in the very fount of mercy itself, that so we too may join with thee in Paradise in blessing that same Heart of JESUS for ever and for ever. Amen.

Act of Praise to the SS. Hearts of Jesus and Mary.

MAY the Divine Heart of JESUS and the Immaculate Heart of Mary be known, praised, blessed, loved, worshipped and glorified always and in all places! Amen.

258. Chaplet of the Immaculate Heart of Mary.

i. 300 Days, once a day.
ii. Plenary, once a month. I, II, III, IV.

(See Instructions, p. 1.)

℣. O GOD, come to our assistance.
℟. O LORD, make haste to help us.
℣. Glory be to the FATHER, *etc.*

I

IMMACULATE Virgin, who, conceived without sin, didst direct every movement of thy pure heart to GOD, ever the object of thy love, and who wast ever most submissive to his will, obtain for me the grace to hate sin with my whole heart, and to learn of thee to live in perfect resignation to the will of GOD. PATER *once*, Ave *seven times.*

Heart of Mary, pierced with grief, set my heart on fire with the love of GOD.

II

Mary, I wonder at thy deep humility when thy blessed heart was troubled at the gracious message brought thee by Gabriel the Archangel how that thou wast chosen to be Mother of the SON of GOD Most High and didst still proclaim thyself his humble handmaid; in great confusion at my pride, I ask thee for the grace of a contrite and humble heart, that, knowing my own misery, I may obtain that crown of glory promised to those who are truly humble of heart. PATER *once*, Ave *seven times;* Heart of Mary, *etc.*

III

Sweetest Heart or Mary, precious treasury, wherein the Blessed Virgin kept the words of

JESUS whilst she thought on the high mysteries which she had heard from the lips of her SON, and whereby she learned to live for GOD alone; how does the coldness of my heart confound me! Dearest Mother, obtain for me grace so to meditate within my heart upon the holy law of GOD, that I may strive to follow thee in the fervent practice of every Christian virtue. PATER *once*, Ave *seven times*; Heart of Mary, *etc.*

IV

Glorious Queen of Martyrs, whose sacred heart was cruelly transfixed in the bitter Passion of thy SON by the sword foretold by the holy old man, Simeon, obtain for my heart true courage and a holy patience to bear well the troubles and adversities of this miserable life, and, by crucifying my flesh with its desires in following the mortification of the Cross, to show myself truly thy son. PATER *once*, Ave *seven times*; Heart of Mary, *etc.*

V

O Mary, Mystic Rose, whose loving heart, burning with the living fire of charity, accepted us for thy children at the foot of the Cross, whereby thou didst become our most tender Mother; make me feel the sweetness of thy maternal heart, and thy power with JESUS in all the perils of this mortal life, and especially in the terrible hour of death, that so my heart, united with thine own, may love JESUS now and throughout all ages. Amen. PATER *once*, Ave *seven times*; Heart of Mary, *etc.*

Let us entreat the Most Sacred Heart of JESUS to inflame us with his holy love.

O DIVINE Heart of JESUS, I consecrate myself to Thee, full of deep gratitude for the many blessings I have received, and daily receive, from thy infinite charity. I thank Thee with my whole heart for having also vouchsafed to give me thine own Mother to be my Mother, consigning me to her in the person of the beloved Disciple. Grant unto me that my heart may ever burn with this love of Thee, and so may find in Thee its peace, its refuge and its happiness.

259. Ejaculation.

i. 300 Days. T.Q.
ii. Plenary, once a month. I, II, III, IV.
> (See Instructions, p. 1.)

S WEET Heart of Mary, be my salvation.

E. OUR LADY OF THE ROSARY

260. The Rosary blessed by Canons Regular of St Augustine of the Order of the Holy Cross.

One *Pater noster* or one *Ave Maria* said on a rosary blessed by the Master General or one of the Canons delegated by him, or by one having this special privilege. See N.B. on next page.

500 Days. T.Q.
> (See Instructions, p. 1.)

261. The Rosary of St Dominic.

This Devotion, called also the Psalter of Mary, consists of the continuous recitation of the *Ave Maria*, said 150 times (as many times as there are Psalms), divided into fifteen decades, each beginning with a *Pater noster*, while at the same time the principal mysteries of the life, death and resurrection of our LORD are meditated on.

To gain the following Indulgences beads must be used, though in the case of several persons saying the Rosary together it is sufficient if the person leading the Devotion uses them. They must, except in the case of i, have been blessed by a Dominican Father or other priest duly authorized.

Persons incapable of meditating may gain the Indulgences by merely saying the Rosary devoutly. Such persons should however endeavour, in some measure, to acquire the power of meditating.

    i. Five Years and five Quarantines, for a third part, five decades, of the Rosary (blessed beads not necessary). T.Q.

    ii. 100 Days, to all who say the fifteen, or at least five decades for every *Pater* and *Ave*.

    iii. Plenary, to all who say five decades every day for a year, on any one day in the year. I, II, IV.

    iv. Ten Years and ten Quarantines, once a day, to all who say five decades in company with others, either in public or in private.

    v. Plenary, on the last Sunday of every month, to all who are in the habit of saying with others, at least three times a week, five decades. I, II, III, IV.

    vi. 100 Years and 100 Quarantines, once a day, to all associates of the confraternity who devoutly carry a rosary about with them.

    vii. Plenary, to all associates who say the Fifteen Mysteries in the course of the natural day, for the triumph of the Church. I, II, III.

N.B.—The Indulgences attached to beads blessed by the Canons Regular of the Holy Cross (see No. 260) can be gained simultaneously with the Dominican Indulgences, i.e., while reciting the Rosary, provided the beads are blessed with the two blessings. (Pius X, June 12, 1907.)

Note. Indulgences vi and vii, with many others not re-corded in the *Raccolta*, can be gained only by members of the Confraternity of the Holy Rosary. To enjoy the privileges of this confraternity it is only requisite that a person's name be entered on the Dominican Register, and that the beads should be blessed as above.

The Joyful Mysteries.

IN the First Joyful Mystery we meditate on the Annunciation made by the angel Gabriel to most holy Mary, that she was to conceive and bear a Son, our Lord Jesus Christ.

PATER *once,* Ave *ten times (a* Gloria *is usually added; so also in all the Mysteries).*

In the Second Joyful Mystery we meditate how, when Mary heard that Elizabeth had conceived, she went to her house to visit her, and stayed with her three months.

In the Third Joyful Mystery we meditate how, when the full time of Mary's delivery was come, she brought forth our Saviour Jesus Christ at midnight, in the city of Bethlehem, and laid Him in a manger between two brute beasts.

In the Fourth Joyful Mystery we meditate how most holy Mary, on the day of her Purification, presented Christ our Lord in the Temple, and placed Him in the hands of the holy old man Simeon.

In the Fifth Joyful Mystery we meditate how the Virgin Mary lost her Son, when twelve years old, sought for Him three days, and at the end of the third day found Him in the Temple amid the doctors, hearing them and asking them questions.

The Sorrowful Mysteries.

IN the First Sorrowful Mystery we meditate how our LORD JESUS CHRIST prayed in the garden of Olives, and sweated blood.

In the Second Sorrowful Mystery we meditate how our LORD JESUS CHRIST was cruelly scourged in Pilate's house with innumerable blows.

In the Third Sorrowful Mystery we meditate how our LORD JESUS CHRIST was crowned with sharp thorns.

In the Fourth Sorrowful Mystery we meditate how JESUS was condemned to die, and, for his greater ignominy and pain, the heavy tree of the Cross was laid upon his shoulder.

In the Fifth Sorrowful Mystery we meditate how, when JESUS arrived at Calvary, He was stripped and nailed with iron nails to the Cross, and died thereon, before the eyes of his afflicted Mother.

The Glorious Mysteries.

IN the First Glorious Mystery we meditate how JESUS CHRIST our LORD rose again in glory, the third day after his Death and Passion, triumphant over death, never more to die.

In the Second Glorious Mystery we meditate how JESUS CHRIST, the fortieth day after his Resurrection, ascended into Heaven with great joy and triumph, in the presence of his most holy Mother and his disciples.

In the Third Glorious Mystery we meditate how JESUS CHRIST sat down on the right hand of the FATHER, and sent from thence the HOLY SPIRIT into the room where the Apostles and the most holy Virgin were assembled.

In the Fourth Glorious Mystery we meditate how, twelve years after our LORD JESUS CHRIST rose from the dead, his Mother herself passed from this mortal life, and was carried into Heaven by the angels.

In the Fifth Glorious Mystery we meditate how, in Heaven, Mary was crowned by her SON; in this Mystery also we meditate upon the glory of the saints.

262. The Month of October.

i. Seven Years and Seven Quarantines daily, if five decades are said either in public or in private.
ii. Plenary, on Rosary Sunday, or during the Octave, if five decades are said on all those days. I, II, III, IV.
iii. Plenary, once during the month, if, after the Octave, five decades are said on any ten days. I, II, III, IV.

(See Instructions, p. 1.)

263. Prayer.

100 Days, once a day.

(See Instructions, p. 1.)

O QUEEN of the most holy Rosary, in these times of brazen impiety, show forth thy power, with the signs which accompanied thy victories of old, and from the throne where thou art seated, dispensing pardon and grace, in pity watch over the Church of thy SON, his Vicar, and every order of the clergy and laity, suffering in grievous warfare. Hasten, O most powerful destroyer of heresy, hasten the hour of mercy, seeing that the hour of judgment is daily challenged by innumerable offences. Obtain for me, the lowest of men, kneeling suppliant in thy presence, the grace which may enable me to live a just life on earth, and reign with the just in Heaven, whilst with the faithful throughout the world, O Queen of the most holy Rosary, I salute thee and cry out: Queen of the most holy Rosary, pray for us.

264. The Fifteen Saturdays.

   i. Plenary, on one Saturday. I, II.
   ii. Seven Years and Seven Quarantines, on each of the
      others. I, II.

            (See Instructions, p. 1.)

On each day five decades must be said, or meditation in some other manner made on the mysteries. In case of lawful hindrance, Sundays may be substituted. In either case they must be consecutive, and may be at any time of the year.

265. Our Lady of the Rosary of Pompeii.

   i. 100 Days, once a day.
   ii. Plenary, on May 8, and on Rosary Sunday. I, II, III,
      IV.

           ((See Instructions, p. 1.)

A visit must be made to a statue of our Lady of Pompeii, in any church or public chapel.

266. Prayer to Our Lady of the Rosary.

300 Days, once a day.

            (See Instructions, p. 1.)

O VIRGIN Mary, grant that the recitation of thy Rosary may be for me each day, in the midst of my manifold duties, a bond of unity in my actions, a tribute of filial piety, a sweet refreshment, an encouragement to walk joyfully along the path of duty. Grant, above all, O Virgin Mary, that the study of thy fifteen mysteries may form in my soul, little by little, a luminous atmosphere, pure, strengthening and fragrant, which may penetrate my understanding, my will, my heart, my memory, my imagination, my whole being. So shall I acquire the habit of praying while I work, without the aid of formal prayers, by interior acts of admiration and of supplication, or by aspirations of love. I ask this of thee, O Queen of the Holy Rosary, through St Dominic, thy son of predilection, the renowned preacher of thy mysteries, and the faithful imitator of thy virtues. Amen.

F. VARIOUS TITLES OF OUR LADY

267. Prayer to Our Lady of Pity.

i. 100 Days, once a day.
ii. Plenary, once a month. I, II, III, IV.
(See Instructions, p. 1.)

KNEELING at thy holy feet, O gracious Queen of Heaven, we offer thee our deepest reverence. We confess that thou art the daughter of the Eternal FATHER, the Mother of the Divine Word, and the Spouse of the HOLY SPIRIT. Full of grace, of virtue and of heavenly gifts, thou art the chaste temple of the Holy Trinity. With thee are treasured GOD's mercies, and thou, too, dost dispense them. And since thy loving heart is filled with charity, sweetness, and tender compassion for us poor sinners, we call thee Mother of Divine Pity. With the greatest trust, then, O most loving Mother, do I come to thee in my sorrow and distress. I beg thee to give me an assurance of thy love, by granting me . . . . if it be GOD's will, and for the welfare of my soul. Cast, then, thy most pure eyes upon me and upon all my kindred. Consider the cruel warfare which the devil, the world, and the flesh wage against our souls, and how many perish in it. Remember, O fondest of mothers, that we are thy children, purchased with the Precious Blood of thy Divine SON. Pray without ceasing that the adorable Trinity may give us the grace to be victorious over the devil, the world, and our own unhallowed passions; that grace by which the just grow in holiness, sinners are converted, and heresy is destroyed; by which unbelievers are enlightened, and Jews brought to the true religion. Bestow on us this boon, O most pure Virgin, through the infinite bounty of the Most High, through the merits of thy most holy SON, by the milk with which thou didst nourish Him, by the devotion with which thou didst serve Him, by the love with which thou didst cherish Him, by thy tears and the anguish endured by thee in his holy Passion. Obtain for us the great favour that the whole world may be made one people and one Church, to give thanks, praise, and glory to the most Holy Trinity, and to thee who art our mediatrix.

May the power of the FATHER, the wisdom of the SON and the virtue of the HOLY SPIRIT grant us this blessing. Amen.

268. Prayers to Our Lady of Perpetual Succour.

100 Days, once a day, for each of the three prayers.
(See Instructions, p. 1.)

I

BEHOLD at thy feet, O Mother of Perpetual Succour, a wretched sinner who has recourse to thee, and confides in thee. O Mother of mercy, have pity on me. I hear thee called by all, the refuge and the hope of sinners: be, then, my refuge and my hope. Assist me, for the love of Jesus Christ; stretch forth thy hand to a miserable fallen creature who recommends himself to thee, and who devotes himself to thy service for ever. I bless and thank Almighty God, who in mercy has given me this confidence in thee, which I hold to be a pledge of my eternal salvation. It is true that in the past I have miserably fallen into sin, because I had not recourse to thee. I know that, with thy help, I shall conquer. I know, too, that thou wilt assist me, if I recommend myself to thee; but I fear that, in time of danger, I may neglect to call on thee, and thus lose my soul. This grace, then, I ask of thee, and this I beg, with all the fervour of my soul, that, in all the attacks of hell, I may ever have recourse to thee. O Mary, help me. O Mother of Perpetual Succour, never suffer me to lose my God.

II

O MOTHER of Perpetual Succour, grant that I may ever invoke thy most powerful name, which is the safeguard of the living and the salvation of the dying. O purest Mary! O sweetest

Mary! let thy name henceforth be ever on my lips. Delay not, O blessed Lady, to succour me, whenever I call on thee; for, in all my temptations, in all my needs, I shall never cease to call on thee, ever repeating thy sacred name, Mary! Mary! Oh, what consolation, what sweetness, what confidence, what emotion fills my soul when I utter thy sacred name, or even only think of thee! I thank the LORD for having given thee, for my good, so sweet, so powerful, so lovely a name. But I will not be content with merely uttering thy name. Let my love for thee prompt me ever to hail thee Mother of Perpetual Succour.

III

O MOTHER of Perpetual Succour, thou art the dispenser of all the gifts which GOD grants to us miserable sinners; and for this end He has made thee so powerful, so rich, and so bountiful, in order that thou mayest help us in our misery. Thou art the advocate of the most wretched and abandoned sinners who have recourse to thee: come to my aid; I commend myself to thee. In thy hands I place my eternal salvation, and to thee I entrust my soul. Count me among thy most devoted servants; take me under thy protection, and it is enough for me. For, if thou protect me, I fear nothing; not from my sins, because thou wilt obtain for me the pardon of them; nor from the devils, because thou art more powerful than all hell together; nor even from JESUS, my Judge, because by one prayer from thee He will be appeased. But one thing I fear: that in the hour of temptation, I may through negligence fail to have recourse to thee, and thus perish miserably. Obtain for me, therefore, the pardon of my sins, love for JESUS, final perseverance, and the grace ever to have recourse to thee, O Mother of Perpetual Succour.

269. Prayer to Our Lady of Good Counsel.

100 Days, once a day.

(See Instructions, p. 1.)

MOST glorious Virgin, chosen by the Eternal Counsel to be the Mother of the Eternal WORD made Man, treasure-house of divine graces and advocate of sinners; I, the most unworthy of thy servants, have recourse to thee, begging of thee to be my guide and counsellor in this vale of tears. Obtain for me, through the most Precious Blood of thy Divine SON, forgiveness of my sins, and the salvation of my soul with all the means necessary to secure it. Obtain for Holy Church triumph over her enemies and the extension of the Kingdom of JESUS CHRIST over the whole earth. Amen.

270. Prayer to Our Lady of Mount Carmel.

200 Days, once a day.

(See Instructions, p. 1.)

O MOST blessed Virgin Immaculate, the beauty and splendour of Carmel, thou who regardest with eyes of special love those who wear thy blessed habit, look kindly upon me and spread over me the mantle of thy maternal protection. Strengthen my weakness with thy power, illuminate the darkness of my mind with thy wisdom, increase in me the virtues of Faith, Hope and Charity. Adorn my soul with such graces and virtues that it may be ever dear to thy divine Son and to thee. Assist me in life, console me in death, with thy dear presence, and present me to the Holy Trinity as thy child and devoted servant, eternally to praise and bless thee in Paradise. Amen. Ave *thrice* and Gloria *once.*

271. Prayer to Our Lady, Mother of Divine Providence.

200 Days, once a day.

(See Instructions, p. 1.)

O IMMACULATE Virgin Mary, Mother of Divine Providence, take possession of my soul with all the fullness of thy favour and protection. Govern thou my life, and direct it along the way of virtue to the fulfilment of the divine will. Do thou obtain for me the pardon of my sins; be my refuge, my protection, my defence, my guide in the pilgrimage of this life; console me in afflictions, sustain me in dangers, and in the storms of adversity afford me the security of thy guardianship. Obtain for me, O Mary, the renewal of my heart within me, so that it may become the holy dwelling place of thy divine Son Jesus; remove far from me, weak and miserable as I am, every kind of sin, negligence, sloth, timidity and human respect; entirely expel from me pride, vain glory, self-love, and all other earthly affections which hinder the efficacy of thy patronage. O sweetest Mother of Providence, turn thy maternal regard

upon me, and if through frailty or malice I have
provoked the menaces of the eternal Judge and
embittered the most Sacred Heart of my loving JESUS, do thou throw over me the mantle of
thy protection, and I shall be safe. Thou art the
watchful Mother, the Virgin of forgiveness, and
my hope on earth; oh, grant that I may have thee
for the Mother of Glory in Heaven. Ave Maria
thrice.

272. Prayer to Our Lady of the Cœnaculum.

i. 100 Days, once a day, for the Prayer.
ii. 50 Days, once a day, for the Ejaculation.
(See Instructions, p. 1.)

MOST holy Virgin of the Cœnaculum and
our Mother, Mary Immaculate, we humbly
beg of thee to obtain for us the gifts of the HOLY
SPIRIT; that living united in charity, and persevering with one mind and heart in prayer, assisted
by thee, our guide and mistress, we may, to the
greater glory of GOD, be worthy to devote ourselves to work by example and deed for the salvation of souls, and so secure for ourselves eternal
life. O blessed Lady of the Cœnaculum, favour
and assist us in our present need, and succour
us with thy power, that by thy prayers GOD, almighty and merciful, may be pleased to grant the
grace we so urgently demand. Amen.
Ejaculation.
    Our Lady of the Cœnaculum, pray for us.

273. Prayer to Our Lady Help of Christians.

100 Days, once a day.

(See Instructions, p. 1.)

MARY, Immaculate Virgin, Mother of GOD and our Mother, thou seest how the Catholic Faith, in which we propose by the help of GOD to live and die, and so attain to eternal glory, is everywhere assailed by the devil and the world. Do thou, Help of Christians, renew thy victories as of old, for the salvation of thy children. To thee we entrust our firm purpose of never joining assemblies of heretics or sectaries. Do thou, all holy, offer to thy divine SON our resolutions, and obtain from him the graces necessary to enable us to remain steadfast in them to the end. Bring consolation to the visible head of the Church; support the Catholic Episcopate; protect the Clergy and the people who proclaim thee Queen; hasten by the power of thy prayers the day when all nations shall be gathered together around the Supreme Pastor. Amen. Mary, help of Christians, pray for us.

274. Prayer to Our Lady Help of Christians.

200 Days, once a day.

(See Instructions, p. 1.)

MOST powerful Virgin, loving help of the Christian people, what thanks are not due to thee from us for the help thou didst give to our fathers, who, when threatened by the infidel Turk, invoked thy maternal aid by devoutly reciting the Rosary. From heaven thou didst behold their danger, thou didst hear their pitiful voices, thou didst lend a favourable ear to the humble prayer suggested by the great Pontiff, St Pius V, and didst promptly run to their assistance. Grant, O dear Mother, that the present and long continued groanings of the holy Spouse of CHRIST may penetrate to thy throne; may they again move thy compassion and arouse thee afresh to free her from the powerful enemies who surround her.

And so from every corner of the earth there rises to thy throne that precious prayer to make thee propitious now, as then, in our present calamity. Perchance our sins hinder, or at least retard, their effect. Therefore, dearest Mother, obtain for us true sorrow for them, and a firm purpose to be ready rather to face death than return to sin. Intolerable is the thought that through our fault the aid we so desperately need should be denied or delayed. Arise then, dear Mother, yielding to the prayers of the Catholic world, and beat down the pride of those wretched men who in their insolence outrage GOD, and would have that Church destroyed against which, by the infallible word of CHRIST, the gates of hell shall never prevail. Let it once more be seen that where thou dost arise to protect her the victory is assured, that though it may be delayed it is certain in the end; for so we are taught by the faith, which bids us hope through thee to be mercifully heard by GOD. Amen.

275. Prayer to Our Lady of Africa for the Conversion of the Mussulmans and other Infidels.

100 Days, once a day.

(See Instructions, p. 1.)

O THOU, our Lady of Africa, whose stainless heart is full of mercy and maternal compassion; consider the deep misery of the Mussulmans and other infidels of Africa; remember that the souls of these poor infidels are the work of the hands of thy divine SON, that they have been created in his image and redeemed at the price of his Precious Blood. Do not allow, O Mother of mercy, that these unhappy people, who are, like us, thy children, should continue to fall into hell, despite the merits of JESUS CHRIST and the most cruel death he suffered for their salvation. Obtain for them knowledge of our holy religion, and the grace to love, to embrace, and to practise it faithfully. And since thou art the mistress and sovereign of Africa, O Queen of the Apostles, be pleased to choose and send legions of holy missionaries to these abandoned countries, to conquer them, to rescue them from death and Satan, and to bring them into the fold of Holy Church. So shall we be all united in one and the same hope and in one and the same love, in thy stainless heart, and in the adorable Heart of thy divine SON our LORD JESUS CHRIST, who was crucified and died for the salvation of all men, and who rose full of glory, and liveth and reigneth in the unity of the FATHER and the HOLY SPIRIT, world without end. Amen.

276. Invocation to be said Morning and Evening.

200 Days, once a day.

(See Instructions, p. 1.)

M Y Mother, preserve me this day from mortal sin. Ave Maria *thrice*.

277. Prayer to Mary our Helper.

300 Days. T.Q.

(See Instructions, p. 1.)

M OST holy and immaculate Virgin Mary, our most tender Mother, and powerful Help of Christians, we dedicate ourselves entirely to thy most sweet love and holy service. We consecrate our minds with all their thoughts, our hearts with all their affections, our bodies with all their senses and powers, and we promise to desire always to work for the greater glory of GOD and for the salvation of souls. Meanwhile do thou, O incomparable Virgin, who hast always been the Help of the Christian people, continue to show thyself such, especially in these days. Humble the enemies of our holy religion, and frustrate their evil purposes. Enlighten and strengthen bishops and priests, and keep them ever united in obedience to the Pope, their infallible master. Preserve incautious youth from irreligion and vice. Promote holy vocations and increase the number of thy sacred ministers, that by means of them the Kingdom of JESUS CHRIST may be preserved among us, and extended to the farthest boundaries of the earth.

We pray thee also, most sweet Mother, to look at all times with compassion upon the young and thoughtless, exposed to so many dangers, and upon poor sinners and the dying; be for all a sweet hope, O Mary, Mother of Mercy and Gate of Heaven.

Also we pray thee for ourselves, O great Mother of GOD. Teach us to copy thy virtues and especially angelic modesty, profound humility, and ardent charity; so that by word and example we may, as far as is possible in our state of life, present in the midst of the world a living image of blessed JESUS thy SON, and may cause thee to be known and loved, and so may succeed in saving many souls.

Obtain for us, O Mary our Helper, that we may be all gathered under thy maternal mantle, that in temptation we may invoke thee promptly and confidently; in short, that the thought of thee, so good, so loving, and so dear, and the remembrance of the love which thou bearest to thy clients may be such a support to us, as to render us victorious over the enemies of our souls in life and in death, so that we may become thy crown in beautiful Paradise. Amen.

278. Prayer to Our Lady, Queen of Prophets.

100 Days, once a day.
(See Instructions, p. 1.)

TO thee, O Queen of Prophets, foreseen by them, Mother of GOD and of his people, to thee we have recourse in our necessities, confident that as thou thyself art the fulfilment of prophecy, so thou wilt desire the fulfilment of thy own words, bringing, out of all generations, N___ to call thee blessed. Say to all the erring for whom we beseech thee, and especially to N___

"Thy light has come." Say but one word to thy SON, and the glory of the LORD shall rise upon them, and the eyes of the blind shall be opened, and so they, wondering at the star, will follow into the house of bread, where, finding thy Child with thee, they will eat of the true bread and live for ever, possessing joy and gladness, while sorrow and sadness will disappear. O thou who art omnipotent in prayer, at whose request thy SON worked his first miracle, beg Him to say: "I the LORD will do this suddenly in its time," and grant to those for whom we pray, that they may draw water with joy at the fountains of the SAVIOUR. May it be granted to us all to be united with thee, O Mother, in singing thy *Magnificat* to Him thy SON, our LORD JESUS CHRIST, who with the FATHER and the HOLY SPIRIT liveth and reigneth one GOD world without end. Ave Maria. Magnificat (No. 215).

279. Prayer to Our Lady, Mother of Confidence.

200 Days, once a day.

(See Instructions, p. 1.)

OIMMACULATE Mary, when we venerate thee under the gracious title of Mother of Confidence, how our hearts overflow with the sweetest consolation, how we are moved to hope for every good gift from thee! That such a name should have been given to thee is a sign that none have recourse to thee in vain. Receive, then, with a mother's compassion these acts of homage, with which we earnestly pray thee to be propitious to us in every necessity. Above all we ask thee to make us live ever united to thee and thy divine Son Jesus.* Under thy escort we shall safely walk along the straight road; and so shall it be our lot to hear on the last day of our lives those consoling words: Come, O faithful servant, enter into the joy of thy Lord. Amen.

*N.B.—Clerics, in order to gain this Indulgence, must insert the following words: "and since in his goodness thy Son has chosen us to labour in his mystical vineyard, do thou, who desirest a rich harvest, bestow thy special care on us miserable creatures, that our work may be abundantly fruitful."

280. Prayer to Our Lady of Lourdes.

300 Days. T.Q.

(See Instructions, p. 1.)

O HOLY Mary, Mother of God, who to reanimate the faith of the world and draw men to thy divine Son, Jesus Christ our Lord, didst deign to appear at Lourdes; thou who, in order to render more manifest thy maternal tenderness, and to inspire our hearts with greater confidence, didst choose a simple little child as the confidant of thy mercy; thou who didst say: "I am the Immaculate Conception," to make us understand the priceless value of that innocence which is the pledge of the friendship of God; thou who by eighteen successive apparitions didst not cease by thy actions and words to urge men to prayer and penance, which alone can appease Heaven and ward off the blows of divine justice; thou who, by a moving appeal to the world, hast reunited before the miraculous grotto an innumerable multitude of thy children; behold us, Our Lady of Lourdes, prostrate at thy feet, and confident of obtaining blessings and graces from GOD by thy most powerful intercession.

Those who love thee, O Mother of JESUS CHRIST, Mother of men, desire above everything to serve GOD faithfully in this world, so as to have the happiness of loving Him eternally in Heaven. Listen to the prayers which we this day address to thee; defend us against the enemies of our salvation, and against our own infirmities; together with the pardon of our sins, obtain for us perseverance in the determination never to fall away again.

We implore thee also to take under thy protection our friends and benefactors, and of these in a very special manner those who have abandoned the practice of their Christian duties. May they be converted and become thy faithful servants.

We beseech thee also to bless our country. She has many failings, for which we must implore pardon; but in the midst of her wanderings from the right path, she has never ceased to proclaim through the best of her sons that thou art for ever her Mother and her Sovereign.

Thou hast always shown her thy love, and we hope that thou wilt not abandon her after having heaped thy favours and benefits upon her.

While we pour forth our hearts in prayer at thy feet, O Virgin Immaculate, Our Lady of Lourdes, we cannot forget our Holy FATHER, the Supreme Pontiff, and in his person the whole Catholic Church, which thy divine SON has entrusted to him to lead along the paths of eternal salvation.

He, too, places his whole trust in thee. Protect and bless him; be his support and consolation in the midst of his trials, and help him to extend the Kingdom of GOD. O Mother of mercy, be for us all "the cause of our joy," and "show unto us" JESUS CHRIST, as thy gift in this life and in eternity. Amen.

281. Ejaculation.

300 Days. T.Q.
          (See Instructions, p. 1.)

OUR Lady of Lourdes, pray for us.

282. Prayer to Our Lady "Reparatrice."

200 Days, once a day.
          (See Instructions, p. 1.)

IMMACULATE Virgin, the refuge of sinners, thou who, to repair the outrages committed against GOD, and the evil inflicted on man by sin, didst resign thyself to the death of thy divine SON, be ever propitious to us, and carry on thy work of zeal and love for us in heaven, where thou reignest so gloriously. We wish to be thy children, do thou show thyself a Mother to us; obtain from the divine Restorer, JESUS, that by applying to our souls the fruits of his Passion and Death, He may free us from the bonds of our iniquities. May He be our light in the darkness, our strength in weakness, our help in danger, so that after He has consoled us by his grace and love in time, He may permit us to see, possess and love Him in eternity. Amen.

283. Prayer to Our Lady of Lourdes for a Sick Person.

300 Days. T.Q.

(See Instructions, p. 1.)

O MARY, conceived without sin, our Lady of Lourdes, who dost draw from all parts thy children to the Grotto of the apparitions; thou never ceasest to encourage, by innumerable benefits, the filial confidence of those who have responded to thy invitation. Suffering in body and soul, I come in the company of thousands and thousands of poor sick people to throw myself at thy feet and implore thee to heal me. O Mother of goodness, and all-powerful with our LORD, grant that I may be delivered from my infirmities, and that I may be able to consecrate my renewed strength to the service of GOD and of my brethren. How sweet it would be for me to proclaim that I owe to thy intercession the restoration of my health, which, while bearing witness to thy goodness to me, might be also a motive of conversion for many a soul.

But I desire, above everything, to abandon myself into thy maternal hands. If it be the will of JESUS CHRIST, my divine SAVIOUR, to which thy will is ever united, that the chalice of my sufferings should not at present depart from me, I desire the grace to say, with resignation and love, that I, too, will the same. Cause me, then, to be penetrated to the depths of my heart with a full and perfect acceptance of that consoling and heaven-sent doctrine: that the GOD of goodness loves us infinitely, always and under all circumstances, but especially without doubt when he associates us with the sufferings of JESUS CHRIST and fastens us to his Cross.

O Immaculate Virgin, our Lady of Lourdes, Mother of a GOD who was a man of sorrows, thy divine SON wished thee to be at his side on Calvary, whilst He suffered and died for us. He loves thee as only GOD could love a mother, and yet He willed that thy soul should be pierced with a sword of grief, so that thy love for Him should be revealed, and expand by sharing in his inexpressible sufferings.

Obtain for me this grace, our Lady of Lourdes, consoler of the afflicted, health of the sick, that I may love GOD more and more, in proportion as He prolongs and aggravates my trials. This would be a miracle greater than my sudden and complete restoration. To restore my health a single word would suffice, spoken by thee in the name and with the power of Him who is thy SON, while He is also thy GOD; but that the grace of resignation in suffering should make me accept with joy my sickness and its many painful consequences, this I feel to be in an eminent degree the work of the Most High. I see that it is in some sort easier for GOD to heal my sufferings than to make me love them. But, if thou desirest it, my weakness will have for support a supernatural force which will render it victorious, and so manifest the extent of thy power.

Would that the pains of my malady, sanctified by submission to the divine will, could be united to the agony of my Divine Saviour; would that my tears, mixed with his tears and his blood, could effect the expiation of my past sins, and draw down the graces of resurrection on poor souls dying or dead in sin. May the abundance of thy gifts, O my God, be granted, I beseech Thee, in the name of thy Mother, especially to those who are united to me by ties of blood or friendship. Grant that my sufferings, until it shall please thee to put an end to them, may open for them a fountain of mercies.

O Mother of Sorrows and Mother of merciful bounty, who stood erect at the foot of the Cross, pray for us, that we may be made worthy of the promises of Christ. Amen.

284. Our Lady of Ransom.

Plenary. I, II, IV, T.Q.

(See Instructions, p. 1.)

This Indulgence, after the manner of the Portiuncula, may be gained between first vespers and sunset on September 24, the Feast of Our Lady of Ransom, as many times as a person visits a church or public chapel of the Order of Ransom, whether of men or women, or of the Third Order, or of confraternities.

285. Seven Saturdays of Our Lady of Ransom.

Plenary, to all who take part in this devotion in public, on one of the seven Saturdays. I, II, III, IV.

The church visited must, if possible, be a church or

chapel of the Religious of the Order of Ransom, as above.

(See Instructions, p. 1.)

286. Ejaculation to Our Lady "del Pilar" of Saragossa.

300 Days. T.Q.

(See Instructions, p. 1.)

MOST blessed Virgin of the Pillar, pray for us.

287. Ejaculation.

200 Days, once a day.

(See Instructions, p. 1.)

OUR LADY, deliverer of slaves, pray for us.

288. Ejaculation.

300 Days, once a day.

(See Instructions, p. 1.)

OUR LADY of Good Studies, pray for us.

XI. THE HOLY ANGELS

ST MICHAEL ARCHANGEL

289. Hymn, Antiphon, *etc.*

i. 200 Days, once a day.
ii. Plenary, once a month. I, II, IV.

(See Instructions, p. 1.)

TE splendor et virtus
  PATRIS,
Te vita JESU, cordium,
Ab ore qui pendent tuo,
Laudamus inter Angelos.

O JESUS! life-spring of
  the soul!
The FATHER's Power and
  Glory bright!
Thee with the Angels
  we extol;
From Thee they draw
  their life and light.

Tibi mille densa millium
Ducum corona militat:
Sed explicat victor
  crucem
Michael salutis signifer.

Thy thousand, thousand
  hosts are spread,
Embattled o'er the azure
  sky;
But Michael bears thy
  standard dread,
And lifts the mighty
  Cross on high.

Draconis hic dirum
  caput
In ima pellit tartara,
Ducemque cum rebel-
  libus
Cœlesti ab arce fulminat.

He in that Sign the rebel
  powers
Did with their Dragon
  Prince expel;
And hurled them from
  the Heaven's high
  towers,
Down like a thunderbolt
  to hell.

Contra ducem superbiæ
Sequamur hunc nos
  Principem,
Ut detur ex AGNI throno
Nobis corona gloriæ.

Grant us with Michael
  still, O LORD,
Against the Prince of
  Pride to fight;
So may a crown be our
  reward,

Patri, simulque Filio,
Tibi que, Sancte
   Spiritus,
Sicut fuit, sit jugiter
Sæclum per omne glo-
   ria. Amen.

Before the Lamb's pure
   throne of light.
To God the Father and
   the Son,
Who rose from death, all
   glory be;
With Thee, O blessed
   Paraclete,
Henceforth through all
   eternity.
Amen.

Ant. Princeps glo-
riosissime, Michael
Archangele, esto mem-
or nostri: hic et ubique
semper precare pro no-
bis Filium Dei.

Ant. Most glorious
Prince, Michael the
Archangel, be mind-
ful of us: pray for us
always both here and
everywhere to the Son
of God.

℣. In conspectu angelo-
rum psallam tibi, Deus
meus.

℣. In the sight of the
Angels I will sing
psalms to Thee, O my
God.

℟. Adorabo ad templum
sanctum tuum, et con-
fitebor nomini tuo.
Oremus.

℟. I will adore at thy
holy temple, and will
confess to thy name.
Let us pray.

Deus, qui miro or-
dine angelorum
ministeria, hominum-
que dispensas: con-
cede propitius, ut a

O God, who dispos-
est the services of
Angels and men in a
wonderful order; mer-
cifully grant that those

quibus tibi ministran-
tibus in cœlo semper
assistitur, ab his in
terra vita nostra mu-
niatur. Per CHRISTUM
DOMINUM, *etc.*

who ever stand before
Thee, ministering to
Thee in Heaven, may
themselves also pro-
tect our life here upon
earth. Through CHRIST
our LORD. Amen.

290. Novena of St Michael.

    i. 300 Days, on each day.
    ii. Plenary, once during the Novena. I, II, IV.
            (See Instructions, p. 1.)
N.B.—The Novena may be made at any time of the
year, and with any form of prayers sanctioned by competent ecclesiastical authority.

291. Angelical Crown.

    i. Seven Years and Seven Quarantines.
    ii. 100 Days, daily, to any one who carries this Chaplet
       about him, or kisses the medal with the represen-
       tation of the Holy Angels appended to the said
       Chaplet.
    iii. Plenary, once a month. I, II, IV.
    iv. Plenary. I, II, IV, on:
     1. The Feast of the Apparition of St Michael, May 8.
     2. The Dedication of St Michael, September 29.
     3. St Gabriel the Archangel, March 18.
     4. St Raphael the Archangel, October 24.
     5. Holy Angel Guardians, October 2.
            (See Instructions, p. 1.)
To gain these Indulgences special beads must be used,
and they must have been blessed by a priest holding
from the Holy See general faculties for blessing rosaries, medals, etc.

℣. O GOD, come to my assistance.
℟. O LORD, make haste to help me.

Glory be to the FATHER, *etc.*

FIRST SALUTATION. PATER *once*, Ave *thrice, to the First Angelic Choir.*

AT the intercession of St Michael and the heavenly choir of the Seraphim, may it please GOD to make us worthy to receive into our hearts the fire of his perfect charity. Amen.

SECOND SALUTATION. PATER *once*, Ave *thrice, to the Second Angelic Choir.*

AT the intercession of St Michael and the heavenly choir of the Cherubim, may GOD grant us grace to abandon the ways of sin, and follow the path of Christian perfection. Amen.

THIRD SALUTATION. PATER *once*, Ave *thrice, to the Third Angelic Choir.*

AT the intercession of St Michael and the sacred choir of the Thrones, may it please GOD to infuse into our hearts a true and earnest spirit of humility. Amen.

FOURTH SALUTATION. PATER *once*, Ave *thrice, to the Fourth Angelic Choir.*

AT the intercession of St Michael and the heavenly choir of the Dominations, may it please GOD to grant us grace to have dominion over our senses, and to correct our depraved passions. Amen.

FIFTH SALUTATION. PATER *once*, Ave *thrice, to the Fifth Angelic Choir.*

AT the intercession of St Michael and the heavenly choir of the Powers, may GOD vouchsafe

to keep our souls from the wiles and temptations
of the devil. Amen.

SIXTH SALUTATION. PATER *once,* Ave *thrice, to the
Sixth Angelic Choir.*

AT the intercession of St Michael and the
choir of the admirable celestial Virtues, may
our LORD keep us from falling into temptations
and deliver us from evil. Amen.

SEVENTH SALUTATION. PATER *once,* Ave *thrice, to the
Seventh Angelic Choir.*

AT the intercession of St Michael and the
heavenly choir of the Principalities, may it
please GOD to fill our souls with the spirit of true
and hearty obedience. Amen.

EIGHTH SALUTATION. PATER *once,* Ave *thrice, to the
Eighth Angelic Choir.*

AT the intercession of St Michael and the
heavenly choir of Archangels, may it please
GOD to grant us the gift of perseverance in the
faith and in all good works, that we may thereby
be enabled to attain unto the glory of Paradise.
Amen.

NINTH SALUTATION. PATER *once,* Ave *thrice, to the
Ninth Angelic Choir.*

AT the intercession of St Michael and the
heavenly choir of Angels, may GOD vouchsafe to grant that the Holy Angels may protect us
during life, and after death may lead us into the
everlasting glory of heaven. Amen.

Then say PATER *noster four times in conclusion, the
first to St Michael, the second to St Gabriel, the third*

to St Raphael, the fourth to our Angel Guardian. Then end with the following Antiphon:

MICHAEL, glorious Prince, chief and champion of the heavenly host, guardian of the souls of men, conqueror of the rebel angels, who art set over the palace of GOD, our worthy captain under JESUS CHRIST, endowed with superhuman excellence and virtue; vouchsafe to free us from every evil, who with full confidence have recourse to thee; and by thy powerful protection enable us to make progress every day in the faithful service of our GOD.

℣. Pray for us, most blessed Michael, Prince of the Church of JESUS CHRIST.

℟. That we may be made worthy of his promises.

Let us pray.

ALMIGHTY and eternal GOD, who in thy own marvellous goodness and pity didst, for the common salvation of man, choose the glorious Archangel Michael to be the Prince of thy Church; make us worthy, we pray Thee, to be delivered by his beneficent protection from all our enemies, that at the hour of our death no one of them may approach to harm us, and that by the same Archangel Michael we may be introduced into the presence of thy high and heavenly Majesty. Through the merits of JESUS CHRIST our LORD, Amen.

292. Prayer to St Michael.

300 Days, once a day.

(See Instructions, p. 1.)

O GLORIOUS Archangel St Michael, Prince of the heavenly host, be our defence in the terrible warfare which we carry on against principalities and Powers, against the rulers of this world of darkness, spirits of evil. Come to the aid of man, whom GOD created immortal, made in his own image and likeness, and redeemed at a great price from the tyranny of the devil. Fight this day the battle of the LORD, together with the holy angels, as already thou hast fought the leader of the proud angels, Lucifer, and his apostate host, who were powerless to resist thee, nor was there place for them any longer in Heaven. That cruel, that ancient serpent, who is called the devil or Satan, who seduces the whole world, was cast into the abyss with his angels. Behold, this primeval enemy and slayer of men has taken courage. Transformed into an angel of light, he wanders about with all the multitude of wicked spirits, invading the earth in order to blot out the name of GOD and of his CHRIST, to seize upon, slay and cast into eternal perdition souls destined for the crown of eternal glory. This wicked dragon pours out, as a most impure flood, the venom of his malice on men of depraved mind and corrupt heart, the spirit of lying, of impiety, of blasphemy, and the pestilent breath of impurity, and of every vice and iniquity. These most crafty enemies have filled and inebriated with gall and bitterness the Church, the spouse of the immaculate Lamb, and have laid impious hands on her most sacred possessions. In the Holy Place itself, where has been set up the See of the most holy Peter and the Chair of Truth for the light of the world, they have raised the throne of their abominable impiety, with the iniquitous design that when the Pastor has been struck, the sheep may be scattered. Arise then, O invincible Prince, bring help against the attacks of the lost spirits to the people of GOD, and give them the victory. They venerate thee as their protector and patron; in thee holy Church glories as her defence against the malicious power of hell; to thee has GOD entrusted the souls of men to be established in heavenly beatitude. Oh, pray to the GOD of peace that He may put Satan under our feet, so far conquered that he may no longer be able to hold men in captivity and harm the Church. Offer our prayers in the sight of the Most High, so that they may quickly conciliate the mercies of the LORD; and beating down the dragon, the ancient serpent, who is the devil and Satan, do thou again make him captive in the abyss, that he may no longer seduce the nations. Amen.

℣. Behold the Cross of the LORD; be scattered ye hostile powers.

℟. The Lion of the tribe of Juda has conquered, the root of David.

℣. Let thy mercies be upon us, O LORD.

℟. As we have hoped in thee.

℣. O LORD, hear my prayer.

℟. And let my cry come unto thee.

Let us pray.

O GOD, the FATHER of our LORD JESUS CHRIST, we call upon thy holy name, and as suppliants we implore thy clemency, that by the intercession of

Mary, ever Virgin immaculate and our Mother, and of the glorious Archangel St Michael, thou wouldst deign to help us against Satan and all other unclean spirits, who wander about the world for the injury of the human race and the ruin of souls. Amen.

293. Antiphon.

100 Days, once a day.

(See Instructions, p. 1.)

ST MICHAEL Archangel, defend us in the day of battle, that we may not be lost in the dreadful judgment.

ST GABRIEL AND ST RAPHAEL

294. Novena.

i. 300 Days, each day.
ii. Plenary once during the Novena. I, II, IV.

(See Instructions, p. 1.)

A Novena to either of these Archangels may be made at any time of the year with any form of prayer sanctioned by competent ecclesiastical authority.

295. Prayer.

100 Days, once a day.

(See Instructions, p. 1.)

O GLORIOUS Archangel, St Raphael, great Prince of the heavenly court, illustrious for thy gifts of wisdom and grace, guide of those who journey by land or sea, consoler of the afflicted, and refuge of sinners; I beg thee to assist me in all my needs and in all the sufferings of this life, as once thou didst help the young Tobias on his travels. And because thou art the medicine of GOD, I humbly pray thee to heal the many infirmities of my soul, and the ills which afflict my body, if it be for my greater good. I specially ask of thee an angelic purity which may fit me to be the temple of the HOLY SPIRIT. Amen.

THE GUARDIAN ANGEL

296. Invocation.

   i. 100 Days. T.Q.
   ii. Plenary on October 2, Feast of the Guardian Angels, if said daily, morning and evening, for a year. I, II, III, IV.
   iii. Plenary, once a month. I, II, III, IV.
   iv. Plenary *in articulo mortis* (at the point of death) if frequently used.

(See Instructions, p. 1.)

ANGELE DEI, qui custos es mei, me tibi commissum pietate superna illumina, custodi, rege, et guberna. Amen.

ANGEL of GOD, whom GOD hath appointed to be my guardian, enlighten and protect, direct and govern me. Amen.

Or:

ANGEL of GOD, my guardian dear,
To whom his love commits me here,
Ever this day be at my side,
To light and guard, to rule and guide. Amen.

297. Novena of the Guardian Angel.

   i. 300 Days, each day.
   ii. Plenary, once during the Novena. I, II, IV.
   The Novena may be made at any time and with any
form of prayer sanctioned by competent ecclesiastical
authority.

XII. ST JOSEPH

298. Responsory, Antiphon, etc.

One Year. T.Q.

(See Instructions, p. 1.)

QUICUMQUE sanus
vivere,
Cursumque vitæ clau-
   dere,
In fine lætus expetit,
   Opem Josephi postulet.

Hic Sponsus almæ
   Virginis,
Paterque Jesu creditus,
Justus, fidelis, integer,
Quod poscit, orans
   impetrat.

TO all who would
holily live,
To all who would hap-
   pily die
St Joseph is ready to
   give,
Sure guidance, and help
   from on high.

Of Mary the spouse
   undefil'd,
Just, holy, and pure of all
   stain,
He asks of his own
   foster Child,
And needs but ask to
   obtain.

Here the first stanza is repeated.
Quicumque, *etc.*   To all, *etc.*

Fœno jacentem parvu-
lum
Adorat, et post exulem
Solatur; inde perditum
Quærit dolens, et
invenit.
    Quicumque, *etc.*

In the manger that Child
he adored
And nursed Him in exile
and flight;
Him, lost in his boy-
hood, deplored,
And found with amaze
and delight.
    To all, *etc.*

Mundi supremus artifex
Ejus labore pascitur,
Summi Parentis Filius
Obedit illi subditus.
    Quicumque, *etc.*

The Maker of heaven
and earth
By the labour of Joseph
was fed;
The Son by an infinite
birth
Submissive to Joseph
was made.
    To all, *etc.*

Adesse morti proximus
Cum Matre Jesum
conspicit,
Et inter ipsos jubilans
Dulci sopore solvitur.
    Quicumque, *etc.*

And when his last hour
drew nigh,
Oh, full of all joy was his
breast,
Seeing Jesus and Mary
close by,
As he tranquilly slum-
bered to rest.
    To all, *etc.*

Gloria Patri, et Filio,
et Spiritui Sancto.

All praise to the
Father above;
All praise to his glori-
ous Son;

All praise to the S<small>PIRIT</small> of love,
While the days of eternity run.

To all, *etc.*

Quicumque, *etc.*

Ant. Ecce fidelis servus, et prudens, quem constituit D<small>OMINUS</small> super familiam suam.
℣. Ora pro nobis, beate Joseph.
℟. Ut digni efficiamur promissionibus C<small>HRISTI</small>.
Oremus.

D<small>EUS</small> qui ineffabili providentia beatum Joseph Sanctissimæ Genitricis tuæ Sponsum eligere dignatus es; præsta, quæsumus, ut quem protectorem veneramur in terris intercessorem habere mereamur in cælis, qui vivis et regnas in sæcula sæculorum. Amen.

Ant. Behold the faithful and prudent servant whom the L<small>ORD</small> set over his house.
℣. Pray for us, holy Joseph.
℟. That we may be made worthy of the promises of C<small>HRIST</small>.
Let us pray.

O G<small>OD</small>, who in thy ineffable providence didst vouchsafe to choose blessed Joseph to be the spouse of thy most holy Mother, grant, we beseech Thee, that we may have him for our intercessor in Heaven, whom on earth we venerate as our most holy protector. Who livest and reignest, *etc.* Amen.

299. Psalms in honour of the Name of St Joseph.

   i. Seven Years and Seven Quarantines. T.Q.
   ii. Plenary once a month. I, II, IV.
  iii. Plenary on the Feast of the Patronage of St Joseph
     (third Sunday after Easter) to those who have fre-
     quently practised this devotion during the year. I,
     II.

(See Instructions, p. 1.)

Ant. Joseph vir Mariæ, de qua natus est JESUS, qui vocatur CHRISTUS.

J. Psalm, xcix.

JUBILATE DEO omnis terra: * servite DOMINO in lætitia.

Introite in conspectu ejus, * in exultatione.

Scitote, quoniam DOMINUS ipse est DEUS: * ipse fecit nos, et non ipsi nos.

Populus ejus, et oves pascuæ ejus: * introite portas ejus in confessione, atria ejus in hymnis; confitemini illi.

Laudate nomen ejus, quoniam suavis est DOMINUS, in æternum misericordia ejus: * et usque in generationem et generationem veritas ejus.

Gloria PATRI, *etc.*

Ant. Joseph vir Mariæ, de qua natus est JESUS, qui vocatur CHRISTUS.

Ant. Joseph de domo David, et nomen Virginis Maria.

O. Psalm, xlvi.

OMNES gentes, plaudite manibus: * jubilate DEO in voce exultationis.

Quoniam DOMINUS excelsus, terribilis, * rex magnus super omnem terram.

Subjecit populos nobis, * et gentes sub pedibus nostris.

Elegit nobis hæreditatem suam, speciem Jacob, quam dilexit.

Ascendit DEUS in jubilo, et DOMINUS in voce tubæ.

Psallite DEO nostro, psallite; *psallite regi nostro psallite.

Quoniam rex omnis terræ DEUS; * psallite sapienter.

Regnabit DEUS super gentes;* DEUS sedet supersedem sanctam suam.

Principes populorum congregati sunt cum DEO Abraham: * quoniam dii fortes terræ vehementer elevati sunt.

Gloria PATRI.

Ant. Joseph de domo David, et nomen Virginis Maria.

Ant. Joseph vir ejus, cum esset justus, et nollet eam traducere.

S. Psalm, cxxviii.

SÆPE expugnaverunt me a juventute mea: * dicat nunc Israel.

Sæpe expugnaverunt me a juventute mea: * etenim non potuerunt mihi.

Supra dorsum meum fabricaverunt peccatores: * prolongaverunt iniquitatem suam.

DOMINUS justus concidit cervices peccatorum: * confundantur, et convertantur retrorsum omnes, qui oderunt Sion.

Fiant sicut fœnum tectorum, * quod priusquam evellatur, exaruit.

De quo non implevit manum suam, qui metit, *
et sinum suum, qui manipulos colligit.

Et non dixerunt, qui præteribant: Benedictio
Domini super vos: * benediximus vobis in nomine
Domini.

Gloria Patri.

Ant. Joseph vir ejus, cum esset justus, et nollet
eam traducere.

Ant. Joseph fili David, noli timere accipere Mariam
conjugem tuum.

E. Psalm. lxxx.

EXULTATE Deo adjutori nostro:*jubilate Deo
Jacob.

Sumite psalmum, et date tympanum, *psalteri-
um jucundum cum cithara.

Buccinate in neomenia tuba, * in insigni die so-
lemnitatis vestræ.

Quia præceptum in Israel est,*et judicium Deo
Jacob.

Testimonium in Joseph posuit illud, cum exiret
de terra Ægypti: * linguam, quam non noverat,
audivit.

Divertit ab oneribus dorsum ejus: * manus ejus
in cophino servierunt.

In tribulatione invocasti me, et liberavi te: * ex-
audivi te in abscondito tempestatis; probavi te
apud aquam contradictionis.

Audi, populus meus, et contestabor te: * Israel
si audieris me, non erit in te Deus recens, neque
adorabis deum alienum.

Ego enim sum Dominus Deus tuus, qui eduxi te
de terra Ægypti; dilata os tuum, et implebo illud.

Et non audivit populus meus vocem meam: * et Israel non intendit mihi.

Et dimisi eos secundum desideria cordis eorum: * ibunt in adinventionibus suis.

Si populus meus audisset me, * Israel si in viis meis ambulasset:

Pro nihilo forsitan inimicos eorum humiliassem: *et super tribulantes eos misissem manum meam.

Inimici DOMINI mentiti sunt ei: * et erit tempus eorum in sæcula.

Et cibavit eos ex adipe frumenti; * et de petra melle saturavit eos.

Gloria PATRI.

Ant. Joseph fili David, noli timere accipere Mariam conjugem tuam.

Ant. Joseph, exurgens a somno, fecit sicut præcepit ei angelus.

PH. Psalm. lxxxvi.

FUNDAMENTA ejus in montibus sanctis: * diligit DOMINUS portas Sion super omnia tabernacula Jacob.

Gloriosa dicta sunt de te, * civitas DEI.

Memor ero Rahab et Babylonis * scientium me.

Ecce alienigenæ, et Tyrus, et populus Æthiopum, * hi fuerunt illic.

Numquid Sion dicet: Homo, et homo natus est in ea, * et ipse fundavit eam altissimus?

DOMINUS narrabit in scripturis populorum, et principum: *horum, qui fuerunt in ea.

Sicut lætantium omnium * habitatio est in te.

Gloria PATRI.

Ant. Joseph, exurgens a somno, fecit sicut præcepit ei angelus.

℣. Constituit eum DOMINUM domus suæ.
℟. Et principem omnis possessionis suæ.
Oremus.

DEUS, qui ineffabili providentia beatum Joseph sanctissimas Genitricis tuæ sponsum eligere dignatus es; præsta, quæsumus, ut quem protectorem veneramur in terris, intercessorem habere mereamur in cœlis. Qui vivis et regnas, *etc.*

HYMNUS.

DEI qui gratiæ impotes
Cœlestium dona expetunt,
Josephi nomen invocent,
Opemque poscant supplices.

Joseph vocato nomine
DEUS adest petentibus,
Auget piis quærentibus
Culpamque delet impiis.

Joseph piis quærentibus
Dantur beata munera,
Datur palma victoriæ
Agonis in certamine.

Amplexus inter Virginis,
Castæque prolis placido
Vitam sopore deserens,
Morientium fit regula.

Illo nihil potentius,
Cujus parentem nutibus,
Et subditum imperiis
DEUM viderunt æthera.

Illo nihil perfectius,

Qui sponsus almæ Virginis
Electus est, Altissimi
Custos, parensque creditus.

O ter beata et amplius
Honor sit tibi, Trinitas,
PATER, VERBUMque, et SPIRITUS,
Sanctoque Joseph nomini. Amen.

Ant. Adjutor est in tribulationibus, et protector omnibus beatus Joseph nomen suum pie invocantibus.

℣. Sit nomen beati Joseph benedictum,

℟. Ex hoc, nunc, et usque in sæculum.

Oremus.

DEUS, qui, mirabilis in sanctis tuis, mirabilior in beato Joseph, eum cælestium donorum dispensatorem super familiam tuam constituisti; præsta, quæsumus, ut cujus nomen devoti veneramur, ejus precibus et meritis adjuti ad portum salutis feliciter perveniamus. Per CHRISTUM DOMINUM nostrum. Amen.

300. Seven Sorrows and Seven Joys.

  i. 100 Days, once a day.
 ii. 300 Days, every Wednesday in the year, and every day of the two Novenas preceding the two Feasts of St Joseph, i.e., his principal Feast, March 19, and the Feast of his Patronage (third Sunday after Easter).
iii. Plenary, on each of these two Feasts, to all who shall say the prayers. I, II.
 iv. Plenary, once a month. I, II.
  v. 300 Days, on each of the first six Sundays, to all the faithful who say the Prayers on any seven consecutive Sundays in the year.

vi. Plenary, on each of the Seven Sundays. The same Indulgence is also granted to the illiterate, wherever this devotion is not publicly practised, provided only they say seven times *Pater noster, Ave Maria* and *Gloria Patri* instead of the Prayers which follow. I, II, III, IV.

(See Instructions, p. 1.)

I

PURE spouse of most holy Mary, glorious St Joseph, the trouble and anguish of thy heart were great when, being in sore perplexity, thou wast minded to put away thy stainless spouse; yet was thy joy inexpressible when the Archangel revealed to thee the sublime mystery of the Incarnation.

By this thy sorrow and thy joy, we pray thee comfort our souls now and in their last pains with the consolation of a well-spent life, and a holy death like unto thy own, with JESUS and Mary at our side. PATER, Ave, Gloria.

II

MOST blessed Patriarch, glorious St Joseph, chosen to the office of FATHER of the Word made Man, the pain was keen that thou didst feel when thou didst see the Infant JESUS born in abject poverty; but thy pain was changed into heavenly joy when thou didst hear the harmony of angel-choirs, and behold the glory of that night.

By this thy sorrow and thy joy, we pray thee obtain for us that, when the journey of our life is ended, we too may pass to that blessed land where we shall hear the angel-chants, and rejoice in the bright light of heavenly glory. PATER, Ave, Gloria.

III

OHOU who wast ever most obedient in exe-
cuting the law of GOD, glorious St Joseph,
thy heart was pierced with pain when the precious Blood of the Infant SAVIOUR was shed at his
Circumcision; but with the Name of JESUS new
life and heavenly joy returned to thee.

By this thy sorrow and thy joy, obtain for us
that, being freed, while we still live, from every
vice, we too may cheerfully die with the sweet
Name of JESUS in our hearts and on our lips.
PATER, Ave, Gloria.

IV

MOST faithful Saint, glorious St Joseph,
who wast admitted to take part in the redemption of man; the prophecy of Simeon foretelling the sufferings of JESUS and Mary caused
thee a pang like that of death, but, at the same
time, by his prediction of the salvation and glorious resurrection of innumerable souls, filled thee
with great joy.

By this thy sorrow and thy joy, help us with thy
prayers to be of the number of those who, by the
merits of JESUS and the intercession of his Virgin
Mother, shall be partakers of the resurrection to
glory. PATER, Ave, Gloria.

V

MOST watchful Guardian, glorious St
Joseph, who wast so intimately familiar
with the Incarnate SON of GOD, greatly thou didst
toil to nurture and to serve the SON of the Most
High, especially in the flight thou madest with
Him into Egypt; greatly also didst thou rejoice to

have God Himself always with thee, and to see the overthrow of the idols of Egypt.

By this thy sorrow and thy joy, obtain for us grace to keep far out of the reach of the enemy of our souls, by quitting all dangerous occasions, that so no idol of earthly affection may any longer occupy a place in our hearts, but that, being entirely devoted to the service of Jesus and Mary, we may live and die for them alone. Pater, Ave, Gloria.

VI

Angel on earth, glorious St Joseph, who didst so wonder to see the King of Heaven obedient to thy bidding, the consolation thou hadst at his return from Egypt was disturbed by the fear of Archelaus, but nevertheless, being reassured by the angel, thou didst go back and dwell happily at Nazareth, in the company of Jesus and Mary.

By this thy sorrow and thy joy, obtain for us that, having our hearts freed from idle fears, we may enjoy the peace of a tranquil conscience, dwelling safely with Jesus and Mary, and dying at last in their arms. Pater, Ave, Gloria.

VII

Example of holy living, glorious St Joseph, when through no fault of thine thou didst lose Jesus, the Holy Child, thou didst search for Him with great sorrow for three days, until with joy unspeakable thou didst find Him, who was thy Life, amidst the doctors in the Temple.

By this thy sorrow and thy joy, we pray thee with our whole hearts so to interpose always in our behalf, that we may never lose Jesus by mor-

tal sin, and if we are at any time so wretched as to
lose Him, then we pray thee to aid us to seek Him
with unwearied sorrow until we find Him, particularly in the hour of our death, that we may pass
from this life to enjoy Him for ever in heaven,
there to sing with thee his divine mercies without
end. PATER, Ave, Gloria.

Ant. JESUS Himself was about thirty years old,
being, as was supposed, the son of Joseph.

℣. Pray for us, holy Joseph.

℟. That we may be made worthy of the promises
of CHRIST.

Let us pray.

O GOD, who in thine ineffable providence didst
vouchsafe to choose blessed Joseph to be the
spouse of thy most holy Mother; grant, we beseech Thee, that we may have him for our intercessor in heaven, whom on earth we venerate
as our holy Protector. Who livest and reignest,
world without end. Amen.

301. Novena of St Joseph.

i. 300 Days, once a day.
ii. Plenary, during the Novena. I, II, IV.

(See Instructions, p. 1.)

This Novena may be made at any time of the year,
and with any form of prayer sanctioned by competent
ecclesiastical authority.

302. Month of March.

i. 300 Days, each day.
ii. Plenary, on any one day. I, II, IV.

(See Instructions, p. 1.)

The month may be either that of March, or a month

terminating on the Feast of St Joseph, March 19.

Persons legitimately hindered from practising this devotion in March may substitute any other month.

The devotion consists of any prayers or other pious practice in honour of the Saint.

303. Prayer.

300 Days, once a day.
(See Instructions, p. 1.)

REMEMBER, most pure spouse of Mary ever Virgin, my loving protector, St Joseph, that never has it been heard that anyone ever invoked thy protection, or besought aid of thee, without being consoled. In this confidence I come before thee, I fervently recommend myself to thee. Despise not my prayer, foster-father of our REDEEMER, but do thou in thy pity receive it. Amen.

304. Prayer.

100 Days, once a day.
(See Instructions, p. 1.)

VIRGINUM custos, et pater Sancte Joseph, cujus fideli custodiæ ipsa innocentia CHRISTUS JESUM, et Virgo virginum, Maria commissa fuit; te per hoc utrumque carissimum

GUARDIAN of virgins, and holy father Joseph, to whose faithful custody CHRIST JESUS, Innocence itself, and Mary, Virgin of virgins, were committed;

pignus, JESUM et Mariam, obsecro, et obtestor, ut me ab omni immunditia præservatum, mente incontaminata, puro corde et casto corpore JESU et Mariæ semper facias castissime famulari. Amen.

I pray and beseech thee, by these dear pledges, JESUS and Mary, that, being preserved from all uncleanness, I may with spotless mind, pure heart and chaste body, ever serve JESUS and Mary most chastely all the days of my life. Amen.

305. Prayer to St Joseph, Patron of the Universal Church.

100 Days, once a day.
(See Instructions, p. 1.)

O MOST powerful Patriarch, St Joseph, Patron of that universal Church which has always invoked thee in anxieties and tribulations; from the lofty seat of thy glory lovingly regard the Catholic world. Let it move thy paternal heart to see the mystical Spouse of CHRIST and his Vicar weakened by sorrow and persecuted by powerful enemies. We beseech thee, by the most bitter suffering thou didst experience on earth, to wipe away in mercy the tears of the revered Pontiff, to defend and liberate him, and to intercede with the Giver of peace and charity, that every hostile power being overcome and every error being destroyed, the whole Church may serve the GOD of

all blessings in perfect liberty: ut destructis ad-
versitatibus et erroribus universa Ecclesia secura
DEO serviat libertate. Amen.

306. Prayer.

300 Days, once a day.

(See Instructions, p. 1.)

O GLORIOUS St Joseph, chosen by GOD to
be the reputed father of JESUS, the most pure
spouse of Mary ever Virgin, and the head of the
Holy Family, and then elected by the Vicar of
CHRIST to be the heavenly Patron and Protector
of the Church founded by JESUS CHRIST; with
the greatest confidence I implore at this time
thy powerful aid for the entire Church militant.
Protect in a special manner with thy truly paternal love the Supreme Pontiff and all the bishops
and priests united to the See of St Peter. Defend
all those who labour for souls in the midst of the
afflictions and tribulations of this life, and obtain
the willing submission of every nation throughout the world to the Church, the necessary means
of salvation for all.

O dearest St Joseph, be pleased to accept the
consecration which I make to thee of myself. I
dedicate myself entirely to thee that thou mayest
ever be my father, my protector, and my guide in
the way of salvation. Obtain for me great purity of heart and a fervent love of the interior life.
Grant that after thy example all my actions may
be directed to the greater glory of GOD, in union
with the divine Heart of JESUS and the immacu-

late heart of Mary, and with thee. Finally, pray for me that I may be able to share in the peace and joy of thy most holy death. Amen.

307. Prayers for those in their Agony.

300 Days, once a day.
(See Instructions, p. 1.)

ETERNAL FATHER, by the love which Thou bearest to St Joseph, chosen by Thee from among all men to represent Thee on earth, have pity on us and on poor souls in their agony. PATER, Ave, Gloria.

Eternal and divine SON, by the love which Thou bearest to St Joseph, thy most faithful guardian on earth, have pity on us and on all poor souls in their agony. PATER, Ave, Gloria.

Eternal and divine SPIRIT, by the love Thou bearest to St Joseph, who with so great solicitude watched over most holy Mary the Spouse of thy predilection, have pity on us and on all poor souls in their agony. PATER, Ave, Gloria.

308. Prayer.

i. Seven Years and Seven Quarantines, if said after the Rosary in October.
ii. 300 Days, once a day, at other times (and in this case the words in italics are omitted).
(See Instructions, p. 1.)

TO thee, O blessed Joseph, do we fly in our tribulation, and having *implored the help of thy most holy spouse*, we confidently crave thy patronage *also*. Through that charity which bound thee to the Immaculate Virgin Mother of GOD, and through the paternal love with which thou didst embrace the Child JESUS, we humbly beseech thee graciously to regard the inheritance which JESUS CHRIST hath purchased by his Blood, and with thy power and strength to aid us in our necessities.

O most watchful Guardian of the Divine Family, defend the chosen children of JESUS CHRIST; O most loving FATHER, ward off from us every contagion of error and corrupting influence; O our most mighty protector, be propitious to us and from Heaven assist us in this our struggle with the power of darkness; and, as once thou didst rescue the Child JESUS from deadly peril, so now protect GOD's holy Church from the snares of the enemy and from all adversity: shield, too, each one of us by thy constant protection, so that, supported by thine example and thine aid, we may be able to live piously, to die holily, and to obtain eternal happiness in Heaven. Amen.

309. Prayer of St Bernadine of Siena.

100 Days, once a day.

(See Instructions, p. 1.)

MEMENTO nostri, beate Joseph; et tuæ orationis suffragio apud tuum putativum Filium intercede; sed et beatissimam Virginem Sponsam

BE mindful of us, O blessed Joseph, and intercede on our behalf with thy reputed SON; and secure for us the favour of thy most holy Virgin tuam nobis propitiam redde, quæ mater est ejus, qui cum PATRE et SPIRITU SANCTO vivit et regnat per infinita sæcula sæculorum. Amen.

Spouse, the Mother of Him who liveth and reigneth with the FATHER and the HOLY SPIRIT, world without end. Amen.

310. Invocation.

300 Days, once a day.
(See Instructions, p. 1.)

FAC nos innocuam, Joseph, decurrere vitam, sitque tuo semper tuta patrocinio.

GRANT, O holy Joseph, that, ever secure under thy protection, we may pass our lives without guilt.

311. Invocation.

300 Days, once a day.
(See Instructions, p. 1.)

ST JOSEPH, foster-father of our LORD JESUS CHRIST, and true spouse of Mary ever Virgin, pray for us.

312. Ejaculation.

100 Days, once a day.
(See Instructions, p. 1.)

ST JOSEPH, model and patron of those who love the Sacred Heart of JESUS, pray for us.

313. Prayer for the Observance of Sundays and Feast Days.

300 Days. T.Q.

(See Instructions, p. 1.)

MOST glorious Patriarch, St Joseph, obtain, we beseech thee, from our LORD JESUS CHRIST a most abundant blessing on all who keep festival days holy; obtain for us that those who profane them may know, in time, the great evil they commit, and the chastisements which they draw down upon themselves in this life and in the next, and may be converted without delay.

O most blessed St Joseph, thou who on the LORD's day didst cease from every labour of thy craft, and with JESUS and Mary didst fulfil the duties of religion with most lively devotion, bless the pious work of the sanctification of feast-days, erected under thy most powerful patronage; cause it to spread to every home, office, and workshop, so that the day may soon come when all the Christian populace may on feast-days abstain from forbidden work, seriously attend to the salvation of their souls, and give glory to GOD, who liveth and reigneth, world without end. Amen.

314. Prayer to St Joseph.

100 Days, twice a day.

(See Instructions, p. 1.)

O JOSEPH, virgo pater JESU, purissime sponse Virginis

O JOSEPH, virgin father of JESUS, most pure spouse of

Mariæ, quotidie dep-
recare pro nobis ipsum
JESUM FILIUM DEI, ut,
armis suæ gratiæ mu-
niti, legitime certantes
in vita ab eodem coro-
nemur in morte.

the Virgin Mary, pray
for us daily to the SON
of GOD, that, armed
with the weapons
of his grace, we may
fight as we ought in
life, and be crowned
by Him in death.

315. Prayer to St Joseph.

300 Days, once a day.
(See Instructions, p. 1.)

GLORIOUS St Joseph, model of all those who
are devoted to labour, obtain for me the grace
to work in a spirit of penance for the expiation of
my many sins; to work conscientiously, putting
the call of duty above my inclinations; to work
with gratitude and joy, considering it an honour to employ and develop, by means of labour,
the gifts received from GOD; to work with order,
peace, moderation and patience, without ever re-
coiling before weariness or difficulties; to work,
above all, with purity of intention, and with detachment from self, having always death before
my eyes and the account which I must render of
time lost, of talents wasted, of good omitted, of
vain complacency in success, so fatal to the work
of GOD. All for JESUS, all for Mary, all after thy
example, O Patriarch Joseph. Such shall be my
watchword in life and in death. Amen.

XIII. VARIOUS SAINTS

ST JOACHIM

316. Prayer.

300 Days, once a day.

(See Instructions, p. 1.)

O GREAT and glorious patriarch St Joachim, how I rejoice to think that thou wast chosen from among all the Saints to co-operate in the divine mysteries, and enrich the world by bestowing on it the great Mother of God, most holy Mary! By this singular privilege thou hast become so powerful with the Mother and the Son as to obtain whatever graces may be necessary for us. With great confidence, then, I have recourse to thy most powerful protection, and I commend to thee all the wants of my family, both spiritual and temporal, as well as my own; and especially I appeal to thee for the particular grace which I desire and expect from thy paternal intercession. And since thou wast a perfect model of the interior life, obtain for me interior recollection and a distaste for the fleeting goods of this earth, with a lively and persevering love of Jesus and Mary. Obtain for me, too, devotion and sincere obedience to Holy Church, and to the Supreme Pontiff who governs her, so that I may live and

die in Faith, Hope, and perfect Charity, invoking
the most holy names of JESUS and Mary, and may
save my soul. Amen. PATER, Ave, Gloria, *thrice.*

317. Prayer.

300 Days, once a day.

(See Instructions, p. 1.)

O JOACHIM sancte, conjux Annæ, PATER almæ Virginis, hic famulis confer salutis opem.

O HOLY Joachim, husband of Anne, father of the Blessed Virgin, bestow on thy servants here help and salvation.

318. Prayer.

300 Days, once a day.

(See Instructions, p. 1.)

O GREAT patriarch St Joachim, by that singular privilege by which thou wast chosen by
Divine Providence to present to the world that
Immaculate Queen in whom all nations should
be blessed, and who should bear in her virginal
bosom the salvation of the human race; we thy
devout clients rejoice with thee over this beautiful privilege, and we implore thy special protection for ourselves and our families. Do not allow,
O dear Saint, the devil or sin to have any place in
our souls, nor the perverse maxims of the world
to seduce us, nor permit us to live unmindful
of that eternity for which we have been created.
Obtain for us from GOD a firm faith, unshaken
by the impieties and errors which are scattered

abroad by sects hostile to the Church and to the Apostolic See, a sincere and constant affection for the Vicar of JESUS CHRIST, the Roman Pontiff, a generous and indomitable courage in refuting the calumnies uttered against everything that is most sacred and revered in our holy religion. Thou who art powerful through the love which thy holy daughter, Mary, bears thee, help on the cause of the Church, obtain for her the long-desired triumph, scatter the powers of darkness, humble their pride, and cause the light of truth and of the Faith to outshine every falsehood. Grant us, above everything, a tender and filial devotion to most holy Mary, thy dear daughter and our Mother, so that daily honouring her with devout homage we may deserve to be counted by her among the happy company of her children, and after the miseries of this exile to be brought by her to Paradise, there to praise the mercies of GOD for ever. Amen. PATER, Ave, Gloria, *thrice.*

ST ANNE

319. Prayer.

300 Days, once a day.
(See Instructions, p. 1.)

WITH deep and heartfelt veneration I prostrate myself before thee, O glorious St Anne. Thou art that creation of privilege and predilection, who through thy extraordinary virtues and sanctity wast worthy to receive from GOD the supreme grace of giving life to the treasure-house of all graces, blessed among women, Mother of the Word Incarnate, the most holy Virgin Mary. Deign, therefore, O most compassionate saint, for the sake of this lofty privilege, to receive me into the number of thy true followers, for such I protest I am and desire to remain so long as I may live. Surround me with thy powerful patronage, and obtain for me from GOD the grace to imitate those virtues with which thou wast so abundantly adorned. Grant that I may know and bitterly lament my sins. Obtain for me a most lively affection for JESUS and Mary, and fidelity and constancy in the practice of the duties of my state. Preserve me from every danger in life, and assist me in the moment of my death, so that, safe in Paradise, I may unite with thee, most blessed Mother, in praising the Word of GOD made man in the bosom of thy most pure child, the Virgin Mary. Amen. PATER, Ave, Gloria, *thrice.*

SS. PETER AND PAUL

320. Prayer.

i. 100 Days, once a day.
ii. Plenary, once on any Feast of St Peter and St Paul, or on one of the nine days preceding or eight days following such Feast. I, II, III, IV.
N.B.—The visit must be made to a church or altar dedicated to these Saints, and there the prayer must be recited.

(See Instructions, p. 1.)

OBLESSED Apostles Peter and Paul, I elect you this day for my special protectors and advo-

cates with GOD. In all humility I rejoice with thee,
blessed Peter, Prince of the Apostles, because
thou art the rock whereon GOD hath built his
Church; and I rejoice with thee, too, blessed Paul,
because thou wast chosen of GOD for a vessel of
election and a preacher of the truth throughout
the world. Obtain for me, I beseech you both, a
lively faith, firm hope, and perfect charity, entire
detachment from myself, contempt of the world,
patience in adversity, humility in prosperity, at-
tention in prayer, purity of heart, right intention
in my works, diligence in the fulfilment of all
the duties of my state of life, constancy in my
good resolutions, resignation to the holy will of
GOD, perseverance in Divine grace unto death;
that, having overcome, by your joint intercession
and your glorious merits, the temptations of the
world, the flesh and the devil, I may be made worthy to appear before the face of the chief and eternal Shepherd of Souls, JESUS CHRIST our LORD, to
enjoy Him and to love Him for all eternity, who
with the FATHER and the HOLY SPIRIT, liveth and
reigneth ever, world without end. Amen. PATER,
Ave, Gloria.

321. Responsory of St Peter.

i. 100 Days, once a day.
ii. Plenary, on the Feast of St Peter's Chair in Rome,
January 18, and also on the Feast of St Peter's
Chains, August I, II, III, IV.

(See Instructions, p. 1.)

N.B.—The visit must be to a church or altar dedicated
to St Peter.

SI vis patronum
quærere,
Si vis potentem vindi-
  cem,
Quid jam moraris?
  invoca
Apostolorum principem.

O sancte cœli Claviger,
Tu nos precando sub-
  leva;
Tu redde nobis pervia
Aulæ supernæ limina

Ut ipse multis pœnitens
Culpam rigasti lacrymis,
Sic nostra tolli poscimus
Fletu perenni crimina.
    O sancte cœli, *etc.*

Sicut fuisti ab angelo
Tuis solutus vinculis,
Tu nos iniquis exue
Tot implicatos nexibus.
    O sancte cœli, *etc.*

SEEK ye a patron to
defend
Your cause?—then, one
  and all,
Without delay upon the
  Prince
Of the Apostles call.

Blest holder of the heav-
  enly keys,
Thy prayers we all
  implore;
Unlock to us the sacred
  bars
Of heaven's eternal door.

By penitential tears thou
  didst
The path of life regain;
Teach us with thee to
  weep our sins,
And wash away their
  stain.
    Blest holder, *etc.*

The angel touch'd thee,
  and forthwith
Thy chains from off thee
  fell;
Oh, loose us from the
  subtle coils
That bind us fast to hell.
    Blest holder, *etc*

O firma Petra Ecclesiæ,
Columna flecti nescia,
Da robur et constantiam,
Error fidem ne subruat.
  O sancte cœli, *etc.*

Firm rock, whereon the
  Church is based,
Pillar that cannot bend,
With strength endue us;
  and the faith
From heresy defend.
      Blest holder, *etc.*

Romam tuo qui san-
  guine
Olim sacrasti, protege;
In teque confidentibus
Præsta salutem gentibus.
  O sancte cœli, *etc.*

Save Rome, which from
  the days of old
Thy blood hath sancti-
  fied;
And help the nations of
  the earth
That in thy help confide.
      Blest holder, *etc.*

Tu rem tuere publicam,
Qui te colunt, fidelium,
Ne læsa sit contagiis,
Ne scissa sit discordiis.
  O sancte cœli, *etc.*

Oh, worshipp'd by all
  Christendom,
Her realms in peace
  maintain;
Let no contagion sap her
  strength,
No discord rend in
  twain.
      Blest holder, *etc.*

Quos hostis antiquus
  dolos
Instruxit in nos, destrue;
Truces et iras comprime,
Ne clade nostra sœviat.
  O sancte cœli, *etc.*

The weapons which our
  ancient foe
Against us doth prepare,
Crush thou; nor suffer
  us to fall
Into his deadly snare.
      Blest holder, *etc.*

Contra furentis impetus
In morte vires suffice,
Ut et supremo vincere
Possimus in certamine.
          O sancte cœli, *etc.*

Guard us through life;
  and in that hour
When our last flight
  draws nigh,
O'er death, o'er hell, o'er
  Satan's power,
Gain us the victory.
          Blest holder, *etc.*

Gloria PATRI et FILIO et
  SPIRITUI SANCTO.
          O sancte cœli, *etc.*

Glory be to the FATHER
  and to the SON and to
  the HOLY SPIRIT.
          Blest holder, *etc.*

Ant. Tu es Pastor ovium,
Princeps Apostolorum;
tibi traditæ sunt claves
regni cœlorum.
℣. Tu es Petrus.
℟. Et super hanc pe-
tram ædificabo eccle-
siam meam.
Oremus.

Ant. Thou art the
Shepherd of the sheep,
Prince of the Apostles;
to thee were given the
keys of the Kingdom
of Heaven.
℣. Thou art Peter
℟. And upon this rock
will I build my Church.
Let us pray.

APOSTOLICIS
nos, DOMINE quæ-
sumus, beati Petri
Apostoli tui attolle
præsidiis: ut quanto
fragiliores sumus, tan-
to ejus intercessione
validioribus auxiliis
foveamur; et jugiter
apostolica defensione

O LORD, we beseech
Thee, raise us
up by the Apostolic
might of blessed Peter,
thy Apostle; that, the
weaker we are in our-
selves, the more pow-
erful may be the assis-
tance whereby we are

muniti, nec succumbamus vitiis, nec opprimamur adversis. Per CHRISTUM, *etc*.

strengthened through his intercession; that thus, ever fortified by the protection of thy Apostle, we may neither yield to sin nor be overwhelmed by adversity. Through CHRIST our LORD. Amen.

322. Responsory of St Paul.

i. 100 Days, once a day.
ii. Plenary, on January 25, the Feast of the Conversion of St Paul, and on June 30, the Feast of his Commemoration. I, II, III, IV.

(See Instructions, p. 1.)

N.B.—The visit must be to a church or altar dedicated to this Saint.

PRESSI malorum pondere
Adite Paulum supplices,
Qui certa largus desuper
Dabit salutis pignora.

ALL ye who groan beneath
A load of ills oppress'd,
Entreat St Paul, and he will pray
The LORD to give you rest.

O grata cœlo Victima
Doctorque, amorque, gentium,
O Paule, nos te vindicem,

O victim dear to Heaven!
O Paul, thou teacher true!

Nos te patronum posci-
mus.
Nam tu beato concitus
Divino amoris impetu,
Quos insecutor oderas,
Defensor inde am-
plecteris.
O grata, *etc.*

Thou love and joy of
Christendom,
To thee for help we sue.
Pierced by the flame of
love,
Descending from on
high,
'Twas thine to preach
the faith which once
Thou soughtest to
destroy.
O victim, *etc.*

Non te procellæ, et
verbera,
Non vincla, et ardor
hostium,
Non dira mors deterruit,
Ne sancto adesses cœtui.
O grata, *etc.*

Nor toil, nor threatened
death,
Nor tempest, scourge,
nor chain,
Could from the assem-
bly of the saints
Thy loving heart detain.
O victim, *etc.*

Amoris eja pristini
Ne sis, precamur, imme-
mor,
Et nos supernæ langui-
dos
In spem reducas gratiæ.
O grata, *etc.*

Oh, by that quenchless
love
Which burnt in thee of
yore,
Take pity on our mis-
eries,
Our fainting hope
restore.
O victim, *etc.*

Te destruantur auspice

True champion of the
LORD,

Sævæ inferorum
  machinæ,
Et nostra templa publicis
Petita votis insonent.
            O grata, etc

Crush thou the schemes
  of hell,
And with adoring mul-
  titudes
Thy sacred temples fill.
            O victim, etc.

Te deprecante floreat
Ignara damni charitas,
Quam nulla turbent
  jurgia,
Nec ullus error sauciet.
            O grata, etc.

Through thy prevailing
  prayer
May charity abound;
Sweet charity, which
  knows no ill,
Which nothing can
  confound.
            O victim, etc

Qua terra cumque
  diditur,
Jungatur uno fœdere,
Tuisque semper affluat
Salubre nectar litteris
            O grata, etc.

To earth's remotest
  shores
May one same faith
  extend;
And thy epistles through
  all climes
Their blessed perfume
  send.
            O victim, etc.

Det velle nos quod
  imperat,
Det posse Summus
  Arbiter,
Ne fluctuantes horridæ
Caligo noctis obruat.
            O grata, etc.

Grant us the will and
  power
To serve Thee, GOD of
  might,
Lest, wav'ring still and
  unprepared,
We sink in depths of
  night.

O victim, *etc.*

Gloria PATRI, et FILIO, *etc.*
O grata, *etc.*

Praise to the FATHER be;
Praise to the SON who
rose;
Praise to the SPIRIT
PARACLETE;
While age on ages flows.
O victim, *etc.*

Ant. Vas Electionis est mihi iste, ut portet nomen meum coram gentibus, et regibus, et filiis Israel.
℣. Ora pro nobis, sancte Paule Apostole.
℟. Ut digni efficiamur promissionibus CHRISTI.
Oremus.

OMNIPOTENS sempiterne DEUS, qui beato Apostolo tuo Paulo, quid faceret ut impleretur SPIRITU SANCTO, divina miseratione præcepisti; ejus dirigentibus monitis, et suffragantibus meritis concede, ut servientes tibi in timore et tremore, cœlestium

Ant. He is my Vessel of Election, to carry my Name among the gentiles and kings and the children of Israel.
℣. Pray for us, O blessed Apostle Paul.
℟. That we may be made worthy of the promises of CHRIST.
Let us pray.

ALMIGHTY and eternal GOD, who in thy divine compassion didst direct thy blessed Apostle Paul what to do that he might be filled with thy HOLY SPIRIT; grant that we may be so counselled by his teaching, and aided by the suffrage of his

donorum consolati-
one repleamur. Per
CHRISTUM DOMINUM
nostrum. Amen.

merits, that, serving
Thee in fear and trem-
bling, we may be filled
with the consolation
of thy heavenly gifts.
Through CHRIST our
LORD. Amen.

323. Veneration of St Peter's Statue.

i. 50 Days, to any one who shall, with contrite heart
and devotion, kiss the foot of the bronze statue of
this Apostle in St Peter's at Rome. IV. T.Q.

ii. 50 Days, once a day, for kissing the foot of a copy
of the said statue, blessed by the Sovereign Pontiff;
available for all the members of the family dwelling
in the house where the statue is kept. IV.

(See Instructions, p. 1.)

324. Prayer to St Paul.

300 Days, once a day.

(See Instructions, p. 1.)

O GLORIOUS St Paul, who from a persecu-
tor of the Christian name didst become an
Apostle of burning zeal, and who, in order that
JESUS CHRIST might be known to the furthermost
bounds of the earth, didst joyfully suffer impris-
onment, scourging, stoning, shipwreck, and every
kind of persecution, and who didst finally shed
thy blood to the last drop; obtain for us the grace
of accepting, as divine favours, the infirmities,
torments and calamities of this life, so that we
may not be drawn from the service of GOD by the
vicissitudes of this our exile, but on the contrary

may prove ourselves more and more faithful and fervent. Amen.

ST JOHN, APOSTLE & EVANGELIST

325. Prayer.

200 Days, once a day.
(See Instructions, p. 1.)

O GLORIOUS Apostle, who, on account of thy virginal purity, wast so beloved by JESUS as to deserve to lay thy head upon his divine breast, and to be left, in his place, as son to his most holy Mother; I beg thee to inflame me with a most ardent love towards JESUS and Mary. Obtain for me from our LORD that I, too, with a heart purified from earthly affections, may be made worthy to be ever united to JESUS as a faithful disciple, and to Mary as a devoted son, both here on earth and eternally in heaven. Amen.

ST EMIGDIUS, BISHOP & MARTYR

326. Prayer.

200 Days, once a day.
(See Instructions, p. 1.)

O GOD of infinite goodness, who hast given the crown of glory and honour to the martyred Bishop St Emigdius, we humbly pray Thee through his merits for that spirit of active faith which he inspired by his word and commended by his example, at last confirming the truth with

his blood. Deign, I beseech Thee, O LORD, to preserve me from ruin by earthquake, through the
intercession of this same glorious saint, to whom
Thou hast given special power to protect his clients from this fearful scourge. Amen.

327. Invocation.

100 Days, once a day.

(See Instructions, p. 1.)

BY the intercession and merits of the holy
FATHER Emigdius, from earthquake and all
evil deliver us, O LORD.

ST CHALCEDONIUS, MARTYR

328. Prayer.

100 Days, once a day.

(See Instructions, p. 1.)

MOST glorious martyr St Chalcedonius,
I rejoice with thee and return thanks to
GOD for the sublime glory to which He has raised
thee in Heaven, and specially for the great power
which He has conferred upon thee of obtaining
graces on behalf of those who are devout to thee.
Behold me, then, O blessed Chalcedonius, suppliant at thy feet, praying thee to come to the aid of
me, a humble client, and to obtain from GOD the
grace I ask of thee (*here insert the grace required*).
Most blessed Saint, be ever my advocate and protector; assist me in every approach of danger; succour me in all my necessities; free me from every

peril of soul and body; keep me under thy powerful patronage all my life long, and specially in the
awful moment of my death; that so, after having
enjoyed thy most powerful protection here on
earth, I may come to thank, praise, and enjoy GOD
with thee above in heaven for all eternity. Amen.

ST GREGORY VII

329. Prayer.

300 Days, once a day.
(See Instructions, p. 1.)

O INVINCIBLE defender of the liberty of the
Church, by that fortitude which thou didst
manifest, O glorious St Gregory, in maintain-
ing her rights against the powers of earth and
hell conspiring together, extend from heaven, we
pray thee, thy powerful arm over the Church, to
strengthen and defend her in the terrible warfare in which she is engaged at this very time.
Above all, encourage in the bitter struggle the august Pontiff, who has inherited with thy episcopal
chair some of the fearlessness of thine own heart,
and obtain that he may see his pious efforts
crowned by the triumph of the Church and the
return of the wandering to the right path. By thy
means let all the earth know, once for all, that it
is in vain to do battle against that faith which has
ever conquered and will ever conquer the world:
"hæc est victoria quæ vincit mundum, fides nostra,"—"this is the victory which overcomes the

world, our faith." This is the prayer which we
with one mind and heart send up to thee, and we
trust that after we have been heard on earth thou
wilt summon us one day to join thee in heaven in
the presence of the Eternal Pontiff, who with the
FATHER and the HOLY SPIRIT liveth and reigneth
for ever and ever. Amen.

ST PIUS V

330. Hymn.

   i. 40 Days, once a day.
   ii. Plenary from First Vespers till sunset on the Feast,
   May 5, if said before an altar or relic of the Saint,
   or in a Dominican church. I, II, IV.

(See Instructions, p. 1.)

BELLI tumultus in-
gruit,
Cultus DEI contemnitur;
Ultrixque culpam perse-
quens
Jam pœna terris im-
minet.

Quem nos in hoc discri-
mine
Cœlestium de sedibus
Præsentiorem vindicem,
Quam te, Pie, invocabi-
mus?

WARS and tu-
mults fill the
earth;
Men the fear of GOD
despise;
Retribution, vengeance,
wrath,
Brood upon the angry
skies.

Holy Pius! Pope sub-
lime!
Whom, in this most evil
time
Whom, of saints in bliss,
can we

Better call to aid than
thee?

Nemo, beate Pontifex,
Intensiore robore
Quam tu superni nu-
minis
Promovit in terris decus.
   Quem nos, etc.

None more mightily
than thou
Hath, by holy deed or
word,
Through the spacious
earth below
Spread the glory of the
LORD.
   Holy Pius, etc.

Ausisve fortioribus
Avertit a cervicibus,
Quod Christianis gen-
tibus
Jugum parabant barbari.
   Quem nos, etc.

Thine it was, O pontiff
brave!
Pontiff of eternal Rome!
From barbaric yoke to
save
Terror-stricken
Christendom.
   Holy Pius, etc.

Tu comparatis classibus,
Votis magis sed fervidis
Ad insulas Echinadas
Fundis tyrannum
 Thraciæ.
   Quem nos, etc.

When Lepanto's gulf
beheld,
Strewn upon its waters
fair,
Turkey's countless navy
yield
To the power of thy
prayer:
   Holy Pius, etc.

Absensque eodem
 tempore

Who meanwhile with
prophet's eye

Hostis fuit quo perditus,
Vides, et adstantes doces
Pugnæ secundos exitus.
    Quem nos, *etc*.

Didst the distant battle
  see,
And announce to stand-
  ers-by
That same moment's
  victory.
    Holy Pius, *etc*.

Majora qui cœlo potes,
Tu supplices nunc
  aspice,
Tu civium discordias
Compesce, et iras hos-
  tium.
    Quem nos, *etc*.

Mightier now and
  glorified,
Hear the suppliant cry
  we pour;
Crush rebellions haugh-
  ty pride;
Quell the din of rising
  war.
    Holy Pius, *etc*.

Precante te, pax aurea
Terras revisat; ut Deo
Tuti queamus reddere
Mox laetiora cantica.
    Quem nos, *etc*.

At thy prayer may gold-
  en peace
Down to earth descend
  again:
Licence, discord, trouble
  cease;
Justice, truth and order
  reign.
    Holy Pius, *etc*.

Tibi, beata Trinitas
Uni Deo sit gloria,
Laus, et potestas omnia
Per saeculorum sæcula.
  Amen.

To the Lord of endless
  days,
One Almighty Trinity,
Sempiternal glory,
  praise,

Honour, might, and
  blessing be.
> Holy Pius, *etc.*

℣. Ora pro nobis, beate
  Pie.
℟. Ut digni efficia-
  mur promissionibus
  Christi.
Oremus.

Deus, qui ad con-
  terendos ecclesiæ
tuæ hostes, et ad di-
vinum cultum repa-
randum beatum Pium
Pontificem Maximum
eligere dignatus es:
fac nos ipsius defendi
præsidiis, et ita tuis
inhærere obsequiis,ut
omnium hostium su-
peratis insidiis perpet-
ua pace lætemur. Per
Christum   Dominum
nostrum.
℟. Amen.

℣. Pray for us, blessed
Pius.
℟. That we may be
made worthy of the
promises of Christ.
Let us pray.

God, who, to the
  destruction of the
enemies of thy Church
and for the restoration
of thy holy worship
didst   vouchsafe   to
elect blessed Pius to
be thy High Priest;
grant us so to be de-
fended by his protec-
tion, and so to remain
steadfast in thy ser-
vice, that, overcoming
the snares of all our
enemies, we may en-
joy perpetual peace.
Through Christ our
Lord. Amen.

ST NICHOLAS OF BARI

331. Prayer.

50 Days, once a day.

(See Instructions, p. 1.)

ST NICHOLAS, my special protector, from that bright throne where thou dost enjoy the vision of thy GOD, in pity turn thine eyes upon me; obtain for me from GOD that grace and assistance of which, in my present necessities, spiritual and temporal, I am most in want, and especially the grace of N—, if such be expedient for my eternal welfare. Remember, moreover, O glorious and holy Bishop, our Sovereign Pontiff, the Holy Church, and this City of Rome. Bring back to the right way of salvation those who live steeped in sin or buried in the darkness of ignorance, error, and heresy. Comfort the sorrowing, provide for the needy, strengthen the weak-hearted, defend the oppressed, help the sick; let all experience the effects of thy powerful intercession with Him who is Supreme Giver of all good. Amen. PATER, Ave, Gloria.

℣. Pray for us, blessed Nicholas.

℟. That we may be made worthy of the promises of CHRIST.

Let us pray.

O GOD, who hast honoured and ceasest not daily to honour thy glorious Confessor and Pontiff, blessed Nicholas, with innumerable miracles; grant, we beseech Thee, that by his merits and prayers we may be delivered from the fire of hell and from all other dangers. Through CHRIST our LORD. Amen.

ST ALPHONSUS LIGUORI

332. Prayer.

200 Days, once a day.
(See Instructions, p. 1.)

O GLORIOUS Saint Alphonsus, my most beloved protector, thou who hast laboured and suffered so much to secure to men the fruits of Redemption, behold the miseries of my poor soul, and have pity on me. Through thy powerful intercession with JESUS and Mary, obtain for me true repentance, together with the pardon of my past faults, a great horror of sin, and strength always to resist temptation. Impart to me, I pray thee, a spark of that ardent charity with which thy heart was ever inflamed; and grant that, imitating thee, I may make the good pleasure of GOD the only rule of my life. Obtain for me, moreover, a fervent and constant love for JESUS CHRIST, and a tender and filial devotion to his Mother Mary, together with the grace to pray always, and to persevere in the service of GOD until my death; so that I may at length join with thee in praising GOD, and the most Blessed Virgin Mary, for all eternity. Amen.

ST LOUIS OF TOULOUSE

333. Prayer.

100 Days, once a day.

(See Instructions, p. 1.)

TO thee, St Louis, lily of virginity, brilliant star, and vessel of sanctity, we have recourse in prayer. Diffuse by thy intercession heavenly graces over the Catholic nations with which thou art united by ties of affinity, and over which thou hast been appointed protector by GOD. Implore of GOD and the Immaculate Virgin that the faith of our ancestors may again be revived among Christian people, that charity may burn, and virtuous living flourish. Obtain true peace for princes and their subjects, the triumph of our holy Mother the Church over her enemies, complete liberty for the Vicar of CHRIST on earth in his sacred government of souls, and for all of us who implore thine aid, eternal happiness in Heaven. Amen.

ST DOMINIC

334. Prayers.

i. 100 Days, once a day.
ii. Plenary, once a month. I, II, III, IV.

(See Instructions, p. 1.)

I

MY LORD JESUS CHRIST, who didst found the Church with thy Precious Blood, and by the preaching of the Apostles didst establish, propagate and extend it throughout the whole world, and thereafter didst commission the holy

Patriarch Dominic to adorn, illustrate, and defend
it with the splendour of his merits and doctrine;
graciously hear the prayers which this Apostolic
man incessantly offers to Thee for the increase of
her treasures, both spiritual and temporal. PATER,
Ave, Gloria.

II

MOST merciful REDEEMER, who didst choose
as thy fellow labourer for the salvation of
souls St Dominic, who by his zeal, aided by thy
grace, gained over to the Church so many heretics
who had been lost to her, and so many sinners
who had grieved her by their obstinacy; send, O
my GOD, ever fresh labourers into thy vineyard
to work for thy glory, and gather in the fruits of
eternal life. PATER, Ave, Gloria.

III

O GOOD JESUS, who didst delight to see St
Dominic prostrate every night before thy
altar, adoring Thee hidden in the most holy
Sacrament with most lively faith, and offering
up, now groans, now prayers, now penances on
behalf of the Church, at that time persecuted by
her enemies and profaned by her servants; defend this thy Spouse through the intercession of
St Dominic from the outrages and plots of the
infernal enemy of mankind. PATER, Ave, Gloria.

℣. Pray for us, St Dominic.

℟. That we may be made worthy of the promises
of CHRIST.

Let us pray.

GRANT, we beseech Thee, Almighty GOD, that
we who are weighed down by the burden of

our sins may be raised up by the patronage of thy blessed Confessor Dominic. Through CHRIST our LORD. Amen.

ST FRANCIS OF ASSISI

335. The Five Sundays.

Plenary, on each of the five Sundays. I, II, III, IV.

(See Instructions, p. 1.)

To all who apply themselves to meditation, vocal prayer or other good works, on any five successive Sundays, in honour of the Sacred Stigmata.

N.B.—Once in the year only.

336. Hymn.

100 Days, once a day.

(See Instructions, p. 1.)

O DIVI amoris victima,
Quino cruenta vulnere,
Francisce, qui vivam crucis
CHRISTI refers imaginem.

Tu caritatis fervidis
Flammis adustus, sanguinem
CHRISTO daturus, barbara
Ter cogitasti littora.

Voti sed impos, non sinis
Languere flammas desides:
Et excitas cœlestia,
Flagrans amore incendia.

In prole vivens efferas
Pervadis oras; algida

Gelu soluto, ut ferveant
Ardore sancto pectora.

Sic pertimendis lividum
Armis Avernum conteris;
Virtutis et firmum latus
Templo labenti subjicis.

Adsis, PATER, precantibus,
Ignemque, late quo tua
Exarsit ingens caritas,
Accende nostris mentibus.

Sit laus PATRI et FILIO,
Sit inclyto PARACLITO,
Qui nos parentis optimi
Det æmulari spiritum. Amen.

337. Feast of St Francis.

i. Plenary, on the Feast or during the Octave. I, II,
   III, IV.
ii. 300 Days, each day of public novena or month dedicated to the Saint.

(See Instructions, p. 1.)

THE SEVEN HOLY FOUNDERS OF
THE SERVANTS OF MARY

338. Prayer.

200 Days, once a day.

(See Instructions, p. 1.)

O MOST glorious Patriarchs, who by your sublime sanctity became worthy to be chosen by
the Mother of GOD herself to propagate the devo-

tion to her Dolours; at her bidding you separated
from the world, and, hidden in the rough caves of
Senario, chastised your bodies with unheard-of
penances and fed your spirit with the continual contemplation of the great mysteries of the
Faith, thus unconsciously preparing for the mission which was afterwards entrusted to you and
your Order, namely to eradicate sin and iniquity
from the hearts of men through compassion for
the Dolours of the Blessed Virgin Mary. Then,
bearing the Passion of JESUS and the sufferings
of his Mother deeply engraven on your hearts,
you strove everywhere to quell civil feuds, move
sinners to repentance, and bring back heretics
to the obedience of the Roman Pontiff. Deign,
O glorious Saints, now that you are reigning in
Heaven with CHRIST, deign from the thrones of
your glory to look down upon us, unfortunate pil-
grims, who have still to fight in this land of trial
and combat. The devil with his suggestions, the
world with its deceits, the flesh with its concupis-
cence, as so many roaring lions, are ever seeking
to devour us. Have then compassion on us, and
pour down into our hearts a portion at least of
that tender devotion to the Dolours of Mary with
which you were constantly penetrated, that the
sight of our Mother so afflicted may enable us to
resist the seductions of temptation, and preserve
us from renewing by sin the Passion of our divine
REDEEMER and Mary's sorrows. Obtain for us, we
beseech you, O powerful protectors, docility and
promptitude to answer the calls of GOD, detachment from the fallacious goods of this world, a

true spirit of mortification and penance, that, following on earth your examples of perfection and sanctity, we may deserve to join you in heaven, to praise for ever the tender mercies of our crucified REDEEMER and the glories of the Queen of Martyrs. Amen.

339. Seven Prayers.

100 Days, once a day.

(See Instructions, p. 1.)

I

O GLORIOUS Patriarchs, who, even in the midst of the corruption of the world, ever kept the fire of divine love burning in your hearts, and fostered a most tender devotion to the Queen of Heaven, thus deserving to be invited by her to leave the world the better to serve GOD; obtain for us, we beseech you, that we too, being inflamed with the fire of charity, may please the Most High, and imitating the love and patience of our sorrowful Mother, may conform ourselves, in adversity as well as in prosperity, to the dispositions of divine Providence. PATER, Ave, Gloria.

II

O BRIGHT models of perfection, who, having turned your backs on the world and renounced whatever it might offer you, did deserve, in answer to your wish of being entirely hidden from men, that Mary herself should point out to you Mount Senario as the place of your retreat and tranquillity; obtain for us, we beseech you, that, despising the false and contemptible pleasures of the earth, we may, after your example, embrace a life of penance to atone for our sins; and if we cannot, like you, serve our Lady in solitude, at least may we show her our sorrow for the grief we have caused her, when by our sins we have renewed the bitter Passion of her Divine SON. PATER, Ave, Gloria.

III

O MOST humble dwellers among the wild rocks of Senario, who, in order the better to imitate the heroic humility of the Handmaid of the LORD, did not only forget the nobility of your birth and the grandeur of your station, but with generosity humbled yourselves so deeply as to go and beg your scanty food in the streets of your native town; obtain for us, we beseech you, that no human respect may deter us from serving GOD, and that, as you, by an unheard of prodigy, merited to be called, by infants still at the breast, "Servants of Mary," so we too may edify and be a light to guide our brethren along the road to heaven; thus showing ourselves by our deeds to be devout servants of the august Mother of GOD. PATER, Ave, Gloria.

IV

O FAITHFUL servants of the Queen of Heaven, who wept so bitterly over the Dolours she suffered during the life and in the Passion and Death of her beloved SON, and were rewarded for it by the miracle of a vine putting forth ripe clusters in the midst of winter, by which she foreshadowed the propagation of the Order of her Servants, whose mission it would be to spread in

the Church compassion for her sorrows; obtain
for us, we beseech you, a most tender devotion
to our Lady of Sorrows, that we may, by this our
compassion, move our neighbour to sincere sorrow for his sins; thus becoming fruitful branches of the mystical vine of our LORD JESUS CHRIST.
PATER, Ave, Gloria.

V

O GLORIOUS Founders of the Order of the
Servants of Mary, who were filled with such
inexpressible sweetness, when you were made
worthy to see the Queen of Martyrs herself, who,
pointing to you the rule to follow and the habit
to wear in memory of her Dolours, showed you
also the palm which should be the reward of
your merits; obtain for us, we beseech you, to be
shown by our heavenly Lady in what manner we
may best serve her Divine SON, and thus attain
more surely to the possession of the eternal happiness which GOD in his mercy has prepared for
us in heaven. PATER, Ave, Gloria.

VI

O MOST austere penitents, who, by continually
chastising your bodies, became so rich in merits and so dear to our LORD that to show how well
pleased he was in you, he made your retreat of
Mount Senario a place of wonders, now causing
it to seem all girt about with fire, now showing it
covered with flowers and lilies of exquisite beauty, which the angels gathered and presented to
Mary; obtain for us, we beseech you, that the fire
of divine love be kindled in our hearts, and that
our souls, purified from all sin, may become to

the Queen of Heaven a garden of delight, from which we may offer to her choice flowers of virtues as so many tokens of our devotion. PATER, Ave, Gloria.

VII

O MOST blessed Patriarchs, angels of purity, seraphs of love, and martyrs of penance, who were all granted the privilege of a most happy death, one dying comforted by the presence of the Child JESUS, another audibly called by Mary herself to his eternal reward, this one taking his flight to Heaven under the appearance of flames, and that under the form of a dazzling lily; obtain for us, we beseech you, that, when the last hour comes for us, we may in that dread moment, through your intercession, be protected by our Lady of Sorrows against the wiles of the infernal foe, and breathing our souls into her maternal hands, be brought by her to Heaven, there to enjoy for ever the possession of GOD, who is the eternal source of all glory and sanctity. PATER, Ave, Gloria.

ST JOHN OF MATHA

340. Prayer.

100 Days, once a day.
                    (See Instructions, p. 1.)

G LORIOUS St John of Matha, thou who wast inflamed with a great love of GOD and a tender compassion for thy neighbour, and wast divinely chosen to found the famous Order of the

Holy Trinity, and didst spend thy days in glorifying that adorable mystery and in redeeming Christians from a miserable slavery; obtain for us, we beseech thee, the grace to pass our lives also in glorifying the most blessed Trinity, and in doing good to our neighbour, by works of Christian charity, so that it may be our happy portion to enjoy in Heaven the blessed vision of the FATHER, the SON, and the HOLY SPIRIT. Amen.

ST FRANCIS OF PAOLA

341. The Thirteen Fridays in honour of Christ and his Twelve Apostles.

    i. Plenary, on any one of the Fridays. I, II, IV.
    ii. Seven Years and Seven Quarantines, on each of the other Fridays. I, II, IV.
           (See Instructions, p. 1.)
  This Devotion consists in visiting on thirteen consecutive Fridays a church of the Minims; or in the case of those who dwell more than a mile from such a church, any church dedicated to St Francis, or an altar where there is a picture of the Saint, or in default of these the parish church.

ST IGNATIUS LOYOLA

342. The Ten Sundays.

  Plenary, on each of the Sundays. I, II, IV.
           (See Instructions, p. 1.)
  This Devotion consists of meditation, vocal prayers, or good works performed for the glory of GOD and in honour of the Saint, with a visit to a Jesuit church, or in

default of such, the parish church, on ten consecutive Sundays.

N.B.—Once in the year only.

343. Prayer.

200 Days, once a day.

(See Instructions, p. 1.)

O GLORIOUS Patriarch St Ignatius, we humbly beseech thee to obtain for us from GOD freedom, above all things, from sin, the greatest of evils, and then escape from the deadly disease of cholera, one of those terrible scourges with which the LORD punishes the sins of the people. May thy example inflame our hearts with an efficacious desire to labour continually for the greater glory of GOD and the good of our neighbour; and obtain from the loving Heart of JESUS, our LORD, the crown of all other graces, the gift of final perseverance, and eternal beatitude.

ST PHILIP NERI

344. Prayers for every Day of the Week.

50 Days, once a day.

(See Instructions, p. 1.)

FOR SUNDAY. *Prayer to obtain the virtue of Humility.*

ST PHILIP, my glorious patron, who on earth didst so love humility as to count the praise and even the good esteem of men as dross; obtain for me also this virtue by thy prayers. Thou knowest how haughty I am in my thoughts, how contemptuous in my words, how ambitious in my works. Ask for me humility of heart, that my mind may be freed from all pride, and impressed with the same low esteem of self which thou hadst of thyself, counting thyself the worst of all men, and for that reason rejoicing when thou didst suffer contempt, and seeking out for thyself occasions of enduring it. Great saint, obtain for me a truly humble heart and the knowledge of my own nothingness; that I may rejoice when I am despised, and chafe not when others are preferred before me; that I may never be vain when I am praised, but may ever seek only to be great in the eyes of GOD, desiring to receive from Him alone all my exaltation. PATER, Ave, Gloria.

FOR MONDAY. *Prayer to obtain the virtue of Patience.*

ST PHILIP, my patron Saint, whose heart was ever so constant in time of trouble, and whose spirit was so loving under suffering that, when persecuted by the jealous, or calumniated by the wicked who thought to discredit thy sanctity, or, when tried by GOD with many long painful infirmities, thou didst always bear thy trials with wonderful tranquillity of heart and mind; pray for me that I may have a spirit of true courage in every adversity. Alas, how much I stand in need of patience! I shrink from every little trouble; I sicken under every light affliction; I fire up at and resent every trifling contradiction; never setting myself to learn that the road to Paradise lies amidst the thorns of tribulation. Yet was this the path our Divine Master deigned to tread, and this too, my saintly patron, was thy path also. Obtain for me, then, this courage, that with good hearty will I may embrace the crosses which every day I receive from GOD, and bear them all with the same endurance and ready will which thou didst manifest on earth; that so I may be made worthy to enjoy the blessed fruit of sufferings with thee in heaven above. PATER, Ave, Gloria.

FOR TUESDAY. *Prayer to obtain the virtue of Purity.*

ST PHILIP, who didst ever keep unsullied the lily of purity, so that the glory of this fair virtue dwelt in thy eyes, shone forth from thy hands, and cast its fragrance over thy whole body, causing it to emit so sweet a perfume that it gave consolation, fervour, and devotion to all who conversed with thee; obtain for me from the HOLY SPIRIT of GOD so true a love for that virtue that neither the words nor bad examples of sinners may ever make any impression upon my soul. Never permit me in any way to lose that lovely virtue; and since avoidance of occasions, prayer, labour, humility, mortification of the senses, frequent use of the Sacraments, were the arms with which thou didst conquer the flesh, which is our worst enemy, so do thou obtain for me grace to use the same arms to vanquish the same foe. Take not away thy help from me; but be as zealous for me as thou wast during thy life for thy penitents, keeping them far removed from all infection of the senses. Do this for me, my holy patron; and be my protector and pattern in this fair virtue. PATER, Ave, Gloria.

FOR WEDNESDAY. *Prayer to obtain the Love of GOD.*

ST PHILIP, I am filled with wonder at the great miracle which was wrought in thee by the HOLY SPIRIT when He poured into thy heart such a flood of heavenly charity that, in order to contain it, two of thy ribs were broken by the power of Divine love; and I am confounded when I compare thy heart with my own. I see thy heart all burning with love, and mine all frozen and taken up with creatures. I see thine inflamed with a fire from heaven, which so filled thy body that it radiated like flames from thy countenance, while mine is full of earthly love. I love the world, which allures me and can never make me happy; I love the flesh, which ever wears me with its cares and can never render me immortal; I love riches, which I can enjoy but for a moment. Oh, when shall I learn of thee to love nothing but GOD, my incomprehensible and only Good. Help me, then, blessed patron, that by thy intercession I may begin at once: obtain for me an efficacious love, manifesting itself by works; a pure love, making me love GOD most perfectly; a strong love, enabling me to surmount all obstacles hindering my union with GOD in life, that so I may be wholly united to Him for ever after my death. PATER, Ave, Gloria.

FOR THURSDAY. *Prayer to obtain the Love of our Neighbor.*

GLORIOUS Saint, who didst devote thyself wholly to the good of thy neighbour, thinking well of all, sympathizing with all, helping all; who throughout thy whole life didst ever try to secure

the salvation of all, never shrinking from labour
or trouble, keeping for thyself no time or comfort, that thou mightest win all hearts to GOD;
pray for me, that, together with the pardon of all
my sins, I may have charity for my neighbour, and
be henceforth more compassionate to him in his
necessities; and obtain for me grace that I may
love every man with pure unselfish love as my
own brother, succouring each one, if I am unable
to do it with temporal good, at least with prayers
and good advice. And teach me too, on every occasion, to defend the honour of my neighbour,
and never to say to him a hurtful or displeasing
word; but ever to maintain, even with my enemies, sweetness of spirit like thy own, whereby
thou didst triumph over thy persecutors. Blessed
Saint, ask of GOD for me also this lovely virtue,
which already thou hast gained for so many of
thy clients; that so we may all one day come to
praise our GOD with thee in an eternity of bliss.
PATER, Ave, Gloria.

FOR FRIDAY. *Prayer to obtain Detachment from
Temporal Goods.*

GREAT Saint, who didst prefer a poor and austere life to the comforts of thy home, despising the honour and glory of thy station; obtain
for me grace ever to keep my heart detached from
the transitory goods of this life. St Philip, whose
desire it ever was to become so poor as one day
to beg thy bread, and not to find the charitable
hand to offer thee a crumb wherewith to support life; ask of GOD for me such love of poverty

that I may turn all my thoughts to goods which
never fail. St Philip, who didst prefer to live un-
known to promotion to the highest honours of
the Holy Church; intercede for me that I may never seek after dignities, but always content myself
with that state where GOD has set me. My heart
is too anxious for the empty fleeting things of
this earth, but do thou obtain for me, that the
great lesson contained in the words "And then?"
whence followed so many wonderful conversions,
may ever be deeply impressed upon my soul; that,
despising the nothingness of earth, GOD alone
may reign sole object of my affections and my
thoughts. PATER, Ave, Gloria.

FOR SATURDAY. *Prayer to obtain Perseverance in
Good Works.*

ST PHILIP, my holy patron, who, ever constant in good works and full of merit, didst
receive from the Most High GOD the crown of
glory in reward of all thy labours, obtain for me
grace never to weary in his service. St Philip, who
didst recompense those who loved thee by acquiring for them the gift of perseverance in good,
ask of GOD this gift for me; stand by me, dear
father, at the last moment of my life, and pray for
me that I may depart this life strengthened with
the grace of the Holy Sacraments. Meanwhile, intercede for me, that I may do penance for my sins,
and deplore them bitterly all my days. St Philip,
who from on high beholdest all my miseries, and
the chains which yet bind me to my sins and to
this earth; pray for me that I may be liberated

from them, and be constantly devoted to my GOD.
Obtain for me an ardent desire to co-operate in
my own salvation, and unshaken firmness in the
good which I have begun; that so, by thy intercession, I may deserve to be for ever in thy company
in an eternity of bliss. PATER, Ave, Gloria.

345. Prayer.

100 Days, once a day.
(See Instructions, p. 1.)

O GLORIOUS St Philip, who wast so favoured
by GOD while consoling and helping thy spiritual children in the hour of their death; be to me
an advocate and father at the awful moment of
my passage to eternity. Obtain for me the grace
that Satan may not overcome me, temptation oppress me, or fear unnerve me in that hour; but
that, fortified by a lively faith, a firm hope, and
a sincere charity, I may bear with patience and
perseverance this last conflict; so that, full of trust
in the mercy of GOD, the infinite merits of JESUS
CHRIST, and the protection of most holy Mary, I
may be worthy to die the death of the just, and
to enter the blessed country of Paradise, there to
love and enjoy GOD, together with thee and all
the saints forever. Amen.

ST JOSEPH CALASANCTIUS

346. Prayer.

200 Days, once a day.

(See Instructions, p. 1.)

O BLESSED St Joseph Calasanctius, protector of the young, great servant of our LORD, who didst perform such great and wondrous works on their behalf; thou who didst make thyself a mirror to them of most ardent charity, of invincible patience, of most profound humility, of angelic purity, and of every other heroic virtue; and who by thy holy words and example, full of the spirit of GOD, didst excite them to fly dangerous occasions, to abhor vice, to hate sin, to love piety and devotion, and so didst guide innumerable souls to Heaven; thou who didst obtain for them the blessing of the infant JESUS and his most blessed Mother, visibly bestowed; O great advocate and most loving father, obtain for us too, thy humble and devout clients, a constant hatred of sin, victory over temptation, help in peril, and profit from study; that so, by acquiring the fullness of true wisdom, which is the holy fear of GOD, we may attain to eternal life. Amen.

ST CAMILLUS OF LELLIS

347. The Seven Sundays.

i. Seven Years and Seven Quarantines on each Sunday,
ii. Plenary, on the seventh Sunday. I, II, III, IV.

(See Instructions, p. 1.)

This devotion consists of any prayer in honour of the Saint, recited on any seven consecutive Sundays.

348. Prayer.

200 Days, once a day.

(See Instructions, p. 1.)

GLORIOUS St Camillus, special protector of poor sick people, who for forty years, with a charity truly heroic, didst devote thyself to alleviating their spiritual and corporal miseries; be pleased to succour them still more generously, now that thou art happy in Heaven and that they have been confided by the Church to thy powerful protection. Obtain for them from GOD either that they may be healed of the evils from which they are suffering, or that by patience and Christian resignation they may be sanctified and strengthened in the hour of their death; and obtain also for us the grace to live and die, after thy example, in the practice of divine love. Amen. PATER, Ave.

ST VINCENT OF PAUL

349. Novena.

i. 300 Days, each day.
ii. Plenary, during the Novena. I, II, IV.

(See Instructions, p. 1.)

This Novena in honour of the saint may be made at any time, and with any form of prayer sanctioned by competent ecclesiastical authority.

350. Prayer.

100 Days, once a day.

(See Instructions, p. 1.)

OGLORIOUS St Vincent, heavenly patron of all charitable associations and father of all the unfortunate, who in thy lifetime didst not reject anyone who had recourse to thee; see now by how many evils we are oppressed, and come to our assistance. Obtain from our Lord help for the poor, solace for the sick, consolation for the afflicted, protection for the abandoned, charity for the rich, conversion for sinners, zeal for priests, peace for the Church, tranquillity among nations, and salvation for all. May all feel the effects of thy merciful intercession, so that, sustained by thee in the miseries of this life, we may be able to join thee above, where there will be no more strife, lamentation or sorrow, but joy, exultation, and beatitude for ever. Amen.

ST PAUL OF THE CROSS

351. Prayer.

i. One Year, once a day.
ii. Plenary, on the Feast (April 28) or within the Octave, if said for a month preceding the Feast. I, II.

(See Instructions, p. 1.)

OGLORIOUS St Paul, thou who, while on earth, wast a mirror of innocence and a model of penance! O hero of sanctity, specially chosen by God to meditate night and day on the

most bitter Passion of his only-begotten Son,
and to propagate the same devotion throughout
the world, by word, by example, and by means
of thy institute! O Apostle, powerful in word
and work, who didst spend thy life in bringing
back the wandering souls of wretched sinners to
the feet of the Crucified, look graciously down
from heaven upon my soul, and hear my prayers.
Obtain for me so great a love of Jesus suffering
that, ever meditating on his Passion, I may make
his sufferings mine; that I may recognize in the
deep wounds of my Saviour the wickedness of
my sins, and may draw from them, as from so
many founts of salvation, the grace of lamenting
them bitterly, and a firm will to imitate thee in
penance, if I have not followed thee in innocence.
Procure for me, O St Paul, the grace which here,
at thy feet, I particularly and earnestly beg of thee
(*here mention the grace desired*). Moreover, obtain
for our holy Mother the Church victory over her
enemies; obtain conversion of sinners, and a return to the Catholic Faith of all heretical nations,
particularly England, for which thou didst pray
so much. Finally, intercede for me with God that
I may die a holy death, and come to enjoy Him
with thee in heaven, for all eternity. Amen. Pater,
Ave, Gloria.

352. Novena.

    i. 300 Days, on each day.
    ii. Plenary, at the end of the Novena. I, II, IV.
               (See Instructions, p. 1.)
   Any form of prayers may be used.

ST PETER FOURIER

353. Prayer.

300 Days, once a day.

(See Instructions, p. 1.)

O GLORIOUS St Peter, lily of purity, example of Christian perfection, model of priestly zeal; by that glory which as a reward of thy merits has been bestowed on thee in heaven, look upon us kindly, and come to our assistance before the throne of the Most High. On earth thou didst make this maxim specially thy own, having it ever on thy lips, "Injure no one, give joy to all," and, armed with this, didst spend thy whole life in succouring the wretched, counselling the doubtful, comforting the afflicted, bringing back the strayed to the path of virtue, restoring to JESUS CHRIST souls redeemed by his Precious Blood. Now that thou art so powerful in heaven, continue thy labour of helping all, and be to us a watchful protector, so that, freed by thy intercession from temporal evils, and confirmed in faith and charity, we may overcome the snares of the enemies of our salvation, and be able one day with thee to praise and bless our LORD in Paradise for ever. Amen.

ST THOMAS AQUINAS

354. Prayer to St Thomas, Patron of Schools.

200 Days, once a day.

(See Instructions, p. 1.)

DOCTOR angelice, Sancte Thoma, theologorum princeps et philosophorum norma, præclarum Christiani orbisdecus et ecclesiæ lumen, scholarum omnium Catholicarum cœlestis patrone, qui sapientiam sine fictione didicisti et sine invidia communicas, ipsam Sapientiam, FILIUM DEI, de precare pro nobis, ut veniente in nos spiritus sapientiæ, ea quæ docuisti intellectu, conspiciamus et quæ egisti imitatione compleamus; doctrinæ et virtutis, quibus in terris solis instar semper eluxisti, participes efficiamur; ac tandem earum suavissimis fructibus perenniter tecum delectemur in cœlis, Divinam Sapientiam collaudantes per infinita sæcula sæculorum. Amen.

ANGELIC Doctor St Thomas, prince of theologians and model of philosophers, bright ornament of the Christian world and light of the Church; O heavenly patron of all Catholic schools, who didst learn wisdom without guile and dost communicate it without envy, intercede for us with the SON of GOD, Wisdom itself, that the spirit of wisdom may descend upon us, and enable us to understand clearly that which thou hast taught, and fulfil it by imitating thy deeds; to become partakers of that doctrine & virtue which caused thee to shine like the sun on earth; and at last to rejoice with thee for ever in their most sweet fruits in Heaven together praising the Divine Wisdom for all eternity. Amen.

355. Little Office of St Thomas Aquinas.

300 Days, once a day.
(See Instructions, p. 1.)
The Latin and English text may be obtained in separate form from Messrs Burns & Oates.

356. The Six Sundays.

Plenary, on each of the Sundays. I, II.
(See Instructions, p. 1.)
This devotion consists in spending some time in meditation, vocal prayer, or other works of piety, on any six consecutive Sundays, in honour of St Thomas.

N.B.—These Indulgences can be gained only once in the year.

357. Invocation, before Lecture or Study.

100 Days, once a day.
(See Instructions, p. 1.)

O BLESSED Thomas, patron of schools, obtain for us from GOD an invincible faith, burning charity, a chaste life, and true knowledge, through CHRIST our LORD. Amen.

ST ANTHONY OF PADUA

358. Responsory.

i. 100 Days. T.Q.
ii. Plenary, once a month. I, II, III, IV.
(See Instructions, p. 1.)

SI quæris miracula,
Mors, error, calami-
tas,

IF then you ask for
miracles,
Death, error, all calamities,

Dæmon, lepra fugiunt,
Ægri surgunt sani.

The leprosy and de-
mons fly,
And health succeeds
infirmities.

Cedunt mare, vincula;
Membra resque perd-
itas
Petunt et accipiunt
Juvenes et cani.

The sea obeys, and fet-
ters break,
And lifeless limbs
thou dost restore;
Whilst treasures lost
are found again,
When young or old
thine aid implore.

Pereunt pericula,
Cessat et necessitas;
Narrent hi, qui senti-
unt,
Dicant Paduani.

All dangers vanish at
thy prayer,
And direst need doth
quickly flee.
Let those who know
thy power proclaim—
Let Paduans say—
These are of thee.

Cedunt mare, vincula
etc.
Gloria Patri et Filio,
Et Spiritui Sancto.
Cedunt mare, vincula
etc.
℣. Ora pro nobis, beate
Antoni.
℟. Ut digni efficia-
mur promissionibus
Christi.

The sea obeys, *etc.*

To Father, Son, may
glory be,
And Holy Spirit eternally.
The sea obeys, *etc.*
℣. Pray for us, blessed
Anthony.
℟. That we may be
made worthy of the
promises of Christ.

Oremus.

ECCLESIAM tuam, DEUS, beati Antonii confessoris tui commemoratio votiva lætificet, ut spiritualibus semper muniatur auxiliis et gaudiis perfrui mereatur æternis. Per CHRISTUM DOMINUM nostrum. Amen.

Let us pray.

GOD, may the votive commemoration of the blessed Anthony, thy Confessor, be a source of joy to thy Church, that she may always be fortified with spiritual assistance, and deserve to enjoy eternal rewards. Through JESUS CHRIST our LORD. Amen.

359. Pater, Ave, and Gloria, thirteen times, in honour of the Saint.

100 Days, once a day.
(See Instructions, p. 1.)

360. St Anthony's Bread. Prayer.

100 Days, once a day.
(See Instructions, p. 1.)

TO thee we have recourse, most powerful worker of miracles, in whose breast burned a sublime fire of charity towards GOD and the poor. To thee, who wast deemed worthy to hold in thy arms the Infant JESUS, who chose to be born poor, to thee, full of confidence, we betake ourselves, that thou mayest pray the good JESUS to have compassion on us in our great tribulations. Oh!

obtain for us the favour which we humbly implore (*here state the favour needed*). If thou dost obtain it for us, O glorious St Anthony, we will offer thee bread for the poor whom thou didst love so greatly on earth. PATER, Ave, Gloria.

361. St Anthony's Bread. Thanksgiving.

100 Days, once a day.
(See Instructions, p. 1.)

O GLORIOUS worker of miracles, father of the poor, who, wondrously gifted with a heart full of compassion for the miseries of the unfortunate, didst by a miracle lay open the heart of a miser steeped in avarice; thou who dost offer our prayers to our LORD and obtain a hearing, accept as a proof of our gratitude the pence we lay at thy feet for the relief of misfortune. May it turn to the benefit of ourselves and of the suffering; hasten with thy usual kindness to help us in our temporal necessities, and still more to provide for our spiritual needs, now and at the hour of our death. Amen.

362. The Thirteen Tuesdays, or Sundays.

Plenary, on each Tuesday, or Sunday. I, II.
(See Instructions, p. 1.)

Some time must be devoted to meditation, vocal prayer or other works of piety, in consecutive weeks, and in honour of the Saint.

These Indulgences can be obtained only once in the year.

363. Prayer to St Anthony.

300 Days, once a day.
(See Instructions, p. 1.)

O WONDERFUL St Anthony, glorious on account of the fame of thy miracles, and through the condescension of JESUS in coming in the form of a little child to repose in thy arms; obtain for me of his bounty the grace which I ardently desire from the depths of my heart. Thou who wast so compassionate towards miserable sinners, regard not the unworthiness of those who pray to thee, but the glory of GOD, that it may be once again magnified by thee, to the salvation of my soul, in connection with the particular request which I now ask for with persevering earnestness. May this small offering of pence, which I make to thee in aid of the poor, be a pledge of my gratitude, and with them may it one day be granted to me, through the grace of JESUS CHRIST and thy intercession, to possess the kingdom of Heaven. Amen.

ST VINCENT FERRER

364. Prayer.

200 Days, once a day.
(See Instructions, p. 1.)

O GLORIOUS Apostle and worker of miracles, St Vincent Ferrer, new angel of the Apocalypse and our kind protector, receive our humble prayers and obtain for us a copious shower of divine favours. By that love with which thy heart was inflamed, obtain for us from the FATHER of mercies the pardon of all our sins, confirmation in the Faith, and perseverance in good works; so that by living as good and fervent Christians we may become worthy of thy powerful patronage. Extend thy patronage also to our bodies, and free us from our infirmities. Protect our lands from the violence of tempest and hail, and keep misfortune far from us. Thus, blessed by thee in the goods of soul and body, we shall be ever devout to thee, and one day see thee in Heaven, there with thee to praise GOD for ever and ever. Amen.

ST JOHN OF THE CROSS

365. Prayer.

 i. 100 Days, once a day.
 ii. Plenary, once a month, on the last day, or within eight days. I, II, III, IV.
   (See Instructions, p. 1.)

O GLORIOUS St John, who, through a pure desire of being like unto JESUS crucified, didst long for nothing so eagerly, up to the last moment of thy holy life, as to be despised and made little of by all, and whose thirst after sufferings was so burning that thy noble heart rejoiced in the midst of the sorest torments and afflictions: vouchsafe, I beseech thee, O dear Saint, by the glory which thy many sufferings have gained for thee, to intercede for me, and obtain for me of GOD a love of suffering, together with grace and strength to bear with firmness of mind all trials and adversities, which are the sure means to the happy attainment of that glorious crown which awaits me in Heaven. Dear Saint, from thy most happy throne of glory, whereon thou art now seated in majesty, hear, I beseech thee, my prayers; so that, after thy example, full of love for the Cross and for suffering, I may deserve to be thy companion in glory. Amen.

ST ANDREW AVELLINO

366. Prayers.

i. 300 Days. T.Q.
ii. Plenary, once a month. I, II.
(See Instructions, p. 1.)

I

O MOST glorious Saint, whom GOD has made our protector against apoplexy, seeing that thou thyself didst die of that disease, we earnestly pray thee to preserve us from an evil so dangerous and so common. PATER, Ave, Gloria.

℣. By the intercession of St Andrew, stricken with apoplexy.

℟. From a sudden and unprovided death deliver us, O LORD.

II

O MOST glorious Saint, if ever by the just judgment of GOD we should be stricken with apoplexy, we earnestly beseech thee to obtain for us time enough to receive the last Sacraments and die in the grace of GOD. PATER, Ave, Gloria.

℣. By the intercession of St Andrew, stricken with apoplexy.

℟. From a sudden and unprovided death deliver us, O LORD.

III

O MOST glorious Saint, who didst endure, before dying, a terrible agony, through the assaults of the devil, from which the Blessed Virgin and St Michael delivered thee, we earnestly beseech thee to assist us in the tremendous moment of our death. PATER, Ave, Gloria.

℣. By the intercession of St Andrew, stricken with apoplexy.

℟. From a sudden and unprovided death deliver us, O LORD.

ST MICHAEL DE' SANTI

367. Prayer.

  i. 300 days, once a day.
 ii. Plenary, on April 10 (the day of the Saint's death), on Corpus CHRISTI, and on July 5, his Feast, provided the prayer has been said at least ten times during the year. I, II, IV.

(See Instructions, p. 1.)

G LORIOUS Michael, Seraph inflamed with burning love of JESUS in the most holy Sacrament; thou who, passing days and nights in his Royal Presence, didst find there those dear delights which, inundating not thy heart alone but thy whole body with surpassing sweetness, threw thee into an ecstasy of joy; and who, rapt in thy GOD, didst feel thyself faint for love, being unable to support the torrent of consolations; vouchsafe, I pray thee, powerful advocate, to obtain for me lively faith, firm hope, and burning charity towards this priceless treasure, the precious pledge of everlasting glory; so that by thy intercession I may, through the whole course of my life, be numbered amongst the true worshippers of JESUS in the Holy Sacrament, and with thee hereafter enjoy Him face to face in an eternity of bliss. Amen. PATER, Ave, Gloria.

ST ANTHONY, ABBOT

368. Prayer.

100 Days, once a day.
(See Instructions, p. 1.)

O GLORIOUS St Anthony, who, on hearing one single precept of the Gospel while assisting at Mass, didst abandon riches and the comforts of home, and retire from thy country and the world into a desert; who, though burdened with years and wasted with penance, didst not hesitate to leave the desert, and make many journeys to Alexandria in Egypt to denounce publicly the impiety of the heretics and to strengthen wavering Christians in the Faith, eager, like a true confessor of JESUS CHRIST, to seize the palm of martyrdom, if only GOD had permitted it; obtain for us, we beseech thee, the grace to be ever zealous for the cause of JESUS CHRIST and his Church, and to persevere to the end of our days in believing the truths, observing the precepts, and practising the counsels of the Catholic Religion, and in imitating thy virtues; so that by faithfully following thy example here on earth we may rejoice in the participation of thy glory in Heaven through all eternity. PATER, Ave, *and* Gloria *thrice.*

ST ALOYSIUS GONZAGA

369. Feast Day.

Plenary. I, II, IV.
(See Instructions, p. 1.)
A visit must be made to an altar at which the Saint is being honoured.
N.B.—The Feast may be celebrated on any day, and in any place, with leave from the Bishop.

370. The Six Sundays.

Plenary, on each Sunday. I, II.
(See Instructions, p. 1.)
Some time must be spent in meditation, vocal prayer or other good works, in honour of the Saint, on six consecutive Sundays, either preceding the Feast, June 21, or otherwise, at discretion.

371. Prayer.

100 Days, once a day.
(See Instructions, p. 1.)

O BLESSED Aloysius, adorned with angelic virtues, I, thy most unworthy suppliant, recommend specially to thee the chastity of my soul and body, praying thee by thy angelic purity to plead for me with JESUS CHRIST, the Immaculate Lamb, and his most Holy Mother, Virgin of virgins, that

they would vouchsafe to keep me from all grievous sin. Never suffer me to be defiled with any
stain of fleshly sin; but when thou dost see me in
temptation, or in danger of falling, then remove
far from my mind all bad thoughts and unclean
desires, and awaken in me the memory of eternity to come and of JESUS crucified; impress deeply
in my heart a sense of the holy fear of GOD; and,
kindling in me the fire of divine love, enable me
so to follow thy footsteps here on earth that in
heaven I may be made worthy to enjoy with thee
the vision of our GOD for ever. Amen. PATER, Ave.

372. Act of Consecration.

   i. 200 Days, once a day.
   ii. Plenary, on the Feast or during the Octave, if said
     every day in June. I, II, III, IV.
        (See Instructions, p. 1.)

O GLORIOUS St Aloysius, honoured by the
Church with the title of Angelic Youth, for the
eminent purity of thy life on earth, to thee I offer
myself this day with all the devotion of my mind
and heart, and to thee I consecrate myself entirely. O perfect example, O kind and powerful protector of youth, how much I have need of thee!
The world and the devil lay snares for me; I feel
the fire of my passions, I know the weakness and
inconstancy of my age. Who can protect me if not
thou, O angelic saint, the glory, ornament, love
and mainstay of the young? To thee, then, with
all my mind and heart I have recourse; in thee I
confide, to thee I consecrate myself. Therefore I
firmly purpose and resolve to be specially devout

to thee, to glorify thee for thy lofty virtues, and especially for thy angelic purity; to imitate thy example, to promote devotion to thee among my companions, and to invoke and bless to the end of my life thy dear and holy name. To thee I consecrate my soul, my senses, my heart, and all my being. O dear St Aloysius, lo! today I am all thine, and thine I wish to remain for ever. Oh! protect, defend, and preserve me as thy possession, that through honouring thee I may be better able to serve and honour JESUS and Mary, and come one day with thee to see and bless my GOD for ever in Paradise. Amen.

ST STANISLAUS KOSTKA

373. Feast Day. Ten Sundays, etc.

i. Plenary, to all who, after First Vespers, visit a church or chapel where the Feast (November 13) is being celebrated. I, II, IV.

ii. Seven Years and Seven Quarantines, on each of the ten Sundays before the Feast, to those who visit a church or public chapel where these Sundays are being kept. IV.

iii. 100 Days, each day for assisting at the Novena for the Feast, IV.

N.B.—These three Indulgences may be gained if the Feast be transferred, with leave from the Bishop.

iv. 100 Days, once a day, to those who say a *Pater* and *Ave* before a representation of the Saint, exposed in any church or chapel, public or private.

v. Plenary, once a month, for the above. I, II, IV.

N.B.—In cases of lawful impediment, the *Pater* and *Ave* may be said anywhere.

vi. 100 Days, to all those who assist at the day's retreat known as "The Retreat of St Stanislaus." IV.

(See Instructions, p. 1.)

374. Prayers.

  i. 300 Days, once a day.
  ii. Plenary, once a month. I, II, III, IV.

(See Instructions, p. 1.)

ST STANISLAUS, my most pure patron, angel of purity, I rejoice with thee at the extraordinary gift of virginal purity which graced thy spotless heart; I humbly pray thee, obtain for me strength to overcome all impure temptations, and inspire me with constant watchfulness in guarding the virtue of holy purity. PATER, Ave, Gloria.

ST STANISLAUS, my most loving patron, Seraph of charity, I rejoice with thee at the ardent fire of charity which kept thy pure and innocent heart always at peace and united to GOD; I humbly pray thee, obtain for me such ardour of divine love that it may consume away every other earthly affection, and kindle in me the fire of his love alone. PATER, Ave, Gloria.

ST STANISLAUS, my most tender and most mighty patron, Angel of purity and Seraph of charity, I rejoice with thee at thy most happy death, which arose from thy desire to contemplate our Lady in heaven, and was at length caused by the excess of thy love for her. I give thanks to Mary because she thus accomplished thy desires; and I pray thee, by the lustre of thy happy death, to be my advocate and patron in my death. Intercede with Mary for me, to obtain for me a death, if not all happiness like thine, yet calm and peaceful, under the protection of Mary my advocate, and thee, my special patron. PATER, Ave, Gloria.

ST JOHN BERCHMANS

375. The Five Sundays.

i. Seven Years and Seven Quarantines, on the first four Sundays. I, II, III, IV.
ii. Plenary on the fifth. I, II, III, IV.
(See Instructions, p. 1.)

Some pious exercise must be performed in honour of the saint on the five Sundays preceding the Feast, August 13.

ST BENEDICT JOSEPH LABRE

376. Prayer.

100 Days, once a day.
(See Instructions, p. 1.)

O ADMIRABLE example of Christian perfection, St Benedict Joseph! From the first use of reason till death thou didst preserve inviolate the immaculate stole of innocence, and abandoning all things, as a wanderer on the face of the earth, didst meet with nothing but suffering, privations and insults. I, a miserable sinner, prostrate at thy feet, return thanks to the infinite goodness of GOD for having impressed on thee so living an image of his crucified SON, while at the same time I am covered with confusion at the sight of my life, so different from thine. I beseech thee, dear Saint, have pity on me; present thy merits at

the throne of GOD, and obtain for me the grace
that, following thy example and regulating my actions by the precepts and teaching of thy divine
Master, I may come to love his suffering and humiliations, and may hold in contempt the pleasures and honours of the world, so that neither
the fear of the one nor the desire of the other
may ever induce me to transgress his holy laws.
And so may I merit one day to be acknowledged
and numbered among the blessed of his FATHER.
PATER, Ave, Gloria.

℣. Pray for us, St Benedict Joseph.

℟. That we may be made worthy of the promises
of CHRIST.

Let us pray.

O GOD, who hast caused blessed Benedict Joseph,
thy Confessor, by practising humility and loving poverty, to cling to Thee alone; grant through
the power of his merits that we may despise all
earthly things and ever seek after the things of
Heaven. Through CHRIST our LORD. Amen.

ST LUCY, VIRGIN AND MARTYR

377. Prayers.

200 Days, once a day.
(See Instructions, p. 1.)

WE contemplate with wonder, O glorious virgin and martyr, St Lucy, that light of living
faith which GOD in his mercy was pleased to infuse into thy fair soul. By the light of this faith
thou didst know how to despise the vain and

fleeting things of this miserable world, and to keep thy eyes fixed on heaven, for which alone we were created. The honours, riches, and pleasures of this seductive world did not obscure thy mind, much less corrupt thy heart, to the injury of thy faith and of divine grace; so that far from consenting to the wicked proposals of the unjust judge, thou didst fearlessly and resolutely encounter even death rather than be unfaithful to thy celestial LORD. What shame for us, who, illumined also by faith and strengthened by grace, know not at all how to resist our guilty passions, despise the perverse maxims of the world, or frustrate the wiles of our enemy the devil! Therefore we beseech thee, dear Saint, to obtain for us greater light from GOD, to understand better that we are not made for earthly things, but for the things of heaven. PATER, Ave, Gloria.

O VICTORIOUS martyr, St Lucy, admirable was thy virtue of hope, which kept alive in thee the desire of heaven and nourished that filial confidence in GOD, our most loving FATHER, which possessed thy heart. Animated with this virtue, while praying fervently for thy mother at the tomb of St Agatha, thou didst obtain for her health in sickness. Full of trust in GOD, in order to become more completely detached from the things of this earth, thou didst willingly distribute to the poor whatever still remained to thee of earthly treasure; and if courage and strength never failed thee in resisting the tyrant, and in standing firm in the faith in the midst of unspeakable torments, it was solely because thou didst place thy hope in Him who has promised never to abandon us in dangers, but to be to us a shield of defence, ready to work even miracles, such as actually happened in thy glorious martyrdom. Let us then freely confess that too great an attachment to things here below and too little confidence in GOD harden our hearts, and so deprive us of courage that we often miserably succumb to occasions of danger. Obtain for us, we beseech thee, O blessed St Lucy, a more firm trust in our LORD and GOD, that we may deserve in every untoward event of our lives to have Him for our helper and consoler. PATER, Ave, Gloria.

O GLORIOUS martyr of JESUS CHRIST, St Lucy, thy living faith and firm hope could not be separated from the fire of most ardent charity which inflamed thy heart, and made thee so ready to shed thy blood and sacrifice thy life for thy spouse JESUS. No wonder the flame of material fire which was applied to thy body by order of the tyrant could not penetrate it or reduce it to ashes. This fire was too weak beside that which burnt in thy breast; and so the impious prefect, seeing that his efforts were vain, ordered that thy throat should be completely severed with a sharp sword. Then it was that thy beautiful soul took its flight to heaven, there to repose on the breast of thy JESUS, and enjoy his heavenly delights for ever. Alas! we love creatures, and so weary ourselves on their account that we find our poor hearts not only void of consolation, but overwhelmed with bitterness. Obtain for us, dear Saint, we beseech thee, that we may be persuaded, once for all, that our true happiness should begin on this earth, in the love of that GOD who will be the true and the sole object of our perfect and eternal beatitude in heaven. PATER, Ave, Gloria.

FULL of confidence in thy powerful intercession, O glorious martyr St Lucy, we beseech thee to intercede with thy divine spouse JESUS, that it may please Him to keep ever healthy the light of our bodily eyes, giving us at the same time the grace to make good use of them, so that on the day of the general resurrection they may become radiant with that heavenly light which will fit them to behold the ineffable beauties of the country of the blessed. Amen.

℣. Pray for us, St Lucy.

℟. That we may be made worthy of the promises of CHRIST.

Let us pray.

HEAR our prayers, O GOD our SAVIOUR, that as we rejoice in the constancy in the faith of the blessed St Lucy, virgin and martyr, so we may be filled with pious and devout affections. Through CHRIST our LORD. Amen.

378. Prayer to St Lucy.

300 Days, once a day.

(See Instructions, p. 1.)

O SAINT, named from the light, full of confidence we present ourselves before thee, to ask of thee a holy light, which may render us cautious in avoiding the ways of sin and escaping the darkness of error. We beg also, through thy intercession, for the preservation of the light of our eyes, together with abundant grace to use it always in accordance with the will of GOD and without injury to our souls. Grant, O blessed Lucy, that, after venerating and thanking thee for thy powerful patronage on earth, we may come at last to rejoice with thee in the paradise of the eternal light of the divine Lamb, thy sweet spouse JESUS. Amen.

ST AGNES, V.M.

379. Prayer.

100 Days, once a day.
(See Instructions, p. 1.)

SWEETEST LORD JESUS CHRIST, Source of all virtue, Lover of virgins, most powerful Conqueror of demons, most severe Extirpator of vice, deign to cast thy eyes upon my weakness, and through the intercession of Mary most blessed, Mother and Virgin, and of thy beloved spouse, St Agnes, glorious virgin and martyr, grant me the aid of thy heavenly grace, in order that I may learn to despise all earthly things, and to love what is heavenly; to oppose vice, and to be proof against temptation; to walk firmly in the path of virtue, not to seek honours, to shun pleasures, to bewail my past offences, to keep far from the occasions of evil, to keep free from bad habits, to seek the company of the good, and persevere in righteousness, so that, by the assistance of thy grace, I may deserve the crown of eternal life, to-

gether with St Agnes and all the saints, for ever
and ever, in thy kingdom. Amen.

380. Prayers.

200 Days, once a day.

(See Instructions, p. 1.)

O SINGULAR example of virtue, glorious St
Agnes, by that lively faith which animated
thee from thy most tender years, and rendered
thee so acceptable to GOD that thou didst merit
the crown of martyrdom; obtain for us the grace
to preserve entire in our hearts the Catholic Faith,
and sincerely to profess ourselves Christians not
only in word but also in deed; so that while we
confess JESUS openly in the face of men, JESUS
may give favourable testimony of us before his
Heavenly FATHER. PATER, Ave, Gloria.

O INVINCIBLE martyr, St Agnes, by that hope
which thou hadst in the divine aid, when being condemned by the impious prefect to see the
lily of thy purity stained and trampled under foot,
thou wast wholly undismayed, firmly trusting in
the GOD who gives his angels charge over those
who trust in Him; we beseech thee to obtain for
us by thy intercession the grace to guard this virtue jealously in our hearts, so that to the many
sins which we commit we may never add that
most hateful sin of distrust in the mercy of GOD.
PATER, Ave, Gloria.

O BRAVE child, most pure St Agnes, by that
ardent charity which enflamed thy heart and
secured thee from being injured by the flames of

passion or of the stake at which the enemies of
JESUS CHRIST sought to destroy thee; obtain for us
from GOD that every fire may be extinguished in
us except that which JESUS CHRIST came on earth
to enkindle; so that after passing a spotless life in
the exercise of this beautiful virtue we may be allowed to share in that glory which is the crown of
thy purity of heart and of thy martyrdom. PATER,
Ave, Gloria.

ST BARBARA, VIRGIN

381. Prayer for a Happy Death.

100 Days, once a day.

(See Instructions, p. 1.)

O GOD, who didst choose St Barbara to bring
consolation to the living and the dying; grant
that through her intercession we may live always
in thy divine love, and place all our hopes in the
merits of the most sorrowful Passion of thy SON;
so that a sinner's death may never overtake us,
but that, armed with the Sacraments of Penance,
the Holy Eucharist, and Extreme Unction, we
may be able to pass without fear to everlasting
glory. We implore this of Thee through the same
JESUS CHRIST our LORD. Amen.

ST JULIANA FALCONIERI

382. Prayer.

200 Days, once a day.

(See Instructions, p. 1.)

O FAITHFUL spouse of JESUS CHRIST and most humble servant of the Virgin Mary, Mother of Sorrows, glorious St Juliana; at the end of a life entirely spent in the exercise of heroic virtues, thou didst undergo one last trial, in that thou couldst not be united in holy Viaticum, to thy Beloved by reason of bodily infirmity. But this trial was so acceptable to thy heavenly Spouse, JESUS, that He deigned Himself to reward it with an extraordinary miracle; for at thy request JESUS in the Blessed Sacrament was placed on thy virginal breast, and He instantly entered within, leaving outwardly impressed the image of Himself crucified, while with a sweet smile thou didst breathe forth thy soul in his holy embrace. O great Saint and my special patroness, obtain from GOD, I beseech thee, that like thee I may live a good life and die a holy death; and that being so prepared for the last passage, fortified with the holy Sacraments, and invigorated by divine grace, I may finish my days in holiness and be preserved from eternal death.

ST THERESA OF AVILA, VIRGIN

383. Prayer of St Alphonsus.

100 Days, once a day.

(See Instructions, p. 1.)

O SERAPHIC virgin, St Theresa, beloved spouse of the Crucified, thou who didst burn

with such great love of GOD while on earth, and
now burnest with a still purer and brighter flame
in Heaven; thou who didst so greatly desire to
see Him loved by all men, obtain for me too, I
pray thee, a spark of that holy fire, whereby I
may oppose the world, creatures, and myself; and
grant that all my thoughts, desires and affections
may be ever employed in pursuing, whether in
the midst of joys or of sufferings, the will of the
Supreme Good, who deserves our unbounded
love and obedience. Oh, obtain for me this grace,
thou who art so powerful with GOD, that, like
thee, I may be all on fire with divine love. Amen.

ST MARY SALOME

384. Prayer.

100 Days, once a day.
(See Instructions, p. 1.)

O BELOVED disciple and true lover of JESUS
CHRIST, St Mary Salome; I thy humble client
thank the Blessed Trinity for the glory bestowed
on thee, making thy family truly a family of
saints. By thy generosity in devoting to the apostolate thy sons and thyself, obtain for me that
throughout my whole life, whatever be the cost, I
may labour efficaciously in promoting the glory
of GOD and the salvation of souls. And when my
end shall come, O my dear protectress, assist me
with that loving pity with which thou didst assist
our dying LORD on Calvary; and grant that in that
terrible hour He may address to me also those

consoling words which He spoke on the Cross to the penitent thief: "This day thou shalt be with Me in Paradise."

ST ELIZABETH OF HUNGARY

385. Prayer.

300 Days, once a day.
(See Instructions, p. 1.)

BLESSED Elizabeth, vessel elect of exalted virtues, thou dost show forth to the world by thy example what the virtues of Faith, Hope, and Charity are able to do in a Christian soul.

Thou didst employ all the powers of thy heart to love thy GOD alone. Thou didst love Him with a love so pure and fervent that it rendered thee worthy to taste upon earth beforehand those favours and those sweetnesses of Paradise which are communicated to souls invited to the nuptials of the Divine adorable LAMB of GOD.

Thou, illuminated by supernatural light and faith immovable, didst show thyself to be a true daughter of the Holy Gospel, by seeing in the person of thy neighbour the Person of our LORD JESUS CHRIST, sole object of thy affections; and therefore didst thou place all thy delight in holding converse with the poor, in serving them, in drying their tears and comforting their spirits, in assisting them with every pious good office, in the midst of pestilence and the miseries to which our human nature is subject.

Thou didst make thyself poor in order to succour thy neighbour in his poverty, poor in the good things of earth, to enrich thyself with the goods of heaven.

Thou wast so humble that, after thou hadst exchanged a throne for a poor hovel, and a royal mantle for the modest habit of St Francis, thou didst subject thyself, innocent though thou wast, to a life of privation and of penance, and with holy joy didst embrace the cross of thy REDEEMER, with goodwill accepting with Him insults and the most unjust persecution: thus didst thou forget the world and thyself, to remember thy GOD alone.

Dearest Saint, who wast so beloved by GOD, vouchsafe to be the heavenly friend of our souls, and help them to become ever more and more acceptable to JESUS. Cast down upon us from the height of heaven one of those tender looks which, when thou wast upon earth, healed the most distressing infirmities. In this our age, so depraved and corrupt, and at the same time so cold and indifferent to the things of GOD, we have recourse to thee with confidence, in order that we may receive from our LORD light for the understanding and strength for the will, and thence obtain peace of soul.

Whilst we bless the LORD for having glorified his name in this world with the splendour of thy heroic virtues and the eternal reward accorded to them, do thou bless them, O dear St Elizabeth, from that blessed throne which thou dost occupy close to the Saint of Saints; protect us in our

dangerous pilgrimage; obtain for us the pardon
of our sins, and open for us the way to enter and
share with thee the Kingdom of GOD. Amen.

ST MARGARET OF CORTONA

386. Prayer.

100 Days, once a day.
(See Instructions, p. 1.)

O MOST glorious Margaret, true gem wrested
by GOD with so much love out of the hands
of the infernal robbers who had seized thee, that
by the example of thy wonderful conversion, holy
life and most precious death all sinners might be
moved to abandon sin and every approximate occasion of evil, and practise virtue; obtain for us
thy clients, we beseech thee, from the lofty throne
of thy glory, to which thy tears and penances have
raised thee, the grace of a sincere conversion of
heart and of a lively sorrow for our sins, and, after
a holy life passed like thine in the love of JESUS
crucified for us, a happy death, and the crown
of glory in the bosom of the Eternal Beatitude.
Amen. PATER, Ave, Gloria.

387. Prayer to St Blaise.

300 Days, once a day.
(See Instructions, p. 1.)

O GLORIOUS St Blaise, who with a short
prayer didst restore to perfect safety a child
at the point of death from a fish-bone fixed in its

throat, grant that we may all feel the power of thy
patronage in every malady of the throat, and may
have the special grace to mortify the dangerous
sense of taste by observing faithfully the precepts
of the Church. Thou also, who in thy martyrdom
hast left to the Church the testimony of a glorious faith, grant that we may keep this divine gift
intact, and that in these times we may be enabled,
by word and deed, without fear of man, to defend
the truths of faith, so grievously obscured and at-
tacked.

ST STEPHEN

388. Antiphon and Prayer.

i. 300 Days, once a day.
ii. Plenary, on August 3 and December 26, or during
the Octaves, if said for nine days preceding the
Feast. I, II, III, IV.

(See Instructions, p. 1.)

Antiphon.

ELEGERUNT Apostoli Stephanum Levitam plenum fide et SPIRITU SANCTO, quem lapidaverunt Judæi orantem et dicentem: DOMINE JESU, accipe spiritum meum, et non statuas illis hoc peccatum.

THE APOSTLES chose the Levite Stephen, full of faith and the HOLY SPIRIT, whom the Jews stoned while he prayed, saying: LORD JESUS, receive my spirit, and lay not this sin to their charge.

℣. Meritis et precibus beati Stephani.
℟. Propitius esto, Domine, populo tuo.

Prayer.

OMNIPOTENS, sempiterne Deus, qui primitias Martyrum in beati Levitæ Stephani sanguine dedicasti: tribue, quæsumus, ut pro nobis intercessor existat, qui pro suis etiam persecutoribus exoravit Dominum nostrum Jesus Christum Filium tuum, qui vivit et regnat in sæcula sæculorum. Amen.

℣. By the merits and prayers of the blessed Stephen.
℟. Be merciful, O Lord, to thy people.

ALMIGHTY and everlasting God, who didst consecrate the first fruits of the Martyrs in the blood of the blessed Levite Stephen, grant, we beseech Thee, that he may become our advocate, who even for his persecutors besought our Lord, thy Son Jesus Christ, who liveth and reigneth world without end. Amen.

ST JOHN THE BAPTIST

389. Prayers.

i. 200 Days, once a day.
ii. 300 Days, once a day, during a triduo or novena.
iii. Plenary, once during the Triduo or Novena, or within eight days. I, II, IV.

(See Instructions, p. 1.)

XIII. VARIOUS SAINTS 419

O GLORIOUS St John the Baptist, of those born of women the greatest of prophets (Luke vii, 28); thou, though sanctified from thy mother's womb and most innocent, didst nevertheless will to retire into the desert, there to practise austerities and penance; obtain for us from our LORD the grace to be detached, at least in the affections of our hearts, from all earthly treasure, and to practise Christian mortification with interior recollection and a spirit of holy prayer. PATER, Ave, Gloria.

O MOST zealous Apostle, who, without working any miracle on others, but solely by the example of thy life of penance and the power of thy words, didst draw after thee crowds, in order to prepare them to worthily receive the MESSIAH, and listen to his heavenly teaching; grant that it may be given to us also, by the example of a holy life and the practice of good works, to lead many souls to GOD, and, above all, those who have been enveloped in the darkness of error and ignorance, and led astray by vice. PATER, Ave, Gloria.

U NCONQUERED martyr, who for the honour of GOD and the salvation of souls, didst, with heroic constancy, and at the cost of life itself, withstand the impious Herod, reproving him openly for his bad and dissolute life; obtain for us a brave and generous heart, so that, overcoming all human respect, we may boldly profess our faith, and follow the teaching of our divine master JESUS CHRIST. PATER, Ave, Gloria.

℣. Pray for us, St John the Baptist.

℟. That we may be made worthy of the promises of CHRIST.

Let us pray.

O GOD, who hast made this day worthy of honour in the nativity (commemoration) of St John, grant to thy people the grace of spiritual joys, and direct the minds of all the faithful into the way of eternal salvation. Through CHRIST our LORD. Amen.

ST FRANCIS XAVIER

390. Novena in honour of the Saint.

    i. 300 Days, each day.
    ii. Plenary, within eight days of the completion. I, II, IV.

(See Instructions, p. 1.)

The following prayer must be said each day or *Pater, Ave* and *Gloria* five times. (N.B.–Twice a year only.)

O GREAT St Francis, well beloved and full of charity, with thee I reverently adore the divine Majesty; and since I specially rejoice in the singular gifts of grace, bestowed on thee in life, and of glory after death, I give thanks to GOD, and beg of thee, with all the affections of my heart, that by thy powerful intercession thou mayest obtain for me above all things the grace to live a holy life and die a holy death. Moreover, I beg of thee to obtain for me (*here insert some special spiritual or temporal favour*), but if what I ask does not tend to the glory of GOD and the greater good of my soul, do thou, I beseech thee, obtain for me what will more certainly attain these ends. Amen.

ST PAUL OF THE CROSS

391. Prayer.

300 Days, once a day.

(See Instructions, p. 1.)

O GLORIOUS St Paul of the Cross, thou who in meditating on the Passion of JESUS CHRIST didst attain to such a high degree of sanctity on earth and of happiness in Heaven, and didst, by preaching the same holy Passion, offer to the world a most efficacious remedy for all its evils; obtain for us that we may ever have that Passion so deeply engraven on our hearts, that we may gather similar fruits in time and in eternity. Amen. PATER, Ave, Gloria.

ST RITA

392. Prayer.

300 Days, once a day.

(See Instructions, p. 1.)

O GLORIOUS St Rita, thou who didst miraculously share in the sorrowful Passion of our LORD JESUS CHRIST, obtain for me that I may bear with resignation the suffering of this life, and protect me in all my necessities.

ST JOHN DE LA SALLE

393. Prayer.

i. 300 Days, once a day.

ii. Plenary, once a month. I, II, III, IV.
(See Instructions, p. 1.)

O GLORIOUS John Baptist de la Salle, Apostle
of infancy and of youth, and, from the height
of Heaven, our guide and our protector, intercede
for us, help us, that, preserved from all the defile-
ment of error and corruption, we may live always
faithful to JESUS CHRIST and to the infallible Head
of his Church. Grant that practising the virtues
of which thou wast so admirable an example, we
may one day partake of thy glory in the heavenly
country. Amen.

SS. BRIDGETT AND CATHARINE OF SWEDEN

394. Prayers.

300 Days, once a day, for either
(See Instructions, p. 1.)

I. *To St Bridgett, Queen of Sweden.*

W ITH confident hearts we fly to thee, blessed Bridgett, and ask, in these times of
darkness and unbelief, thy intercession on behalf of those who are separated from the Church
of JESUS CHRIST. By the clear knowledge which
thou hadst of the cruel sufferings of our crucified
SAVIOUR, the price of our redemption, we beg of
thee to obtain for those who are outside the one
fold the grace of faith, so that the scattered sheep
may return to the one true Shepherd. Through
CHRIST our LORD. Amen.
St Bridgett, fearless servant of GOD, pray for us.

St Bridgett, patient in sufferings and humiliations, pray for us.
St Bridgett, wonderful in thy love towards JESUS
and Mary, pray for us. PATER, Ave, Gloria.
II. *To St Catharine, Virgin.*

O GOD, who didst adorn blessed Catharine in an
especial manner with the virtues of humility,
charity, and angelic purity, we humbly beseech
Thee, by her merits and example, to make us so
firm in faith and so ardent in charity that we may
obtain the rewards of eternity. Through JESUS
CHRIST our LORD. Amen.
St Catharine, lily of purity, pray for us.
St Catharine, model of humility, pray for us.
St Catharine, admirable in the love of JESUS and
Mary, pray for us. PATER, Ave, Gloria.

ST CATHARINE OF ALEXANDRIA

395. Prayers for the Promotion of Studies.

100 Days, once a day for each prayer.
(See Instructions, p. 1.)

I

L ORD JESUS CHRIST, the Way, the Truth and the
Life, Thou who so lovest souls, and who, not
content with giving us an example, hast made
such magnificent promises to those who shall
teach the truth; fill with thy spirit of wisdom,
knowledge, and fear, all those who teach; fill with
thy grace those who are taught, so that, instructed in a profitable and useful manner, their minds
may receive the truth, their hearts cling to what

is right, and their lives be full of good works; and may thy holy Name be glorified in everything. O JESUS, teacher, who, moved to compassion for thy children, like sheep without a shepherd, didst say to thy disciples, *Pray to the Lord of the harvest that He send labourers*; deign, we beseech Thee, to multiply worthy instructors of youth; sanctify them in truth, and increase in them faith, hope and charity.

O good JESUS, who hast said, *Suffer little children to come unto Me*, let not one of these little ones, purchased with thy Precious Blood, perish; remove them from all scandal of impiety, of vice, and error; we ask this from Thee in the name of thy holy Passion, of the sorrows of thy holy Mother, and by the intercession of the angels and saints. Amen.

II

PRAYER TO ST CATHARINE OF ALEXANDRIA, PATRONESS OF STUDIES.

O GLORIOUS Virgin and Martyr, St Catharine, who by thy admirable learning, thy zeal for the Faith, and by thy glorious martyrdom didst gain so many souls for JESUS CHRIST; thou whose patronage has been so often claimed by the most learned, we choose thee for the patroness and protector of our studies and our teaching.

Obtain for us who are thy clients a generous love for JESUS CHRIST our SAVIOUR, an ardent zeal to make Him known and loved, an inviolable fidelity to the Catholic Faith and to the teaching of Holy Church.

May our LORD deign, through thy intercession, to grant to all who teach, the plenitude of the gifts of the HOLY SPIRIT. May they join to true knowledge sure and effective methods, purity of faith, integrity of life, and a humble distrust of themselves.

Beg of JESUS, thy Spouse, that He take pity on all those who are taught; that He preserve them from impious or indifferent masters, and perverse or erroneous doctrines; that He give them an upright character, and docile heart, and the grace to make progress in their studies according to the designs of his sovereign wisdom.

And lastly, O glorious Saint, beg the FATHER of lights for such an outpouring of grace on the instruction of youth that, after having studied, loved and practised the divine law, all masters and disciples may together come to the holy Mount, which is JESUS CHRIST. Amen.

III

ANOTHER PRAYER TO ST CATHARINE.

O GLORIOUS St Catharine, wise and prudent virgin, who didst place the knowledge of JESUS CHRIST above all knowledge, obtain for us the grace to live inviolably attached to the Catholic Faith, and to seek in our studies and teaching but one thing, to extend in ourselves and in others the kingdom of JESUS CHRIST our SAVIOUR, and of his holy Church. Amen.

396. Blessed Francus, Carmelite Confessor.

Plenary, on the Feast, from First Vespers, to those who visit a Carmelite church or public chapel. I, II, III, IV.

(See Instructions, p. 1.)

XIV. BLESSED CROSSES, CRUCIFIXES, ROSARIES, MEDALS, ETC., FROM THE HOLY LAND

397.

The following Indulgences may be gained by persons who possess blessed objects which have touched the holy places and sacred relics of the Holy Land.

    i. Plenary, *in articulo mortis*, at the point of death. I, II.

Should Confession and Communion be impossible, the invocation of the holy Name of JESUS with contrition, at least in the heart, suffices.

    ii. Plenary, on Christmas Day, the Epiphany, Easter Day, Ascension Day, Pentecost, Trinity Sunday, Corpus CHRISTI, the Purification, Annunciation, Nativity B.V.M., Nativity of St John Baptist, SS. Peter and Paul, Andrew, James, John, Thomas, Philip and James, Bartholomew, Matthew, Simon and Jude, Matthias, and All Saints, to those who say at least once a week a Chaplet of our LORD, or of our Lady, the Rosary or a third part thereof, the Divine Office, or the Office of the B.V.M. or of the Dead, the Penitential or Gradual Psalms; or whose custom it is to teach the Catechism, visit prisoners, or the sick in hospitals, or help the poor, or hear Mass, or say Mass. I, II, III.

    iii. Seven Years and Seven Quarantines, for the above pious exercises on other Feasts of our LORD or of our Lady.

    iv. Five Years and Five Quarantines, for the same on any Sunday or Feast in the year.

    v. 100 Days, for the same, on any day of the year.

    vi. 200 Days, to those who visit prisoners, or the sick in hospitals, or teach the Catechism in church, or at home to their own children, relations or servants, or who are accustomed to say at least once a week, the Chaplet or Rosary, or Office B.V.M or of the Dead, or Vespers of the Dead, or one Nocturn with Lauds of the same, or who shall say the Penitential Psalms with the Litanies and Prayers.

vii. 100 Days, to those who at the sound of the bell say the *Angelus*, or not knowing it, a *Pater* and *Ave*, or in like manner say the *De Profundis* at night, or not knowing it, a *Pater* and *Ave*, or who every Friday meditate on the Passion and Death of our LORD and say the *Pater* and *Ave* thrice, or who with contrition and purpose of amendment examine their consciences and say *Pater* and *Ave* thrice, or who say the *Pater* and *Ave* thrice in honour of the Holy Trinity, or the *Pater* and *Ave* five times in memory of the Five Wounds of our LORD.

viii. 50 Days, to those who say any prayer in preparation before saying Mass or receiving Holy Communion, or before saying the Divine Office or the Office B.V.M.

ix. 50 Days, to those who pray for the dying, saying for them at least the *Pater noster* and *Ave Maria*.

(See Instructions, p. 1.)

N.B.—Indulgences following the same lines and practically identical with the above are attached to similar objects blessed by the Pope or a priest with the requisite faculties. The list of these Indulgences, with slight variations, is published anew by successive Pontiffs. The following conditions, however, must be observed:

i. The blessed object must be carried about on the person, or kept in the bedroom, or other suitable place, and reverently used for the prescribed devotions.

ii. It must not be made of fragile material.

iii. Pictures, whether printed or painted, are not admissible, and images must be of saints canonized or inscribed in approved martyrologies.

See also *Decisions*, No. 38. For precise particulars, cf. Acta S. Sedis xxxvi, 125.

XV. THE DYING AND THE APOSTOLIC BLESSING

398. Praying for the Dying.

100 Days.

(See Instructions, p. 1.)

This may be gained by priests saying Mass, or the laity assisting thereat, who commend to GOD all the sinners of the world who are "at that moment in their agony, or who are to die that day."

399. Offering of Masses for the Dying.

300 Days. T.Q.

(See Instructions, p. 1.)

MY GOD, I offer Thee all the Masses which are being celebrated today throughout the whole world, for sinners who are in their agony and who are to die this day. May the Precious Blood of JESUS, their REDEEMER, obtain mercy for them.

400. The Apostolic Blessing.

Plenary Indulgence, at the point of death to those who receive the blessing given by the Pope, or those who have the necessary faculties, who must in all cases use the prescribed form. (See Ritual.)

N.B.—The dying person must renew his sorrow for sin and fervent love of GOD; and especially he must accept death from the hands of GOD with resignation and in conformity to the divine pleasure, invoking the holy Name of Jesus in his heart, if unable to do so with his lips. This Indulgence is not suspended in the year of Jubilee.

401. Plenary Indulgence in Articulo Mortis.

To all who, with sincere love towards GOD, after Confession and Communion, made on any day they may choose, say the following prayer:

O LORD my GOD, I now, at this moment, readily and willingly accept at thy hand whatever kind of death it may please Thee to send me, with all its pains, penalties, and sorrows.

XVI. THE FAITHFUL DEPARTED

402. The Office of the Dead.

  i. 100 Days, on days prescribed by the Rubrics.
  ii. 50 Days, at other times.
         (See Instructions, p. 1.)

403. The Heroic Act.

This heroic act of charity in behalf of the souls in purgatory consists in a voluntary offering, made by any one of the faithful in their favour, of all works of satisfaction done by him in this life, as well as of all suffrages which shall be offered for him after his death; by this act he deposits all these works and suffrages into the hands of the Blessed Virgin, that she may distribute them in behalf of those holy souls whom it is her good pleasure to deliver from the pains of purgatory, at the same time that he declares that by this personal offering he only forgoes in their behalf the special and personal benefit

of these works of satisfaction, so that, if he is a priest,
he is not hindered from applying the Holy Sacrifice of
the Mass according to the intention of those who give
him alms for that purpose.

This heroic act of charity, called also a vow of oblation,
was instituted by F. Caspar Oliden, a Theatine. It was he
who propagated it, and it was at his prayer that it was
enriched with many Indulgences.

    i. An Indult of a privileged altar, personally, every
       day in the year to all priests who have made this
       offering.

   ii. Plenary, daily, applicable only to the departed, II,
       III, IV.

  iii. Plenary, every Monday to all who hear Mass in suf-
       frage for the souls in purgatory, II, III, IV.

          (See Instructions, p. 1.)

N.B.—All Indulgences granted, or to be granted and
gained by the faithful who have made this offering, are
applicable to the holy souls in purgatory.

For all the faithful who cannot hear Mass on Monday,
the Mass heard on Sundays is available for gaining Indulgence No. iii. In the case of those who are not yet
communicants, or who are hindered from communicating, their respective ordinaries may authorize confessors to commute the works enjoined.

Lastly, although this act of charity is denominated a
vow in some printed tracts, in which also is given a
formula for making the offering, no inference is to be
drawn therefrom that this offering binds under sin; neither is it necessary to make use of the said formula,
since, in order to share in the said Indulgences, no more
is required than a hearty act of our will.

N.B.—This act, or offering, may be at any time revoked.

404. The De Profundis.

    i. 100 Days, to all the faithful, every time that, at the
       sound of the bell at nightfall, they say devotedly on

their knees the Psalm *De profundis* or *Pater, Ave* and *Requiem æternam.*

ii. Plenary, once a year, if said daily. I, II, IV.

N.B.—In places where no bell is rung, these Indulgences may be gained by reciting the above at nightfall.

iii. 50 Days, three times a day to all who say the *De profundis* with ℣. and ℟. *Requiem æternam.*

(See Instructions, p. 1.)

Psalm. cxxix.

DE profundis clamavi ad te, DOMINE: * DOMINE, exaudi vocem meam.

Fiant aures tuæ intendentes * in vocem deprecationis meæ.

Si iniquitates observaveris, DOMINE: * DOMINE, quis sustinebit?

Quia apud te propitiatio est: * et propter legem tuam sustinui te, DOMINE.

Sustinuit anima mea in verbo ejus: speravit anima mea in DOMINO.

A custodia matutina usque ad noctem * speret Israel in DOMINO.

Psalm. cxxix.

OUT of the depths I have cried unto Thee, O LORD: LORD, hear my voice.

Let thine ears be attentive: to the voice of my supplication.

If Thou, O LORD, shalt mark our iniquities: O LORD, who can abide it?

For with Thee there is mercy: and by reason of thy law I have waited on Thee, O LORD.

My soul hath waited on his word: my soul hath hoped in the LORD.

From the morning watch even unto night: let Israel hope in the LORD.

Quia apud DOMINUM misericordia, * et copiosa apud eum redemptio.

Et ipse redimet Israel * ex omnibus iniquitatibus ejus.

℣. Requiem æternam * dona eis, DOMINE.

℟. Et lux perpetua luceat eis.

For with the LORD there is mercy: and with Him is plenteous redemption.

And He shall redeem Israel: from all his iniquities.

℣. Eternal rest give to them, O LORD.

℟. And let perpetual light shine upon them.

405. Holy Week.

Seven Years and Seven Quarantines, on Holy Thursday, Good Friday, and Holy Saturday.
(See Instructions, p. 1.)

To those who, on Thursday, Friday and Saturday in Holy Week make one hour's mental or vocal prayer, or who assist at the functions and services of Holy Week by way of suffrage for the holy souls, seeing that on these days they are deprived of the benefit of holy Mass.

406. Pater and Ave five times, etc.

i. 300 Days, once a day, to all who, devoutly meditating on the Passion, shall say for the departed the *Pater* and *Ave* five times with the following versicle or ejaculation, etc.

ii. Plenary, once a month. I, II, IV.
(See Instructions, p. 1.)

℣. TE ergo quæsumus, tuis famulis subveni, quos pretioso sanguine redemisti.

℣. WE therefore beseech Thee, help thy servants, whom Thou hast redeemed with thy Precious Blood.

Ejaculation.

Eternal Father, by the Precious Blood of Jesus, Mercy!

Eternal rest give unto them, O Lord, and let perpetual light shine upon them.

407. All Souls Day.

Plenary Indulgence, T.Q. I, II, IV.

(See Instructions, p. 1.)

This Indulgence, like that of the Portiuncula, may be gained as often as a person visits a church or public chapel of the Benedictines, whether monks or nuns, between first Vespers on November 1 and sunset on November 2. I, II, IV. Communities and those dwelling with them may use a semi-public chapel.

Those who wear a duly blessed medal of St Benedict, and are hindered from visiting a church or public chapel of the Benedictines by infirmity, enclosure or distance (more than a mile), may gain the same Indulgence by visiting any church or public chapel. I, II, IV.

408. Prayers.

100 Days, once a day. IV.

(See Instructions, p. 1.)

For Sunday.

O Lord God Almighty, I pray Thee, by the Precious Blood which thy Divine Son Jesus shed in the garden, deliver the souls in purgatory, and especially that soul amongst them all which is most destitute of spiritual aid; and vouchsafe to bring it to thy glory, there to praise and bless Thee for ever. Amen. Pater, Ave, De profundis. (No. 404).

For Monday.

O Lord God Almighty, I pray Thee, by the Precious Blood which thy Divine Son Jesus shed in his cruel scourging, deliver the souls in purgatory, and that soul especially amongst them all which is nearest to its entrance into thy glory; that so it may forthwith begin to praise and bless Thee for ever. Amen. Pater, Ave, De profundis.

For Tuesday.

O Lord God Almighty, I pray Thee, by the Precious Blood which thy Divine Son Jesus shed in his bitter crowning with thorns, deliver the souls in purgatory, and in particular that one amongst them all which would be the last to depart out of those pains, that it may not tarry so long a time before it come to praise Thee in thy glory and bless Thee for ever. Amen. Pater, Ave, De profundis.

For Wednesday.

O Lord God Almighty, I pray Thee, by the Precious Blood which thy Divine Son Jesus shed in the streets of Jerusalem, when He carried the Cross upon his sacred shoulders, deliver the souls in purgatory, and especially that soul which is richest in merits before Thee; that so, in that throne of glory which awaits it, it may magnify Thee and bless Thee for ever. Amen. Pater, Ave, De profundis.

For Thursday.

O Lord God Almighty, I pray Thee, by the Precious Body and Blood of thy Divine Son Jesus, which He gave with his own hands upon the eve of his Passion to his beloved Apostles to be their meat and drink, and which He left to his whole Church to be a perpetual sacrifice and the life-giving food of his own faithful people, deliver the souls in purgatory, and especially that one which was most devoted to this mystery of infinite love, that it may with the same thy Divine SON, and with thy HOLY SPIRIT, ever praise Thee for thy love therein in eternal glory. Amen. PATER, Ave, De profundis.

FOR FRIDAY.

O LORD GOD ALMIGHTY, I pray Thee, by the Precious Blood which thy Divine SON shed on this day upon the wood of the Cross, especially from his most sacred hands and feet, deliver the souls in purgatory, and in particular that soul for which I am most bound to pray; that no neglect of mine may hinder it from praising Thee in thy glory and blessing Thee for ever. Amen. PATER, Ave, De profundis.

FOR SATURDAY.

O LORD GOD ALMIGHTY, I beseech Thee, by the Precious Blood which gushed forth from the side of thy Divine SON JESUS, in the sight of, and to the extreme pain of his most holy Mother, deliver the souls in purgatory, and especially that one amongst them all which was the most devout to her; that it may soon attain unto thy glory, there to praise Thee in her, and her in Thee, world without end. Amen. PATER, Ave, De profundis.

409. Prayers for Nine or Seven Days.

i. 300 Days, each day.
ii. Plenary, during the period. I, II, IV.

(See Instructions, p. 1.)

Any form of prayers for the Holy Souls, sanctioned by competent ecclesiastical authority, may be used.

410. League of Perpetual Suffrage.

200 Days, once a day, to all who say thrice daily the versicle below.

(See Instructions, p. 1.)

REQUIEM æternam dona eis DOMINE, et lux perpetua luceat eis. Requiescant in pace, Amen.

ETERNAL rest give unto them, O LORD, and let perpetual light shine upon them. May they rest in peace. Amen.

411. Month of November.

i. Seven Years and Seven Quarantines, each day.
ii. Plenary, once during the month. I, II, III, IV.
(See Instructions, p. 1.)

Any daily devotions for the Holy Souls, public or private, will suffice.

412. Devotion to the Five Wounds.

200 Days, once a day.
(See Instructions, p. 1.)

GO before our actions, we beseech Thee, O LORD, with thy inspiration, and follow after them with thy help, that every prayer and work of ours may begin from Thee and through Thee be likewise ended. Through CHRIST our LORD. Amen.

Eternal rest give unto them, O LORD, and let perpetual light shine upon them.

WE offer unto Thee, O eternal FATHER, FATHER of mercies, for those souls so dear to Thee in purgatory, the most Precious Blood shed on Calvary from the wound in the left foot of JESUS thy SON, our SAVIOUR, and the sorrow of Mary his most loving Mother in beholding it. PATER, Ave, Requiem æternam.

II. We offer unto Thee, O eternal FATHER, FATHER of mercies, for those souls so dear to Thee in purgatory, the most Precious Blood shed on Calvary from the wound in the right foot of JESUS thy SON, our SAVIOUR, and the sorrow of Mary his most loving Mother in beholding it. PATER, Ave, Requiem æternam.

III. We offer unto Thee, O eternal FATHER, FATHER of mercies, for those souls so dear to Thee in purgatory, the most Precious Blood shed on Calvary from the wound in the left hand of JESUS thy SON, our SAVIOUR, and the sorrow of Mary his most loving Mother in beholding it. PATER, Ave, Requiem æternam.

IV. We offer unto Thee, O eternal FATHER, FATHER of mercies, for those souls so dear to Thee in purgatory, the most Precious Blood shed on Calvary from the wound in the right hand of JESUS thy SON, our SAVIOUR, and the sorrow of Mary his most loving Mother in beholding it. PATER, Ave, Requiem æternam.

V. We offer unto Thee, O eternal FATHER, FATHER of mercies, for those souls so dear to Thee in purgatory, the most Precious Blood and water flowing on Calvary from the pierced side of JESUS thy SON, our SAVIOUR, and the sorrow of Mary his most loving Mother in beholding it. PATER, Ave, Requiem æternam.

Let us pray.

AND now to give greater value to our feeble prayers, turning to Thee, most loving JESUS, we humbly pray Thee thyself to offer to the eternal FATHER the sacred wounds of thy feet, hands and side, together with thy most Precious Blood, and thy agony and death; and do thou also, Mary, Virgin of sorrows, present, together with the most sorrowful Passion of thy well-beloved SON, the sighs, tears and all the sorrows suffered by thee through his sufferings, so that through their merits the souls who suffer in the most ardent flames of purgatory may obtain refreshment, and, freed from this prison of torment, may be clothed with glory in heaven, there to sing the mercies of GOD for ever. Amen.

Absolve, O LORD, the souls of all the faithful departed from every bond of sin, so that by thy aid they may deserve to escape the judgment of wrath, and come to the enjoyment of beatitude in eternal light.

℣. Eternal rest give unto them, O LORD.

℞. And let perpetual light shine upon them.

℣. From the gate of hell.

℞. Deliver their souls, O LORD.

℣. May they rest in peace.

℞. Amen.

℣. O LORD, hear my prayer.

℞. And let my cry come unto Thee.

℣. The LORD be with you.

℞. And with thy spirit.

Let us pray.

O GOD, the CREATOR and REDEEMER of all the faithful, grant to the souls of thy servants departed the remission of all their sins, that through pious supplications they may obtain the pardon they have always desired. Who livest and reignest world without end. Amen.

Eternal rest, *etc.*

413. Prayers.

100 Days, once a day.

(See Instructions, p. 1.)

MY JESUS, by that copious sweat of blood with which Thou didst bedew the ground in the garden, have mercy on the souls of my nearest relations who are suffering in purgatory. PATER, Ave, Requiem æternam.

MY JESUS, by that cruel scourging which Thou didst suffer, bound to the column, have pity on the souls of my other relations and friends who are suffering in purgatory. PATER, Ave, Requiem æternam.

MY JESUS, by that crown of sharpest thorns which pierced thy sacred temples, have mercy on that soul which is most neglected and least prayed for, and on that soul which is furthest from being released from the pains of purgatory. PATER, Ave, Requiem æternam.

MY JESUS, by those sorrowful steps which Thou didst take with the Cross on thy shoulders, have mercy on that soul which is nearest to its departure from purgatory; and by the pains which Thou didst suffer together with thy most holy Mother Mary, when Thou didst meet her on the road to Calvary, deliver from the pains of purgatory those souls who were devout to this beloved Mother. PATER, Ave, Requiem æternam.

MY JESUS, by thy most holy body stretched on the Cross, by thy most holy hands and feet pierced with hard nails, by thy most cruel death, and by thy most holy side laid open with a lance, have pity and mercy on those poor souls; free them from the awful pains they suffer, call and admit them to thy most sweet embrace in Paradise. PATER, Ave, Requiem æternam.

O HOLY souls, tormented in most cruel pains, as one truly devoted to you, I promise never to forget you, and continually to pray to the Most High for your release. I beseech you to respond to this offering which I make to you, and obtain for me from GOD, with whom you are so powerful on behalf of the living, that I may be freed from all dangers of soul and body; I beg both for myself and for my relations and benefactors, friends and enemies, pardon for our sins, and the grace of perseverance in good, whereby we may save our souls. Set us free from all misfortunes, miseries, sicknesses, trials and labours. Obtain for us peace of heart; assist us in all our actions; succour us promptly in all our spiritual and temporal needs; console and defend us in our dangers. Pray for the supreme PONTIFF, for the exaltation of holy Church, for peace between nations, for Christian princes, and for tranquillity among peoples; and obtain that we may one day all rejoice together in Paradise. Amen.

414. Prayer for the Dead.

50 Days. T.Q. Applicable only to the dead.
(See Instructions, p. 1.)

℣. Requiem æternam dona eis, Domine.
℟. Et lux perpetua luceat eis.

℣. Eternal rest give to them, O Lord.
℟. And let perpetual light shine upon them.

415. ℣℣. & ℟℟. for the Dead.

300 Days. T.Q. Applicable only to the dead.
(See Instructions, p. 1.)

℣. Requiem æternam dona eis, Domine.
℟. Et lux perpetua luceat eis.
℣. Requiescant in pace.
℟. Amen.

℣. Eternal rest give to them, O Lord.
℟. And let perpetual light shine upon them.
℣. May they rest in peace. ℟. Amen.

XVII. MISCELLANEOUS

416. Visits to the Churches of the Stations.

i. 40 Years and as many Quarantines, to all the faithful, every time that during Lent, with contrite hearts and devotion, they visit the Churches of the Stations in the manner prescribed in the book printed for the purpose in Rome.

ii. Plenary, to all persons who shall have made the visit as above three times, each visit on a different day. I, II, III, IV.

The method prescribed to be used is as follows: First, to visit some church, and say there the prayers appointed in the book to the Blessed Sacrament, to the Blessed Virgin, and to the holy martyrs; then to go to the Church of the Station, saying on the way the Psalm *Miserere, Pater, Ave,* and *Gloria,* five times, and then the *Steps of the Passion of our Lord Jesus Christ;* and lastly, whilst at the Church itself, to say the Litanies of the Saints, with the versicles and prayers assigned, and at the end the Psalm *De profundis,* etc. All unlearned persons, however, and others who do not possess this book of the Stations, may gain the same Indulgences by saying at the two churches which they visit such prayers as their own devotion suggests to them, and as are suitable to their capacity; and while they go from one church to the other they are to say a third part of their Rosary with the Litanies, and on leaving the Church of the Station to end their visit with the Psalm *De profundis,* or else with one *Pater noster,* one *Ave Maria* and a *Requiem æternam* for the holy souls in purgatory.

N.B.—Nuns and others dwelling in monasteries and communities may participate in the benefit of these

Indulgences, provided that they keep the method pre-scribed and visit their own churches; these Indulgences may also be gained by the sick and prisoners, provided they supply what they are unable to perform by doing some good work enjoined them by their own confessor.

To gain the specific Indulgence attached to the church-es and days specified below, a simple visit is all that is required for partial Indulgences; Confession and Com-munion must be made for Plenary Indulgences.

These Indulgences may be gained in certain churches and chapels out of Rome, to which this special privilege has been granted.

Days and Churches of the Stations in Rome.

January 1. *Circumcision of our Lord Jesus Christ.* Station, St Mary beyond the Tiber. Thirty Years and Thirty Quarantines. The same Indulgence for the next four Stations.

January 6. *The Epiphany of our Lord.* St Peter on the Vatican.

Septuagesima Sunday. St Laurence outside the Walls.

Sexagesima. St Paul outside the Walls.

Quinquagesima. St Peter on the Vatican.

Ash Wednesday. St Sabina in St Alexius, and St Mary in Cosmedin, called Bocca della Verità. Fifteen Years and Fifteen Quarantines.

Thursday after Ash Wednesday. St George in Velabro, and the Church of JESUS and Mary. Ten Years and Ten Quarantines. The same Indulgence is granted for all the following days till the fourth Sunday in Lent.

—*Friday after Ash Wednesday.* SS. John and Paul, and St Gregory on the Celian Hill.

—*Saturday.* St Tryphon and St Augustine.

First Sunday in Lent. St John Lateran.

—*Monday.* St Peter's Chains and St John della Pigna.

—*Tuesday.* St Anastasia.

—*Wednesday (Ember Day).* St Mary Major.

—*Thursday.* St Laurence in Panisperna.

—*Friday (Ember Day).* The Twelve Holy Apostles.

—*Saturday* (Ember Day). St Peter on the Vatican.
Second Sunday in Lent. St Mary in Domnica, called the Church of the Navicella, and St Gregory on the Celian.
—*Monday.* St Mary Major and St Clement.
—*Tuesday.* St Balbina.
—*Wednesday.* St Cecilia beyond the Tiber.
—*Thursday.* St Mary beyond the Tiber.
—*Friday.* St Vitalis.
—*Saturday.* SS. Marcellinus and Peter, near the Lateran Basilica.
Third Sunday in Lent. St Laurence outside the Walls.
—*Monday.* St Mark.
—*Tuesday.* St Pudentiana.
—*Wednesday.* SS. Sixtus, Nereus and Achilleus.
—*Thursday.* SS. Cosmas and Damian, in the Forum.
—*Friday.* St Laurence in Lucina.
—*Saturday.* SS. Caius and Susanna, and St Mary of the Angels at the Baths.
Fourth Sunday in Lent. The Holy Cross in Jerusalem. Fifteen Years and Fifteen Quarantines.
—*Monday.* The Four Saints crowned with Martyrdom. Ten Years and Ten Quarantines.
—The same Indulgences for all the Stations following till Palm Sunday.
—*Tuesday.* St Laurence in St Damasus, and St Andrew della Valle.
—*Wednesday.* St Paul outside the Walls.
—*Thursday.* SS. Martin and Silvester on the Hills, and St Silvester in Capite.
—*Friday.* St Eusebius and St Bibiana.
—*Saturday.* St Nicholas in Carcere.
Passion Sunday. St Peter on the Vatican, and St Lazarus.
—*Monday.* St Chrysogonus beyond the Tiber.
—*Tuesday.* St Cyriacus in St Mary in Viâ Latâ, and SS. Quiricus and Julitta on the Hills.
—*Wednesday.* St Marcellus.
—*Thursday.* St Apollinaris.
—*Friday.* St Stephen on the Celian.

—*Saturday*. St John before the Latin Gate, and St Cæsareus.

Palm Sunday. St John Lateran. Twenty-five Years and Twenty-five Quarantines.

Monday in Holy Week. St Praxede. Ten Years and Ten Quarantines, also for next three days.

Tuesday in Holy Week. St Prisca, and St Mary at the Gate of the People.

Wednesday in Holy Week. St Mary Major.

Thursday in Holy Week. St John Lateran. Plenary. I, II.

Good Friday. Holy Cross in Jerusalem. Thirty Years and Thirty Quarantines.

Holy Saturday. St John Lateran. The same Indulgence.

Easter Day. St Mary Major. Plenary. I, II.

Easter Monday. St Peter on the Vatican, and St Onuphrius. Thirty Years and Thirty Quarantines. The same till Ascension Day.

Easter Tuesday. St Paul outside the Walls.

Wednesday in Easter Week. St Laurence outside the Walls.

Thursday in Easter Week. The Twelve Holy Apostles.

Friday in Easter Week. St Mary of the Martyrs, called La Rotonda.

Saturday in Easter Week. St John Lateran.

Low Sunday. St Pancratius and St Mary della Scala.

April 25. *Feast of St Mark the Evangelist*. St Peter on the Vatican.

Rogation Monday. St Mary Major.

Rogation Tuesday. St John Lateran.

Rogation Wednesday. St Peter on the Vatican.

Ascension Day. St Peter on the Vatican. Plenary. I, II.

Saturday, Vigil of Pentecost. St John Lateran. Ten Years and Ten Quarantines.

Whit Sunday. St Peter on the Vatican. Thirty Years and Thirty Quarantines. The same to Saturday in Whitsun Week.

Whit Monday. St Peters Chains.

Whit Tuesday. St Anastasia.

Wednesday in Whitsun Week (Ember Day). St Mary Major.

Thursday in Whitsun Week. St Laurence outside the Walls.

Friday in Whitsun Week (Ember Day). The Twelve Holy Apostles.

Saturday in Whitsun Week (Ember Day). St Peter on the Vatican.

Wednesday in September (Ember Day). St Mary Major. Ten Years and Ten Quarantines. The same to Third Sunday in Advent.

Friday in September (Ember Day). The Twelve Holy Apostles.

Saturday in September (Ember Day). St Peter on the Vatican.

First Sunday in Advent. St Mary Major.

Second Sunday in Advent. Holy Cross in Jerusalem.

Third Sunday in Advent. St Peter on the Vatican. Fifteen Years and Fifteen Quarantines.

Wednesday in December (Ember Day). St Mary Major. Ten Years and Ten Quarantines. The same up to Christmas Eve.

Friday in December (Ember Day). The Twelve Holy Apostles.

Saturday in December (Ember Day). St Peter on the Vatican.

Fourth Sunday in Advent. The Twelve Holy Apostles.

December 24. *Christmas Eve.* St Mary Major. Fifteen Years and Fifteen Quarantines. The same up to the Third Mass on Christmas Day.

December 25. *Christmas Day. First Mass.* The Altar of the Holy Crib, in St Mary Major.

Second Mass. St Anastasia.

Third Mass, and the rest of the day. St Peter on the Vatican, and St Mary Major. Plenary. I, II.

December 26. *St Stephen the first Martyr.* St Stephen on the Celian. Thirty Years and Thirty Quarantines. The same on two following days.

December 27. *St John the Apostle and Evangelist.* St Mary Major.
December 28. *Holy Innocents, Martyrs.* St Paul outside the Walls.

417. Visit to the Seven Churches and the Seven Privileged Altars.

The custom of visiting the seven principal Churches in Rome is of most ancient institution. They are as follows: St Peter on the Vatican; St Paul and Sebastian outside the Walls; St John Lateran; the Holy Cross in Jerusalem; St Laurence outside the Walls; and St Mary Major. Whoever between first Vespers and sunset of the day following, shall visit these Seven Churches, may gain the many Indulgences with which these Churches have been enriched for every day in the year, and a Plenary Indulgence. I, II, III.

Most ancient also is the custom of visiting in these Churches, but especially in St Peter on the Vatican, the seven privileged Altars. The seven Altars in St Peters are:

1. The Altar of Our Lady, commonly called the "Gregoriana";
2. Of SS. Processus and Martinianus;
3. Of St Michael the Archangel;
4. Of St Petronilla, Virgin;
5. Of Our Lady, commonly called "of the Pillar";
6. Of the Holy Apostles SS. Simon and Jude;
7. Of St Gregory the Great.

Any of the faithful who shall visit devoutly these seven Altars may obtain the numerous Indulgences granted to these seven Altars by successive Pontiffs.

The same Indulgences may be gained outside Rome in churches to which the privileges of the Seven Churches or the Seven Altars have been extended.

418. The Portiuncula.

Plenary, to all as often as they visit any one of the churches of the three Orders of St Francis, and many other churches and chapels having this privilege, between first Vespers on August 1 and sunset on August 2. I, II, IV. T.Q.

(See Instructions, p. 1.)

N.B.—The time for Confession is extended to July 30.

419. The Gradual or Penitential Psalms.

50 Days, on the days prescribed by the Rubric of the Roman Breviary.

(See Instructions, p. 1.)

420. Christian Doctrine.

   i. Seven Years to all masters of schools who, on Feast days, shall take their scholars to be instructed in Christian Doctrine, and shall themselves instruct them in it.

  ii. 100 Days, to those masters who, on working days, explain Christian Doctrine in their schools.

 iii. 100 Days, to fathers and mothers, every time they instruct their children and servants in Christian Doctrine.

 iv. 100 Days, to all the faithful, every time they employ themselves for half an hour in studying the Catechism.

  v. Seven Years and Seven Quarantines, to adults every time they assist at public Catechism, in church or chapel.

 vi. Plenary, on Christmas Day, Easter Day and SS. Peter and Paul, to adults who make a practice of assisting at public Catechism. I. II, IV.

vii. Three Years, on all Feasts of our Lady, to those of every age who make a practice of assisting in school or church at instruction in Christian Doctrine. I.

viii. Seven Years, for the same. I, II

(See Instructions, p. 1.)

421. Mental Prayer.

i. Plenary, once a month, to all the faithful who make mental prayer devoutly for half an hour, or at least a quarter of an hour, a day. I, II, IV.

ii. Plenary, once a month, to those who frequently teach or learn how to make mental prayer. I, II, IV.

iii. Seven Years and Seven Quarantines, every time, for teaching or learning, in public or private, how to make mental prayer. I, II.

(See Instructions, p. 1.)

422. Explanation of the Gospel.

i. Seven Years, to all who assist at the same in their parish church on Sundays and festivals.

ii. Plenary, on Christmas Day, Epiphany, Easter Day, Pentecost, and SS. Peter and Paul, to those who make a practice of assisting at the same. I, II.

(See Instructions, p. 1.)

423. Prayer after saying Office.

The remission, in the case of persons under obligation to say Office, of temporal punishment due for defects and faults committed through human frailty in the recital of Office, whether the Divine Office or that of our Lady.

The prayer must be said kneeling, except in cases of inability.

(See Instructions, p. 1.)

SACROSANCTÆ et Individuæ Trinitati, Crucifixi Domini nostri Jesu Christi humani-

tati, beatissimæ et gloriosissimæ semperque
Virginis Mariæ fœcundæ integritati, et omnium
Sanctorum universitati sit sempiterna laus, hon-
or, virtus, et gloria ab omni creatura, nobisque
remissio omnium peccatorum, per infinita sæcula
sæculorum. Amen.

℣. Beata viscera Mariæ Virginis, quæ portaverunt
æterni PATRIS FILIUM.

℟. Et beata ubera quæ lactaverunt CHRISTUM DO-
MINUM. PATER noster, Ave Maria.

424. Prayers to be said after the Sacrosanctæ

   i. 300 Days, once a day, for each prayer.
   ii. Plenary, once a month (I, II, IV) for each prayer.
          (See Instructions, p. 1.)

I

OCLEMENTISSIME JESU, gratias ago tibi ex
toto corde meo. Propitius esto mihi vilissimo
peccatori. Ego hanc actionem offero divino Cordi
tuo emendandam atque perficiendam, ad laudem
et gloriam sanctissimi Nominis tui et beatissimæ
Matris tuæ, ad salutem animæ meæ totiusque
Ecclesiæ tuæ. Amen.

II

BENEDICTUM sit Cor amantissimum et dul-
cissimum Nomen DOMINI nostri JESU CHRISTI
et gloriosissimæ Virginis Mariæ Matris ejus in
æternum et ultra.

425. Prayer for the Conversion of the Dutch.

   i. 200 Days.
   ii. Plenary, once a month.
  Any form of prayer may be used.
          (See Instructions, p. 1.)

426. The Divine Praises.

   i. One Year. T.Q.
   ii. Two Years, when said publicly after Mass or Benediction.
   iii. Plenary, once a month. I, II, III, IV.
(See Instructions, p. 1.)

BLESSED be GOD.
Blessed be his holy Name.
Blessed be JESUS CHRIST, true GOD and true Man.
Blessed be the Name of JESUS.
Blessed be his most Sacred Heart.
Blessed be JESUS in the most holy Sacrament of the Altar.
Blessed be the great Mother of GOD, Mary most holy.
Blessed be her holy and immaculate Conception.
Blessed be the name of Mary, Virgin and Mother.
Blessed be GOD in his Angels and in his Saints.

427. Ejaculations for a Happy Death.

   i. 300 Days. T.Q.
   ii. 100 Days, for saying one of the same.
(See Instructions, p. 1.)

JESUS, Mary, Joseph, I give you my heart and my soul.
JESUS, Mary, Joseph, assist me in my last agony.
JESUS, Mary, Joseph, may I breathe forth my soul in peace with you.

428. Beati Mortui, *etc.*

300 Days. T.Q.
(See Instructions, p. 1.)

BEATI mortui, qui in DOMINO moriuntur.

O mi DEUS, moriendum mihi est certo, sed nescio quando, quomodo, ubi moriar; hoc unum scio, me in æternum periturum, si in peccato lethali expirem.

Beatissima Virgo Maria, Mater DEI sancta, ora pro me peccatore, nunc et in hora mortis meæ. Amen.

BLESSED are the dead who die in the LORD.

O my GOD, I have certainly to die, but I know not when, how, or where I shall die; this only I know: that if I die in mortal sin, I shall be lost forever.

Most blessed Virgin Mary, holy Mother of GOD, pray for me a sinner, now and at the hour of my death. Amen.

429. Prayer for those in their Agony.

i. 300 Days, T.Q.
ii. Plenary, once a month. I, II, IV.

(See Instructions, p. 1.)

Pater noster thrice in memory of the Passion of Christ, and *Ave Maria* thrice in memory of the Sorrows of Mary assisting at the same. They are to be said kneeling unless physical infirmity makes it impossible.

430. Visiting the Sick in Hospitals.

100 Days, each visit.

(See Instructions, p. 1.)

431. Almsgiving.

i. Seven Years and Seven Quarantines.
ii. Plenary, on the day itself. I, II, IV.

iii. 100 Days, to members of the family and servants assisting at least by their presence.

(See Instructions, p. 1.)

This Devotion consists in giving food to three poor persons in honour of JESUS, Mary and Joseph.

432. Prayer for Deaf-Mutes.

100 Days, T.Q.

(See Instructions, p. 1.)

O MOST merciful JESUS, who didst show such tenderness towards little children, who enjoyed the privilege of being caressed by thy divine hands, and didst say that whoever received one such innocent child, received Thee; extend, we pray Thee, the hand of thy providence over the little ones who, through being deprived of hearing and speech, are exposed to so many dangers of soul and body. Diffuse the spirit of thy ardent charity into Christian hearts, that they may come to their aid, and send down abundant graces on those who help in providing for this portion of thy flock a refuge where their innocence can be secure, and they can find food and affection. Amen.

433. Propagation of the Faith.

i. 100 Days, T.Q.
ii. Plenary, on or during the Octaves of the Immaculate Conception, the Feast of St Joseph, and that of St Francis Xavier. I, II, IV.

(See Instructions, p. 1.)

This Devotion consists in giving help, by contributions or personal service to the Missions, or by exhorting others to help them, together with the recital of the *Ave Maria* thrice.

434. Against an Unprovided Death.

i. 100 Days. T.Q.
ii. Plenary, on Holy Thursday and Good Friday, and on the two Feasts of the Holy Cross, May 3 and September 14, to those who, having made the Devotion every day for a year, visit the Holy Sepulchre, or the Blessed Sacrament in Church. I, II, III, IV.

(See Instructions, p. 1.)

HEAR us, O GOD of our salvation, and issue not the decree for the completion of our days before Thou forgivest us our sins; and because penance avails not in hell, and there is no room for amendment in the pit, therefore we humbly pray and beseech Thee here on earth that, giving us time to pray for pardon, Thou wouldst give us also forgiveness of our sins. Through CHRIST our LORD. Amen.

Take away, merciful LORD, all errors from thy faithful people, avert from them the sudden destruction of the wasting pestilence; and those whose wanderings Thou dost justly chastise, do Thou mercifully pity when corrected. Through CHRIST our LORD. Amen.

Ant. Sin no longer, O my soul; think upon the sudden change from sin to endless torments. There, in hell, penance is not accepted, and tears profit not. Turn, then, whilst thou hast time; cry out and say, Have mercy upon me, O my GOD.

Ant. In the midst of life we are in death; but to whom can we look to be our helper save Thee, O LORD, who art justly angry with us because of our sins? O holy GOD, holy and strong, holy and merciful SAVIOUR, deliver us not over to a bitter death.

℣. Lest, overtaken by the day of death, we seek time for penance, and be unable to find it:

℟. Hearken, O LORD, and have mercy on us, for we have sinned against Thee.

WE beseech Thee, ALMIGHTY GOD, receive in thy fatherly pity thy people who flee unto Thee from thine anger; that those who fear to be chastised by the rod of thy majesty through sudden death, may be made worthy to rejoice in thy pardon. Through CHRIST our LORD. Amen.

We beseech Thee, ALMIGHTY GOD, graciously incline thine ear to the assembly of thy Church, and let thy mercy to us prevent thine anger, for if Thou shouldst mark iniquities there shall no creature be able to stand before Thee; and in that same admirable charity whereby Thou didst create us, pardon us sinners, and destroy not the work of thy own hands by sudden death. Through CHRIST our LORD. Amen.

Hear our prayers, O LORD, and enter not into judgment with thy servants; for, knowing that there is no justice in us on which we can dare to presume, we acknowledge no other fount of mercy whereby we can be washed from our sins, delivered from our infirmities, and especially from sudden death, but only Thee, O GOD. Through CHRIST our LORD. Amen.

O GOD, in whose sight every heart trembles and every conscience is awed; show forth thy mercy upon us, thy suppliants, that we, who trust not in the excellence of our own merit, may never experience thy judgments by suddenness of death, but may receive Thy pardon. Through CHRIST our LORD. Amen.

Prayer.

MOST merciful LORD JESUS, by thy agony and bloody sweat, and by thy death, deliver me, I beseech Thee, from sudden and unprepared death. O most gentle LORD JESUS, by thy cruel and ignominious scourging and crowning with thorns, by thy Cross and bitter Passion, and by thy own great goodness, I humbly pray Thee let me not die unprepared and pass from this life without the Holy Sacraments. JESUS, my best beloved, my LORD! by all thy travails and all thy sorrows, by thy Precious Blood, and by thy most holy wounds, and by those last words spoken by Thee upon the Cross—"My GOD, my GOD, why hast Thou forsaken Me?"and again, "FATHER, into thy hands I commend my spirit"—most ardently I pray Thee, free me from sudden death. Thy hands, O my REDEEMER, have wholly made and formed me; oh, suffer not death to take me unawares; grant me, I beseech Thee, time for penance; vouchsafe me a happy passage when I am in thy grace, that in the world to come I may love Thee with my whole heart, and praise and bless Thee for ever and for ever. Amen.

PATER *and* Ave *five times, in memory of the Passion of our Lord Jesus Christ, and* Ave *thrice, to the Blessed Virgin, Mother of Sorrows.*

435. Ejaculation.

50 Days. T.Q.

(See Instructions, p. 1.)

Nos, Jesu, Maria, et Joseph bone,
Benedicite nunc et in mortis agone.

436. In Honour of the Blessed Trinity, etc.

100 Days, on every Sunday.
(See Instructions, p. 1.)

I. THE BLESSED TRINITY.

WITH our whole hearts and lips we acknowledge, praise and bless Thee, O FATHER unbegotten; Thee, O only begotten SON; Thee, O HOLY SPIRIT and PARACLETE; O holy and undivided Trinity; to Thee be glory for ever.

℣. Let us bless the FATHER, SON, and HOLY SPIRIT.

℟. Let us praise and exalt Him for ever.

Let us pray.

ALMIGHTY and everlasting GOD, who hast granted to thy servants in the confession of the true faith to acknowledge the glory of the eternal Trinity, and in the power of thy Majesty to adore the Unity; we beseech Thee that by the strength of the same faith we may ever be defended from all adversity; through CHRIST our LORD. Amen.

II. ALL ANGELS AND SAINTS.

ANGELS, Archangels, Thrones and Dominations, Principalities and Powers, and Virtues of Heaven, Cherubim and Seraphim, Patriarchs and Prophets, holy Doctors of the Law, Apostles, all Martyrs of CHRIST, holy Confessors, Virgins of the LORD, Anchorites, and all Saints, intercede for us.

℣. All ye holy men and women, saints of GOD.
℟. Intercede for us.

Let us pray.

ALMIGHTY and everlasting GOD, who hast willed that we should profit by the merits of all thy saints, we beseech Thee that, as our intercessors are multiplied, so thou wouldst bestow upon us that abundance of mercy which we desire. Through CHRIST our LORD. Amen.

437. Spiritual Canticles.

i. One Year, to all the faithful every time they promote the singing of the Spiritual Canticles.
ii. 100 Days, every time anyone practises this devotion.
iii. Plenary, once a month, for promoting and practising this exercise, during the month. I, II, IV.

(See Instructions, p. 1.)

438. Prayer, with Ejaculation.

i. 40 Days, once a day.
ii. Plenary, once a month. I, II, III, IV.

(See Instructions, p. 1.)

O FATHER of mercies, and source of every good! I humbly beg Thee, through the most sacred and most loving Heart of JESUS, thy well-beloved SON, our LORD and REDEEMER, in whom Thou art always well pleased, vouchsafe to grant me the grace of a lively faith, a firm hope, and an ardent charity for Thee and for my neighbour. Grant me, besides, the grace of a true sorrow for all my sins, together with a most firm purpose of never offending Thee in the future, that I may always live according to thy divine good pleasure, fulfil thy most holy will in all things with a generous and willing heart, and persevere in thy love unto the end of my life. Amen.

O MOST blessed Virgin Mary, Mother of my LORD and REDEEMER, I entreat thee and beseech thee to effect by thy mercy that, in all the dangers and necessities of my soul, I may flee to thee, pray to thee, and call upon thee for help.

439. Prayers for a Happy Death.

i. 100 Days, once a day.
ii. Plenary, once a month. I, II, III, IV.
(See Instructions, p. 1.)

O LORD JESUS, GOD of goodness, and FATHER of mercies, I draw nigh to Thee with a contrite and humble heart; to Thee I recommend the last hour of my life, and that judgment which awaits me afterwards.

When my feet, benumbed with death, shall admonish me, that my course in this life is drawing to an end, merciful JESUS, have mercy on me.

When my hands, cold and trembling, shall no longer be able to clasp the crucifix, and shall let it fall against my will on my bed of suffering, merciful JESUS, have mercy on me.

When my eyes, dim and troubled at the approach of death, shall fix themselves on Thee, my last and only support, merciful JESUS, have mercy on me.

When my lips, cold and trembling, pronounce for the last time thy adorable Name, merciful JESUS, have mercy on me.

When my face, pale and livid, shall inspire the beholders with pity and dismay; when my hair, bathed in the sweat of death, and stiffening on my head, shall forebode my approaching end, merciful JESUS, have mercy on me.

When my ears, soon to be for ever shut to the discourse of men, shall be open to that irrevocable decree which is to fix my doom for all eternity, merciful JESUS, have mercy on me.

When my imagination, agitated by dreadful spectres, shall be sunk in an abyss of anguish; when my soul, affrighted with the sight of my iniquities and the terrors of thy judgments, shall have to fight against the angels of darkness, who will endeavour to conceal thy mercies from my eyes, and plunge me into despair, merciful JESUS, have mercy on me.

When my poor heart, oppressed with suffering and exhausted by its continual struggles with the enemies of its salvation, shall feel the pangs of death, merciful JESUS, have mercy on me.

When the last tear, the forerunner of my dissolution, shall drop from my eyes, receive it as a sacrifice of expiation for my sins; grant that I may expire the victim of penance; and then, in that dreadful moment, merciful JESUS, have mercy on me.

When my friends and relations, encircling my bed, shall be moved with compassion for me, and invoke thy clemency in my behalf, merciful JESUS, have mercy on me.

When I shall have lost the use of my senses, when the world shall have vanished from my sight, when I shall groan with anguish in my last agony and the pangs of death, merciful JESUS, have mercy on me.

When my last sighs shall force my soul to issue from my body, accept them as born of a loving impatience to come to thee; merciful JESUS, have mercy on me.

When my soul, trembling on my lips, shall bid adieu to the world, and leave my body lifeless, pale and cold, receive this separation as a homage which I willingly pay to thy Divine Majesty, and in that last moment of my mortal life, merciful JESUS, have mercy on me.

When at length my soul, admitted to thy presence, shall first behold the immortal splendour of thy Majesty, reject it not, but receive me into the loving embrace of thy mercy, where I may for ever sing thy praises; merciful JESUS, have mercy on me.

Let us pray.

O GOD, who hast doomed all men to die, but hast concealed from all the hour of their death, grant that I may pass my days in the practice of holiness and justice, and that I may be made worthy to quit this world in the embrace of thy love, through the merits of our LORD JESUS CHRIST, who liveth and reigneth with Thee in the unity of the HOLY SPIRIT. Amen.

440. Invocations and Petitions.

  i. 300 Days, once a day. IV.
  ii. Plenary, once a month on any of the three last days of the month. I, II, III, IV.

(See Instructions, p. 1.)

O FATHER! O SON! O HOLY SPIRIT! O Holy Trinity! O JESUS! O Mary!

O ye blessed Angels of GOD, all ye Saints of Paradise, men and women, obtain for me these graces, which I ask through the Precious Blood of JESUS CHRIST:

1. Ever to do the holy will of GOD.
2. Ever to live in union with GOD.
3. Not to think of anything but GOD.
4. To love GOD alone.
5. To do all for GOD.
6. To seek only the glory of GOD.
7. To sanctify myself solely for GOD.
8. To know well my own utter nothingness.
9. Ever to know more and more the will of my GOD.
10. (*Here ask for any special grace.*)

MARY most holy, offer to the Eternal FATHER the most Precious Blood of JESUS CHRIST for my soul, for the holy souls in purgatory, for the needs of Holy Church, for the conversion of sinners, and for all the world.

Then say Gloria PATRI *thrice to the most holy Blood of Jesus Christ,* Ave Maria *once to most holy Mary sorrowing, and* Requiem æternam *once for the holy souls in purgatory.*

441. Prayers in Times of Calamity.

40 Days, once a day.

(See Instructions, p. 1.)

MERCY of our GOD, encompass us, and deliver us from every plague. Gloria PATRI.

ETERNAL FATHER, sign us with the Blood of the Immaculate Lamb, as Thou didst sign the dwellings of thy people. Gloria PATRI.

MOST Precious Blood of JESUS our Love, cry for mercy for us from thy Divine FATHER, and deliver us. Gloria PATRI.

WOUNDS of my JESUS, mouths of love and mercy, speak for us in pity to the Eternal FATHER; hide us within yourselves and deliver us. Gloria PATRI.

ETERNAL FATHER, JESUS is ours; ours his Blood, ours his infinite merits; to Thee we offer ourselves wholly: then, if Thou lovest Him, and holdest precious this gift we make Thee, Thou oughtest to deliver us: for this we hope with fullest confidence. Gloria PATRI.

ETERNAL FATHER, Thou desirest not the death of a sinner, but rather that he should be converted and live: in thy mercy grant that we may live before Thee and be for ever thine. Gloria PATRI.

SAVE us, CHRIST our SAVIOUR, by the virtue of thy holy Cross; Thou who didst save Peter in the sea, have mercy upon us.

MARY, Mother of mercy, pray for us, and we shall be delivered; Mary, our advocate, speak for us, and we shall be saved.

The LORD justly scourgeth us for our sins; but do thou, Mary, plead for us, for thou art our most tender Mother.

Mary, in thy JESUS, and in thee, have we put our hope; oh, let us never be confounded. Salve Regina (No. 184).

442. Prayers for the Conversion of Japan.

i. 40 Days. T.Q.
ii. Plenary, twice a year, on any days they choose, to those who have prayed for this intention at least once a week, or have frequently exhorted others to do so. I, II, III, IV.

(See Instructions, p. 1.)

Prayer for this intention must be said at the visit.

443. Prayer in any Plague or Trouble.

100 Days. T.Q.

(See Instructions, p. 1.)

HELP us, O GOD of our salvation, and for the glory of thy name deliver us: be merciful to our sins for thy name's sake.

Psalm liii.

SAVE me, O LORD, in thy name; and judge me in thy strength.

O GOD, hear my prayer; give ear to the words of my mouth;

For strangers have risen up against me, and the mighty have sought after my soul, and they have not set GOD before their eyes.

For, behold, GOD is my helper, and the LORD is the protector of my soul.

Turn away evil from me upon my enemies, and scatter them in thy truth.

I will freely sacrifice to Thee; and will give praise, O GOD, to thy name, because it is good.

For Thou hast delivered me out of all my trouble, and mine eye hath looked down upon mine enemies.

Gloria Patri.

℣. For the glory of thy name, deliver us.

℟. And deal mercifully with our sins for thy name's sake.

Let us pray.

LORD, we beseech Thee, in thy pity hear the prayers of thy people; that we who suffer justly for our sins may, for the glory of thy name, mercifully be delivered. Through Christ our Lord.

℟. Amen.

We beseech Thee, therefore, help thy servants, whom Thou hast redeemed with thy Precious Blood.

444. Three Offerings.

i. 300 Days. T.Q.
ii. Plenary, once a month. I, II, III, IV.
(See Instructions, p. 1.)

ETERNAL FATHER, in union with the most holy and Immaculate Virgin, all the blessed in heaven and all the elect upon earth, I offer to Thee the most Precious Blood of JESUS CHRIST, in thanksgiving for the gifts and privileges with which Thou hast enriched Mary, thy most obedient daughter, particularly in her Immaculate Conception. I offer to Thee also this Precious Blood for the conversion of poor sinners, for the propagation and exaltation of thy Holy Church, for the safety and prosperity of our chief pastor, the Bishop of Rome, and according to his intentions. Gloria PATRI.

ETERNAL and Incarnate Word! in union with the most holy and Immaculate Virgin, all the blessed in heaven, and all the elect upon earth, I offer to thee thine own most Precious Blood, in thanksgiving for the gifts and privileges with which Thou hast enriched Mary, thy most loving Mother, particularly in her Immaculate Conception. I offer to thee also this Precious Blood for the conversion of poor sinners, for the propagation and exaltation of thy Holy Church, for the safety and prosperity of our chief pastor, the Bishop of Rome, and according to his intentions. Gloria PATRI.

HOLY and Eternal Spirit! in union with the most holy and Immaculate Virgin, all the blessed in Heaven, and all the elect upon earth, I offer to Thee the most Precious Blood of JESUS, in thanksgiving for the gifts and privileges with which Thou hast enriched Mary, thy most faithful Spouse, particularly in her Immaculate Conception. I offer to Thee also this Precious Blood for the conversion of poor sinners, for the propagation and exaltation of thy Holy Church, for the safety and prosperity of our chief pastor, the Bishop of Rome, and according to his intentions. Gloria PATRI.

PRAYER TO THE MOST HOLY VIRGIN.

MARY, Mother of GOD, most holy and Immaculate Virgin, by the love thou dost ever bear to GOD, by the gratitude thou hast towards Him for the manifold graces and favours with which thou wast enriched by Him, particularly for the privilege of Immaculate Conception granted to thee alone, and by the infinite merits of JESUS CHRIST, thy Divine SON our LORD, we pray thee most earnestly to obtain for us a most perfect and constant devotion towards thyself, and a full trust that through thy most mighty intercession we shall receive all the graces which we ask. Certain henceforth of obtaining them from thy great goodness, with hearts overflowing with joy and thankfulness, we venerate thee, and say the salutation which the holy archangel Gabriel made to thee. Ave Maria.

445. Prayer of St Benedict Joseph Labre for Times of Necessity.

100 Days. T.Q.

(See Instructions, p. 1.)

JESUS CHRISTUS, Rex gloriæ, venit in pace. DEUS homo factus est. Verbum caro factum est. CHRISTUS de Maria Virgine natus est. CHRISTUS per medium illorum ibat in pace. CHRISTUS crucifixus est. CHRISTUS mortuus est. CHRISTUS sepultus est.

JESUS CHRIST, the King of Glory, hath come in peace. GOD was made man. The Word was made flesh. CHRIST was born of Mary the Virgin. CHRIST went thro the midst of them in peace. CHRIST was crucified. CHRIST died. CHRIST was buried.

CHRISTUS resurrexit.	CHRIST rose from the dead.
CHRISTUS ascendit in cœlum.	CHRIST ascended into heaven.
CHRISTUS vincit.	CHRIST is victorious.
CHRISTUS regnat.	CHRIST reigns.
CHRISTUS imperat.	CHRIST is LORD of all.
CHRISTUS ab omni malo nos defendat.	May CHRIST defend us from all evil.
JESUS nobiscum est.	JESUS is with us.
PATER, Ave, Gloria.	PATER, Ave, Gloria.

ETERNAL FATHER, by the Blood of JESUS have mercy; sign us with the Blood of the Immaculate Lamb JESUS CHRIST, as Thou didst sign the people of Israel, in order to deliver them from death: and do thou, Mary, Mother of Mercy, pray to GOD and appease Him for us, and obtain for us the grace we ask. Gloria PATRI.

ETERNAL FATHER, by the Blood of JESUS have mercy; save us from the shipwreck of the world, as Thou didst save Noe from the universal deluge: and do thou, Mary, Ark of salvation, pray to GOD and appease Him for us, and obtain for us the grace we ask. Gloria PATRI.

ETERNAL FATHER, by the Blood of JESUS have mercy; deliver us from the plagues which we have deserved for our sins, as Thou didst deliver Lot from the flames of Sodom. And do thou, Mary, our Advocate, pray to GOD and appease Him for us, and obtain for us the grace we ask. Gloria PATRI.

ETERNAL FATHER, by the Blood of JESUS have mercy; comfort us under our present necessities and troubles, as Thou didst comfort Job, Anna and Tobias in their afflictions. And do thou, Mary, Comforter of the afflicted, pray to GOD and appease Him for us, and obtain for us the grace we ask. Gloria PATRI.

ETERNAL FATHER, by the Blood of JESUS have mercy; Thou who wouldst not the death of a sinner, but rather that he should be converted and live, grant us through thy mercy time for penance; that, filled with contrition and penance for our sins, which are the cause of all our evils, we may live in the holy faith, hope, charity and peace of our LORD JESUS CHRIST. And do thou, Mary, Refuge of sinners, pray to GOD and appease Him for us, and obtain for us the grace we ask. Gloria PATRI.

PRECIOUS Blood of JESUS, our Love, cry unto the Divine FATHER for mercy, pardon, grace and peace for us, for N., and for all the world. Gloria PATRI.

MARY, our Mother and our Hope, pray to GOD for us, for N., and for all, and obtain for us the grace we ask. Gloria PATRI.

ETERNAL FATHER, I offer Thee the Blood of JESUS CHRIST in discharge of all my debt of sin, for the wants of Holy Church, and for the conversion of sinners. Gloria PATRI.

MARY Immaculate, Mother of GOD, pray to JESUS for us, for N., and for all. JESUS, Mary, mercy!

St Michael Archangel, St Joseph, SS. Peter and Paul, protectors of all the faithful in the Church of GOD, and all ye Angels and Saints of Paradise, men and women, pray to GOD, and by your intercession obtain grace and mercy for me, for N., and for all. Amen.

446. Prayers for Purity.

i. 300 Days. T.Q.
ii. Plenary, once a month. I, II.
(See Instructions, p. 1.)

O JESUS, SON of the living GOD, brightness of eternal light, who from all eternity wast begotten most pure in the bosom of the Eternal FATHER, and who in time didst will to be born of a most pure and immaculate Virgin, I, thy creature full of infirmity, beg of Thee, with all my heart, to preserve me pure in mind and body; and do Thou cause to be renewed most abundantly in thy holy Church the virtue of holy Purity for thy greater glory and the salvation of the souls Thou hast redeemed.

O most pure and ever-immaculate Virgin Mary, Daughter of the Eternal FATHER, Mother of the Eternal SON, and Spouse of the HOLY SPIRIT, august and living temple of the most adorable Trinity, lily of purity and mirror without stain, obtain for me, dear Mother, I beseech thee, from the good JESUS, purity of mind and body, and beg of Him to cause this beautiful virtue to flourish more and more among all classes of the faithful.

O most chaste Spouse of Mary Immaculate, glorious St Joseph, who didst merit to receive from

GOD the singular privilege of being the reputed
FATHER of Innocence itself, JESUS CHRIST, and
spotless guardian of the Virgin of virgins, obtain for me, I beseech thee, the love of JESUS, my
SAVIOUR and GOD, and the special protection of
Mary my most blessed Mother; grant, O blessed
Joseph, protector of all chaste souls, that this thy
beloved virtue of holy purity may be better loved
by me and by all men.

And thou who didst so deeply love JESUS, Mary
and Joseph, St Bernadine, my special advocate
and example, model of Christian modesty, restorer in our times of piety and holy living, present
my prayers, I beseech thee, to the Holy Family,
and implore that, together with piety and the fear
of GOD, holy purity of soul and body may reign
in all Christian families and in all children of our
Mother, the holy Roman Church. Amen.

447. Temperance Pledge.

300 Days.

(See Instructions, p. 1.)

GOD, my FATHER, to show my love for Thee,
to make reparation to thy wounded honour,
to obtain the salvation of souls, I firmly purpose
to take this day neither wine, nor beer, nor any
intoxicating drink.

I offer Thee this act of mortification in union
with the sacrifice of thy SON JESUS CHRIST, who
daily offers Himself a Victim on the altar for thy
greater glory. Amen.

448. Salutation and Answer.

50 Days. T.Q.

(See Instructions, p. 1.)

PRAISED be Jesus and Mary.—Now and for ever.

449. For the Sovereign Pontiff.

    i. 300 Days, once a day.
    ii. Plenary, once a month. I, II, III, IV.

(See Instructions, p. 1.)

℣. Oremus pro Pontifice nostro N.

℟. Dominus conservet eum, et vivificet eum, et beatum faciat eum in terra, et non tradat eum in animam inimicorum ejus.

℣. Let us pray for our Pontiff N.

℟. The Lord preserve him and give him life, and make him blessed upon earth, and deliver him not up to the will of his enemies.

Pater noster. Ave Maria.

450. Prayer for Pope Pius X.

Composed by H.E. Cardinal Capecelatro, Archbishop of Capua.

300 Days. T.Q.

(See Instructions, p. 1.)

O JESUS, Divine Redeemer, Father of the great family called the Catholic Church, in these days of fear and bitter trial come to our aid. We pray Thee for all the Church, but especially for him who holds thy place here on earth, Pope Pius

X. He loves Thee fervently, and desires to restore all things to Thee. Now having completed his fifty years of the priesthood, he strives with all his might to imitate Thee in his life, praying, loving and sacrificing himself for the salvation of souls. O JESUS, mercifully hear the prayers which we offer to Thee for thy Vicar, true apostle of faith and charity. Respond to the ardent desire which he has to see our lives and the lives of all our brethren in the Church reformed. Give ever more and more light of supernatural wisdom to his intellect, and inflame more and more in him that burning charity which Thou hast diffused into his heart by the HOLY SPIRIT. Grant that he may have the longed-for consolation of seeing accomplished in his day that strict union of the sons of the Church for which Thou didst pray shortly before thy death, saying: Grant, O FATHER, that all my followers may be one with Me, as I am one with Thee. Unite then, O JESUS, around the shepherd of shepherds, thy Vicar, all the flock of the Church in the unity of faith and love. Grant that each of her children may remember that Thou didst empty thyself, becoming obedient unto death, even the death of the Cross. Thus will all who glory in the name of Catholic be humble, obedient and devoted to thy Vicar. Grant him, O LORD, this consolation, so earnestly desired by him, and by us all. O LORD, LORD JESUS, we hope in Thee. Grant us (in this year of Jubilee) to sing the hymn of thy peace, that hymn of peace which the angels sing in Heaven. Amen.

451. For the Conversion of Africa.

    i. 300 Days. T.Q.
    ii. Plenary, once a month. I, II, III, IV.
               (See Instructions, p. 1.)

   N.B.—Persons unable to read or otherwise hindered may substitute *Pater*, *Ave* and *Gloria* twice.

LET us pray also that for the most unhappy peoples of Africa, that Almighty GOD may at length remove the curse of Cham from their hearts, and give them that blessing which can only be obtained in JESUS CHRIST, our GOD and LORD.

Let us pray.

LORD JESUS CHRIST, the one and only SAVIOUR of the whole human race, "who reignest from sea to sea and from the river unto the boundaries of the world," open thy most Sacred Heart in mercy to those wretched souls in Africa who still sit in darkness and in the shadow of death, that through the intercession of the Blessed Virgin Mary, thy immaculate Mother, and of blessed Joseph her most glorious spouse, they may abandon their idols, and prostrating themselves before Thee, be admitted into thy holy Church, who livest and reignest, *etc.* PATER, Ave, Gloria.

452. Praises to Jesus Christ and most Holy Mary.

   100 Days, once a day.
               (See Instructions, p. 1.)

PRAISED be JESUS CHRIST, SON OF GOD;
May JESUS be ever praised.

Praised be Jesus,

May Jesus be ever praised.

true GOD and true man;
author of life;
eternal Wisdom;
infinite goodness;
GOD of peace;
Good Shepherd;
most loving FATHER;
our SAVIOUR;
our Hope;
our Love;
our Life;
our beginning;
our end;

MOST HOLY MARY.

PRAISED be Mary, daughter of the Eternal FATHER; May Mary be ever praised.

Praised be Mary,

May Mary be ever praised.

Mother of the Word Incarnate;
Spouse of the Divine SPIRIT;
co-redemptress of the world;
Immaculate Queen;
full of grace;
refuge of sinners;
Mother most merciful;
consoler of the sorrowful;
refuge of the afflicted;
star of promise in the midst of evil;
safe harbour for travellers;
our comfort in life;
our hope in death;

453. Christian Acts.

i. 300 Days, once a day.
ii. Plenary, once a month, on a Sunday. I, II, III, IV.

(See Instructions, p. 1.)

The prayer must be repeated thirty-three times, with a *Gloria* after each eleven.

MY GOD, I believe in Thee, I hope in Thee, I love Thee above all things with all my soul, with all my heart, with all my strength: I love Thee because Thou art infinitely good and worthy to be loved; and because I love Thee, I repent with my whole heart for having offended Thee; be merciful to me a sinner. Amen.

454. Assisting at a First Mass.

   i. Plenary, for blood relations to the third degree. I, II, IV.
   ii. Seven Years and Seven Quarantines for others. IV.
(See Instructions, p. 1.)

455. Prayer of St Thomas Aquinas for grace to lead a holy life.

Three Years, once a day.
(See Instructions, p. 1.)

CONCEDE mihi, misericors DEUS, quæ tibi sunt placita, ardenter concupiscere, prudenter investigare, veraciter agnoscere et perfecte adimplere ad laudem et gloriam nominis tui. Ordina, DEUS meus, statum meum: et quod a me

MERCIFUL GOD, grant that I may eagerly desire, carefully search out, truthfully acknowledge, and ever perfectly fulfil all things which are pleasing to Thee. Order, O my GOD, all my state and grant me to know what Thou requiris, ut faciam, tribue ut sciam; et da exequi sicut oportet et expedit animæ meæ.

Da mihi, Dominus Deus meus, inter prospera et adversa non deficere, ut in illis non extollar, et in istis non deprimar. De nullo gaudeam vel doleam nisi quod ducat ad te, vel abducat ate. Nulli placere appetam, vel displicere timeam nisi tibi.

Vilescant mihi DOMINE, omnia transitoria, et cara mihi sint omnia æterna. Tædeat me gaudii quod est sine te, nec aliud cupiam quod est extra te. Delectet me DOMINE, labor, qui est pro te; et tædiosa sit mihi omnis quies, quæ est sine te.

dost require me to do, and give me to do it as is fitting and profitable to my soul.

Grant, O LORD my GOD, that I may not fail either in prosperity or adversity, that I be not lifted up by the one or cast down by the other. Let me joy in nothing but what leads to Thee, nor grieve for anything but what leads away from Thee; let men either seek to please, nor fear to displease any but Thee alone.

May all transitory things grow vile in my eyes, O LORD, and may all that is eternal be dear to me. May all joy be irksome to me that is without Thee, nor may I desire anything that is apart from Thee. May all labour and toil delight me which is for Thee, and all rest be weariness which is not in Thee.

Da mihi, DEUS meus, cor meum ad te dirigere, et in defectione meacum emendationis proposito constanter dolere.

Fac me, DOMINE DEUS meus, obedientem sine contradictione, pauperem sine dejectione, castum sine corruptione, patientem sine murmuratione; humilem sine fictione, hilarem sine dissolutione, maturum sine gravidine, agilem sine levitate, timentem te sine desperatione, veracem sine duplicitate, operantem bona sine præsumptione, proximum corripere sine elatione, ipsum ædificare verbo et exemplo sine simulatione.

Da mihi, DOMINE DEUS, cor pervigil, quod nulla abducat a te curiosa cogitatio: da nobile, quod nulla deorsum trahat

Grant me, O LORD, continually to lift up my heart towards Thee, and to bring sorrowfully to mind my many short comings with full purpose of amendment.

Make me, O LORD, obedient without demur, poor without repining, chaste without stain, patient without murmur, humble without pretence, joyous without frivolity, fearful without abjectness, truthful without disguise, given to good works without presumption, faithful to rebuke my neighbour without arrogance, and ever careful to edify him by word and example without pretension.

Give me, O LORD, an ever watchful heart, which no subtle speculation may lure from Thee. Give me a noble heart, which no unworthy affection can draw downwards to the earth. Give indigna affectio: da rectum, quod nulla seorsum obliquet sinistra intentio: da firmum, quod nulla frangat tribulatio: da liberum, quod nulla sibi vindicet violenta affectio.

Largire mihi, DOMINE DEUS meus, intellectum te cognoscentem, diligenti am te quærentem, sapientiam te invenientem, conversationem tibi placentem, perseverantiam fidenter te expectantem, et fiduciam te finaliter amplectentem. Da tuis pœnis hic affligi per pœnitentiam, tuis beneficiis in via uti per gratiam, tuis gaudiis in patria perfrui per gloriam. Qui vivis et regnas DEUS per omnia sæcula sæculorum. Amen,

me an upright heart, which no insincere intention can warp aside. Give me a firm heart, which no tribulation can crush or quell. Give me a free heart, which no perverted or impetuous affection can claim for its own.

Bestow on me, O LORD, my God, understanding to know Thee, diligence to seek Thee, wisdom to find Thee, a life and conversation which may please Thee, perseverance in waiting patiently for Thee, and a hope which may embrace Thee at the last. Grant me to be pierced with compunction by thy sorrows through true repentance, to improve all thy gifts and benefits during this my pilgrimage through thy grace, and so in glory to rejoice together with Thee in the heavenly country. Who livest and reignest God, for ever and ever. Amen.

456. Prayer in Times of Calamity.

100 Days, once a day.
(See Instructions, p. 1.)

O LORD JESUS CHRIST, true GOD and true Man, GOD of Sanctity, GOD of Majesty, GOD Everlasting, have pity on us and upon the whole human race; now and always purify us from our sins and infirmities with thy Precious Blood, so that we may be able to live in thy holy peace and charity, now and for ever. Amen.

457. Prayer for the Christian Family.

200 Days, once a day.
(See Instructions, p. 1.)

GOD of bounty and of mercy, to thy almighty protection we commend our home, our family and all we possess. Bless us all, as Thou didst bless the Holy Family at Nazareth.

O JESUS, our most blessed SAVIOUR, by the love with which Thou didst become man for our salvation, by thy mercy in dying for us on the Cross, bless, we beseech thee, our home, our family and our household; preserve us from every evil and from the snares of men; protect us from lightning and hail, from fire, flood and tempest; preserve us from thy wrath, from the hatred and the evil designs of our enemies, from pestilence, famine and war. Let not any one of us die without the holy Sacraments; grant us thy blessing, that we may bravely confess that faith by which we are sanctified, that we may preserve our hope in sorrow and in affliction, and that we may redouble our love of Thee and our charity towards our neighbour.

O JESUS, bless and protect us.

O Mary, mother of grace and of mercy, bless us, defend us against the evil spirit, lead us by the hand across this vale of tears, reconcile us with thy SON, and commend us to Him that we may be made worthy of his promises. O holy Joseph, reputed father of our SAVIOUR, guardian of his most blessed Mother, head of the Holy Family, intercede for us, and bless and protect our habitation at all times.

St Michael, defend us against all the malice of hell.

St Gabriel, make us ever to seek the holy will of GOD.

St Raphael, preserve us from sickness and all danger of death.

Ye holy angels, our guardians, keep us day and night in the way of salvation.

Ye holy saints, our patrons, pray for us before the throne of GOD.

Bless this our home, O GOD the FATHER, who hast created us; O GOD the SON, who hast suffered for us on the Cross; O GOD the HOLY SPIRIT, who hast sanctified us in baptism. May GOD in his three divine Persons preserve our bodies, purify our souls, guide our hearts and lead us to eternal life.

Glory be to the FATHER, glory be to the SON, glory be to the HOLY SPIRIT. Amen.

458. Prayers to the Holy Family.

300 Days, once a day.
(See Instructions, p. 1.)

JESUS, Mary and Joseph, bless us and grant us the grace to love the Church, as we ought, above every other earthly thing, and always to show forth our love by deeds. PATER, Ave, Gloria.

JESUS, Mary and Joseph, bless us and grant us the grace without fear or human respect openly to profess, as we ought, the faith which was given to us in baptism. PATER, Ave, Gloria.

JESUS, Mary and Joseph, bless us and grant us the grace to share, as we ought, in the defence and propagation of the Faith, when duty calls, whether by word or by the sacrifice of our fortunes and our lives. PATER, Ave, Gloria.

JESUS, Mary and Joseph, bless us and grant us the grace to love one another, as we ought, and to live together in perfect harmony of thought, will and action, under the rule and guidance of our pastors. PATER, Ave, Gloria.

JESUS, Mary and Joseph, bless us and grant us the grace to conform our lives, as we ought, to the precepts of GOD and of the Church, so as to live always in that charity which they set forth. PATER, Ave, Gloria.

459. Prayer for Benefactors.

50 Days, twice a day.
(See Instructions, p. 1.)

RETRIBUERE dignare Domine, omnibus nobis bona facientibus propter nomen tuum vitam æternam. Amen.

REWARD, O Lord, with eternal life all those who do us good for thy name's sake. Amen.

460. Prayer of St Alphonsus.

To be said before retiring to rest.
60 Days, once a day.

(See Instructions, p. 1.)

JESUS CHRIST, my God, I adore Thee and I thank Thee for the many favours Thou hast bestowed on me this day. I offer Thee my sleep and all the moments of this night, and I pray Thee to preserve me from sin. Therefore I place myself in thy most sacred side, and under the mantle of our blessed Lady my Mother. May the holy angels assist me and keep me in peace, and may thy blessing be upon me.

461. Prayer for the Conversion of the Jews.

100 Days, once a day.

(See Instructions, p. 1.)

GOD of goodness and FATHER of mercies, we beseech Thee, by the immaculate heart of Mary, and by the intercession of the Patriarchs and holy Apostles, to look with compassion upon the remnant of Israel, so that they may come to a knowledge of our only SAVIOUR JESUS CHRIST, and share in the precious graces of Redemption. Amen.

462. Prayer for the Propagation of Faith and Piety.

i. Seven Years and Seven Quarantines, once a day.
ii. Plenary, once a month. I, II, IV.

(See Instructions, p. 1.)

ETERNAL FATHER, by thy infinite mercy and by the infinite merits of thy divine SON JESUS, make thyself known and loved by all souls, since it is thy will that all should be saved. Gloria PATRI.

Through the sacred mysteries of human redemption send, O LORD, labourers into thy harvest, and spare thy people.

Eternal Word incarnate, REDEEMER of the human race, convert all souls to thyself, since for them Thou wast obedient even to the death of the Cross. Gloria PATRI.

Through the merits and intercession of thy most holy Mother, and of all the Angels and Saints, send, O LORD, labourers into thy harvest, and spare thy people.

O HOLY SPIRIT of GOD, by the infinite merits of the Passion and Death of JESUS CHRIST, diffuse thy most ardent and all-powerful charity in all hearts, that there may be one Fold and one Shepherd throughout the world, and that all may come to sing thy divine mercies in Heaven for ever. Amen. Gloria PATRI.

Queen of Apostles, and all ye Angels and Saints, pray the LORD of the harvest to send labourers into his harvest and spare his people, that we may all rejoice with Him and the FATHER and the HOLY SPIRIT for ever and ever. Amen.

Immaculate Mother of GOD, Queen of Apostles, I know that the divine precept, by which I am bound to love my neighbour as myself, obliges me to procure by every possible means not only my eternal salvation, but also that of my neighbour. But I confess that through my sins I am not worthy of the grace to labour effectually and constantly for the eternal salvation of my soul and of the souls of my relations and neighbours; much less am I worthy of the grace to promote good works and increase the means, both spiritual and temporal, of restoring Faith and rekindling Charity among Catholics, and propagating the truth throughout the world. Do thou then, O Mother, obtain for me this grace through the mercy of GOD and the infinite merits of JESUS CHRIST; and in union with the heavenly court and all the just, who are or will be in the Church of GOD, from henceforth I intend to offer these same merits of JESUS as a thanksgiving in anticipation of this grace obtained by thee for us and for all, as thou didst obtain it for the holy Apostles. And so, I, N.N., trusting in thy powerful intercession, resolve from henceforth to use whatever I have from GOD of power, talents, learning, riches, position, health, sickness or sorrow, for the greater glory of GOD and the salvation of my soul, and that of my neighbour, more especially by working for the propagation of piety and the holy faith throughout the world. And when all other means to this end fail me, I will never cease to pray, that there may be one Fold and one Shepherd. By so doing I hope to reach Paradise, there to enjoy the fruit of the Apostolate of JESUS CHRIST for all eternity. Amen. Ave Maria *thrice*, Gloria PATRI *once*.

463. Prayer for the Sanctification of Priests.

i. Seven Years and Seven Quarantines. T.Q.
ii. Plenary, once a month. I, II, III, IV.
(See Instructions, p. 1.)

O JESUS, eternal pastor of souls, hear our prayer on behalf of our priests and hear in it thy own eternal desire. Are not priests the object of thy most tender and exquisite care, that profound love in which are summed up all thy affections for souls? Let us confess our unworthiness to have good priests. But thy mercy is infinitely greater than our folly and wickedness.

O JESUS, grant that only those ascend to thy priesthood who are called by Thee; enlighten pastors in their choice, inspire directors with a spirit of counsel, and teachers in the cultivation of vocations. Give us priests who are angels of purity, models of humility, seraphs of holy love, heroes of self-sacrifice, apostles of thy glory, and saviours and sanctifiers of souls.

Have pity on the ignorant who should be enlightened, on the sons of toil who call for someone to save them from error and redeem them in thy name, on all the children and youths who cry for such as may save them and bring them to Thee, on so many who suffer and have need of a heart which will find them consolation in thine. What a number of souls would arrive at perfection through the ministry of holy priests! Then, O JESUS, have compassion again on the crowds who hunger and thirst. Grant that thy priesthood may bring to Thee fainting humanity, and let the earth be once again renewed, the Church exalted, and the reign of thy Heart established in peace.

Immaculate Virgin, Mother of the Eternal Priest, and thou thyself a priest at the altar, who hadst for thy first son of adoption St John, the beloved priest of JESUS, who didst preside in the cœnaculum, mistress and queen of the Apostles; deign to utter with thy sacred lips this our humble prayer; do thou make its accents to penetrate to the Heart of thy divine SON, and, all-powerful in thy supplication, obtain for the Church of thy SON JESUS a perennial renewal of Pentecost. Amen.

464. Two Prayers for the Increase and Preservation of the Clergy.

300 Days for each.*
(See Instructions, p. 1.)

I. FOR THE INCREASE OF LABOURERS.

Ant. Quid statis tota die otiosi? Ite in vineam meam.

℣. Rogate DOMINUM messis.

℟. Ut mittat operarios in vineam suam.

Oremus.

Ant. Why stand ye all the day idle, go ye into my vineyard.

℣. Ask the LORD of the harvest.

℟. That He send labourers into his vineyard.

Let us pray.

DEUS qui non vis mortem peccatoris, sed magis ut convertatur et vivat, da, quæsumus, per intercessionem beatæ Mariæ semper Virginis et omnium sanctorum, operarios Ecclesiæ tuæ, qui sunt cooperatores CHRISTI, ut se impendant et superimpendant pro animabus. Per eundem DOMINUM, *etc.* Amen.

GOD who willest not the death of the sinner, but rather that he be converted and live; grant, by the intercession of blessed Mary ever Virgin and of all the saints, labourers for thy Church, fellow labourers with Christ, to spend and consume themselves for souls. Through the same JESUS CHRIST, *etc.* Amen.

II. FOR THE PRESERVATION OF THE CLERGY.

Ant. Nemo mittens manum suam ad aratrum et respiciens retro aptus est regno DEI.
℣. Nemo militans DEO implicat se negotiis sæcularibus.
℟. Ut ei placeat, cui se probavit.

Ant. No one putting his hand to the plough and looking back is fit for the Kingdom of GOD.
℣. No soldier of GOD involves himself in worldly affairs.
℟. That he may please Him to whom he has approved himself.
Let us pray.

Oremus.
DEUS infirmitatis humanæ singulare præsidium, exaudi,

GOD, the sole protection of human weakness, hear, we

quæsumus, preces quas pro fratribus in discrimine positis humiliter fundimus, ut famulos tuos ab omni eruas peccatorum nequitia et in tua protectionis securitate constituas. Per DOMINUM, *etc.* Amen.

beseech Thee, the prayers which we humbly address to Thee for our brethren who are in danger, and do Thou rescue them from all evil of sin, and establish them in the security of thy protection. Through JESUS CHRIST our LORD. Amen.

465. For Clerics and Students putting on a Cotta.

300 Days. T.Q.

(See Instructions, p. 1.)

Make the Sign of the Cross and say:

INDUE me, DOMINE, novum hominem, qui secundum DEUM creatus est, in justitia et sanctitate veritatis. Amen.

CLOTHE me, O LORD, with the new man, who was created according to GOD, in justice and the sanctity of truth. Amen.

FOR SPECIAL CLASSES

I. FOR PRIESTS

466. Intention before Mass.

50 Days.

(See Instructions, p. 1.)

EGO volo celebrare Missam, et conficere Corpus et Sanguinem DOMINI nostri JESU CHRISTI, juxta ritum sanctæ Romanæ Ecclesiæ, ad laudem omnipotentis DEI, totiusque curiæ triumphantis, ad utilitatem meam, totiusque curiæ militantis, pro omnibus, qui se commendaverunt orationibus meis in genere et in specie, et pro felici statu sanctæ Romanæ Ecclesiæ. Amen.

GAUDIUM cum pace, emendationem vitæ, spatium veræ pœnitentiæ, gratiam et consolationem SANCTI SPIRITUS, perseverantiam in bonis operibus, tribuat nobis omnipotens et misericors DOMINUS. Amen.

467. Prayer after Mass.

Three Years.

(See Instructions, p. 1.)

OBSECRO te dulcissime, DOMINE JESU CHRISTE, ut passio tua sit mihi virtus qua muniar, protegar, atque defendar: vulnera tua sint mihi cibus potusque, quibus pascar, inebrier atque delecter: aspersio sanguinis tui sit mihi gloria sempiterna. In his sit mihi refectio, exsultatio, sanitas et dulcedo cordis mei: qui vivis et regnas in sæcula sæculorum. Amen.

468. Prayer to St Joseph, before Mass.

100 Days.

(See Instructions, p. 1.)

O FELICEM virum beatum Joseph, cui datum est DEUM, quem multi reges voluerunt videre, et non viderunt, audire, et non audierunt, non solum videre et audire, sed portare, deosculari, vestire et custodire.

℣. Ora pro nobis, beate Joseph.

℟. Ut digni efficiamur promissionibus CHRISTI.

Oremus.

DEUS, qui dedisti nobis regale sacerdotium, præsta quæsumus, ut sicut beatus Joseph unigenitum FILIUM tuum natum ex Maria Virgine, suis manibus reverenter tractare meruit et portare, ita nos facias cum cordis munditia et operis innocentia tuis sanctis altaribus deservire, ut sacrosanctum FILII tui Corpus et Sanguinem hodie digne sumamus, et in future sæculo præmium habere mereamur æternum. Per eumdem CHRISTUM DOMINUM nostrum. Amen.

469. Prayer to our Lady before Mass.

100 Days.

(See Instructions, p. 1.)

O MATER pietatis et misericordiæ, beatissima Virgo Maria, ego miser et indignus peccator ad te confugio toto corde et affectu, et precor pietatem tuam: ut sicut dulcissimo Filio tuo in crucependenti astitisti, ita et mihi misero peccatori, et sacerdotibus omnibus hic et in tota sancta Ecclesia hodie offerentibus, clementer assistere digneris, ut tua gratia adjuti, dignam et accept-

abilem hostiam in conspectu summæ et individuæ Trinitatis offere valeamus. Amen.

470. Preparation and Thanksgiving.

i. One Year, for the Antiphon, Psalms, Versicles and
Prayers contained in the *Præparatio ad Missam*,
with one of the seven prayers of St Ambrose.
ii. One Year for the Antiphon, Canticle, Psalm,
Versicles and Prayers contained in the *Gratiarum
Actio post Missam*, together with the prayers of St
Thomas and St Bonaventure.
iii. 100 Days, for each of the other prayers, to be said
in Preparation and Thanksgiving (see Table below).
iv. Plenary, once a month, for saying daily all the
Psalms, Prayers, etc., given below (see Table).

(See Instructions, p. 1.)

TABLE OF INDULGENCED PSALMS, PRAYERS, ETC.,
TO BE SAID IN PREPARATION FOR MASS OR IN
THANKSGIVING:

Preparation:

1. *Antiphon,* Ne reminiscaris, Psalms lxxxiii, lxxx-
iv, lxxxv, cxv, cxxix, *with* ℣.℣., ℟.℟. *and Prayers.*
2. *Prayers of St Ambrose for every day of the week.*
3. *Prayer of St Thomas Aquinas,* Gratias tibi ago.
4. *Prayer of St Ambrose,* Ad mensam dulcissimi.
5. *Prayer to the Angels and Saints,* Angeli,
Archangeli.
6. *Prayer when about to offer the Mass in honour of
a Saint or Beatus.*

Thanksgiving:

1. *Antiphon,* Trium puerorum; *Canticle,* Benedicite;
Psalm cl. ℣.℣., ℟.℟. *and Prayers.*
2. *Prayer of St Thomas Aquinas,* Gratias tibi ago.
3. *Prayer of St Bonaventure,* Transfige dulcissime.
4. *Adoro te devote.*

5. *Prayers of St Alphonsus for every Day of the Week.*
6. *Prayer to our Lady,* O Maria, Virgo et Mater.
  N.B.—All these are to be found in Missals, Breviaries
and other books used by Priests.

471. Prayer before Hearing Confessions.

100 Days, once a day.

(See Instructions, p. 1.)

DA mihi, DOMINE, sedium tuarum assistricem
sapientiam, ut sciam judicare populum tuum
in justitia, et pauperes tuos in judicio. Fac me ita
tractare claves regni cælorum, ut nulli aperiam, cui
claudendum sit, nulli claudam, cui aperiendum
sit. Sit intentio mea pura, zelus meus sincerus,
caritas mea patiens, labor meus fructuosus. Sit
in me lenitas non remissa, asperitas non severa,
pauperem ne despiciam, diviti ne aduler. Fac me
ad alliciendos peccatores suavem, ad interrogan-
dos prudentem, ad instruendos peritum. Tribue,
quæso, ad retrahendos a malo solertiam, ad con-
firmandos in bono sedulitatem, ad promovendos
ad meliora industriam, in responsis maturitatem,
in consiliis rectitudinem, in obscuris lumen, in
implexis sagacitatem, in arduis victoriam, inutili-
bus colloquiis ne detinear, pravis ne contaminer,
alios salvem, meipsum non perdam. Amen.

472. Prayers before and after Confession.

200 Days.

(See Instructions, p. 1.)

Before.

SUSCIPE Confessionem meam, piissime ac clementissime DOMINE JESU CHRISTE, unica spes salutis animæ meæ, et da mihi, obsecro, contritionem cordis, et lacrimas oculis meis, ut defleam diebus ac noctibus omnes negligentias meas cum humilitate et puritate cordis. DOMINE DEUS meus, suscipe preces meas. SALVATOR mundi, JESU bone, qui te crucis morti dedisti, ut peccatores salvos faceres, respice me miserum peccatorem invocantem nomen tuum, et noli sic attendere malum meum ut obliviscaris bonum tuum; et si commisi unde me damnare potes, tu non amisisti unde salvare soles. Parce ergo mihi qui es SALVATOR meus, et miserere peccatrici animæ meæ. Solve vincula ejus, sana vulnera. Emitte igitur, piissime DOMINE, meritis purissimæ et immaculatæ semper Virginis Genitricis tuæ Mariæ, et Sanctorum tuorum, lucem tuam, veritatem tuam in animam meam, quæ omnes defectus meos in veritate mihi ostendat, de quibus confiteri me oportet, atque juvet et doceat ipsos plene et contrite corde explicare. Qui vivis et regnas DEUS, per omnia sæcula sæculorum. Amen.

After.

SIT tibi DOMINE, obsecro, meritis beatæ semper Virginis Genitricis tuæ Mariæ et omnium Sanctorum, grata et accepta ista confessio mea; et quid quid mihi defuit nunc et alias de sufficientia contritionis, de puritate et integritate confessionis, suppleat pietas et misericordia tua, et secundum illam digneris me habere plenius et perfectius absolutum in cælo: Qui vivis et regnas DEUS per omnia sæcula sæculorum. Amen.

473. First Mass.

Plenary, for the Celebrant. I, III, IV.
(See Instructions, p. 1.)

II. FOR PRIESTS AND OTHERS IN
SACRED ORDERS

474. Prayer to our Lord.

300 Days, once a day.
(See Instructions, p. 1.)

JESU dilectissime, qui ex singulari benevolentia me præ millenis hominibus ad tui sequelam et ad eximiam Sacerdotii dignitatem vocasti, largiri mihi, precor, opem tuam divinam ad officia mea obeunda. Oro te, DOMINE JESU, ut resuscites hodie et semper in me gratiam tuam, quæ fuit in me per impositionem manuum episcopalium. O potentissime animarum medice, sana me taliter, ne revolvar in vitia; et cuncta peccata fugiam tibique usque ad mortem placere possim. Amen.

475. Ejaculation.

100 Days, once a day.
(See Instructions, p. 1.)

BONE JESU, rogo te per dilectionem, qua diligis Matrem tuam, ut sicut vere eam diligis et diligi vis, ita mihi des, ut vere eam diligam.

476. Prayer for the Preservation of Chastity.

100 Days, once a day.
(See Instructions, p. 1.)

DOMINE JESU CHRISTE, sponse animæ meæ,
deliciæ cordis mei, imo cor meum et anima
mea, ante conspectum tuum genibus me provolvo, et maximo animi ardore te oro et obtestor,
ut mihi des servare fidem a me tibi solemniter
datam in receptione Subdiaconatus. Ideo O dulcissime JESU, abnegem omnem impietatem, sim
semper alienus a carnalibus desideriis et terrenis
concupiscentiis, quæ militant adversus animam,
et castitatem te adjuvante intemerate servem.

O sanctissima et immaculata Maria, Virgo
Virginum et Mater nostra amantissima, munda
in dies cor meum et animam meam, impetra mihi
timorem DOMINI et singularem mei diffidentiam.

Sancte Joseph, custos Virginitatis Mariæ, custodi animam meam ab omni peccato.

Omnes sanctæ Virgines divinum Agnum quo-
cunque sequentes, estote mei peccatoris semper
sollicitæ, ne cogitatione, verbo aut opere delin-
quam et a castissimo Corde JESU unquam disce-
dam. Amen.

III. FOR YOUNG STUDENTS

477. Consecration of Studies to Mary Immacu-
late.

100 Days, once a day.
(See Instructions, p. 1.)

SUB patrocinio tuo, Mater dulcissima, et in-
vocato Immaculatæ Conceptionis tuæ mys-
terio, studia mea laboresque litterarios prosequi

volo: quibus me protestor hunc maxime ob finem incumbere, ut melius divino honori tuoque cultui propagando inserviam. Oro te igitur, Mater amantissima, sedes sapientiæ, ut laboribus meis benigne faveas. Ego vero, quod justum est, pie libenterque promitto, quidquid boni mihi inde successerit, id me tuæ apud DEUM intercessioni totum acceptum relaturum. Amen.

478. Prayer in Choosing a State of Life.

300 Days, once a day.
(See Instructions, p. 1.)

O My GOD, Thou who art the GOD of wisdom and of counsel, Thou who readest in my heart the sincere will to please Thee alone, and to govern myself with regard to my choice of a state of life, entirely in conformity with thy most holy desire; grant me, by the intercession of the most blessed Virgin, my Mother, and of my holy patrons, specially of St Joseph and St Aloysius, the grace to know what state I ought to choose, and when known to embrace it, so that in it I may be able to pursue and increase thy glory, work out my salvation, and merit that heavenly reward which Thou hast promised to those who do thy holy will. Amen.

479. Prayer for one aspiring to the Priesthood.

200 Days, once a day.
(See Instructions, p. 1.)

O My GOD, I am unworthy, most unworthy, to serve in the ministry of the priesthood,

through which is offered on thy altars the Body
and Blood of thy SON JESUS CHRIST. I am in no way
worthy of this honour, being a miserable sinner,
a mere nothing, even less than nothing by reason
of my malice, fit for nothing but to commit sin.
But while I feel within me an impulse drawing
me to the ecclesiastical state, and of myself cannot tell whether it be presumption on my part or
an inspiration from Thee, I humble myself before
Thee, and I pray Thee to enlighten me to know if
it be in accordance with thy good pleasure, for I
would do nothing contrary to thy will. Do Thou,
therefore, who art the Light of the world, shine
forth in my heart, and if this thought is a call
from Thee, give me the grace to obey it promptly, and worthily to correspond with it. But if, O
LORD, Thou dost not call me to the priestly ministry, or Thou seest that as a member of it I should
not be a good priest, but rather a disedification
and a scandal to the Church, never permit me to
enter a state which would be my damnation.

Most holy Virgin, Mother of GOD, and Mother
of good counsel, do thou support my poor prayer,
and may I have the grace from our LORD by thy
merits and intercession in all things to regulate
my actions, not by my own, but by thy holy Will.
PATER, Ave, Gloria.

480. Prayer to Our Lady.

300 Days, once a day.
(See Instructions)

O GREAT Queen of Heaven, most pure Virgin,
look, I beseech thee from thy throne with eyes

of pity upon my tender age. How many insidious and seductive maxims are abroad, to rob me of the holy faith, which was infused into my soul in Baptism, in order to enlighten my understanding and render my will upright and holy! In how many ways do the evil examples of men, the various arts and endless displays strive with their alluring images to destroy the precious germs of virtue in my tender heart! O thou who wast chosen by the GOD of mercy to give to the world the REDEEMER of the human race, which had fallen victim to the insidious promises of the rebellious and crafty Lucifer, protect me from the malicious snares which he is ever laying for the regenerate children of Adam. O thou who didst receive me on Calvary as thy son, let me not succumb to the suggestions of evil passions, or fall a victim to the crafty enemies of my eternal salvation; let not the ministers of Satan, proud of the laurels they have already gained, acquire fresh courage and strength for bolder and more fatal schemes. O sweet and powerful Mother Mary, may I never be guilty of renewing by my sins the Passion of thy SON, my most loving REDEEMER, and of piercing thy most loving heart with sharp swords. May all my actions, O dear Mother, thanks to thy patronage, be ever directed to the glory of GOD and the salvation of my soul. Amen. Ave Maria *thrice*.

481. Prayer for Children in Purgatory.

i. 100 Days, once a day, for children who say this prayer.

ii. Plenary, on All Saints Day, to those who recite it daily for at least half the year. I, II, III, IV.

N.B.—Bishops can authorize confessors to commute the Communion in case of children who have not made their first Communion.

(See Instructions, p. 1.)

SWEET Saviour Jesus, who during thy life didst show such great love for children; we who as children share with them thy blessing, beseech Thee to open the gate of Heaven to our companions who are lamenting in the place of sorrow and penance. Grant also their protection to us, to our relations, and to our common Father, the supreme Pontiff.

Holy Virgin, good Mother, pray for us and for the children who suffer. Ave Maria.

APPENDIX

482. Prayer for the Conversion of Freemasons.

100 Days, once a day.

(See Instructions, p. 1.)

O LORD JESUS CHRIST, who showest forth thy omnipotence most manifestly when Thou sparest and hast compassion; Thou who didst say, "Pray for those who persecute and calumniate you," we implore the clemency of thy Sacred Heart on behalf of souls, made in the image of GOD, but most miserably deceived by the treacherous snares of Freemasons, and going more and more astray in the way of perdition. Let not the Church, thy spouse, any longer be oppressed by them; but, appeased by the intercession of the blessed Virgin thy Mother and the prayers of the just, be mindful of thy infinite mercy; and, disregarding their perversity, cause these very men to return to Thee, that they may bring consolation to the Church by a most abundant penance, make reparation for their misdeeds, and secure for themselves a glorious eternity; who livest and reignest world without end. Amen.

483. Pious Reading of the Gospel.

i. 300 Days, once a day.
ii. Plenary, once a month. I, II, IV.
These Indulgences are gained by reading the Gospel

for at least a quarter of an hour.

484. Prayer to the Sacred Heart for Pope Pius X.

i. 300 Days. T.Q.
ii. Seven Years and Seven Quarantines, if said before
the Blessed Sacrament exposed.
iii. Plenary, if said every day in June, on the last day of
the month. I, II, III, IV.

(See Instructions, p. 1.)

MOST Sacred Heart of JESUS, with humble
confidence we earnestly pray to Thee for
thy Vicar, our Holy FATHER Pius X, to whom on
earth Thou hast been pleased to confide thy joys
and thy sorrows. O good JESUS, Thou didst make
a special promise to all priests who are devout to
thy Heart, that they should enjoy the gift of moving the most hardened hearts, and should gather marvellous fruits from their apostolic labours.
Oh, may that promise be realized to the full in
the Pontiff of thy Eucharist and of thy adorable
Heart. And since he is the universal High Priest,
give him power to stir the hardened hearts of the
entire human family; may his words, inspired by
thy Divine Heart, fill with light, humility and love
all who are hardened by ignorance, rebellious
pride, or earthly lusts; and with strenuous zeal
all who are feeble, slothful, or lukewarm in thy
service. O sweetest Heart, renew in him the joys
of the sacerdotal unction; lighten the burdens of
the Pontifical Office; and do Thou hasten on the
fulfilment of his apostolic desire to "restore all
things in Thee." Grant that the Holy FATHER, who
has so well understood the love of thy Heart in its
desire for sacramental union with men, may see

the accomplishment of that other desire of thine, the prayer of the Cenaculum, "that they may be one." O Heart infinitely powerful and merciful, unite round him all those committed to Thee by the FATHER, and to thy Vicar by Thee; so that we may be all one among ourselves by the love which alone makes us brethren, and one with the Pontiff by the obedience which alone makes us free, and one with Thee, as Thou art one with the FATHER. Amen.

485. Prayer to the Queen of Angels by the Ven. Louis Edward Cestac.

300 Days, once a day.

(See Instructions, p. 1.)

AUGUST Queen of Heaven and Mistress of Angels, who hast been commissioned by GOD with power to crush the head of Satan, we humbly beseech thee to send forth the legions of Heaven, that under thy command they may seek out all evil spirits, everywhere put them to flight, curb their insolence, and hurl them back into the abyss.

Who is like unto GOD?

Holy Angels and Archangels, defend and keep us.

O good and tender Mother, thou shalt ever be our love and our hope.

O Mother of GOD, send the holy Angels to defend me, and drive far away from me the cruel enemy.

486. Ejaculation to the Sacred Heart.

300 Days. T.Q.

(See Instructions, p. 1.)

ALL for Thee, most Sacred Heart of JESUS.

487. The Twelve Saturdays immediately preceding the Immaculate Conception.

Plenary on each Saturday. I, II, IV.

(See Instructions, p. 1.)

Some time must be spent in prayer or pious meditation in honour of the Immaculate Conception.

488. Prayer to St Paul.

300 Days once a day.

(See Instructions, p. 1.)

O MOST glorious Apostle, who didst labour with so much zeal at Ephesus to destroy the writings which thou knewest full well would pervert the minds of the faithful; deign in these times to turn upon us thy loving regard. Thou seest how an unbelieving and unbridled press endeavours to steal from mans heart its precious treasures of faith and moral purity. We beseech thee, O great Apostle, to enlighten the minds of all these perverse writers, that at length they may cease from injuring souls by their wicked doctrines and perfidious suggestions; move their hearts to renounce the evil which they do to the chosen sheep of CHRIST's fold; obtain for us the grace that, being always obedient to the voice of the supreme Pastor, we may never give ourselves up to the reading of evil books, but may, on the contrary, seek to read, and, as far as possible, diffuse, such works as may by their wholesome influence help all to promote the greater glory of God, the exaltation of the Church, and the salvation of souls. Amen.

489. Litany of St Joseph.

300 Days, once a day.

(See Instructions, p. 1.)

N.B.—The public recitation of this Litany is now authorized.

Latin	English
Kyrie, eleison.	Lord, have mercy.
Christe, eleison	Christ, have mercy.
Kyrie, eleison.	Lord, have mercy.
Christe, audi nos.	Christ, hear us.
Christe, exaudi nos.	Christ, graciously hear us

Pater de cælis, Deus, *miserere nobis.*
Fili Redemptor mundi, Deus,
Spiritus Sancte, Deus,
Sancta Trinitas, unus Deus,

God, the Father of Heaven, *have mercy on us.*
God the Son, Redeemer of the world
God, the Holy Spirit,
Holy Trinity one God,

Sancta Maria, *ora pro nobis.*
Sancte Joseph,
Proles David inclyta,
Lumen Patriarcharum,
Dei Genitricis sponse,

Holy Mary, *pray for us.*
St Joseph
Renowned offspring of David,
Light of Patriarchs,
Spouse of the Mother of God,

Custos pudice Virginis,	Chaste guardian of the Virgin,
Filii Dei nutritie,	Foster father of the Son of God,
Christi defensor sedule,	Diligent protector of Christ,
Almæ Familiæ præses,	Head of the Holy Family,
Joseph justissime,	Joseph most just,
Joseph castissime,	Joseph most chaste,
Joseph prudentissime,	Joseph most prudent,
Joseph fortissime,	Joseph most strong,
Joseph obedientissime,	Joseph most obedient,
Joseph fidelissime,	Joseph most faithful,
Speculum patientissime,	Mirror of patience,
Amator paupertatis,	Lover of poverty,
Exemplar opificum,	Model of artisans,
Domesticæ vitæ decus,	Glory of home life,
Custos virginum,	Guardian of virgins,
Familiarum columen,	Pillar of families,
Solatium miserorum,	Solace of the wretched,
Spes ægrotantium,	Hope of the sick,
Patrone morientium,	Patron of the dying,
Terror dæmonum,	Terror of demons,
Protector sanctæ Ecclesiæ,	Protector of Holy Church,

ora pro nobis.   *pray for us.*

Agnus Dei, qui tollis peccata mundi, parce nobis Domine.

Lamb of God, who takest away the sins of the world, spare us, O Lord.

Agnus Dei, qui tollis peccata mundi, exaudi nos Domine.

Lamb of God, who takest away the sins of the world, graciously hear us, O Lord.

Agnus DEI, qui tollis peccata mundi, miserere nobis.

℣. Constituit eum dominum domus suæ
℞. Et principem omnis possessionis suæ.

Oremus.

DEUS, qui ineffabili providentia beatum Joseph sanctissimæ Genitricis tuæ sponsum eligere dignatus es: præsta quæsumus ut quem protectorem veneramur in terris, intercessorem habere mereamur in cœlis: qui vivis et regnas in sæcula sæculorum. Amen.

Lamb of GOD, who takest away the sins of the world, have mercy on us
℣. He made him the lord of his household,
℞. And prince over all his possessions.

Let us pray.

O GOD, who in thy ineffable providence didst vouchsafe to choose blessed Joseph to be the spouse of thy most holy Mother; grant, we beseech thee, that we may have him for our intercessor in Heaven, whom we venerate as our protector on earth: who livest and reignest world without end. Amen.

490. Medals of the Child Jesus.

i. 50 Days. T.Q.
ii. Plenary, *in articulo mortis.*

(See Instructions, p. 1.)

The medals must be blessed by one having faculties for bestowing the apostolic benediction on rosaries, crosses, etc.

For the partial Indulgence, the medal must be reverently kissed with the invocation below.

The conditions for the plenary Indulgence are Confession and Communion if possible, the invocation of the Holy Name, and the patient acceptance, at the hand of GOD, of death as the wages of sin.

HOLY Child JESUS, bless us.

491. Kissing the Ring of a Cardinal or Bishop.

50 Days.

(See Instructions, p. 1.)

Addendum.

492. Invocation

Seven Years and Seven Quarantines. T.Q.
Plenary once a month.

JESUS, Mary, Joseph.

REFERENCE NOTES

See p. 1, No. 5

1. Clement XIV, June 6, 1769; June 26, 1770.
2. Pius VI. May 15, 1784.
3. Pius VII, Rit. April 15, June 13, July 13, 1815; Mem. Jan. 10, 1817.
4. Pius VII, July 11, 1815.
5. Pius VII, Mem. July 19, 1822.
6. Leo XII, Pr. Ma., October 21, 1823; Pius IX, June 18, 1876.
7. Pius IX, August 8, 1847.
8. Pius IX, Br. July 28, 1863. Br. March 23, 1865.
9. Pius IX, Br. December 5, 1876.
10. Leo XIII, March 15, 1890. N. B.—All existing Indulgences for the same are abrogated.
11. Pius X, March 22, 1905.
12. Pius X, April 18, 1906.
13. Pius X, June 1, 1906.
14. Benedict XIII, January 15, 1728; Benedict XIV, January 28, 1756.
15. Pius VII, August 11, 1818.
16. Leo XII. Pr. Ma. July 9, 1828.
17. Pius IX, Pr. Ma. May 24, 1847.
18. Pius IX, May 18, 1848.
19. Pius IX, Br. April 11, 1860; May 5, 1890.
20. Pius IX, Pr. Ma. April 30, 1860.
21. Pius IX, Br. September 6, 1867.
22. Pius IX, Aff. January 10, 1871.
23. Pius IX, Res. aut. April 11, 1874.

24. Pius IX, June 15, 1862; Leo XIII, July 19, 1879.

25. Leo XIII, May 26, 1883.

26. Leo XIII, January 19, 1889.

27. Leo XIII, December 14, 1889.

28. Leo XIII, May 8, 1896.

29. Pius VII, May 19, 1818.

30. Leo XIII, May 4, 1888.

31. Leo XIII, March 15, 1890.

32. Leo XIII, Br. March 13,1902.

33. Pius X, November 28, 1903.

34. Pius X, January 21, 1905 ; May 30, 1908.

35. Pius VI, Br. May 26, 1796.

36. Pius IX, Res. January 5, 1849 ; November 26, 1876.

37. Leo XIII, Br. May 5, 1895 ; Enc. May 9, 1897.

38. Pius IX, Prop. March 12, 1857.

39. Leo XIII, August 26, 1889.

40. Leo XIII, July 31, 1897.

41. Pius X, May 8, 1907.

42. Leo XIII, Br. March 24, 1902.

43. Pius X, June 5, 1908.

44. Clement X Br. July 20, 1674 ; Leo XII, August 11, 1824.

45. Clement XIII, September 5, 1759.

46. Pius VII, June 13, 1815 ; Nov. 13, 1821.

47. Pius IX, June 10, 1856.

48. Pius IX, Pr. Ma. October 14, 1859.

49. Pius IX, October 6, 1870.

50. Pius IX, November 26, 1876.

51. Leo XIII, June 21, 1879.

52. Leo XIII, February 21, 1880.

53. Leo XIII, Br. September 25, 1883.

54. Leo XIII, April 18, 1885.

55. Pius X, November 26, 1906.

56. Leo XIII, January 16, 1886.

57. From the *Imitation of Christ*, iii, 15 ; v, 3. Leo XIII, February 27, 1886.
58. Leo XIII, April 11, 1888.
59. Leo XIII, February 6, 1893.
60. Leo XIII, March 25, 1897.
61. Pius IX, September 24, 1846.
62. Pius IX, August 11, 1851. November 29, 1853.
63. Pius IX, Pr. Ma. May 7, 1854.
64. Leo XIII, February 27, 1886.
65. Pius X, March 20, 1908.
66. Leo XIII, February 21, 1891.
67. Leo XIII, September 13, 1893.
68. Leo XIII, May 13, 1903.
69. Pius X, October 10, 1904.
70. Pius X, November 22, 1905.
71. Pius X, March 15, 1907.
72. Pius X, March 15, 1906.
73. Sixtus V, Br. October 22, 1586.
74. Pius VII, Mem., August 12, 1815; Pius VIII, July 9, 1830.
75. Pius XII, November 23, 1819.
76. Pius IX, September 23, 1846.
77. Pius IX, Br. October 1, 1861.
78. Leo XIII, January 18, 1894.
79. Leo XIII, Br, December 21, 1901.
80. Pius X, May 8, 1907.
81. Urban IV, Con. August 11, 1264 ; Martin V, Con. May 26, 1429 ; Eugenius IV, Con. May 26, 1433.
82. Pius X, April 10, 1907.
83. Pius X, Br. July 30, 1906.
84. Gregory XIII, Con. April 10, 1580.
85. Gregory XIII, April 10, 1580.
86. Pius IX, November 26, 1876 ; Leo XIII, December 8, 1897 ; Pius VII, Card. Vic. May 10, 1807.

87. Benedict XIV, Br. June 14, 1749 ; Clement XIII, July 23, 1765.
88. Pius VI, Mem. October 17, 1796.
89. Pius XII, Rit. August 26, 1814.
90. Pius VII, January 21, 1815.
91. Pius VII, Mem. February 14, 1815 ; April 6, 1816 ; Pius IX, June 18, 1876.
92. Pius VII, March 7, 1815.
93. Pius VII, Mem. February 9, 1818.
94. Pius VII, August 24, 1818.
95. Pius IX, January 9, 1854.
96. Pius IX, Pr. Ma. September 7, 1854.
97. Pius IX, Pr. Ma. January 1, 1866.
98. Pius IX, Br. September 15, 1876.
99 Pius IX, February 4, 1877.
100 Pius IX, July 18, 1877.
101. Innocent XII, Cons. January 5, 1695.
102. Leo XIII, June 30, 1893.
103. Pius X, July 3, 1908.
104. Leo XIII, June 30, 1893.
105. Leo XIII, February 15, 1895.
106. Leo XIII, Ind. June 15, 1895.
107. Leo XIII, June 3, 1896.
108. Pius VI, Mem. May 24, 1776. Pius VII, June 30, 1818 ; December 7, 1819.
109. Pius X, June 17, 1904 ; August 19, 1904.
110. Pius X, July 12, 1905.
111. Pius X, June 3, 1905.
112. Pius X, January 23, 1907.
113. Pius X, July 6, 1906.
114. Pius X, August 11, 1906.
115. Pius X Aff. July 8, 1904.
116. Pius X, May 18, 1907.

117. Clement XIV, Res. January 26, 1773 ; Pius IX, Br. August 11, 1863 ; Leo XIII, January 19, March 15, 1884.
118. Pius X, November 2, 1906 ; December 1, 1907.
119. Pius VII, September 2, 1817 : Leo XIII, July 23, 1898 ; Pius X, February 26, 1908.
120. Benedict XIV, Br. December 13, 1740. Leo XIII, May 15, 1886.
121. Pius VII, September 29, 1807.
122. Leo XIII, December 8, 1897.
123. Pius VII, February 14, 1815.
124. Gregory XVI, August 4, 1837.
125. Pius VII, August 25, 1820.
126. Leo XII, December 20, 1823 ; Pius IX, August 11, 1851.
127. Pius IX, July 31, 1858.
128. Pius IX, Pr. Ma. May 24, 1859.
129. Pius IX, Pr. Ma. January 21, 1874.
130. Leo XIII, November 21, 1885.
131. Leo XIII, January 16, 1886.
132. Leo XIII, Card. Vie. May 15, 1996.
133. Leo XIII, March 4, 1882.
134. Leo XIII, May 21, 1892.
135. Pius X, September 4, 1903.
136. Pius X, February 16, 1906.
137. Leo XIII, July 16, 1902.
138. Pius VII, Res. October 18, 1815 ; Gregory XVI, July 5, 1843.
139. Pius VII, Res. October 18, 1815.
140. Pius VII, Res. October 18, 1815.
141. Pius VII, Res. September 22, 1817.
142. Leo XII, Res. October 25, 1823.
143. Pius IX, June 4, 1850.
144. Leo III, June 26, 1894.
145. Pius X, January 27, 1908.

146. Pius VII, Res. September 22, 1817.

147. Pius VI, Res. January 2, 1799.

148. Pius VII, Mem. June 9, 1807.

149. Pius VII, Res. February 12, 1808 ; Pius IX, June 18, 1876.

150. Pius VII, March 20, 1815.

151. Pius VII, Mem. July 7, 1815 ; Leo XIII, Rit. June 28, 1889.

152. Pius IX, Res. January 5, 1849 ; November 26, 1876.

153. Pius IX, February 2, 1850.

154. Leo XIII, May 30, 1902 ; Pius X, January 26, 1908.

155. Leo XIII, Br. February 6, 1899.

156. Leo XIII, December 19, 1885.

157. Leo XIII, January 13, 1898 ; Pius X, May 30, 1908.

158. Leo XIII, September 7, 1897.

159. Pius IX, Pr. Ma. September 23, 1860.

160. Pius IX, Pr. Ma. January 25, 1868 ; Pius X, September 15, 1905.

161. Pius IX, Pr. Ma. February 29, 1868.

162. Pius IX, November 26, 1876.

163. Leo XIII, May 21, 1892.

164. Leo XIII, July 16, 1893.

165. Leo XIII, Rit. April 2, 1899.

166. Leo XIII, Br. December 18, 1899.

167. Leo XIII. Br. March 13, 1901.

168. Leo XIII, June 14, 1901.

169. Leo XIII, Br. December 12, 1901 ; Pius X, Br. March 1, 1904.

170. Leo XIII, Br. June 2, 1902.

171. Pius X, June 16, 1906.

172. Pius X, June 15, 1908.

173. Pius X, Br. December 19, 1904.

174. Pius X, Br. July 9, 1904.

175. Pius X, August 19, 1905 ; June 27, 1906.

176. Pius X, July 26, 1907 ; December 26, 1907.

177. Pius X, September 11, 1907.

178. Pius X, May 4, 1906.

179. Pius X, November 6, 1906.

180. Pius X, June 3, 1908.

181. Leo X, Bl. July 10, 1515 ; Clement XI, Bl. September 22, 1714 ; Benedict XIV, Br. January 15, 1743 ; Leo XIII, Br. January 16, 1886, December 8, 1897.

182. Benedict XIII, Br. September 14, 1724 ; December 5, 1727 ; Benedict XIV, Card. Vic. April 20, 1742 ; Pius VI, Prop. March 18, 1781. Leo XIII, April 3, 1884 ; May 20, 1896.

183. Clement XIII, September 5, 1759.

184. Pius VI, April 5, 1786.

185. Pius VII, June 21, 1808 ; Pius IX, June 18, 1876.

186. Pius VII, Mem. March 21, 1815 ; June 18, 1822.

187. Pius VII, June 13, 1815.

188. Pius VII, November 14, 1815.

189. Pius VII, September 30, 1817.

190. Pius VII, May 15, 1821.

191. Leo XII, Pr. Ma. October 21, 1832 ; Pius IX, June 18, 1876.

192. Leo XII, August 11, 1824.

193. Leo XII, January 30, 1828.

194. Leo XII, January 30, 1828.

195. Gregory XVI, January 8, 1838 ; Pius IX, March 17, 1856; Leo XIII, July 23, 1898.

196. Pius IX, 11 Dec., 1846.

197. Pius IX, September 23, 1846.

198. Pius X, 23 Mar. 1904.

199. Pius VII, Res. August 4, 1808 ; Res. November 24, 1808 ; Res. January 11, 1809.

200. Pius IX, Res., January 5, 1849; Bps., January 28, 1850; Indul., November 26, 1876.

201. Pius IX, August 5, 1851.

202. Pius IX, Mem. May 19, 1854.

203. Pius IX, Pr. Ma. September 7, 1854.

204. Pius IX, Brs. March 11, 1856.

205. Pius IX, Br. December 9. 1856.

206. Pius IX, Br. June 26, 1860.

207. Pius IX, Prop. December 30, 1868.

208. Pius IX, Br. June 11, 1869.

209. Leo XIII, March 21, 1885.

210. Leo XIII, December 19, 1885.

211. Pius X, June 2, 1905.

212. Leo XIII, November 27, 1887 ; December 8, 1897 ; Pius X, August 28, 1903 ; December 18, 1906.

213. Leo XIII, January 27, 1888.

214. Pius X, March 21, 1905.

215. Leo XIII, September 20, 1879 ; February 22, 1888.

216. Leo XIII, March 15, 1890.

217. Leo XIII, Lit. Apos., April 15, 1895.

218. Leo XIII, February 1, 1896.

219. Pius IX, August 5, 1851.

220. Leo XIII, Card. Vie. December 15, 1883.

221. Leo XIII, May 20, 1893.

222. Leo XIII, March 29, 1894.

223. Pius X, Br. September 15, July 22, 1905.

224. Pius X, January 10, 190?

225. Pius X, January 8, 1906.

226. Pius X, June 27, 1906.

227. Pius X, May 30, 1908.

228. Pius X, December 19, 1906.

229. Pius X, January 9, 1907.

230. Benedict XIII, Br. September 26, 1724 ; Clement XII, Br. December 12, 1734 ; Pius IX, July 18, 1877 ; Leo XIII, May 15, 1886 ; June 8, 1898.

231. Clement XII, February 4, 1736.

232. Pius VII, Res. January 14, 1815.

233. Pius VII, Mem. February 25, March 21, 1815, June 18, 1822.

234. Pius VII, Br. December 1, 1815 ; Pius IX, June 18, 1876.

235. Pius VII, June 18, 1822.

236. Gregory XIV, Br. July 13, 1837 ; Leo XIII, Br. May 8, 1884, July 23, 1898.

237. Pius IX, Br. April 3, 1857, November 26, 1876 ; Leo XIII, Jan.27, 1888.

238. Pius IX, June 18, 1876.

239. Leo XIII, March 26, 1887.

240. Pius X, February 3, 1906.

241. Pius IX, Br. June 22, 1855.

242. Pius IX, Prop. September 21, 1865 ; Leo XIII, July 23, 1898.

243. Pius IX, Br. March 31, 1876.

244. Pius IX, Br. March 31, 1876.

245. Pius VI, November 21, 1793.

246. Pius IX, Prop. November 26, 1854.

247. Pius IX, Bfs. March 27, 1863.

248. Leo XIII, Br. September 10, 1878.

249. Leo XIII, March 15, 1884.

250. Leo XIII, December 20, 1890.

251. Pius X, September 9, 1904.

252. Pius X, January 11, 1905.

253. Pius X, July 1, 1905.

254. Leo XIII, February 25, 1896 ; Pius X, January 22, 1908.

255. Pius X, Br. June 6, 1904.

256. Pius X, Br. December 5, 1904.

257. Pius VII, August 18, 1807 ; February 1, 1816.

258. Pius IX, December 11, 1854.

259. Pius IX, September 30, 1852.

260. Leo X, Br. August 20, 1516; Gregory XVI, Prop. July 13, 1845 ; Pius IX, Prop. January 9, 1848 ; Leo XIII, March 14, 1884.

261. Sixtus IV, Bl. May 12, 1479; Benedict XIII, April 13, August 13, 1726, May 26, 1727 ; Pius IX, May 12, 1851, January 22, 1858 ; Pius X, July 31, 1906 ; June 12, 1907.

262. Leo XIII, Enc. Sep   tember, 1, 1883 ; Rit. August 20, 1885 : Indul. July 23, 1898.

263. Leo XIII, Card. Vic. July 3, 1886.

264. Leo XIII, September 21, 1889 ; September 17, 1892.

265. Leo XIII, June 21, 1890.

266. Pius X, March 15, 1907.

267. Pius IX, March 26, 1860.

268. Pius IX, Rit. May 17, 1866.

269. Leo XIII, Aff. Nov. 23, 1880.

270. Leo XIII, January 16, 1886.

271. Leo XIII, February 27, 1886.

272. Leo XIII, December 14, 1889.

273. Leo XIII, December 20, 1890.

274. Leo XIII, June 20, 1891.

275. Leo XIII, June 30, 1896.

276. Leo XIII, Br. February 8, 1900.

277. Leo XIII, Br. March 10, 1900.

278. Leo XIII, January 24, 1901.

279. Leo XIII, January 26, 1901.

280. Leo XIII, Br. June 23, 1902.

281. Pius X, November 9, 1907.

282. Pius X, August 24, 1904.

283. Pius X, November 20, 1907.

284. Pius X, August 10, 1904.

285. Pius X, Br. May 25, 1908.

286. Pius X, January 23, 1907.

287. Pius X, January 31, 1906.

288. Pius X, May 22, 1906.

289. Pius VII, May 6, 1817.

290. Pius IX, November 26, 1876.

291. Pius IX, Rit. August 8, 1851.

292. Leo XIII, Mot. Pr. September 25, 1888.

293. Leo XIII, August 19, 1893.

294. Pius IX, November 26, 1876.

295. Leo XIII, June 21, 1890.

296. Pius VI, Br. October 2, 1795; June 11, 1796; Pius VI, May 15, 1821.

297. Pius IX, November 26, 1876.

298. Pius VII, Res. Card. Vic. September 6, 1804.

299. Pius VII, Res. Card. Provicar. June 26, 1809; Indul. June 13, 1815.

300. Pius VII, Card. Vic. December 9, 1819 ; Gregory XVI, January 22, 1836 ; Pius IX, February 1, 1847, March 22, 1847.

301. Pius IX, November 26, 1876.

302. Pius IX, April 27, 1865 ; July 18, 1877.

303. Pius IX, Br. June 26, 1863.

304. Pius IX, February 4, 1877.

305. Leo XIII, March, 1882.

306. Leo XIII, July 18, 1885.

307. Leo XIII, May 17, 1884.

308. Leo XIII, Enc. August 15, 1889; Indul. September 21, 1889.

309. Leo XIII, December 14, 1889.

310. Leo XIII, March 18, 1882.

311. Leo XIII, Mot. Pr. May 15, 1891.

312. Leo XIII, December 19, 1891.

313. Pius X, December 1, 1905.

314. Pius X, November 26, 1906.

315. Pius X, March 15, 1907.

316. Leo XIII, March 20, 1886.

317. Pius X, June 16, 1906.

318. Leo XIII, Mot. Pr. August 16, 1890.

319. Leo XIII, March 20, 1886.

320. Pius VI, Mem. July 28, 1778 ; Pius IX, June 18, 1876.

321. Pius VI, June 22, 1782.

322. Pius VII, Card. Vic., January 23, 1806.

323. Pius IX, Br. May 15, 1857; February 4, 1877; Leo XIII, Bfs. April 27, 1880.

324. Pius X, January 18, 1905.

325. Leo XIII, December 8, 1897.

326. Leo XIII, June 26, 1894.

327. Leo XIII, June 26, 1894.

328. Leo XIII, September 17, 1892.

329. Pius IX, February 4, 1873.

330. Pius VIII, October 2, 1830.

331. Gregory XVI, December 22, 1832.

332. Leo XIII, June 18, 1887.

333. Leo XIII, June 12, 1894.

334. Leo XIII, July 21, 1883.

335. Leo XIII, November 21, 1885.

336. Leo XIII, September 13, 1893.

337. Pius X, Br. February 28, 1904.

338. Leo XIII, February 22, 1888.

339. Leo XIII, April 21, 1888.

340. Leo XIII, March 16, 1897.

341. Clement XII, Br. December 2, 1738; March 20, 1739.

342. Clement XIII, January 27, 1767; Gregory XVI, December 10, 1841.

343. Leo XIII, February 5, 1885.

344. Pius IX, May 17, 1852.
345. Leo XIII, April 22, 1887.
346. Leo XIII, Card. Vic. October 19, 1897.
347. Pius IX, August 8, 1853.
348. Leo XIII, February 27, 1894.
349. Pius IX, November 26, 1876.
350. Leo XIII, June 23, 1885.
351. Pius IX, Pr. Ma. April 24, 1863 ; April 20, 1868.
352. Pius IX, Pr. Ma. October 17, 1867.
353. Leo XIII, May 27, 1897.
354. Leo XIII, July 3, 1885.
355. Leo XIII, March 26, 1887.
356. Leo XIII, August 21, 1886.
357. Leo XIII, December 14, 1889.
358. Pius IX, January 25, 1866.
359. Leo XIII, June 9, 1896.
360. Leo XIII, May 11, 1897.
361. Leo XIII, July 13, 1896.
362. Leo XIII, Br. March 1, 1898.
363. Leo XIII, May 6, 1899.
364. Leo XIII, September 17, 1887.
365. Leo XII, January 30, 1828.
366. Pius IX, Br. June 25, 1869.
367. Pius IX, Pr. Ma. May 20, 1862.
368. Leo XIII, June 3, 1895.
369. Benedict XIII, November 22, 1729 ; Clement XII, November 21, 1737 ; Benedict XIV, April 12, 1742.
370. Clement XII, December 11, 1739 ; January 7, 1740.
371. Pius VII, March 6, 1802.
372. Leo XIII, June 12, 1894.
373. Leo XII, March 3, 1827.
374. Pius IX, Pr. Ma. March 21, 1847 ; Indul. July 10, 1854.
375. Leo XIII, May 17, 1890.

376. Leo XIII, January 21, 1882.

377. Leo XIII, February 27, 1886.

378. Pius X, December 29, 1907.

379. Pius IX, Pr. Ma. October 30, 1854.

380. Leo XIII, January 16, 1886.

381. Leo XIII, Br. March 21, 1879.

382. Leo XIII, July 20, 1889.

383. Leo XIII, April 22, 1898.

384. Leo XIII, February 27, 1894.

385. Pius IX, Br. August 9, 1861.

386. Leo XIII, January 12, 1897.

387. Leo XIII, May 13, 1903.

388. Pius X, January 23, and June 8, 1904.

389. Pius X, January 11, 1904.

390. Pius X, March 23, 1904.

391. Pius X, September 17, 1904.

392. Pius X, August 11, 1906.

393. Pius X, November 28, 1906.

394. Pius X, July 5, 1905.

395. Pius X, April 29, 1907.

396. Pius X, Br. February 11, 1905.

397. Ven. Innocent XI, Br. January 28, 1688 ; Innocent XIII, June 4, 1721 ; Leo XIII, August 19, 1895.

398. Pius X, December 10, 1907.

399. Pius X, December 18, 1907.

400. Benedict XIV, Con. April 5, 1747; Indul. September 23, 1775; February 5, 1841; March 22, 1879.

401. Pius X, March 9, 1904.

402. St Pius V, Bl. July 9, 1568 ; Bl. April 5, 1571.

403. Benedict XIII, August 23, 1728 ; Pius VI, December 12, 1788 ; Pius IX, September 30, 1852, November 20, 1854 ; Pius X, February 20, 1907.

404. Clement XII, Br. August 11, 1736; Pius VI, Prop. March 18, 1781 ; Pius IX, July 18, 1877; Leo XIII, February 3, 1888.

405. Benedict XIV, April 10, 1745 ; April 3, 1751.

406. Pius VII, Br. February 6, 1817.

407. Pius X, February 27, 1907; September 2 & 11, 1907.

408. Leo XII, November 18, 1826.

409. Pius IX, Res. January 5, 1849: Bps. January 28, 1850; November 26, 1876.

410. Leo XIII, August 19, 1880.

411. Leo XIII, January 17, 1888.

412. Leo XIII, September 15, 1888.

413. Leo XIII, December 14, 1889.

414. Leo XIII, Br. March 22, 1902.

415. Pius X, February 13, 1908.

416. Pius VI, July 9, 1777; Leo XII, February 28, 1827.

417. Pius IX, Br. January 26, 1866.

418. Honorius III, 1223; Gregory XV, Br. July 4, 1622; Ven. Innocent XI, Br. January 12, 1687; Pius IX, July 12, 1847; Leo XIII, July 14, 1894.

419. Pius V, Bl. July 9, 1568; April 15, 1571.

420. Paul V, Br. October 6, 1607; Clement XII, Br. May 16, 1736; Pius IX, July 18, 1877.

421. Benedict XIV, Br. December 16, 1746.

422. Benedict XIV, July 31, 1756; Pius VI, December 12, 1784.

423. Leo X ; Pius IX, July 26, 1855.

424. Pius X, December 2, 1905.

425. Pius X, March 14, 1906.

426. Pius VII, Card. Vic. July 23, 1801 ; Pius IX, August 8, 1847 ; Leo XIII, February 2, 1897.

427. Pius VII, April 28, 1807.

428. Pius X, January 12, 1906.

429. Pius VII, Card. Pro-Vic., April 18, 1809.

430. Pius VI, Card. Vic., February 28, 1778.

431. Pius VII, June 13, 1815.

432. Pius X, December 5, 1906.

433. Pius IX, Prop., April 26, 1857.

434. Pius VII, March 2, 1816.

435. Pius X, June 9, 1906.

436. Pius VII, July 2, 1816.

437. Pius VII, Mem. January 16, 1817.

438. Pius VII, April 21, 1818.

439. Leo XII, August 11, 1824.

440. Leo XII, March 3, 1827.

441. Gregory XVI, August 21, 1837.

442. Pius IX, Prop. November 14, 1847.

443. Pius IX, November 8, 1849.

444. Pius IX, Pr. Ma. June 18, 1854.

445. Pius IX, Card. Vic. August 5, 1854.

446. Pius IX, Penit. February 26, 1862.

447. Pius X, Br. March 29, 1904.

448. Pius IX, September 26, 1864.

449. Pius IX, November 26, 1876.

450. Pius X, March 1, 1908.

451. Leo XIII, June 23, 1885 ; March 29, 1889.

452. Leo XIII, July 18, 1885.

453. Leo XIII, November 21, 1885.

454. Leo XIII, January 16, 1886.

455. Leo XIII, January 17, 1888.

456. Leo XIII, June 22, 1888.

457. Leo XIII, January 19, 1889.

458. Leo XIII, May 17, 1890.

459. Leo XIII, December 17, 1892.

460. Leo XIII, June 30, 1893.

461. Leo XIII, July 15, 1893.

462. Leo XIII, January 23, 1894.
463. Pius X, November 9, 1907.
464. Pius X, March 30, 1908.
465. Pius X, December 1, 1907.
466. Gregory XIII.
467. Pius IX, December 11, 1846.
468. Pius IX, February 4, 1877.
469. Leo XIII, February 17, 1883.
470. Leo XIII, December 20, 1884.
471. Pius IX, March 27, 1854.
472. Leo XIII, August 19, 1882.
473. Leo XIII, January 16, 1886.
474. Leo XIII, August 14, 1884.
475. Leo XIII, August 16, 1884.
476. Leo XIII, March 16, 1889.
477. Leo XIII, November 18, 1882.
478. Pius X, May 6, 1905.
479. Leo XIII, Off. February 8, 1901.
480. Leo XIII, May 9, 1895.
481. Leo XIII, May 15, 1886.
482. Leo XIII, Br. August 16, 1898.
483. Leo XIII, December 13, 1898.
484. Pius X, May 27, 1908.
485. Pius X, July 8. 1908.
486. Pius X, Off. November 26, 1908.
487. Pius X, Off. November 26, 1908.
488. Pius X, Off. December 10, 1908.
489. Pius X, Rit. March 18, 1909.
490. Pius X, Off. March 18, 1909.
491. Pius X, Off. March 18, 1909.
492. Pius X, June 8, 1906.

EXTENDED TABLE OF CONTENTS

THE RACCOLTA

II. ALMIGHTY GOD

V. THE CHILD JESUS

VI. THE BLESSED SACRAMENT

VII. JESUS CRUCIFIED

IX. THE SACRED HEART

X. MARY

A. GENERAL

XI. THE HOLY ANGELS

397. XIV. BLESSED CROSSES, CRUCIFIXES, ROSARIES, MEDALS, ETC., FROM THE HOLY LAND

XV. THE DYING AND THE APOSTOLIC BLESSING

XVI. THE FAITHFUL DEPARTED

XVII. MISCELLANEOUS

FOR SPECIAL CLASSES

I. FOR PRIESTS

www.ingramcontent.com/pod-product-compliance
Lightning Source LLC
Chambersburg PA
CBHW032051090426
42744CB00005B/165